"From Our Special Correspondent" Dispatches from the 1875 Black Hills

Nebraska
STATE HISTORICAL SOCIETY

"From Our Special Correspondent"

Dispatches from the 1875 Black Hills Council at Red Cloud Agency, Nebraska

Edited by James E. Potter

Nebraska State Historical Society Books / Lincoln

ISBN 978-0-933307-37-7
Library of Congress Control Number: 2015957299
Index by Kylie Kinley; book design by David Bristow; map by Dell Darling
Printed in the United States of America

Front cover: Oglala and Brulé leaders from the Nebraska agencies were photographed in Omaha on May 14, 1875, while on their way to Washington, D.C. to meet with government officials. They visited Julius Meyer's "Indian Wigwam" curio store during their stop in the city. Standing, l. to r.: Meyer; Red Cloud, Oglala. Seated, l. to r.: Sitting Bull, Oglala; Swift Bear, Brulé; Spotted Tail, Brulé. Nebraska State Historical Society RG 2246-8a

Contents

List of Illustrations

Unless otherwise credited, photos are from the collections of the Nebraska State Historical Society and are credited where they appear as "NSHS" followed by a Record Group number.

Acknowledgments

This project began when I was living in Chadron, and the staff of the Reta King Library at Chadron State College was most accommodating in arranging for the interlibrary loan of microfilmed newspapers not available at the Nebraska State Historical Society. Once I had transcribed the dispatches, I sent them to Kingsley M. Bray of Manchester, England, biographer of Crazy Horse and an authority on Lakota history. Although a full collaboration by the two of us to edit the Black Hills Council dispatches did not materialize, Kingsley provided key biographical information on several council participants and offered additional insights that were very helpful. I also relied heavily on his books and articles relating to Lakota history. Because my goal for this project was to provide access to an underused body of source material, I trust that any editorial shortcomings will be forgiven.

James E. Potter
Nebraska State Historical Society

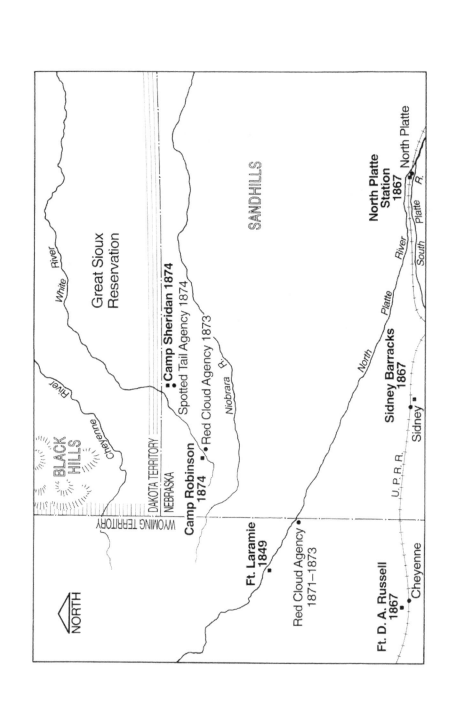

Introduction

❧

For a month in late summer 1875 the nation's gaze was drawn to proceedings at the remote Red Cloud Agency in northwestern Nebraska. Home to Red Cloud's Oglala division of the Lakota (Western Sioux), the agency had been chosen as the site for important negotiations between U. S. Government commissioners and the Indians. The so-called "Grand Council" would focus on gaining the Indians' agreement to cede ownership of the Black Hills, then a part of the Great Sioux Reservation. It was the second of two councils held in western Nebraska that were noteworthy for the issues involved, their effect on the future of Indian-white relations, and because they were among the largest such gatherings in American history.

The first council took place in September 1851 at Horse Creek, just east of the modern Nebraska-Wyoming state line in today's Scotts Bluff County. Originally set for Fort Laramie, the council was moved to Horse Creek because the ponies of the assembled Indians had consumed all the grass near the fort while the delegations were waiting for government officials to arrive. Plains and mountain tribes, including the Lakota, Crow, Shoshone, Arapaho, Cheyenne, Assiniboine, and Arikara attended the eighteen-day council (some estimates say eight to ten thousand Indians were present). The resulting treaty was known officially as the Fort Laramie Treaty of 1851, but it is often called the Horse Creek Treaty.[1]

In return for government compensation in the form of rations and presents, the Indians would accept tribal boundaries, keep the peace among themselves and with the whites, permit the government to build forts in their country, and refrain from molesting emigrants along the Oregon-California trails. As in other instances where the negotiating parties did not speak the same language, represented vastly different cultures, and did not share similar concepts of land possession and use,

9

the whites likely overestimated the extent to which the Indian signatories (band chiefs and headmen) understood the treaty and the ability of those leaders to bind their followers to its terms. It would not be long before conflict occurred.[2]

August 1854 saw the first significant fracture in the tenuous peace the treaty sought to secure. Ironically, the event occurred near Fort Laramie when Bvt. 2d Lt. John Grattan led a detail from the fort to arrest an Indian who had butchered an emigrant's cow and taken refuge in a massive Lakota village. When Brulé headman Scattering Bear was unable to deliver the alleged offender as Grattan demanded, the inexperienced and headstrong officer ordered his twenty-nine soldiers to open fire. Grattan and his party were quickly killed after Scattering Bear was struck down by the soldiers' initial volley. This episode led to the army's retaliatory attack on Little Thunder's Brulé village near Ash Hollow, Nebraska Territory, in September 1855.[3]

After the notorious November 1864 massacre by Colorado volunteers of a peaceful Southern Cheyenne village at Sand Creek, Colorado Territory, the Lakota and Cheyenne responded by attacking settlements and travelers along the Platte Valley travel and communications corridor. During the summer of 1865 the U.S. Army mounted a punitive campaign against the Indians, who by then had concentrated in the Powder River region of today's Wyoming and Montana. The army's subsequent construction of forts along the Bozeman Trail, which arrowed through the heart of Lakota country from Fort Laramie to the new Montana gold fields, sparked Red Cloud's war against the U.S. Army. In December 1866 near Fort Phil Kearny, Red Cloud's followers and allied Northern Cheyenne and Arapaho warriors wiped out Capt. William J. Fetterman and the eighty men under his command. For months afterwards the Indians besieged the soldiers in their trailside enclaves and attacked them when they ventured forth. Indian resistance finally forced the U.S. government to the bargaining table, leading to the 1868 Fort Laramie treaty.[4]

The treaty offered something for both parties. In addition to bringing peace by ending "Red Cloud's War" and removing the troops from the Bozeman Trail forts, it established the "Great Sioux Reservation" in Dakota Territory north of Nebraska and west of the Missouri River, (the western portion of today's South Dakota), from which whites would be permanently excluded. In return for the Lakota giving up the right to roam and hunt wherever they chose and accepting a designated reservation, the government would provide them with rations for four years, and educational and agricultural assistance for longer periods to help them adapt to the inevitable end of their hunting lifestyle. The government's largess would be distributed at agencies located on the reservation and administered by agents appointed by religious denominations under President Ulysses S. Grant's so-called "Peace Policy." Eventually, it was hoped, the Indians would learn to become self supporting, i.e. "civilized," agriculturalists and could then receive individual allotments of land to farm within the reservation.

The region "north of the North Platte River and east of the summits of the Big Horn Mountains," which included the Bozeman Trail and the protective U.S. military posts, was declared to be "unceded Indian territory" not open to white settlement. The treaty provided that although the Indians would not have the right to occupy this region permanently, they could continue to hunt there and on the Republican River in Nebraska for as long as buffalo ranged "in such numbers as to justify the chase." Once the forts were abandoned and the Bozeman Trail closed, the treaty was finally consummated when Red Cloud signed it on November 6, 1868. The Senate ratified the document on February 16, 1869.[5]

Unlike several of the treaty's more straightforward provisions, those relating to the process of "civilization" seemed vague and tenuous to a people who had long supported themselves by hunting and were seemingly being encouraged to continue doing so by the treaty's grant of hunting rights outside the reservation. The treaty also anticipated the prospect of future cessions of reservation land to the government but only with the agreement of three-fourths of the adult males of the bands who had been parties to the treaty.[6]

Some of the Lakota proved more amenable to a reservation future than others, particularly those whose places of habitation had brought them into contact with white overland migration, incipient settlements, and railroad construction already compromising the game resources on which they depended. Notwithstanding the recent victory over the army, Red Cloud and other leaders, such as Spotted Tail of the Brulé, had concluded that fighting the whites in the future would be futile. These men represented Lakota bands that had mostly given up the chase, or were soon to do so. Several of these same chiefs and headmen had been exposed to the United States' seemingly limitless population and technological prowess during visits to meet with government officials in Washington, D.C. Although they recognized that the nomadic life was unsustainable, they sought to extend the inevitable transition to the reservation over a generation or two to give their people time to adapt. In

Red Cloud's view, the change should occur "on Lakota terms, at Lakota speed."[7]

Even the leaders of the more geographically isolated Lakota bands, such as Sitting Bull and Crazy Horse, who had had much less contact with the whites, had not signed the 1868 treaty, and wanted nothing to do with reservations, understood that the nomadic life could not last forever. Nevertheless, they determined to maintain it for the present, rejecting the government's annuities and reservations and resisting white encroachment on their hunting grounds west of the designated reservation for as long as game held out there. Maintaining control of the Black Hills was central to this approach. The Black Hills represented a "food pack" that could sustain the people in times of scarcity and allow them to delay accepting the government handouts that had already become essential to the reservation bands' survival.[8]

It was gold that upset the rather indefinite timetable for transforming the Lakota from hunters to farmers and precipitated the 1875 council, the first in a series of dramatic developments that would rapidly and forever change Lakota life and relations with the government. Rumors of gold in the Black Hills had been circulating for years, and occasional exploring parties had given the rumors credence as early as the 1850s.[9] In 1875 former fur trader Geminien Beauvais recalled acquiring gold dust from the Corn band of the Brulé in 1858, which the Indians had taken from Black Hills streams.[10] Although interest in these potential mineral riches continued to grow, whites were barred from entering the Black Hills, part of the reservation set aside by the 1868 Fort Laramie Treaty. Lacking an incentive more powerful than the fear of Indian retaliation for trespass on the reservation, only the boldest of whites would dare enter this relatively unknown and somewhat forbidding region. That powerful incentive was soon provided.

The 1874 establishment of Camps Robinson and Sheridan near Nebraska's Red Cloud and Spotted Tail agencies in response to disruptions by non-agency and non-treaty Lakota visitors revived Department of the Missouri commander Gen. Philip Sheridan's interest in establishing additional military posts to further encircle the Great Sioux Reservation. Forts Randall and Sully already lay to the east, while Forts Lincoln and Rice were to the north. Sheridan proposed establishing a post or posts west of the reservation in the Lakota hunting grounds of the Yellowstone Valley, along with another in or near the Black Hills. The Indian bureau was also considering the idea of establishing a separate agency in the vicinity to exert more control over the non-agency bands using the Hills as a refuge. After gaining approval from the President and the War and Interior Departments, Sheridan ordered Lt. Col. George Armstrong Custer and the Seventh U.S. Cavalry to explore the Black Hills for appropriate sites. Most observers, however, believed the reconnaissance was to determine whether the Black Hills contained gold in paying quantities.[11]

When the journalists and scientists with Custer reported that gold had indeed been found, "gold fever" sent miners pouring into the Black Hills despite the army's efforts to keep them out. There were simply too few troops available and too many routes by which trespassers could slip into the Hills un-noticed. In the summer of 1875 the government sent geologist Walter P. Jenney's scientific party to the Black Hills, accompanied by a military escort under Lt. Col. Richard Irving Dodge, to confirm or discount the region's mineral endowment once and for all.[12]

In the meantime, rather than continuing a seemingly futile policy to cordon off the Black Hills from white encroachment, the government decided that the best solution lay in negotiating a new agreement with the Lakota for their purchase. Many westerners thought that was the reason Red Cloud, Spotted Tail, and other agency leaders had been taken to Washington D. C. in May 1875 to meet with Commissioner of Indian Affairs Edward P. Smith, Secretary of the Interior Columbus P. Delano, and President Ulysses S. Grant. The Indians did not see it that way, however, focusing instead on their complaints about conditions at their agencies and the question of surrendering their hunting rights in Nebraska. If ceding the Black Hills were to be discussed, said the Native leaders, the government should send commissioners to meet with them in their own country and in the presence of their own people. Hence, on June 18, 1875, with President Grant's approval, Secretary Delano appointed a commission "to treat with the Sioux for the Relinquishment of the Black Hills."[13]

The commission would be chaired by U.S. Senator William B. Allison of Iowa and was popularly known as the Allison Commission. The other appointees who agreed to serve were former Congressman Abram B. Comingo of Independence, Missouri; Brig. Gen. Alfred H. Terry; Rev. Samuel D. Hinman of Nebraska's Santee Agency; former fur trader Geminien P. Beauvais of St. Louis; William H. Ashby of Beatrice, Nebraska; and A. G. Lawrence of Providence, Rhode Island. Fort Laramie post trader John S. Collins, formerly of Omaha, would be the secretary and Robert Lines of Washington, D.C. the stenographer.

The commission hoped to get all the Lakota bands' agreement to hold the council at some point on the Missouri River, enabling the commissioners to travel there by steamboat. A sub-commission consisting of Comingo, Hinman, Ashby, and Collins went out in July and August to make the arrangements. They first visited Red Cloud's agency and the nearby agency for Spotted Tail's Brulé but both Red Cloud and Spotted Tail categorically refused to attend a council held on the Missouri River. The commissioners then trekked north from Spotted Tail Agency via the Black Hills to the less populous Cheyenne River, Crow Creek, and Standing Rock agencies on the Missouri River, where they managed to persuade representatives of the Yanktonai, Miniconjou, Hunkpapa, Two Kettle, Sihasapa, Lower Brulé, and Sans Arc bands to attend a council near the Nebraska agencies. The exact site was not designated, but the commissioners implied that the council would convene on Chadron Creek, about midway between the Red Cloud and Spotted Tail agencies. These hints about the council site would come back to haunt the full commission in early September when it arrived at Red Cloud Agency and sought to get the negotiations underway.

At the government's request, the agency Oglala sent runners into the Powder River and Tongue River country to invite the non-agency bands under Sitting Bull and Crazy Horse to the council. Some Northern Lakota, who had previously visited the agencies to accept government annuities when game became scarce, had begun to consider settling down on the reservation. This softening attitude toward reservation life came to an end in the summer of 1875 when it became clear that the miners' invasion of the Black Hills was continuing with the government's apparent blessing. Neither Sitting Bull and Crazy Horse, nor most of those who followed them, would subsequently attend the 1875 council, although Little Big Man was chosen to lead a delegation of Northern Oglala to monitor and, if necessary, disrupt the proceedings.[14]

By early September 1875 the number of Indians assembled within a fifty-mile radius of Red Cloud Agency, including women and children, may have approached 20,000 although estimates vary. They included the Oglala, Brulé, and associated Northern Arapaho and Northern Cheyenne from the Nebraska agencies, significant delegations from the Missouri River agencies, and a much smaller number of representatives from the non-agency bands. The White River valley and its tributaries must have offered an impressive sight, dotted as they would have been with hundreds of tepees and thousands of ponies. One reporter called it "the last grand gathering of the greatest of the surviving Indian nations."[15]

The commissioners reached Red Cloud Agency on September 4, 1875, having traveled from Omaha to Cheyenne on the Union Pacific Railroad, then overland via Fort Laramie. The first formal session of the Grand Council would not convene for more than two weeks, delayed by wrangling between the commissioners, Red Cloud, and Spotted Tail about exactly where the meeting should take place. Red Cloud wanted the talks held at his agency, while Spotted Tail demanded a site on Chadron Creek, which the sub-commission had seemingly promised during its July-August visit to the agencies. Having settled into quarters within the Red Cloud Agency stockade and under the protective shadow of nearby Camp Robinson, the commissioners were unwilling to travel the thirty or so miles to Chadron Creek to sit down with the Indians. After much discussion among the parties, the commissioners finally fixed the council site on the White River plain about six miles northeast of Red Cloud Agency and just north of the rugged landmark known as Crow Butte.[16]

Because the Black Hills gold discoveries had already received wide publicity and miners were already prospecting and building settlements there illegally, the government's purchase of the Hills seemed crucial to preventing the outbreak of an Indian war. The council and its outcome became national news, and several newspapers sent correspondents to report both on the arrangements leading up to the council and on the council itself. They included the *Omaha Bee, Omaha Herald, Chicago Tribune, New York Herald, Cheyenne Daily Leader,* and *New York Tribune,* along with a few smaller newspapers. Some correspondents were professional journalists, while others were army officers or civilian attachés of the Allison Commission hired by the papers to report on the proceedings.

Homer Stull, city editor of the *Omaha Herald,* covered the travels of the sub-commission in July and August for his own paper and for the *Chicago Tribune.* His letters during that time offer insight to how the agency Lakota felt about the miners' invasion of the Black Hills and provide a glimpse of the miners themselves and the frantic activity that characterized the early months of the Black Hills gold rush. Stull also recorded conditions at the Missouri River agencies and their inhabitants' response to the pending negotiations.

John T. Bell, a former newspaperman who in 1875 worked as a court stenographer in Omaha, took over as the *Omaha Herald* correspondent during the council itself. Charles Collins, editor of the *Sioux City Times,* who for several years had promoted opening the Black Hills for mining, even organizing expeditions for that purpose, wrote dispatches for the *Omaha Bee*.[17] Reuben Davenport of the *New York Herald* accompanied the Jenney/Dodge scientific exploration of the Black Hills during the summer of 1875 before leaving to attend the Grand Council. Capt. Andrew S. Burt of the Ninth U.S. Infantry had also been with the Dodge expedition and traveled with Davenport to Red Cloud Agency, where Burt reported for the *New York Tribune*. Iowa newspaperman Albert Swalm, Senator Allison's confidante and the commission's assistant secretary, penned reports both for the *Chicago Tribune* and for his own paper, the *Fort Dodge Messenger*.[18] Other accounts, unsigned or bearing only initials, appeared in the *Cheyenne Daily Leader* and may have originated with Red Cloud Agency traders or other civilian employees. Even the North Platte *Western Nebraskian* briefly had a special correspondent at the council, identified only as "Mart."

After the correspondents reached Red Cloud Agency in early September, the slow pace of getting the formal talks underway forced them to write about anything and everything associated with the council and its participants, both to occupy their time and to satisfy the public's interest. Their lengthy dispatches were carried by courier from Red Cloud Agency to Fort Laramie or Cheyenne, and sent on from there by telegraph.

The correspondents' reports provide a fascinating glimpse of the personalities, interactions, and cultures of the Indian, mixed-blood, and white participants in the 1875 Black Hills negotiations. They also reveal the depth of dependency and loss of autonomy that characterized the agency Lakota less than a decade after Red Cloud's war had forced the U.S. government to negotiate the 1868 treaty and abandon the Bozeman Trail forts. Nevertheless, the Allison Commission's instructions signaled that the government considered itself bound by the terms of the 1868 treaty confirming Lakota ownership of the Black Hills, even though the treaty's annuity provisions had expired and the government was now feeding the agency Indians gratuitously. Moreover, Article 12 required the consent of three-fourths of all adult male Lakota for land cessions from the Great Sioux Reservation. This was the major hurdle that the Allison Commission would attempt to overcome, particularly since large numbers of the non-agency Lakota declined to attend the council.[19]

As they penned their letters for their respective newspapers, the reporters made little pretense of objectivity, even according to the slack journalistic standards of the day. Much of their writing reflects both the biases against and stereotypes of Indians that many Americans shared.

Although Indians had sometimes been portrayed as innocent children of nature or "noble savages," by 1875 their resistance to American expansion into their homelands and their refusal to adopt white values and ways of living made it easy, particularly on the part of westerners, to characterize them as vicious, immoral, and lazy among other epithets, and almost sub-human. What's more, while the Indians resisted efforts to "civilize" them according to the standards of white society, they were seen as being perfectly willing to adopt the whites' worst vices, degrading themselves even further.[20]

Although the correspondents condemned most aspects of Indian life and culture they observed at the agencies, some of what they wrote concerning the "uncivilized savages" standing in the way of American progress served, even if inadvertently, to highlight the Indians' humanity and undercut the stereotypes. While the reporters were quick to characterize the Indians as "rascals" or "lazy, shiftless dogs" with "untutored minds," and portray leaders such as Red Cloud and Spotted Tail as crafty, sullen, treacherous, or greedy, the accounts also revealed them to be rational and intelligent human beings with a hearty sense of humor who employed considerable diplomatic skill in defending their land and way of life in the face of great odds.

Preliminaries occupied the first two weeks, including informal meetings between the commissioners and band chiefs or headmen. While the correspondents were killing time waiting for the actual council to begin, they observed and recorded some of the more picturesque aspects of agency life, such as the beef issue, dances, and feasts. They interviewed Indian leaders, including Red Cloud and Spotted Tail, and visited with the government commissioners, agency employees, soldiers from nearby Camp Robinson, and the so-called "squaw men," whites who had married Indian women and lived in the Indian camps. As they whiled away the hours and days, the correspondents also had a good deal of fun at their own expense, and took jabs at the commissioners as well. They sometimes highlighted the wry sense of humor that several of the Indians displayed.

After settling the thorny issue of the precise site of the council, the first session was called for noon on September 20. The initial meeting was devoted largely to Senator Allison's speech in which he first proposed that the government would like to lease the Black Hills. This proposal surprised the Indians, who indulged in hearty laughter when Allison said that once all the gold had been dug out, the land would be returned to them to do with as they chose.

Some of the most dramatic newspaper stories describe the September 23 meeting, at which Little Big Man and other northern warriors opposed to ceding the Black Hills threw the council into turmoil. Little Big Man and his followers, painted and armed, surrounded the commissioners and the small detachment of Camp Robinson soldiers and threatened agency leaders, such as Red Cloud and Spotted Tail, who seemed favorable to negotiating the sale of the Black Hills. As the armed groups stood glaring at each other with cocked rifles at the ready, Young Man Afraid of His Horse and Sitting Bull, the Oglala, ordered agency "soldiers" to disperse the northern tribesmen. Had a single shot been fired, it is likely that all of the whites and many Indians would have been killed. Although the shaken commissioners returned safely to Red Cloud Agency, it must have become clear, both to them and to most other participants, that the Grand Council was doomed to failure.

The commissioners and the leading men of the various bands met several more times before the final session convened on September 29. The commissioners had been authorized to offer six million dollars to buy the Black Hills outright, and the Lakota speakers held out for seven million or more (some reports mentioned seventy million), as well as guarantees that the government would subsist their people for seven generations or for as long as any Indian remained alive. And these were the Indians who were willing to sell if the price was right; factions within the agency bands, as well as the northern followers of Sitting Bull and Crazy Horse, opposed ceding the Black Hills under any circumstances.[21]

The correspondents recorded the Indian side of the discussions in some detail, and their dispatches reflect that, while the newspapermen thought most of the Indians' claims were excessive, a compromise might have been possible had the commission been more competent and had the government allowed it more flexibility and more time to conduct the negotiations. The reporters and the editors back home credited the Indians' demands to coaching by "squaw men" and "half-breeds" and the potential profiteering that the government payment for the Black Hills might bring to the alleged "Indian Ring" of conniving politicians, bureaucrats, Indian agents, and contractors who administered and supplied the agencies.[22]

While some of the reporters harped on the Indians' "preposterous" demands, others laid the council's failure, in part, to misunderstanding and poor interpretation, problems that plagued many negotiations between Indians and the government. It seems clear, however, that Lakota leaders were capable of assessing the value of the Black Hills on their own, perhaps not strictly in monetary terms, but according to what giving up the region would mean to their peoples' future. That realization helps explain why many of the Lakota spokesmen insisted on government support during what was sure to be a lengthy transition to a new and problematic way of life. Leaders such as Red Cloud and Spotted Tail were well aware that the rationing period provided in the 1868 Treaty had expired, yet even the agency Lakota remained manifestly unready to support themselves. Therefore they were willing to follow the precedent set in 1868 by exchanging land (in this case the Black Hills) for continued government support.

After the talks had reached an impasse, most of the commissioners and reporters left for home. Commissioners Ashby and Beauvais remained at Red Cloud Agency for another week or so to oversee the distribution of one hundred horses promised as a reward to the Oglala delegates who had gone north in August to notify the non-agency Lakota of the pending council. Newspaperman Albert Swalm also stayed behind and penned a few more letters to the Chicago and Fort Dodge, Iowa, papers. One of his letters described a Sun Dance he attended, while another told of an evening visit, along with Ashby and Beauvais, to the lodge of the Oglala shirt-wearer Sword Owner, where the men had been invited to partake of a dog feast.[23] Swalm's last letter from Red Cloud Agency described some of the problems the commissioners encountered during the distribution of the horses to the Indians.

One the council ended, several of the newspapers that had covered it weighed-in editorially, putting much of the blame for the collapse of the negotiations on the commissioners and, by implication, on the government's Indian policy. Although the *New York Tribune* noted that the Lakota had asked an exorbitant price for the Black Hills, "they were really seeking honest dealings at the agencies. . . During this council that subject was occasionally brought up despite the efforts of the Commissioners to stifle it. . . . It is the real cause of the failure of the council. Indians have as much common sense as white men, and they perceive clearly that until the whole Agency system is remodeled or swept away, they will never get more than a fraction of what belongs to them."[24] Indeed, earlier that summer another government commission had visited Red Cloud Agency to investigate charges of fraud and mismanagement raised by Yale paleontologist Prof. Othniel Marsh.[25]

The *Omaha Herald* (a Democratic paper only too glad to blast the policies of Grant's Republican administration) laid the Grand Council's failure squarely on the Allison Commission's doorstep. The commissioners "assumed the airs of men who neither understood the gravity of their mission nor the means whereby its objects could be accomplished."[26] One of the commission's shortcomings was having inadequate time to conciliate those Lakota who were opposed to the sale of the Black Hills. Some of the northern Indians barely had time to learn about the council before it got underway and only a few attended.

The leasing proposition, too, was another blunder, according to the *Omaha Herald.* "It was entirely worthy of the average stupidity of the heavy men of the Commission and produced universal disgust among both white men and Indians. The political Cheap Johns sent out to meet men of more character and sense than they possess, supposed that these Indians were a set of fools, and that they could be induced to part with a vast and valuable country for a song."[27]

A significant oversight with respect to the 1875 council was alluded to by some of the correspondents; no presents were distributed to the Indians. Providing presents was a standard feature of what Ethnohistorian Raymond DeMallie has termed a minimal model for plains treaty councils. To the Indians, receiving presents was one of the most significant parts of such a council and a prerequisite to serious negotiations.[28] The Allison Commission and the bigwigs in the Office of Indian Affairs should have known this. They had only to read the reports of earlier Indian councils or listen to the advice of their own members, Geminien P. Beauvais and Samuel D. Hinman, both of whom had experience in previous negotiations with Indians. In fact, while engaged with the sub-commission in August to arrange for the council, Hinman had advised Washington officials, "it is important that presents be sent for them."[29]

As the council drew to a close, remarks by Indian leaders such as Spotted Tail and Red Cloud signaled that an agreement to cede the Black Hills might still be possible if negotiations could be kept open. After all, it had taken the government some seven years to persuade those same leaders to surrender the hunting rights granted by the 1868 treaty. But the Allison Commission rejected any such possibility in its report, which one scholar termed "an exhibition of spite" because the initial effort to conclude an agreement had failed.[30]

The consequences of the termination of negotiations were significant. At a White House meeting on November 3 attended by the President, the secretaries of war and interior, and leading army officers, the army was relieved of its assignment to keep miners out of the Black Hills. The decision also played into the army's often-expressed opinion that the solution to the "Indian problem" was military action against the non-agency and non-treaty bands, whom the Allison Commission had blamed for the failure of the Black Hills negotiations. On December 3, the administration issued an order for all Lakota, including the non-treaty bands, to report to an agency by January 31, 1876, or face military action. This ultimatum, and the ridiculously short time provided for the Indians to comply with it, precipitated the Great Sioux War of 1876-77.[31]

Shortly after the Lakota and their allies defeated Lt. Col. George Armstrong Custer's Seventh Cavalry at the June 25-26, 1876, Battle of the Little Bighorn with the loss of some 268 officers and men, the government changed course on its dealings with both the agency and non-agency Lakota. The former were to be subjected to direct military supervision, including disarming and dismounting, while the bands still fighting the army were to be pursued until forced to surrender. On July 18, the Interior Department agreed to transfer authority over all the agencies to the army.

In August 1876 Congress adopted recommendations presented by the Commissioner of Indian Affairs and the Allison Commission with respect to the Black Hills. Because the majority of the Lakota bands could no longer support themselves by hunting and were "absolute pensioners of the government," the government "is entitled to ask something of them in return." This "something" would be the cession of the Black Hills as an equivalent for "the free rations now granted." A new commission was appointed to visit the agencies and inform the Indians that unless they agreed to relinquish all claims to the Black Hills, the government would cut off the rations and other commodities it had been providing them.[32]

The commission, headed by George P. Manypenny, went west in the fall of 1876, arriving at Red Cloud Agency in September, almost exactly a year after the Allison Commission reached there in 1875. It then proceeded to the Spotted Tail Agency and to those along the Missouri River. This time there was no effort at negotiation and no Grand Council.[33] The commission simply presented the Indians with the government's "sell or starve" ultimatum. Even under this pressure, the commission secured signatures only from agency band leaders and headmen, far fewer than the three-fourths of all male Indians required by Article 12 of the Fort Laramie Treaty. Nevertheless, on February 28, 1877, Congress ratified the so-called Manypenny Agreement and the Black Hills ceased to be part of the Sioux Reservation.[34]

Later that spring, following a winter campaign by the army, the last of the fighting Indians fled to Canada or came in to surrender at the agencies, including the band led by Crazy Horse, which arrived at Red Cloud Agency in early May 1877. On September 5 the Oglala leader would die at nearby Camp Robinson after being mortally wounded by a soldier as he resisted being forced into the post guardhouse. A month later the people living at the Red Cloud and Spotted Tail agencies were moved from Nebraska to the Dakota reservation. The Sioux War, along with the Indians' old way of life, was over.

Edward Lazarus in his 1991 book, *Black Hills/White Justice* noted, "The greatest weapon the Sioux possessed had never been their formidable skill as warriors but the way they reminded Americans of the yawning gulf between their high ideals and their political actions."[35] Beginning in the 1890s and continuing into the early twentieth century, elderly survivors of the Red Cloud generation and then younger, more progressive Lakota began agitating to gain compensation for the loss of the Black Hills. A 1920 Congressional act authorized a Court of Claims to adjudicate tribes' claims against the United States. In 1923 attorney Ralph Case filed the Black Hills Claim on behalf of the Lakota. Litigation relating to the claim proceeded for decades until 1974, when the Indian Claims Commission finally ruled that the Lakota were entitled to monetary compensation for the loss of the Black Hills. The U. S. Supreme Court upheld the award in 1980.

As for the so-called preposterous Indian demands at the 1875 council, the judgment valued the Black Hills at $17.5 million in 1877 dollars which, with interest, totaled 106 million by 1980. By this time, however, more militant Lakota had adopted the position that only the return of the land itself would be appropriate compensation. The monetary award under the successful Black Hills Claim remains in the U.S. Treasury, untouched and drawing interest. For the Lakota people, the unclaimed payment signals how the legacy of the failed Grand Council and the loss of the Black Hills during the nineteenth century remains alive well into the twenty-first.[36]

Editor's Note:

The correspondents' dispatches from the 1875 council have been transcribed as they were published except for the subheadings the newspaper compositors inserted below the main headline and within the text, which have been removed. The use of *sic* has been reserved for those instances when, in the editor's judgment, a date or statement was clearly erroneous. During the process of rendering the correspondents' handwritten letters into telegraphic dispatches or setting them in type for the printed page, errors such as misspelled names and terms inevitably resulted. These have been silently corrected when the correct spelling was known or could be determined. The editor has also added annotation as he determined necessary or helpful.

The dispatches are grouped chronologically by the byline date so that accounts written at approximately the same time or describing the same events appear together, regardless of the date they were published in the respective newspapers. In his September 10, 1875, letter appearing below, John T. Bell of the *Omaha Herald* described the difficulties involved in sending dispatches from Red Cloud Agency. First they had to be carried to Fort Laramie, the nearest telegraph office. If the line was temporarily inoperative, they went on to Cheyenne by courier, the whole process taking up to five days. If a dispatch reached Cheyenne after 2:30 p.m. and was being mailed from there, two more days elapsed before it arrived in Omaha. It no doubt took even longer for messages from Red Cloud Agency to reach the eastern newspapers.

The editor is not convinced that the byline dates are strictly accurate for some of the dispatches but has left them as the correspondents rendered them. As day after day unfolded during their lengthy sojourn at Red Cloud Agency, the correspondents may simply have lost track of the days or dates. Moreover, it is not always clear whether a letter written over the course of several days before being sent off bears the starting date or the date it was finished. It is also possible that the newspaper editors back home confused the byline date with the date the message may have been sent by telegraph from Fort Laramie or Cheyenne. The editor has taken the view that minor discrepancies involving the exact date an Indian dance took place, or when a particular individual arrived at or departed from Red Cloud Agency (as examples) do not detract from the value of these fascinating narratives of a major episode in Indian-U.S. Government diplomacy.

---

[1] Douglas C. McChristian, *Fort Laramie: Military Bastion of the High Plains* (Norman, OK: Arthur H. Clark Co., 2008), 51-61.

[2] James C. Olson, *Red Cloud and the Sioux Problem* (Lincoln: University of Nebraska Press, 1965), 6-8.

[3] McChristian, *Fort Laramie*, Chap. 3, "The Unfortunate Affair," and 91-93.

[4] For the story of the Bozeman Trail and warfare in 1866-68, see John D. McDermott, *Red Cloud's War: The Bozeman Trail, 1866-1868*, 2 vols. (Norman, OK: Arthur H. Clark Co., 2010).

[5] Olson, *Red Cloud*, 79-81. The text of the treaty appears in Charles J. Kappler, comp., *Indian Affairs: Laws and Treaties*, 2 vols. (Washington, DC: GPO, 1904), 2: 998-1007.

[6] For an analysis of the 1868 Treaty as an exchange with neither side gaining everything it wanted, see Jill St. Germain, *Broken Treaties: United States and Canadian Relations with the Lakotas and the Plains Cree, 1868-1885* (Lincoln: University of Nebraska Press, 2009), 59-66.

[7] Kingsley M. Bray, *Crazy Horse: A Lakota Life* (Norman: University of Oklahoma Press, 2006), 152.

[8] These themes are noted in ibid., 132, 154, 187-89.

[9] The documented and undocumented accounts of early gold discoveries are reviewed in Watson Parker, *Gold in the Black Hills* (1966; reprint, with new introduction, Pierre: South Dakota State Historical Society Press, 2003), Chap. 1, "Geography and Early Exploration."

[10] G. P. Beauvais, St. Louis, Missouri, Mar. 25, 1875, to William F. Lee, Cheyenne, Wyoming Territory, published in *Cheyenne Daily Leader*, Mar. 30, 1875.

[11] Paul Andrew Hutton, *Phil Sheridan and His Army* (Norman: University of Oklahoma Press, 1985), 290-91.

[12] Wayne R. Kime, ed., *The Black Hills Journals of Colonel Richard Irving Dodge* (Norman: University of Oklahoma Press, 1996), records the day-by-day activities of this expedition.

[13] Much of the foregoing summary is based on "Fiasco in Washington," Chap. 10 of Olson, *Red Cloud*.

[14] Bray, *Crazy Horse*, 181, 189-90.

[15] Reuben Davenport letter, Red Cloud Agency, Sept. 24, 1875, in *New York Herald*, Oct. 7, 1875.

[16] See "Failure of a Commission," Chap. 11 in Olson, *Red Cloud*.

[17] Jane Conard, "Charles Collins: The Sioux City Promotion of the Black Hills," *South Dakota History* 2 (Spring 1972): 131-71.

[18] The *Fort Dodge Messenger* on Oct. 28, 1875, noted Swalm's return from the council. "During his absence, Mr. S. was commissioned as the special correspondent of the *Chicago Tribune* and a portion of the time for the *New York Tribune*—sufficient work to keep him busy when not engaged in his clerical duties."

[19] St. Germain, *Broken Treaties*, 265-68.

[20] See Robert F. Berkhofer Jr., *The White Man's Indian: Images of the American Indian from Columbus to the Present* (New York: Alfred A. Knopf, 1978), 25-31; Hugh J. Reilly, *Bound to Have Blood: Frontier Newspapers and the Plains Indian Wars* (Lincoln: University of Nebraska Press Bison Books, 2011).

[21] "Failure of a Commission," in Olson, *Red Cloud.*

[22] Although there is little doubt that fraud and waste was associated with the administration of Indian affairs, Paul Andrew Hutton concluded "there is no evidence of an organized conspiracy." Hutton, *Phil Sheridan*, 98.

[23] Bray, *Crazy Horse*, 449n.25

[24] Editorial, *New York Tribune*, Oct. 1, 1875.

[25] For the Red Cloud Agency investigation, see Olson, *Red Cloud*, 189-98; *Report of the Special Commission Appointed to Investigate the Affairs of the Red Cloud Indian Agency, July 1875*, 3 vols. (Washington, DC: GPO, 1875) (hereafter, *Report of the Special Commission*).

[26] Editorial, *Omaha Daily Herald*, Sept. 30, 1875.

[27] Ibid.

[28] Raymond J. DeMallie, "Touching the Pen: Plains Indian Treaty Councils in Ethnohistorical Perspective," in Frederick C. Luebke, ed., *Ethnicity on the Great Plains* (Lincoln: University of Nebraska Press, 1980).

[29] Quoted in Grant K. Anderson, "Samuel D. Hinman and the Opening of the Black Hills," *Nebraska History* 60 (Winter 1979): 532.

[30] St. Germain, *Broken Treaties*, 270-71. The Allison Commission's report was published in the Nov. 18, 1875, edition of the *Chicago Tribune*, apparently before the commissioner of Indian affairs received it. The *Tribune's* "scoop" was probably due to Albert Swalm, who had been the paper's special correspondent during the council.

[31] St. Germain, *Broken Treaties*, 278-80; Hutton, *Phil Sheridan*, 298-300.

[32] *Annual Report of the Commissioner of Indian Affairs, 1875* (Washington, DC: GPO, 1875), 510, 701.

[33] As interpreter William Garnett put it, "[T]hey brought a treaty fully cooked containing schemes for schools, children, rations, mixed bloods, etc." Richard E. Jensen, ed., *Voices of the American West, Volume 1: The Indian Interviews of Eli S. Ricker, 1903-1919* (Lincoln: University of Nebraska Press, 2005), 87.

[34] Olson, *Red Cloud*, 224-30.

[35] Edward F. Lazarus, *Black Hills, White Justice: The Sioux Nation versus the United States, 1775 to the Present* (New York: Harper Collins Publishers, 1991), 117.

[36] Ibid., 146, 319, 402.

Part 1

Making the Arrangements,
June 27 – August 29, 1875

❧

The first step in arranging the pending negotiations between the Allison Commission and the Lakota was to send a sub-commission to meet with the agency bands and invite them to the council. Homer Stull, city editor of the *Omaha Herald*, accompanied the sub-commission during its two month sojourn in the Indian country and submitted similar dispatches both to his own newspaper and to the *Chicago Tribune*. The *Omaha Herald* dispatches appear here, along with one of Stull's *Chicago Tribune* dispatches and a few other related articles for which no comparable counterparts appeared in the Omaha paper.

[June 27, 1875 – Homer Stull, from Cheyenne, Wyoming Territory]
Fresh Gold
Cheyenne [Sunday], June 27, 1875
To the Editor of *The Herald*
    The four United States Commissioners who left Omaha on Saturday arrived here to-day at 2 p.m., and soon after received a dispatch from the commissioner of Indian affairs. Dr. [J. W.] Daniels also came in this afternoon. He has been successful in his negotiations with the agency Indians at Spotted Tail and Red Cloud agencies and they have already signed a treaty in which they relinquish their right to hunt in Nebraska. As these are the only Indians who possessed that right this question may be considered settled. The consideration is the $25,000 appropriated for that purpose, which is to be invested for the benefit of the Indians, according to their direction, in horses, harness and wagons.[1]

Another board of commissioners appointed to investigate the affairs of Dr. [John J.] Saville is expected here soon. It consists of Mr. [George W.] Lane, president of the chamber of commerce in New York, Ex-Governor [Thomas] Fletcher, of Missouri, and Ex-Governor [Alexander] Bullock, of Massachusetts.[2] Saville's fate is in their hands, for although he has tendered his resignation, it will not be accepted unless the commissioners report against him. The principal charge prepared by Prof. Marsh, of Yale, that Saville issued bad provisions, coffee, sugar and tobacco that were unsound will be met by Saville by the answer that if so, the government inspector is to blame, for all these goods were passed by that official, accepted by the government and paid for on that official's certificate, sent to Saville to issue, and that he could do nothing more than give them to the Indians. Another charge against Saville is that when buildings were to be erected at his agency he let the contract without advertising to his brother-in-law, at an extravagant price, who at once brought on gangs of workmen, who were fed out of stores that belonged to the Indians. Not less than twelve thousand Indians are fed at Red Cloud, and the pickings in the hands of a dishonest official would be considerable.[3]

I learned to-day from a prominent cattle raiser, a gentleman well known and much respected in Omaha, Judge [William A.] Carter, that a letter was lately received from some miners in the Black Hills who were with the first prospectors that succeeded in getting in this spring. The letter contained small specimens of gold and was addressed to some men who attempted to go to the hills country but were driven back. It stated that they had found good paying diggings—and advised their friends outside not to give up and go away but to stick by and come in as soon as possible. I asked Judge Carter if he thought the letter and the specimens were genuine. He answered: "I know it."[4]

While taking a ride this afternoon I learned that a military man had received a letter sent from the Hills with some very handsome enclosures. *The Herald* always goes to headquarters for news and it was not long before I had obtained an introduction to the gentleman. Of course I was well received. Any man who has sense enough to get gold out of the Black Hills may be trusted to treat a representative of the press courteously. After some general talk I said, "What can you tell me about the Black Hills?" "Nothing—except what you already know. There is gold there." "Is it there in paying quantities?" "Yes." "I was told that you have just received a letter from the mines."

After a pause he said that he had a letter from a man in the hills, that I might say that such a letter had been written, but I was not to use his name. He then showed me three nuggets saying that they came in the

28

letter and were fresh. They are of dull gold, resembling in color the large Alder Gulch nugget of John Creighton, and, contains, I judge, eight or nine dollars worth of the precious stuff.[5] The man who went into the hills and sent out these nuggets was sent to prospect by outside backers. My informant said, "The man who sent them is one of the best practical miners and prospectors in the United States. I have known him a good many years; he tells me there is plenty of gold there and I know he tells me the truth."

"You have no objections to my using these facts?"

"No; if there were only gold enough for one man to go and get, the mines would be a humbug. I could not control the Black Hills—nor could anybody. But there are special reasons why I do not wish my name to be published."

The United States Commissioners will leave for Fort Laramie in the morning and they will be accompanied by Mr. G. A. [Gilbert H.] Collins and your correspondent.[6]

Cheyenne is growing handsomely. B. L. Ford is building a brick block costing $30,000, at the corner of Sixteenth and Hill streets, to be the Inter-Ocean Hotel. Mr. [J. C.] Abney, the enterprising stage proprietor, will erect a brick building on the opposite corner, and George Leighton is building a three story brick store on the corner of 15th and Ferguson, opposite the post office.[7] These are specimen facts that show the prosperous state of affairs. Back of the town on an elevation one hundred feet above [the] city are two very pretty lakes, deep and clear, each about half a mile long. From these the city is to receive her water supply.

Dr. Daniels, who has just left the agencies, says the Indians never felt better than they do now. They appear to be perfectly satisfied, and he tells me that he thinks there will be no difficulty in negotiating a treaty with all the peaceable Indians who receive rations at the agencies. If there is any trouble it will be with the wild northern bands who have always been more or less hostile.[8]

H. S.

[*Omaha Daily Herald*, Wednesday, June 30, 1875]

[June 30, 1875 – Homer Stull, from Fort Laramie, Wyoming Territory]

The Land of Gold

Fort Laramie [Wednesday], June 30, 1875

To the editor of *The Herald*

The four members of the Sioux commission with which I left Omaha, Col. A. Comingo, of Independence, Mo., Hon. W. H. Ashby, of Beatrice, Neb., Rev. S. P. Hinman, of Santee Agency, and Mr. J. S. Collins, of Omaha, left Cheyenne Monday morning at 8 o'clock in a coach. Mr. G. H. Collins and your correspondent accompanied them in a top buggy with a good team. No traveling, except perhaps in a Pullman car, could be pleasanter than this; we invariably reached stations on our route ahead of time and arrived here at 3 p.m. Thursday [Tuesday].

The road from Cheyenne to Fort Laramie is the best I have ever seen in a new country and I doubt if as good a stretch of equal distance, ninety miles, can be found in the west. The qualities of soil which renders the land almost valueless make the road superb. It seems to be a natural turnpike along a great part of the route. A hard, firm road bed sustains your wheels so that they roll lightly forward and you can see that your horses are pushing rapidly onward without apparent effort. There is a little sand in two places but not enough to offer any serious impediment to loaded teams. It is noticeable that Cheyenne stands on much higher ground than Fort Laramie and the descent is made in the sand so that loaded teams coming this way find it easier on that account. This may not be true of quite all the sand on the route, but it is nearly so, and indeed there is so little sand on the road that nobody need be afraid of it. There are plenty of teams that can drive from Cheyenne to Fort Laramie or return in one day. Freighters receive from one cent to a cent and a half per pound for hauling merchandise over this route and this in a country that has no inhabitants except a few ranch men who charge a dollar per meal, with other prices in proportion.

These ranchmen are very friendly, but they take twenty-five cents for a glass of sour beer, which shows how a man may smile and be a villain. Portugese Philip [John Phillips], whose ranch is forty-five miles from Cheyenne is entitled to praise for the really fine meals that he serves up to travelers. Such milk, butter, bread, and coffee are not seen every day. But Philip has a lunacy which he inflicts upon strangers who tarry with him. It is his firm belief that the Clay, a creek about six feet wide which irrigates this part of Gen. [John M.] Thayer's kingdom, contains fish. This is to warn a confiding public against the delusion.[9]

I have neglected no opportunity to learn reliable facts concerning the state of affairs in the Black Hills. I have seen some men who have come out after provisions and while they freely state there are good paying diggings in the hills, and they know it, they are not disposed to tell where they are. They are going back immediately with supplies. I do not think this indisposition to tell where the best claims are located a bad sign but it prevents my giving as precise information as I wish to.

The lack of provisions is the great want among the miners. I heard last night of one company of men who stuck to their claims and worked quietly several days after they had nothing but "venison straight" to eat.

Ed. Smith and Jesse Potts wrote to a friend that they are taking out about seventeen cents to the pan, not far below the surface, and they urge their friend to come at once. Experienced miners say this is at the rate of $18 to $20 per day.[10]

An officer in the escort to Jenney's expedition writes to a brother officer here that he has found some fine gold himself though the officers refrained from working any claims or encouraging the men to do so. I hear that sixteen men deserted in one night. The officer alluded to in his letter said that it would be of no use to state the truth concerning the gold in the Black Hills; that he feared he might not be believed; that no man had attempted to prospect on the bank of the creek without finding more or less gold.

Jim Sanders is a frontiersman who is well known to the military in this department. He left St. Louis in 1843, when only 16 years of age, to go up the Arkansas valley, and he has with rare intervals been on the frontier ever since. He has encountered many trying scenes in this long experience but the love of adventure and the free air has always kept him on the border in front of the advance guard of civilization. He has the appearance of a truth-teller and I learn that he had charge of the pack train for Gen. Myers. He has lately come out of the Black Hills and I have been so fortunate as to meet him and be introduced by a mutual friend.[11]

After a little preliminary talk I asked him to tell me the true state of affairs in the Hills country. He said:

"I went out with the command as far as the east fork of the Beaver River where we made the first permanent camp. Four of us took French leave one night and struck in at the head of what they call Custer's Park. We prospected down through the park and in all the old shafts that had been made by miners last winter. We found gold in them all; fine float gold. I can't tell how much; we had no way to weigh it. I judge it went eight and ten cents to the pan. But that was not the biggest prospect we made."

"What would that pay per day per man?"

"If we had facilities to work, which we haven't got, we could make fifty dollars per day. There is some water, but it would be better if there was more. I haven't seen bed rock but once in the valley and the richest diggings and the heaviest gold is generally found just above the bed rock. I got ten cents to the panful in the gravel."

By further questioning I learned that there are now about three hundred men in the Hills working and prospecting; that they are not molested by the military, though it is common for the miners to visit the soldiers' camp fires. Sanders said, "An old gentleman from Sioux City," whose name he did not know, had found a good place about ten miles above the stockade and staked off a "discoverer's claim." About twenty-five miners are up there working. Others are working ten miles west of Harney City, towards the head of the gulch.[12] Sanders says that a mistake has been made in names; that the real French Creek is 13 miles north of the stream that the miners have given this name.

"When are you going back?" I asked.

"As soon as I can get some provisions—in a few days."

"Have you any gold?"

"What dust I had I left with an officer to send to General Crook."

In answer to questions as to routes and distances Sanders said: "From Spotted Tail Agency to the mining district is about 130 or 140 miles, from Fort Laramie it is 130 miles and the best route is by the fort. I left there (the mines) Wednesday morning and got to the post (Fort Laramie) Friday afternoon at 3 o'clock. I had a riding horse and pack horse. You can drive there in three days easy. The road down to the Beaver, from the ford, beyond that I don't know, they have made a new road. There is plenty of game. I met the party of eighty men going in north of Raw Hide Buttes."

"It is my opinion that there is going to be a big town at what is call[ed] Crow Foot Butte.[13] It is as pretty a country as you ever saw, plenty of timber, oak and pine and they say it is extensive. There is plenty of grass and fine black soil that will raise anything." Mr. Sanders said that the miners were not, he thought, now working the best part of the hill country. He has staked off a claim for himself but was not very definite in describing it, only saying that it was on the "east slope." The statements made by Sanders about the gold and the country have been confirmed by others.

Mr. J. S. Collins, the post trader at this fort, sent a quantity of goods into the Black Hills with Col. Dodge's command. Mr. H. Willard, in charge, has taken some gold in exchange for goods at the rate of $18 per ounce and has written for more goods which will be forwarded with the first train. Flour designed for the Black Hills arrived here this morning from Cheyenne and is now being unloaded by Mr. Collins's freighters. His store here is supplied with a large stock of all goods needed by any man in the field including mining tools. Being the only licensed trader in this section he is known to all the freighters who come to him for employment, giving him extra facilities in hauling goods. Miners will find this a good place to purchase either an entire outfit or anything that may be needed to complete it.

The commissioners will leave to-morrow morning for Red Cloud Agency and after transacting some business there and sending couriers after distant Indians they will go to the mining district to make a personal examination of the ground. They will be accompanied by a military escort and your correspondent.

Some of the Indians are sullen, and show bad temper because so many white men are in the Black Hills. I learn from a private letter that they have had a little fight with a few miners from Montana, who went into the Black Hills country from the north. The writer of the letter, Louis Richard, the interpreter, says he don't know if any were killed.[14]

An agent of Mr. J. S. Collins, in the Black Hills, writes that a quantity of his goods, valued at about $200, were left in a stockade, for want of transportation, to be sent for. When the wagons went back for them the goods were scattered about, burned and destroyed. A small quantity of government forage in the stockade shared the same fate.

H. S.

[*Omaha Daily Herald*, Tuesday, July 6, 1875]

[July 4, 1875 – Homer Stull, from Red Cloud Agency, Nebraska]

The Sioux at Home

Red Cloud Agency [Sunday], July 4, 1875

To the editor of *The Herald*

The members of the Sioux commission, who are doing the practical work in the field, left Fort Laramie on Thursday about noon, accompanied by an escort of fourteen cavalrymen, under command of Lieutenant O'Brien.[15] The camp on the Rawhide was easily reached that evening and formed a most agreeable resting place. This stream is narrow, and winds about through lofty divides, and magnificent stretches of rolling prairie, so that it appears to be a mere brook, but its waters are clear and abundant for all practical uses and its banks are skirted with trees. This last is a rare feature in that part of Wyoming, unfortunately, and these trees, so highly prized by the Indians, have made this a favorite ground. Here most of the devilment of this part of the country has been committed. It was under this shade that the skulking villains hid who shot seven bullets into the body of a harmless mail carrier, and the catalogue might be continued into a long chapter.[16]

The North Platte River which divides the Indian country from the free federal domain runs in sight of Fort Laramie and beyond this it is not considered safe for white men, not protected by an escort to go.[17] It is true that considerable numbers of Black Hills adventurers are crossing the Platte above and below the fort, and daily entering the Indian country in small parties, but they take their lives in their hands. The driver of our coach is a man not easily frightened; he has been sixteen years on the frontier, and has had abundant opportunity to learn what Indian signs mean, and I noticed that he was very fond of having the soldiers in sight. He seemed to be lonesome without them. He drove a carriage not long ago on this same road that contained a party of Sioux chiefs.[18] So long as they were with him all was well. After he had discharged his load and had turned back to Fort Laramie, he was accompanied by seven white men. They rode over the magnificent divides, each of which appears to be almost an empire without interruption, but all at once when he approached the Rawhide two hundred and fifty Cheyennes and Arapahoes seemed to rise out of the ground. They were all men in the vigor of life, no women and children were in sight. Their manner was that of an angry spoiled child. They came to his horses and looked at each as though they had a quarrel to settle, picked up the harness and threw it down again angrily. Every Indian carried a good rifle and many had revolvers, of course there was no hope that seven white men could fight with them successfully and the only course for the driver and his companions was to submit. The Indians went through the outfit, took out the provisions, and finally, after much debate among themselves, allowed the travelers to proceed.

The Sioux comprise the great body of the Indians in the northern country. They are divided into many bands, all numbering eight or nine thousand, but they are generally friendly and peaceable. They are intelligent, manly, and all things considered, are doubtless the best specimens of the aborigines now on the continent. They recognize the fact that they can no longer subsist by game and while they are proud and feel their power to make a strong fight, they know that they cannot successfully contend with the government. They therefore give their adherence to the agency system. But there are some hot heads among them who say that their men who have been to Washington and New York have been bewitched so that when they tell of the numbers and power of the white men, they are not capable of speaking the truth. Another element of the Indian character which must be counted is despair. Indians who know they cannot win final victory may still be terrible enemies to the people on the thinly settled border. Such are the southern Cheyennes and Arapahoes who lately came north after a series of fights in Gen. [John] Pope's department.[19] When told that they must return or they would be killed, they said they would die first. The Sioux as a body will have nothing to do with them, and they are now charging about the prairies, well armed and mounted, a species of land pirates.

They lately passed near Fort Fetterman and stole two hundred and fifty horses on the northern border of Colorado.[20] We saw medicine bags containing little round pebbles and a lot of other mysterious trash that they had hung on little crosses by their camp fires. They believe that the medicine bag guards them from evil and brings good luck.

The grass this side of the Platte is much better than we found before crossing the river. The land is undoubtedly poor but as a stock country it is desirable. Game is said to exist in quantity to reward the patient and skillful hunter but it is not plentiful by the route we came. On the first day out Captain Ashby killed an antelope and yesterday Col. Comingo wounded a deer.

On the second night we camped on the head waters of the Niobrara, where it is only a small creek, and at ten o'clock yesterday entered the White River valley. The soil here is dry but buffalo grass exists in abundance with plenty of water accessible. This land is now almost unoccupied and the horses and cattle of the Sioux do not half consume the grass. The scenery is picturesque with high natural walls on both sides and, although the valley is by no means a garden spot, it appears to great advantage in comparison to what we saw in northern Wyoming.

About noon yesterday we came to Sioux lodges grouped four or five in a place in some natural camping ground at the foot of a canyon. The inmates looked at our coach and escort with great curiosity and soon after we had passed we could see an Indian galloping towards the agency. The commissioners had been expected and these were messengers going to the headquarters after news. How much trouble might be spared these people if they could read *The Herald*.

Our coach drove to Dr. Saville's house and we were cordially received by him.[21] He left his family in Sioux City on his last visit to the east and we found him as cheerful as a man in his condition could be expected to be. Shortly after our arrival a tap was heard at the door and when it was answered an Indian in full dress stalked into the room robed in an air of importance and a coarse blanket, bearing a good sized hatchet on his left arm. He was first introduced to each one of the party and after he had shaken hands with each, and the usual "how-how" had been exchanged he walked to the middle of the room where he stood bolt upright, waving his right hand slightly as if to say: "Commence at me now." This was Red Dog, a Sioux chief.[22]

"Tell him," said Col. Comingo, "that we are glad to see him."

This being duly interpreted, Hon. Red Dog replied: "It ought to give anybody pleasure to meet a wise man." A good deal of this sort followed, but I presume this is enough.

During the evening at least a dozen head men called to pay their respects and as all were introduced to each white man present, we had considerable hand-shaking and "how-ing" to do. All were told that they were to come to-day, after noon, and hear what the commissioners had to say. At the appointed time they appeared, filled the room relit their pipes and a regular preliminary council was held. They were asked when and where they would be ready to meet the Indians of Spotted Tail's Agency. This led to considerable talk, during which the Indians fixed upon "twelve nights" as the time they would require to get their bands together here, and they further agreed to notify Spotted Tail of the time and place and to secure the attendance of his people.

To-morrow morning we shall leave here, with an escort, for Spotted Tail Agency and expect to pass the night there. Tuesday we shall set out for the Black Hills.

The weather here is so cold that a fire is necessary in the house, and the atmosphere out of doors is that of a November day in Omaha.

I was at a "squaw dance" last night where it was hot enough. Madame Red Cloud presided at her favorite instrument, the drum, with that ease and grace for which she is so justly celebrated.

H. S.

[*Omaha Daily Herald*, Tuesday, July 13, 1875]

[July 6, 1875 – Homer Stull, from Spotted Tail Agency, Nebraska]
Still Pow-Wowing
Spotted Tail Agency [Tuesday], July 6
To the Editor of *The Herald*

The Sioux Commission was delayed one day at Red Cloud and therefore did not arrive here until last night. If the time occupied in these negotiations concerned only the Indians the delay would suit exactly. The laziness of these people approaches the sublime. They have absolutely nothing to do and they do it with a competence that defies imitation.

But they are a queer set. Monday night a number of gentlemen, who met by chance at Red Cloud's, were enjoying a friendly union and the hospitality of Mr. J. W. Dear, who had just arrived from Cheyenne, and when Col. Comingo was reminding a group of friends that it was ninety-nine years or thereabouts since our forefathers landed at Plymouth Rock, a messenger arrived who said a number of Spotted Tail's men were outside and they wanted to talk.[23]

It was then 10 o'clock, but it was thought best to hear what the Indians had to say. Mr. Dear's billiard hall was cleared for the purpose, a table provided for the secretary and reporter, the commissioners assumed a proper air of deep solemnity and the interpreter appeared, conducting ten big Indians to the council. They proved to be not Spotted Tail's men, as we had been informed, but Black Bear and men from his band of Kiyuksa Sioux. Black Bear and "Pawnee Killer," who came with him, had both been in the council held on the 4th inst. (reported in my last letter) and they know all that was to be learned by them.[24]

"Ask them," said the chairman, "what they want."

Black Bear straightened himself in an attitude of great dignity, as though about to address the Roman senate, his hatchet resting on his left arm which was bent at the elbow to support it, his blanket falling in graceful folds about his breast. I was expecting a tremendous development and had prepared myself with three pencils beside my note book, sharpened at both ends, to see that nothing valuable should be lost to history.

"We have heard," said Black Bear, "that you are going away. Our hearts are sad. We do not want you to go away."

Just imagine that great overgrown lubber coming in parade dress at 10 o'clock at night, an hour when any sensible Indian ought to be reposing in the bosom of his numerous family, to weep at the departure of a few roving commissioners.

"Tell him," said the chairman, "that we must go to-morrow, but we will return in twelve nights."

This appeared to heal the lacerated affections of Black Bear. He then went on to say that he had told his people the talk at the council on Sunday, and they didn't believe him. The matter was explained again by the chairman, and the Indians, after a number of good, hearty assenting grunts, took their leave.

Joe Merrivale, the army guide, came into Red Cloud yesterday, direct from Colonel Dodge's camp in the Black Hills. He says that it rains there every day—he never saw such a country for that. About two hundred and fifty miners are in the Hills, and all are satisfied. He saw none who talked of leaving and did not know of any going away. He saw one little nugget worth, he thinks $3, and a number of pieces worth ninety cents each. All the men have some gold, but they are afraid to develop their claims because they expect to be removed by military sent from Fort Laramie for that purpose. The gold they have is therefore taken from the surface or very near that. Some gold has been taken to the sutler's store and traded but he thinks not much.[25]

Dr. [John L.] Mills, the physician at this agency, has a very handsome nugget lately brought from French Creek, and the same reports circulate here as we heard at Red Cloud.[26] Every man in the Hills has gold, they say, and no one has been known to have much. I notice that men here who know most about miners are not discouraged by this fact. They say that the circumstances under which the miners and prospectors have been placed makes it reasonable that they should not have much time for actual mining. They have spent a considerable portion of their time in prospecting and have had to watch for Indians, the soldiers, and for something to eat all at once. If they had been shoemakers and compelled to make their own boots under such circumstances they would be barefooted to-day.

Messengers were sent to Spotted Tail and all his bands, numbering about nine thousand Indians. They were notified of the council to be held at Red Cloud on the 17th inst. Our escort will camp to-night ten miles from here on the way to French Creek. We start at daylight to-morrow for the Black Hills. The distance from this place to Col. Dodge's camp on French Creek is about sixty-five miles.

I wish to warn all *Herald* readers not to go to the Black Hills alone. We have met more than one man who was pushing for the mines without company. "I am an outfit by myself," said such a man to me, and I felt more interest in him because when I asked him where he was from, he said "Nebraska." "What part?" "Omaha."

It is true that the agency Indians, comprising the greater portion of the Sioux, are more tolerant and friendly to whites than they have ever been. Last year they would not allow any white man or any half-breed to go to the Black Hills and any attempt to do so would have caused blood-shed. They have just brought in a man and his family who were going to the mines. They were angry at the man's presumption, but did nothing more than compel him to come to the agency. Nick Janis, our guide, says that they are seldom so lenient, that when they meet a lone man on the prairie in their county, they are apt to take all that he has, even his clothing.[27]

The country in the White [River] valley, northwestern Nebraska, where the present Sioux reservation is located, is much better than any we saw in Wyoming.[28] The soldiers moving from Fort Laramie took wood for cooking in their wagons. This country is well wooded. I am informed that over five thousand cords could be cut within one mile of Red Cloud Agency, and it is still plentier here. Men are now getting out lumber for a church and other buildings, and it is found in abundance though the quality is not of the best.

Lieutenant [William E.] Hofman, who has charge of the garden at this post, Camp Sheridan, has a fine thrifty crop of over four hundred bushels of turnips; he has already gathered over five thousand radishes, has a great quantity left and has eight thousand cabbage plants doing well. There has been no irrigation, and no necessity for any. There is an abundance of grass throughout the valley and it is very fresh and bright. A heavy rain fell yesterday.[29]

Another council has been held with Spotted Tail and his band, and the time of the council at Red Cloud Agency changed to next Friday. We will therefore return to Red Cloud to-morrow. I am very sorry for the delay in starting for the Black Hills. My heart is on the ground.

H. S.

[*Omaha Daily Herald,* Thursday, July 15, 1875]

[July 6, 1875 - "Mart," from Spotted Tail Agency, Nebraska]

Letter from Spotted Tail

From our Special Correspondent. Spotted Tail, [Tuesday] July 6, 1875

Editors *Nebraskian*

The interviews with the Indians thus far have been of a very airy and unsatisfactory character. The commission had a talk at Red Cloud on the 5th, which consisted mainly in the exchange of words of friendship and the like, but failed to elicit any very hearty affirmative response to the idea of a council over on the Missouri River. At Spotted Tail on the 6th, [Red Cloud Agency, July 5] Black Bear and some of his braves had a talk with the commission, but which amounted to nothing, save an expression on the part of the Indians that they are sad because the commission intended leaving on the morrow. The Indians are cunning in some respects, but are disgustingly thin when it comes to talking business, especially that kind of business which engages the attention of the commission.

We get word from General Dodge's camp, in the Black Hills, nearly every day. It is currently reported that there are over two hundred miners in the hills, who are putting their time for the greater part in prospecting, not wishing to develop their claims until after it is known whether the government will interfere with their operations. The largest nugget reported as having been taken out is valued at three dollars. The sutlers have traded for a goodly number of nuggets worth ninety cents, and considering the amount of mining that has been done, considerable dust has been exchanged for stores. It is nearly all surface gold, which would indicate that a little delving down would turn out big money.

The miners are said to have had a pretty hard time, on account of rains, watching Indians, dodging the soldiers, and hunting grub. We have seen men alone on their way to the mines seemingly regardless of the actual danger that beset them at every step. This is an act of rashness one would suppose the most inexperienced scarcely capable of. Such, however, is man's love of gold and fair woman that no undertaking for their possession deters him. Parties numbering less than ten men should not undertake the trip. Only a few days since the Indians captured a family consisting of four persons, and forced them to come into the agency. The Indians are more lenient than is their wont to be, but just how long they will be able to support this degree of civilization the gods have not revealed, and it is safe to presume that somebody's scalp will pay the penalty of such folly.

This is a fine country viewed from other standing points than that of the gold-seeker. It is well timbered and watered with fertile valleys and rich grazing lands. Cattle do well here the entire year without any artificial protection or hay or grain. The producing qualities of the soil have been demonstrated by Lieutenant Hofman and others with highly gratifying results. If the mines are thrown open and large numbers of people go there many of them will doubtless find as much profit in agricultural pursuits as in mining. And this very feature of the country is destined to attract thousands who would not otherwise think of emigrating to the Black Hills region.

The commissioners think it is more than possible that the final "big talk" will take place at Red Cloud, and not on the Missouri River, as was at first announced. The chiefs are very reticent on the subject, yet have said sufficient to indicate an unwillingness on their part to go that distance to enjoy the luxury of a pow-wow. The outcome of this effort to get the big Injuns together is thus far so clearly a fragment of chaos that your correspondent deposeth not.[30]

Mart

[North Platte *Western Nebraskian*, Friday, July 23, 1875]

[July 9, 1875 – Homer Stull, from Red Cloud Agency, Nebraska]
The War Path

Red Cloud Agency, [Friday] July 9, 1875

To the Editor of *The Herald*

The Sioux Commissioners arrived here last night from Spotted Tail, having left that agency yesterday. Bissonette's ranch is located thirteen miles west of the post, Camp Sheridan, and in a little group of Sioux lodges.[31] We found Bissonette and a number of Indians consulting over a report that had just been brought in by a Sioux runner that the Hunkpapas had come down from the north on the war path. He had seen twenty-five Hunkpapa "soldiers" who told him they would be revenged on the whites for trespassing in the Black Hills. They had killed three white men in one place and seven in another. These twenty-five soon left him and headed towards Spotted Tail Agency. He saw the trail of another small band leading directly to the route between the two agencies commonly traveled by white men with wagons.[32] He thought

40

they were aiming to strike the road and attack the first travelers they met. The Sioux at Bissonette's were alarmed for the safety of their horses and while they were telling us the news, we saw Indians out running over the prairie to bring them in. The Hunkpapas are a band of wild northern Sioux who have never, as a body, acknowledged any treaty relations with the government. We afterwards heard through another friendly Indian that the Hunkpapas now declare that they will fill the Black Hills with the tracks of their horses' feet; by which they mean that they will overrun the mining district and drive out the white men. We also learn from two sources (both Indian) that this war party lately encountered two small bands of miners and that they killed seven white men in one party and three in another.

Our escort that had been ordered out from Camp Robinson to accompany us to the Black Hills had been sent back to await the conclusion of the next council with the chiefs and head men representing both branches of "The Great Sioux Nation." We were therefore without protection except by his own arms. Our baggage wagon had gone on ahead and might then be in the hands of the Hunkpapas. This was not very comforting for we had generally packed our good clothes in the wagon and were wearing old hunting dresses. I was wondering whether my suit would fit any young brave and where he would find room for the long red cloth that all the Sioux generally drag behind them on the grass.

But would the rebellious rascals be so lost to grace as to attack the United States commissioners? Bissonette thought they might. Their hearts were bad and they might go for us if they came in our way. I always did like soldiers and if we could have seen our cavalry escort just then they would have been positively handsome. There was only one alternative, either to go ahead and protect ourselves, or remain in the Sioux village and camp there with no tents, blankets, or provisions. It was decided to move on. Our guns were loaded, belts filled with cartridges buckled on, and every precaution taken for defence. A friendly Sioux, who was known to be a true man, came forward mounted on his pony and took the lead, riding ten or fifteen rods in advance. The bushes at the crossing were considered the first dangerous place and after that it was thought the sharp turns and precipices in a little strip of bad lands on our road afforded the best place for attack.[33] On the open broad prairies, which constituted the great portion of the route, no danger was apprehended.

Our Sioux friend usually rode ahead, sitting very erect on his pony, his sixteen shooting Winchester rifle well in hand. When the open ground was reached he came back to talk. I have no doubt that what he meant to say was very interesting. Coming to scat he said, "Celah," and wanted to shake hands in a very cordial manner.[34] I was going to ask him to call at *The Herald* building when he came to town but could not quite make it. When he put his uncivilized finger in his mouth and blew it away, I showed him a box of fine imported cigars, manufactured by West & Fritscher, with a look that said, "How is that for high?" His great broad bronze features lit up with a smile of true inwardness, which replied, "It is away up." He lit his cigar, took a fresh grip of his rifle, and went on to form, by himself, our skirmish line.

A rain storm appeared ahead of us and we drew into [John] Bridgman's ranch. This is a most unpromising place, but it was here that Captain [Guy V.] Henry and his men found protection from the storm last winter, when they had been to the Black Hills and came out so badly frozen. Doubtless many of the men owe their lives to this friendly log cabin. Captain Henry has received a year's leave on account of his injuries. His hands are ruined, and I hear he will be retired. Bridgman is an Alabama man, who was in the Confederate army, captured at Missionary Ridge, and then volunteered to guard the frontier. He long ago married an Indian girl and five dusky pledges of affection now stub their toes and chase ponies in that immediate vicinity. They say that he is in difficulty, and nothing but the onward march of civilization will ever help him out. Last year he bought a brand new horse rake. If course it was the kind that goes on wheels and has a comfortable seat for the driver. But the Indians wanted the spokes for whip handles, and that revolving back action hay rake now looks like a hen that has been through a three days rain. And they say that if Bridgman ever gets anything to eat in his ranch, eight or nine of his cousins come and stay with him.[35]

"You seem to have a good place for trading." Said he, "Yes, but I can't make anything at it." "Why not?" "Because any Indian is likely to ask me for fifty dollars worth of goods and stay here till he gets it." "Can't you make him understand that an article worth fifty dollars costs money." "That is why he wants it."

We left Spotted Tail Agency so soon after the close of the last council that I did not have time to write about it. And I am informed that reasons of public policy demand that my report of the council should not be published. There can be no harm, however, in saying that old Spotted Tail loomed up like a morning star. It was fun for me to see that old pagan wrestling with four Christian gentlemen, and as a specimen of mutual gymnastics it was superb. The old chief is a natural orator, and is, beyond that, an astute thinker with a mind that cuts clear through subterfuges and evasions. Finally he told the commissioners that if they would adopt his plan in holding the next council he would do all in his power to facilitate the negotiations. They agreed to it and Spotted Tail is now here with two hundred of his men. Half-breeds say that a great visit is going on and we are to have feasts and horse races, but we know that "Old Spot" is not entirely occupied in social pleasures.

It is expected that the council with Red Cloud's and Spotted Tail's people united will commence Monday afternoon [July 12]. We expect to leave for the Black Hills as soon as it is closed.

H. S.

[*Omaha Daily Herald*, Saturday, July 17, 1875]

[July 12, 1875 – Homer Stull, from Red Cloud Agency, Nebraska]

The Black Hills Treaty

Red Cloud Agency, [Monday] July 12, 1875

To the Editor of *The Herald*

Yesterday afternoon a report circulated here among the great number of Indians present to attend the feasts preceding the expected council that a party of Sioux had been fired into by a company of soldiers and at least two killed. It was known also that a number had been wounded and that several young men of the party had not been seen since the affray. Excitement soon ran high. Tall Lance, an influential chief lately returned from Washington, appeared in mourning, his brother having been one of the slain. He threw away his clothes and, except one piece of a blanket drawn completely over his shoulders, he was entirely naked. After Indian custom, his horses, his tent, and everything he possessed on earth were divided among his tribe. His heart was very bad. Young men in bands of forty and fifty began to gather on the prairie well armed and mounted. They finally all rallied around Young-Man-Afraid-of-his-Horses, and it was said that his brother was among the Indians fired upon, and not since seen. Spotted Tail sent word to the commissioners that there could be no council with him or his people until this murder should be explained.[36]

Meanwhile three confidential agents of the commissioners were among the Indians seeking to learn the exact facts of the killing and the temper of the tribes. I am informed that in a secret council of the Sioux held last evening he [Spotted Tail] said: "I have tried all I could to be a white man, but I am not willing to go further in that direction. I want to do what is right, but I will not meet the white men in council until this murder of our young men is investigated." "And," said my informant, "when he said that, all the Indians hallooed 'how, how.'" Then Spotted

Tail advised them to be calm and patient until all the facts were learned.

To-day the first crude rumors have been crystallized into the facts as they appear from the Indian stand point, and fortunately some of the young men, whose fate was in doubt, have come into camp. This is the story they tell. About six weeks ago a horse-stealing expedition, called a war party, was organized out of the wildest young men at Red Cloud and Spotted Tail agencies to go against the Poncas. They say there was just one man less than two hundred, and yet they were not missed at either agency. They had been to the Poncas where they had a little fight, stole some horses, and were on their way back when they came to the Little White River crossing, 132 miles from Spotted Tail Agency. Here they unexpectedly came upon a camp of forty soldiers. An interpreter with the soldiers called out to them, "Have you a paper?" meaning a pass showing that they had a right to be away from their agency. "Yes, we have a paper," said the leader, "but it is in possession of one of our men who has not come up yet." "The soldiers will shoot any Indian they find here without a pass," said the interpreter. The Indians said, "We are agency men and don't want any trouble with white men," but seeing a piece of timber at hand they ran for it. Then the soldiers fired, killing two and wounding three, one seriously. Their fire was not returned.[37]

This is the Indian version. The soldiers, who are from Fort Randall, might give a different account. In order to comprehend the Indian's feeling on this matter you must understand that he does not consider that it is not at all proper for the government to interfere with any little diversion that the Sioux may have with the Poncas. They agree not to kill white men and consider that they are good Indians if they keep their word. They say that their 199 young men were as well armed as the 40 soldiers and they could have got away with them had they been disposed.

The young men who came in this morning say that after the firing the interpreter who was with the soldiers came to them in the timber and said, "If it is really true that you have not been against white men, the soldiers have made a mistake. If you come to camp the soldiers will give you rations and some horses." The Indians did not go out, fearing treachery, and so did not get the rations, but the interpreter brought them two horses, which they rode into the agency. The most important part of the day's news is that the brother of Young-Man-Afraid-of-his-Horses is one of the men returned this morning. There is much rejoicing over this one fact. The Indians say that the young men who were charging about yesterday in squadrons were getting ready to avenge his fall, had he been killed they would have commenced a general war at once. One of them told the commissioners that in that case, "it would have been black all around."

Old Red Cloud is losing his influence with his people. He was not asked to sign the late treaty relinquishing the right to hunt in Nebraska and he did not sign it. The late council with his people was opened and closed by the young chief whom I have mentioned. His name is erroneously translated. It signifies They Fear His Horse. His father won it in battle and the title and rank were lately conferred on the young chief. Red Cloud feels his position keenly, and has but little to say.

A curious exhibition of one phase of Indian character was seen in a visit of Tall Lance to the commissioners this afternoon. He came in mourning, and entirely naked except a piece of a coarse black blanket. His eyes were on the floor and he did not speak for a long time. Finally he said, "I learned long ago that the Poncas and the Omahas were the enemies of my tribe. I learned that they had arms and I went to try them. I was successful in getting some of their horses, though I was wounded eight times. Wise men of our tribe told me that I better not go to war. I listened to them. Wise men told me to be a friend to the white people. I listened to them. I stood lately in the presence of the Great Father and I heard white men, great chiefs, say before the Great Spirit that they meant to deal justly and kindly with the Indians. I believed them. Now they tell me that it was a mistake when my brother was killed. I have a great heart and though the heaven and the earth come together on me today, I do not mean to be bad. But there is sorrow in my lodge. If my father will give me six beeves so that my children shall not be hungry while they cry, they will feel better."

His father, the same is Dr. Saville, told him he should have the six cattle. Tall Lance then cast his mournful eye on a very fine blanket and suggested that he might feel better if he had that too. Dr. Saville gave that to him also.

You will see that we are not to have an outbreak just yet on account of this tragedy on Little Whitewater, but with hundreds of adventurers overrunning Indian country, it is likely to occur almost any day. Bridgman, the owner of a ranche that has been described to *Herald* readers, and the husband of an Indian wife, says he does not dare to remain in his home but will move to the agency. Only a few days ago Col. [Capt. Anson] Mills, commanding at Camp Sheridan, told me of an incident that illustrates the situation. Some Indian hunters came suddenly upon some Black Hills men and received a volley. Luckily nobody was hit but the Indians showed Col. Mills holes through their blankets cut by the miners' bullets. And they asked Col. Mills if they might retain the horses and other goods of the miners if they would go and capture them. Col. Mills told them they could not, and they said they could not understand the position of a government that burned miners' outfits but would not let Indians have them.[38]

Our readers will remember Sitting Bull [the Oglala]. He has been the fighting friend of this agency and on one occasion he rallied his young men to its defense, himself taking the post of danger, when two thousand hostile Indians threatened to burn the buildings and murder their occupants. The fact was reported to the authorities at Washington and on his late visit there he received a very handsome present. He brought it here to-day, a Winchester rifle with the following engraved on the stock, viz: "To Sitting Bull from the president for bravery and true friendship." Mr. Bull was in a bad humor. I asked him how he liked his sixteen-shooter, and he gave me a look that seemed to say, "That's none of your business." Then he added with great deliberation, "It's all I have."[39]

But Sitting Bull had business on hand. He told Dr. Saville that he was going to bring the miners out of the Black Hills and he wanted to borrow a horse. The doctor told him he had no horse that he could spare and a commissioner urged him to wait in patience a little while and the soldiers would bring the miners out.

We shall have some talk tomorrow looking towards a council, but the prospect for business is not at all flattering. The commissioners have told the Indians that after the preliminary council here they will go to the Black Hills to define the boundaries of the purchase.

H. S.

[*Omaha Daily Herald*, Tuesday, July 20, 1875]

[July 14, 1875 – Homer Stull, from Red Cloud Agency, Nebraska]

Seven Millions

Red Cloud Agency, [Wednesday] July 14, 1875

To the Editor of *The Herald*

Since my last letter on the 12th the hearts of the Indians have been getting better very fast. They have not forgotten the killing of two of their young men at Little White River crossing by the soldiers, but they are not disposed to let that interfere with the pending negotiations for the sale of the Black Hills. A half-breed told me last night that some of the older Indians said yesterday that the young scamps were themselves to blame; that if they had stayed at home they would not have been hurt. Mr. J. H. Bosler, the contractor, has arrived with a herd of cattle, and Tall Lance, of whose happy conversion I wrote you, is not the only brave whose heart is mollified by the prospect of beef. There is not game enough in this beautiful White River valley to support one-fiftieth of its population, and the Indian does not need to be informed of the fact.[40]

The home of the Sioux in this valley is a charming place. We are told that we have witnessed more rain than usually falls in July, but be that as it may, this reservation is a garden spot compared with northern Wyoming. I have not seen that part of northern Nebraska adjacent to the reservation, but I am told that it does not compare favorably with the Indian lands. Here, there appears to be no need of irrigation, there is a great abundance of grass suitable for winter grazing, and at Camp Sheridan (at Spotted Tail Agency) I saw a most thrifty and productive garden, on a very large scale, that had not been irrigated at all. Col. Comingo, a member of the commission, who was reared in Kentucky and is familiar with the famous Blue Grass region, lately penetrated the canons that lie several miles south of the main traveled road between the agencies in search of deer, and came back bringing most enthusiastic reports concerning the beauty and fertility of the natural meadows that he found there. He rode for miles over pasture lands that could support and fatten large herds. Bridgman, whose ranch is in that vicinity, says that the land there will raise fine crops of every kind grown in Nebraska.

Captain Ashby, who resides at Beatrice, Nebraska, was on the same hunt. He says that the lower portion of the White River valley (nearest the stream) is very similar to the valley of the Blue, and of the Republican, while the higher table lands, the natural meadows I have mentioned, are superior to either. The soil is rich and black and the ground closely covered with thrifty grass fifteen inches high. The climate here is charming, clear, bright days and cool nights. Three bounteous rains have fallen within ten days, but there has been very little cloudy weather.

The Indians here are doing nothing and they are really suffering for want of something to do. There is no game worth mentioning, they seldom hunt, and I do not wonder that the young men are easily persuaded to go on horse-stealing expeditions by the wild northern Indians who visit them. Twenty thousand average whites placed in this valley and confined here without tools or stock or implements of any kind except an abundance of horses and Winchester rifles, would do more mischief before the close of the first year.

A number of Cheyennes and Arapahoes yesterday sent word to the commissioners that they would like to shake hands with them. A conference was granted, and Little Wolf (head chief of the northern Cheyennes), Wild Hog, Magpie, The Limber, The White Maned Horse,

Bear Robe, The Elk that Sits Up, and The Man That Comes in Sight were ushered into the presence of "the great white chiefs." The Arapahoes were represented by Friday, their chief, White Horse, Iron, and Spotted Crow.

A glance at these Indians revealed that they are inferior to the Sioux. They are the men who might be selected for desperate deeds. If deviltry is not written in the countenances of these Arapahoes, I have mistaken their expression. Certainly they are of the people that one would prefer to meet by daylight.

There are now about one hundred lodges here of the Cheyennes and their poverty has caused them to double up so that each contains an average of nine people. The Arapahoes average 9 ½ to a lodge, three families sometimes occupying one tepee. There is now no law or treaty which provides for feeding these people. They apply to Dr. Saville for rations and present a knotty problem to him. If he does not give them provisions the women and children will starve and the men will raid the frontier and punish the white settlers; if he does issue rations it is without authority of law, and at his own risk. He is feeding them at present, and the commissioners assured them yesterday that at the grand council they would try to place them on the same footing as the Sioux. This was immensely satisfactory to the chiefs. Their plea for help was really pathetic. I hope they may be fed for a limited time with the distinct understanding that they are to learn to work and earn their own living.

I cannot say whether Dr. Saville has in all things conducted the affairs of his agency honestly or not. I have seen enough to know that injustice has been done him in one important particular. Prof. Marsh says that on a certain day Dr. Saville pretended to issue a certain number of cattle to the Indians and next day he looked for the hides and found that their number did not correspond with the number of cattle. On this ground he supposed that he had discovered a fraud. But he was too fast. These Indians live all over this valley, some of them ten miles from the agency, camped on the streams and wherever they choose to locate, grouped in bands each of which has a chief or head man. Beef is issued to them in the form of live cattle. Sometimes the steers are shot by the Indians near the corral, but in the majority of cases the animal is driven off to the camp before it is killed. The hides belong to the Indians and are brought to the traders whenever it pleases them. It is not at all surprising that Prof. Marsh could not find anything like the full number of hides soon after the issue. A few cattle are butchered by the employees of the agency for a company of widows, but the great bulk of the beef is issued as I have stated.

The Great Sioux Nation met the commissioners in council this afternoon in Dr. Saville's large warehouse. Numerous representatives were present from all the tribes belonging to Red Cloud and Spotted Tail agencies. The speakers on the part of the Indians were Spotted Tail, Red Cloud, Red Dog, Baptiste Good, and Fast [Swift] Bear. They opened the council and indulged in a great deal of random talk.[41] They said that last winter they did not receive their rations regularly and during a part of the time they were without food. They then gave a list of half breeds and squaw men whom they wished appointed as Dr. Saville's book-keepers and assistants. The commissioners submitted two questions. First, when shall the grand council to negotiate for the sale of the Black Hills be held? And second, where shall that council be held?

A loud laugh of scorn arose from the Indians at the proposition that the Commissioner of Indian Affairs would prefer to have the grand council held on the Missouri River. It was too much to think of this great Sioux Nation going away from home to hold a council. Spotted Tail prayed the Great Spirit to watch these white men, to look at them before and behind because he knew that they had come to steal his country. Baptiste Good said the Indians had determined to ask seven millions of dollars for the Black Hills and added they would never sell any more country for two dollars and a half. In spite of Baptiste's very good name, he told the chairman of the commission, who stated that the four years during which the government had agreed to feed the Sioux had expired, that he lied. The Indians have always understood that the time was thirty years, though it reads four in the document.[42]

The place at which the grand council is to be held was fixed, subject to the approval of the Commissioner of Indian affairs, is on the bank of a creek half way between the Spotted Tail and Red Cloud agencies.[43] The date was not settled. It will be as soon as all the different tribes interested in the Black Hills can be brought together. The commissioners will leave to-morrow morning for the Missouri River agencies, by way of the Black Hills, and a delegation of Indians will accompany them. Another delegation of Indians will leave to-morrow on a similar mission to the wild northern tribes, now camped on Tongue River and the Yellowstone.[44] A military escort under command of Capt. [James] Egan, of the Second Cavalry, will accompany us to the Black Hills. Maj. [Capt. William H.] Jordon, commanding at Camp Robinson, has placed us under obligations for the prompt and courteous manner in which he is doing everything that can add to the comfort of the expedition. The officers from Camp Robinson attended the council to-day and appeared much interested.[45]

I close my letter in the midst of a busy scene; the packing of our wagons and the preparations for Indian feasts. Lo is in a pleasant excitement. He is not very complimentary when he bends over my table and asks me to write no lies on my paper but, bless his big Pagan heart, he means well.

We are only sixty miles from the mining district and I hope soon to be investigating the diggings so that I can describe them as they appear to the naked eye.

H. S.

[*Omaha Daily Herald*, Thursday, July 22, 1875]

[July 15 and July 16, 1875 – Rev. Samuel D. Hinman, from Red Cloud Agency and Chadron Creek, Nebraska]

Advices from The Sioux Commission

Washington, D.C., July 19—The following dispatches were received at the Indian Bureau this morning from the Rev. S. D. Hinman of the Special Sioux Commission:

Red Cloud Agency, July 15—We met the Brulés and Oglalas in council to-day. They desire a general council to be held at Chadron Creek, midway between Spotted Tail and Red Cloud agencies, Sept. 1, and positively refuse to go to the Missouri River. They will aid in bringing in the Northern Sioux and Cheyenne. We have assented to the place and time designated by them, subject to your approval.

Camp on the Chadron, July 19 [16]—The young Chief Afraid of his Horses, with fifty of his best men, have gone to bring in the Northern Sioux. Red Dog and others are accompanying us to the Missouri to influence the Indians there.

[Unsigned]

[*Chicago Daily Tribune*, Tuesday, July 20, 1875]

[July 20, 1875 – Homer Stull, from Custer's Gulch on French Creek, Black Hills, Dakota Territory]

Gold! Gold! Gold!

Custer's Gulch on French Creek in the Black Hills, [Tuesday] July 20, 1875

To the editor of *The Herald*

I write in the midst of the excitement and contradictory reports of a mining camp. One man tells me that the Black Hills as a gold producing region has been greatly exaggerated; another who be equally honest and familiar with the facts assures me that the half has not been told. It is admitted on all hands that nobody has yet secured any quantity of gold that would support the reputation of the mines. I shall examine the facts and write more in detail as to the gold yield hereafter, only premising that the great body of men in the hills are still prospecting, and that but very little work has yet been done. Just now there is a stampede to a new discovery on Spring Creek, twenty miles from here. Prof. Jenney informs me that the new gulch promises well, and he has just come from there.

If people could enter the Black Hills by railroad, and passengers could be set down at once in the heart of the gold region, they would be delighted with its pure mountain streams, as clear as crystal, its fine forests, and its natural meadows that are not surpassed, but they would not feel that enthusiasm that is common among all who approach the Hills by the only routes now practicable. I have seen enough to know that the country between the two forks of the Cheyenne [River] would be a valuable addition to the white man if no ounce of gold were ever found here.

The speedy settlement of the Black Hills is now beyond question. It therefore becomes important that the public be correctly informed as to the routes. I am prepared to describe one of the entrances to the hills, and I promise to follow my friend Spotted Tail's advice and not put any lies on my paper.

On the 15th inst. the commissioners, who are to negotiate the purchase of the Black Hills, accompanied by your correspondent, left Red Cloud Agency and marched for Chadron Creek. It is on the banks of this stream, twenty-five miles from Red Cloud and twenty miles from Spotted Tail Agency, that it is proposed to hold the final grand council with all the tribes and bands of Indians interested in the Black Hills as soon as they can be brought together. The road here may be called good. It is such as is found on the better class of prairies where no fords or bridges have been provided. You get bounced somewhat on the hummocks, and it is fun to see a wagon plunge into a creek. It is more fun if you don't happen to be in the wagon.[46]

July 16th. Marched to old Spotted Tail Agency, a deserted place given up to rank weeds and the energetic mosquitoes to [obliterated by crease in the paper] camped on a little creek not named, about three miles west of Slim Butte.[47] Captain Egan proposes to christen the creek Slim Butte Creek. The grass here is of the best and abundant; water of the creek is sweet and not fit to drink. Marched to-day twenty-four miles, upset one army wagon and broke two wagon tongues. There don't appear to have been any county commissioners in this part of the country.

The "original inhabitants," that is what their Great Father calls them, seemed pleased with the proposed sale of the Black Hills. They are satisfied that the white man will have it and are glad of the chance to drive a good bargain with them. But they have so long been in the habit of objecting to anybody's entering the hills country that they can't quite get over it. Spotted Tail agreed to the commissioners going there, provided they would first return to Red Cloud and hold a council there. The Oglalas and Brulés then named the representatives, five from each, that should accompany the commissioners to the Missouri River agencies, a measure that was advocated by the commissioners on the ground that the presence of these Indians would show to others that they were in full accord with them.

Red Dog and No Flesh seem to be the chairmen of the two delegations. A few days ago No Flesh was in mourning and absolutely destitute, having given away all that he possessed in the world. Since then somebody has given him a calico shirt and his spirits are improving. He is my friend. He says he is and I have no doubt he knows how it is. Several times a day, since we have been in the hills, he brings me bright stones, some of which are quartz with mineral deposits. One of these specimens appeared as if somebody had been present when the stone was in process of formation from the heated lava, or something of that sort, and sparkled fine gold dust in it. If No Flesh and I don't get a quartz lead before we leave this country, we are going to know the reason why.[48]

Red Dog is the medicine man of his tribe and though he does not appear to be very active in finding gold, he seems to know very well what it is. He says the proper thing to do is to gather a hat-full of nuggets and then go to the Grand Central [Hotel, in Omaha] to live. He esteems himself a great traveler, having been in Washington. He says that white women are "away up, heap nice," and when he gets his nuggets doubtless he will have no occasion to change his opinion.[49]

But Red Dog is an orator, and nothing delights him so much as to extol his own wisdom. He was delighted with the idea that he was going to the Black Hills with "the Great White Chiefs," but he conceived that for home effect he must object. Our first intimation of what was coming was when [Francis C.] Boucher, a Frenchman, and Spotted Tail's son-in-law, put his head into our tent on the evening of the 16th inst. and said, "The Indians object to the route you are traveling." "Tell them," said Col. Comingo, "that we and not they, selected the route by which we shall travel."[50]

After supper Boucher returned and said the Indians were in council and would like to see the commissioners. We found them seated in the semi-circle on the grass, smoking a pipe at turns, and Red Dog looking very grand. He said, "I am a great man. I am going to make a speech.

But before I do, please look at my papers." He then unfolded a leather case, showed us a discharge from the U.S. Army, in which he had been a soldier, and a silver medal given him in Washington when he went there in 1873 [1872], on a visit that he made with Dr. Daniels. One side contains President Grant's likeness and the motto, "Let Us Have Peace." The other has in the center a design representing agriculture and its fruits, and the words, "Liberty, Justice, and Equality. On earth peace, good will toward men." The council that followed was little more than a protest from Red Dog and No Flesh, who said that no Indians lived in the Black Hills and the commissioners should not go there. They were informed that the president had sent the commissioners and have given them a route to travel, that it was necessary for them to go to the Missouri by way of the Black Hills, and if the Indians thought it best to return, they were at liberty to do so.

Capt. Egan, who commands our escort, had no patience with the Indians when they attempted to dictate to the commissioners, and was at no pains to conceal his views, though he did not formally take part in the council.

The Indians having seen what they knew before, that the "white chiefs" would not be bluffed, spent a pleasant evening about their camp fire telling each other of the grand times they were about to have, hunting grizzlys in the Black Hills.

Game at the two Sioux agencies is very scarce. As we move away from them more is found and it becomes plentier with every day's march. We have had plenty of antelope, deer, and curlew. Capt. Ashby is a fine shot and hunting is a passion with him. Yesterday he and a soldier fired at an antelope at long range at the same instant. The animal fell dead. The soldier said, "If I hit him it was in the head." Capt. Ashby said, "I aimed at his neck." It was found that the antelope's neck was broken, and that he also had a bullet hole in his head. The army needle gun, which all use here, is a splendid weapon against large game.[51]

Our last day's march before reaching the Cheyenne [River] was very bad. We broke camp at 5 o'clock in the morning, and came late to the south bank, having made thirty-one miles. The prospect before us was grand; in front the Black Hills, at the right the Dakota Bad Lands, while at the south and west an interminable plain, covered in nearly all places with rich gramma grass. Some of this land is barren, but those worthless spots are but a small part of the whole. The streams and sloughs are hard to cross. I do not see how an ordinary wagon, drawn by four mules, could get through without help. Travelers should cross this plain with not less than two teams of four mules each so that each can assist the other. Look out for sand at Wood Island Creek.

As to safety of the route for small parties without protection, I cannot speak with certainty. Gen. [Lt. Col. Luther P.] Bradley told the commissioners that if they marched with an escort they would not be molested, while they might be if alone; that Indians are accustomed to watch all movements in their country, and they will not attack soldiers.[52] A party of twenty-five Indians appeared on our right, but they claimed to be hunters, as Indians always do when found on the plains. There appears to be no doubt that the entrance to the hills by way of Fort Laramie is safer than that by way of the reservations. Travelers without protection find it for their interest to see as little of the Indians as possible. Old Spotted Tail and Red Cloud are all right, but the "young busters" are easily seduced.

The south fork of the Cheyenne, which forms the southern boundary of the Black Hills, is sixty yards wide, three feet deep, very dirty, has a hard bottom and swift current. We crossed it early on Sunday morning, the 18th, and struck off to the right along the range of foot hills, where we rode eleven and a quarter miles, and at 10 a.m. went into noon camp just beyond the entrance to Buffalo Gate. We rested at Turkey Creek, a clear stream that affords plenty of good water. There is plenty of gramma grass here, and Capt. Egan says that it is equal to a feed of oats for his stock.

A party of miners numbering sixteen men and three teams preceded us and marched in through the opening to the Hills country called Buffalo Gate.[53] While the command was resting and our stock feeding, the region was reconnoitered for the best road to the stockade, near which we expected to find Col. Dodge's camp.[54] Boucher brought in a specimen stone which he says is "blossom" rock, and indication of gold quartz. It certainly has a number of particles that appear to be gold. A lively dispute arose as to whether the yellow metal in the stone is gold or not and we have no acids to test it. Meanwhile every fellow has his own opinion and I have the stone.

The open ground upon which we took our Sunday dinner is called Pine Prairie and is a pretty place. At 2 p.m. we started again and turned into the Hills through Hinman Pass, so named in honor of Rev. S. D. Hinman, the chairman of the commission, who was in the Hills and discovered it last year.[55] The ascent toward Harney Peak is gentle, through a delightful valley that is bordered on the right by a precipitous bluff, and on the left by a succession of fine groves. Game, buffalo grass, and clear water abundant. Marched fourteen miles in the afternoon and camped on a creek the Indians very appropriately named "Swift Water."

On Monday, the 19th, we started early up an ascent so steep that it was barely possible to draw the wagons. We are now in a canyon with fine forests on both sides, and as we advance, the trees increase in size. At 8 o'clock, about two miles from camp, while we were resting our horses, a soldier found gold in the bottom of a dry creek at our left. It was in very small particles, but was doubtless the genuine stuff. He carried off his hat full of earth to be washed at the nearest water. This is, judging from all indications, entirely fresh ground that has never been prospected. Jim Sanders, an old mountaineer, who was formerly superintendent of Gen. Myers' pack train, told me that he had found richer placer diggings on the east slope than elsewhere, and that he had marked it so that he could find the place again, but in a manner to hide it from observation.

Two miles further up the canyon, we came to a place that forms a natural location for a mountain home. Here the pass opens to a greater width, and Swift Water Creek falls into a beautiful basin cut long ago by its waters from the solid rock. Here we found on a pine tree a leaf from a memorandum on which was the following writing:

"To whom it may concern:

I, Charles Elwood, left the stockade on Friday, May 28, 1875, for Spotted Tail Agency and reached Camp Success on the same day at 12 o'clock. Gold is plenty at the stockade if you only work to get it. The stockade is fifteen miles due west.

Charles Elwood."

Still on up the canyon we came soon to a place where the trail led to the left, and up the side of a mountain. Mr. Collins and I climbed the height with some difficulty, and with many pauses for breath. Fresh air is very plenty in this country, but in order to enjoy it when climbing mountains you need a liberal measure of what the Indian has most of, time.

A serious question now presented itself. What should be done with our wagons? The cavalry men could lead their horses over the height, but the wagons contained our rations, and none of us could very well live on air. Capt. Egan rode on to see if there was any way out at the head of the canyon and found there was not. Twelve mules could not pull a light wagon over the road we had to go. Finally, hand barrows were made and our supplies carried up one piece at a time, by the soldiers. Then long ropes were attached to the empty wagons and men and mules working together brought them over. Camped in a pretty park, where at night it was so cold that with all our robes and blankets we could hardly make ourselves comfortable.

This morning, [July 20] at 10 o'clock, we reached a mining camp, Custer's Gulch, on French Creek, and near the famous stockade built by the party who remained here last winter.

I have to-day seen several practical miners at work in their pits, talked with them all, and this evening interviewed Prof. Jenney. Particulars in my next.

H. S.

[*Omaha Daily Herald*, Sunday, August 8, 1875]

[July 21, 1875 – Acting Assistant Surgeon J. R. Lane, from Camp Harney, Black Hills, Dakota Territory] [56]

[The following excerpt from an article entitled "The Black Hills," with several subtitles including "Arrival of the Commissioners to Negotiate the Purchase of the Black Hills," is included because it relates to the agency Indians and commissioners' arrival in the Black Hills. Ed.]

Special Correspondence of *The Chicago Tribune*, Black Hills, [Wednesday] July 21, 1875

. . . The beatific quietude of Camp Harney was broken yesterday, the 20th, by the arrival of the Indian Commissioners and Red Dog, No Flesh, Little Eagle, The-Man-Who-Kills-The-Hawk, and eight other red devils with fantastic names, escorted by Captain Egan's company of the Third [Second] Cavalry.[57] To-day eighty more Indians are expected to arrive, who are on their way to Tongue River and the Powder River country to induce, if possible, the wild tribes of Sioux, Cheyennes, and Arapahoes that inhabit that portion of Wyoming to meet at Red Cloud on or about the 1st of September of the present year to negotiate sale of the Black Hills.

The Indians of the Red Cloud and Spotted Tail agencies are willing and anxious to sell the Hills; but the commissioners are not satisfied with the title unless the sale is concurred in by the Miniconjou, Brulé, Yanktonai, and other northern tribes that outnumber twenty to one the agency Indians. The commissioners are now here to determine the value of the goldfields, and will push on north to the Cheyenne [River] Agency, on the Missouri River, and from there still further north 160 miles, to another tribe.[58] An attempt is to be made to consolidate the Cheyenne, Arapahoes, and all the different bands of Sioux, into one Sioux Nation; and the commissioners are vested with authority to pardon the Cheyennes who fled from their reservation in Kansas last spring, if they signify a willingness to adopt this plan, and hereafter behave themselves; and it is with a view to the accomplishment of this project that the commissioners, accompanied by so large a party of the representative Sioux Indians, are now moving northward. The Indians selected for this purpose are those who have relatives or have married into the northern tribes, and in that way are supposed to have some influence among them. These Indians objected strongly to coming through the Black Hills, and, after arriving here, wanted to hold a council to advise the commanding officer to have all the white men stop digging holes and washing dirt. These savages think they own this country and do not stop to consider that the real owners (if an Indian's ownership is valid) are the Crows, who were driven from this territory twenty or twenty-five years ago.

Some doubts are guardedly expressed by the commission as to the success of the project now on foot to purchase the Black Hills and consolidate the northern tribes; and, now that the Indians have sold all their rights to live or hunt within the limits of the State of Nebraska, many are looking forward with considerable curiosity to see how that is to be reconciled with their refusal to leave the present reservations on the White River, which are within the limits of that state. The contract is binding between the United States and the State of Nebraska, and in the event of a demand for the removal of these Indians out of the boundaries of the latter, the national government would be compelled to fulfill its contract and move them, which would be the signal for another bloody Indian war. The government has no right to impose any additional agencies within the boundaries of any state, other than those specified at the time that the territory is admitted as a state.[59]

J. R. L.

[*Chicago Daily Tribune*, Tuesday, August 10, 1875]

[July 21, 1875 – Homer Stull, from French Creek, Black Hills, Dakota Territory]

Gold Budget Number Two

French Creek, Black Hills, [Wednesday] July 21, 1875

To the Editor of *The Herald*

The appearance of this gulch is that of a military and mining camp combined. Here the first gold was found and the miners who know the most of the history of other countries still have faith in the valley of this creek. But Camp Harney is now on the site of the town that was founded by Long and Bishop and their companions, and their stockade is within a stone's throw of the soldiers' tent. This fact is important in enabling one to understand the situation.[60]

I spent the greater part of yesterday in visiting the miners who are actually at work here. Being well mounted and accompanied by a good guide I was enabled to get over a good deal of ground and yet stay with each miner long enough to get all the gold news that he was willing to communicate. In almost every instance I found the men anxious as to the movements of the military. "Do you know when the soldiers will leave?" "Will they try to take us out with them?" and similar questions were put to me frequently. I asked if they were willing to stay after the army should withdraw; if they did not fear that the hostile northern Indians would come in to drive them out. They answered that they only asked the military to be let alone, that they would take care of the Indians themselves. I found that parties are leaving bound for "the states," but that a great many more are coming in. A miner told me last evening that 128 men came into this valley to his knowledge day before yesterday.

The presence of the soldiers and the uncertainty as to the future is having a very damaging effect on the development of claims. Nobody is willing to commence work with the idea that he may be just opening the way for some stranger to reap the benefit of his labor and discovery. True, there is no interference and every man is at liberty to stake off any place not occupied and commence at once. But the fear of an unsettled state of affairs in the near future prevents the construction of flumes and sluices, except to a very limited extent, and I find that experienced miners have little confidence in any work done in placer diggings without these facilities. New comers go about digging little holes here and there and washing a few pansful of dirt from each place. They find gold almost always, but it is in small particles. Custer told the truth, no doubt, when he said that his men found gold in the grass roots. A great excitement was created here a few days ago by an exaggerated story of something very rich found in the roots of a rose bush that had been accidentally pulled up by a darkey. But those who expected to find sudden fortune by digging in the neighborhood were disappointed. There is gold here, and much of it will remain here for some time to come. I have not the least doubt that considerable quantities of the precious metal will yet be taken out of the valley of French Creek. But it will be done by men who do not fear military interference, by men who are not "pilgrims" or "tender feet," but miners; by men who have patience, some capital and habits of persistent industry. Men who go about scratching a little here and there, like a hen with one chicken, will succeed as well in the Black Hills as anywhere else.

I would like to give *Herald* readers a pen picture of the gold district as I see it, and therefore shall use some facts which would seem trifling with any other object in view. Yesterday morning found our party in camp on French Creek, and about seven miles below the diggings in

Harney's Gulch. After an early breakfast I set out on foot in company with two commissioners, but soon became separated from them. They wanted to hunt for deer or elk; my object was to inspect the bottom of the creek, thinking that, perhaps, I might find a nugget. All were well armed, and it was understood that we were to move to Camp Harney, which was known to be in the vicinity, and there remain at least one day. The mountain air, the cool morning, and the prospect of soon reaching the mining camp, had an exhilarating effect on us all. I was walking quietly forward through a thick pine forest, and supposed myself entirely alone, when I suddenly came upon Hon. A. Comingo, an ex-congressman and a distinguished lawyer from Missouri, a member of the commission, who is known among the original proprietors of the Black Hills as "the old man." Born under a happy star, the counselor has been the life of our party, never lacking a joke to relieve the most awkward predicament, as when he suddenly remarked of a stale egg that popped in his face and completely demoralized his breakfast: "Gentlemen, that was not the fault of the hen." This time he was in a serious mood. He said, "Hush—I saw an Indian. He is concealed behind one of those rocks, and he was looking directly at you." I was very confident that I had not lost any Indians, and intimated as much to Col. Comingo. He said, "I think he means mischief." At this juncture Mr. Collins came up and was consulted. He advised that we should go to the place where the Indian was said to be lurking and see what he meant. Accordingly we advanced and found one of our Oglalas stretched on the ground behind a rock. He said he was sick and wanted some medicine. A most alarming state of health seemed to prevail here among what the president calls the original inhabitants. Red Dog puts it thus:

"We are negotiating a sale of the Black Hills country?"

"Yes."

"This is very important business?"

"Yes."

"We ought to be very friendly?"

"Yes."

"I shall be sick this evening, when we camp, and I shall come to your tent for medicine. I want white man's medicine."

I hurried to the creek and spent an hour carefully searching for gold, using no spade or shovel, but wading in the stream and inspecting the bottom, which the clearness of the water enabled me to do with ease. I found a number of bright particulars, but none that I believed on examination to be gold. Seeing that I was using valuable time to no purpose, I hurried on, overtook Mr. Collins and Col. Comingo, and were all furnished horses by Capt. [Gerald] Russell of the 3d Cavalry, whom we met in a beautiful glen about two miles up the creek. We were soon at the trader's store in Camp Harney, which had been sent out from Fort Laramie by Mr. Collins, who is post trader there, in charge of Mr. Willard.

Mr. Willard came in with Col. Dodge on the ____, [blank in original] and has kept open store since. He had always offered to buy gold at $18 per ounce, and yet he had only about six dollars worth. I asked him how he could account for the quantity being so small. He said that everybody was anxious to send specimens home; that officers and soldiers had bought dust of the miners for that purpose at more than its market value; that miners had bought rations of soldiers to such an extent that an order had been issued to prevent their coming to camp, and although some did come, the great majority kept away from the soldiers as much as possible. After all he considered that the main reason that he had not bought more gold was that excitement had been high all the time, that rumors were constantly in circulation to the effect that the best diggings were not on French Creek but in some gulch just beyond and that as yet, there had been far more prospecting than mining.

The miner's gold pan is made of sheet iron and is about as large, though not so deep, as a common dish pan. Mr. Willard produced one, and we went to the gulch to try our luck. Our first effort was on Russell's claim near the stockade. A hole had been opened, five or six feet, and a drift made two or three feet in coarse gravel at the bottom. A panful of the gravel was then taken out and Mr. Collins, who spent three years in a mining camp in Montana, washed it out. The result was twelve "colors" or small particles of very fine gold that stuck to the bottom of the pan when the last earth and water had been poured away. Capt. Ashby tried the same experiment on another claim and found some gold, but it was also very fine and the pieces not so numerous. One miner made $1.00 out of eleven pans.

A military order has prevented any sluicing within two miles of camp for the reason that the soldiers depend on French Creek for water. We were told that a number of men had united and put in a sluice about two miles and a half up the creek and we galloped out to see it. The sluice is a very simple arrangement. Three boards about a foot wide are nailed together as to make an open box. This empties again into another box just like it, and so the string is extended ten or twelve rods. Slate is placed in the bottom so that particles of gold may fall in and be saved. A narrow ditch is then dug so as to throw as much water to the sluice as the claim is entitled to by miners' law. Earth to be washed is then shoveled into the boxes and the water let in on it. The "clean up" is when the shoveling ceases and the slates at the bottom are taken up and the gold taken out.

We found the owners of the sluice in some rocks in a rough mountain gorge nearby where they made their camp. A shelving of rock formed their only protection as they were without hut or tent. Mr. Harrison, a New York man, the recorder of the mining district, was there with his books spread out on a stone, and a miner was having a claim recorded as we rode up.[61] Harrison first asked me if I knew the intentions of the military, whether an attempt would be made to remove the miners, and having possessed himself of all the information I had on the subject answered my questions courteously. He said that the sluice was just finished a day or two ago and had only been worked one day, when two men shoveled into it, and the clean up at night yielded $26.14. He showed me a four-ounce vial, about a third full of very handsome gold dust of coarser gold than is found down the creek, and said he had used part of his dust to buy "grub." He said it was almost impossible to hire men to shovel for wages, he had not found any man who could be hired to shovel all day. About one hundred claims are recorded in his book, all on French Creek. His district extends from the stockade up to the headwaters. He and his companions will lay out a town if the military will withdraw and leave them. They do not fear any conflict with the Indians and are ready to protect themselves. He and his companions are confident of success. Mr. Tainer, whom I met there, told me that he could make five dollars every half day on his claim with a rocker, and he was sure of it. His claim is four miles higher up the creek.[62]

I asked Harrison if he had worked his sluice boxes yesterday. He said "No, most of our men are prospecting and I have walked a good many miles to-day myself." "What will you do in the winter when you can't work your boxes?"

"That will be a good time to prospect for quartz. I have located a quartz claim today."

"Where?"

"That we don't tell. We are going to let Jenney find it if he can."

"Is it gold quartz?"

"Gold and silver quartz."

Five miles of claims extend along the creek and most of them have been more or less prospected. Generally they have been "gophered" by little holes cut in here and there. All the men I talked with had found gold, but it was always in small quantities. Miners are found in camps of five or eight men, and they told me generally that a part of the company was prospecting. Seeing one fellow kiting through the bushes ahead of me with a pan on his shoulder, I called to him. "Been working?" "Yes." "What luck?" "D—d bad," he answered, without stopping or looking around.

H. S.

[*Omaha Daily Herald*, [Sunday] August 8, 1875]

[July 23, 1875 – Homer Stull, from Jenney's Gulch, Spring Creek, Black Hills, Dakota Territory]

Gold! Gold! Gold!

Jenney's Gulch, Spring Creek, Black Hills, [Friday] July 23, 1875

To the Editor of *The Herald*

While I was interviewing the miners on French Creek (about which I wrote you in my last letter) I learned that Prof. Jenney had discovered something rich on Spring Creek, about twenty miles distant and that the crowd was setting in that direction. That evening I heard that Prof. Jenney had just arrived in Camp Harney and I was going to see him when he came over to call on the commissioners.

He is a young man, apparently about thirty years of age, tall and thin, with a blond mustache, has a rapid manner in speaking and bears the indefinable look of a scholar. He is deeply interested in the study of mineralogy and has visited the mines of New Mexico, Nevada, and other districts to perfect himself in it, though I am told that his only practical experience in mining was while he was engaged a short ____ in North Carolina. He owes his appointment to the important post he now occupies as chief of the scientific expedition in the Black Hills, to the following circumstance. While President Grant and his advisers were looking about for a suitable man for the position, Bishop [William H.] Hare wrote to the president of the Columbia College (New York City) for advice on the subject and received in reply a letter naming Walter Jenney, a graduate of the School of Mines connected with the college, for the place. He was appointed on the recommendation of Bishop Hare.[63]

I soon had an opportunity to engage Professor Jenney in conversation and asked what was the character of his late discovery.

Prof. Jenney – "The gold up there is coarse, ragged ore, and some of it is rusty gold with pieces of iron attached to it. It shows that it has been derived from the rocks close by and has not been subjected to pounding."

Correspondent –"How many days had they been at work there when you left?"

Prof. Jenney – "They went in on Wednesday and I left on Sunday. They had staked off the whole country at that time. It was quite interesting. They knew that I had made a discovery and when they saw me buying lumber they started for it. The man of whom I purchased the lumber came rushing up to me after I had reached the place, all out of breath, and said, 'I was a fool to sell the lumber and not to follow the boards. I might have known you had found something.' The first day I went in there was no end of fun. Men followed me in all manner of shapes, some with little pack mules, and some with ponies, and in all imaginable confusion. Nobody had any idea of going into camp. California Joe, as they call him (Joe Milner is his name) came to me and said, 'Prof., when did you do your prospecting. I saw one or two little holes but you did not get to bed rock.'[64] I waded into the creek, turned over a rock, and got him a pan full of plastic clay. He went to panning it, got coarse color, and began to get excited. He had thin scales of gold but the pieces were large enough to make a big show in the pan. He said, 'Where is your last stake?' and staked him off a claim. Miners and soldiers could not sharpen stakes enough, in two hours they had miles staked off. Then they began to jump each other's claims in the most absurd manner. One man staked from the middle of another man's claim to the middle of the next claim. A soldier panned out a piece three quarters of an inch across, a thin scale, and the excitement increased. I watched others and found that one pan gave two cents and one ten cents. This was last Wednesday.

"My men staked off claims, but I told them distinctly that I would have nothing to do with it, that the whole proceeding was illegal. I told the miners that they could acquire no title to land until the country was open to settlement, but that if they wanted to amuse themselves in that way they might do so. They held a miners' meeting and I told them that I thought it would be only fair that my men who had dug the first pits should be allowed to hold claims. They agreed to it, but the claims have since been jumped. They could not stay to watch them.

"I would not be at all surprised to hear of trouble there. Powerful parties of twenty or twenty-five men jump claims from men who cannot think of resisting them, but they have begun to hold meetings and we may hear of a disturbance there at any time.

"A great many of the men rushing in here are mere pilgrims who know nothing whatsoever about mining. Some of them expect to pick up gold with case knives. They don't mine at all, but sit down on their claim till they can sell it. The greater portion of them never saw a sluice in their lives.

"An old man came to me with a piece of rock in his hand. He was all excitement and said, 'Professor, what do you think of that?' I said 'I think that is good quartz.' He said, 'I have got a ledge of that and I tell you it is rich.' An army officer standing by asked him what he would take for his ledge. He did not know what to answer at first, but finally said he would sell it for three sacks of flour. Of course, the officer did not want to buy, but only laughed at him.

"Miners bring me every stone and rock, and men are coming to me every hour with specimens. I like that and always encourage it. I have now many hundred pairs of eyes helping me to discover what these hills contain, and some of these men are sharp and experienced gold miners. They are watching now for minerals, and they scrutinize everything that looks like mineral. The consequence is, that I have an unlimited number of assistants and they seem to have confidence in me. They have found out that I don't want to grab anything."

Correspondent – "Have you discovered any good quartz leads?"

Prof. Jenney – "When we say good quartz, we mean a ledge that will warrant a company erecting a quartz mill now, with the country half developed. To that I say no, but there is an immense ledge up here at the miners' camp. It is what they call in California a great belt ledge. It is filled with little fissures. It has been traced four miles in one direction and is two hundred and fifty miles [feet] wide. Then there is fifty feet of barren rock; after that it is seventy-five feet wide."

Correspondent – "Will these men stay here and develop their claims?"

Prof. Jenney – "The cold weather will compel most of them to go out in the winter but nothing but the permanent occupation of the country will keep them out. They came here from every possible direction. Many crossed the Laramie in rude dugouts; some came straight through the Indian country and entered the hills by way of Bear Butte, and one party that came direct from Sioux City, were ten or twelve weeks on the road, and encountered the most formidable difficulties; one party came in from Harney Peak.[65]

"Mountains were nothing to them. Those who took guides got here last of all. One German who came in had two kegs of whisky that he was dreadfully afraid would be taken away from him. He came in from Sioux City and had been more than two months on the road. He had twice turned back from impassable sands and came in at last over the most frightful country. He was going to Custer's Park and had no idea of where the park was.

"I said to the captains of two companies that if they would help me make a dam that they might have the gold for their company fund. My object was to demonstrate the quality of gold that existed there, and show the public whether it was in paying quantities. They are engaged in it now. I got four cents to the pan at six feet. It was a rough ragged surface. Nine or ten inches of clay along the top of the bed rock yielded four cents to the pan. Soldiers got from two cents up. The largest piece was worth one dollar and twenty-five cents, roughly estimated. It is hard to estimate an irregular piece. I saw about half a dozen soldiers get about two dollars from twenty buckets. All they did was to turn over stones and scrape off two inches of earth and they would have to work it like putty."

[Stull continues] Next morning after my interview with Prof. Jenney, we started for the gulch that bears his name, on Spring Creek. The distance is twenty-three miles from Custer's Gulch, nearly north. We were never quite alone on the whole route, with miners moving about in all directions. I saw some who had been prospecting on Cherry Creek. They said they had not been long at work but were doing well. Others have been to the north on Inyan Kara, on the west side. They went as high as Bear Lodge, and say they had better prospects there to the pan than in Custer's gulch.[66] They are from Colorado. We were approached to-day by a man who said he belonged to a company of three hundred and five men who had come in from Montana and camped above us. He had been sent down to learn the intentions of the military. If it was the purpose of Col. Dodge to remove the miners from the hills his party did not mean to be found.

Maj. [Andrew S.] Burt is in command of the camp at Custer's Gulch.[67] His son, Gano, who was struck by lightning a few days ago and had a narrow escape, has recovered. Maj. Burt's own company was among the soldiers that built the dam mentioned above. He tells me that he thinks there are no poor man's diggings here, but that the gulch will pay well if iron pipe and hydraulic works are constructed for heavy mining.

I saw a member of Co. H, 9th infantry, who said he had tried thirteen pansful in a rocker and did not find more than a few fine specks of gold. Another soldier said he had some nice gold, coarser than the French Creek gold, had sent it off, and did not know what it was worth.

C company and H company of the 9th infantry made a ditch a thousand feet long, built a dam above and turned the water so as to clear the stream and enable them to put in a bed rock drain and run sixty feet of sluice boxes. The result was as follows, viz: First day one dollar; second day, twenty-five cents. It is just possible that there were too many cooks engaged in making the broth, and too many hands fingering the sluice boxes, but it may be all right.

I am told that five soldiers worked two days in Custer's Gulch with result of two dollars and nineteen cents first day and one dollar and ten cents the next. The earth cleaned the last day came from the bed rock. It is considered very remarkable that the bed rock earth should not be so good as the gravel.

While I'm writing, Mr. Carlin, a practical miner from Montana, comes to our tent in company with one of our party and brings a very handsome little nugget of rusty gold which he has taken to-day from his claim about half a mile north of the dam I have mentioned. He is well satisfied with his pay streak.[68]

H. S.

[*Omaha Daily Herald*, Tuesday, August 10, 1875]

[July 31, 1875 – "Mart," from Camp Sheridan, Nebraska]

Our Black Hills Letter

From our special correspondent, Camp Sheridan, [Saturday] July 31, 1875

Editors *Nebraskian*

Since my last letter, two weeks ago, nothing of special interest has occurred in this "neck 'o woods," except the arrival at Red Cloud of the commissioners to investigate the alleged frauds of certain government agents at that place. So far we have not been able to learn anything definite as to the action of the commission, but presume that not unlike similar commissions that have been sent out before, they are putting in their time very leisurely, and eliciting very little that has not already appeared a hundred times in print. One thing I feel very certain of, so far as Dr. Saville, agent at Red Cloud, is involved in the trouble, and that is, the record of that gentleman will be found as straight as a string. No one here, so far as I know, has any idea that Saville has done anything purposely that can be twisted to mean fraud or corruption. Saville came here for his health, and having agreed to do his duty as agent to the best of his ability, he will do it.[69]

I have read a great deal of late, one piece in the *Nebraskian*, about the barest possibility of this country turning out "thin" on the gold question but I tell you that there is gold here in paying quantities. A young man was in yesterday from the Jenney party, and exhibited specimens of scale gold that were taken out right under the nose of the doubting professor. This man's name is Simpson, and he has been with the Jenney party since it started. He informed me that the professor had written a long letter to Washington, which he heard read, in which the old gentleman reported that there was no longer any ground for withholding confirmation to the fact that gold exists in the Black Hills in paying quantities. The party is about thirty-five miles northwest of Harney's Peak where the deposits are reported to be the richest yet found, and so situated that the miners will have no trouble gaining abundance of water for mining purposes. Simpson says that the quartz deposits where the party is now operating are simply immense, and that Professor Jenney was completely surprised at the discovery, which he acknowledged was simply "wonderful," and beyond anything he had thought possible to exist there. The quartz is found in a belt of what the professor calls clay, slate, and quartzites. The belt is over twenty miles wide. Besides this report of Simpson we are constantly hearing and seeing from other quarters such evidence as no longer leaves any doubt in the minds of those here as to the truthfulness of former reports of the richness of the mines.

The Indians do not seem to care very much about the occupation of the hills, except so far as it affects their purpose of make a good "dicker" with Uncle Sam in selling out their right to them. The redskins talk [more] about the forthcoming pow-wow near Red Cloud, to come off in September, than they do about the miners sneaking into their gold country. The truth is the lazy beggars don't care a rush for the gold, for they wouldn't wash out a pan of dirt for a dollar's worth of gold, and the idea of an Indian washing out dirt for from seven to twelve cents to the pan is simply preposterous. He is too aristocratic for that. For this reason nothing could be more absurd than to keep this country locked up against the ingress of the white man whose industry in a few years would render it one of the most inviting and wealthiest parts of America. I have never heard anyone who had been into the Hills say other than that the very best opportunities abound there for farming. The soil is deep and rich, the grass abundant and nutritious, the water plentiful and of the purest and sweetest kind, and inexhaustible quantities of fine timber. We have rain here just about as I have seen it in Georgia, so regularly and in such well proportioned quantities that no irrigation would be needful, but if it was I have never been in a country that affords better natural advantages for irrigation than this. But it is not needed. I hear reports of parties going into the Hills every day, and I don't think I should overshoot the mark very much by placing the number of miners in the Hills at 1,500.

Orders have been received here directing the establishment of a military post near Harney's Peak, to be called Camp Harney. Two of the companies detached from Fort McPherson are to garrison the post.[70]

Everything is quiet here at the post. Colonel Mills is much liked here, and seems to be very well satisfied with his present station.

I shall probably get another letter to you for the issue of week after next. I hope then to be with the Jenney party and to be able to give more facts in detail.

Mart

[North Platte *Western Nebraskian*, Friday, August 6, 1875]

[August 2, 1875 – Homer Stull, from Cheyenne River Agency, Dakota Territory]

The Black Hills Indian Commission and Their Movements
Cheyenne Agency, D. T. [Monday] August 2, 1875
To the Editor of *The Herald*

The commissioners who are negotiating a treaty with the Sioux came out of the Black Hills on the 24th ult. [Saturday, July 24] and headed towards the agencies on the Missouri. Before leaving the hills and after the date of my last letter we visited the camp of Col. Dodge on Rapid Creek.[71] We found the command in a delightful camping place to which they had come only two days before, and all in fine health and spirits. There I met Lieutenant [John F.] Trout, whom many of your readers will gratefully remember as the hard-working and self-sacrificing secretary of the State Relief and Aid society last winter.[72] Omaha is a favorite winter retreat for army officers who come to the city to seek relaxation and social enjoyments denied them on the frontier. It was hardly fair to Lieutenant Trout that he should work gratuitously while so many rested. Col. Dodge commands all the troops in the Black Hills, and I found him employing his leisure most usefully in making a map for the guidance of future pilgrims in this region.

The Indian delegates who are sent from the Brulés and Oglalas to accompany the commissioners to the Missouri River agencies signified a wish to talk with Col. Dodge. Arrangements for a council were soon made and a circle formed in front of the headquarters tents with Col. Dodge, his officers, and the commissioners on one side, Black Bear, Blue Horse, The Dawn, Round Thunder, Whirlwind Soldier, Red Dog, No Flesh, Little Eagle, Ghost Shield, and Eagle Hawk on the other, supported by correspondents of the *New York Tribune*, the *Toledo Blade*, and the *Omaha Herald*.[73]

Red Dog told Col. Dodge that the agents at Spotted Tail and Red Cloud had lied to him. They said he (Col. Dodge) had come in the spring with his soldiers to drive the white men out of the Black Hills. Now he found them in all the valleys as thick as grasshoppers. "You are here and nobody gone."

Col. Dodge answered that the white people of the United States surround the Hills in every direction except the north and there are so many that the Indians could not realize their numbers, that the number of troops is very small, located at different posts, not with reference to keeping the white men out of the Black Hills, but to protecting the settlements. The generals commanding the departments of Dakota and the

Platte have both given orders to the troops to keep miners out of the Black Hills so far as they can, but the miners come in by many ways so that the soldiers cannot see them. He continued, "The Great Father wishes to buy this country from the Indians and in order to be able to make a fair bargain, the white men sent here a party of gentlemen to see what the country was worth before they bought it. The troops under me came in here for the purpose of protecting these gentlemen and to prevent Indians or white men from hurting them or taking their stock. In order to do that I keep my men together. I have no men to scatter around and pick up these miners. I have nothing to feed them if I should take them prisoners and no means to carry them to the posts. I do not trouble them, nor do I intend to because I have just troops enough for the special purpose for which I came here. The troops at the different posts will probably be sent in here after these miners."[74]

The Indians made no reply but with significant grunts and scowling looks folded their long blankets about them and strode down the valley. They feel that they are in the power of the white man. One of the chiefs lately said in my presence, "I know I cannot protect my country. I must depend upon my Great Father." The beef ration at the agencies is solving the Indian problem. The scarcity of game on the plains has shown the Sioux that they cannot live by the chase. They care but little for flour or any of the extras; if they could be assured of a fair supply of meat from any other source than the government bounty they would be on the war-path in twenty-four hours. Little Eagle, a young Brulé chief, lately said at one of our camp fires, when speaking of the Black Hills invasion, "If the white men do not listen to me, I will give them ears."

The value of the Black Hills is a question about which good men will be divided in opinion. I notice, however, that experienced miners and men best acquainted with the surroundings and indications of other gold districts have, after personal examination of the Black Hills, the greatest confidence in their value. This is a most encouraging fact. Nobody is more mistaken than he who supposes that gold mining is a haphazard game in which experience counts for nothing. Only a few days ago I was witness to a neat illustration of this. While adventurers of the "pilgrim" and "tender feet" order were pitching about the wide valley in Spring Creek like a blind horse in a ten acre lot, a number of practical men from Montana settled on a "bar" not more than a mile distant and drew out a number of little nuggets of rusty gold that, to their practical eyes, were imminently satisfactory. One of them told me that Alder Gulch, the richest diggings in Montana, did not open up, at first, as well as this bar in Jenney's gulch. Yet a gentleman told me that he saw one hundred and ninety-seven thousand dollars taken from a string of sluice boxes in a single clean up in Alder Gulch.

The contrast which the traveler encounters in coming down from the Black Hills to journey on the arid plains is most disagreeable. In the Hills country he finds refreshing shade in deep forests of pines and lighter groves of oak, ash and elm with a profusion of the most beautiful glens and vales, through each of which flows a mountain stream as pure as sunlight. The most noticeable feature of the prairie of Dakota at this season of the year is the warm wind, which, of itself, would make comfort impossible, the next is the utter absence of all trees and bushes, their place supplied with a white gravelly soil that produces little else than millions of prickly pears and acres on acres of deserted prairie dog holes apparently occupied by the owl and the rattlesnake. Water fit for the use of man or animals is seldom found. The creeks laid down on the maps and depended upon for camping places are far apart, and when found are discovered to be mere dried up lanes and the tourist esteems himself fortunate if he finds a little alkali, stagnant water in holes on the plain where it lies exposed to the scorching rays of the sun without motion to protect it. Coming on to the forks of the Cheyenne, one climbs with a burning thirst, a series of almost impassable hills, that tower one above another opening new vistas of misery as he advances and finally, from the parched summit, looks down upon a vast area of as worthless a country as was ever inflicted upon a people. One is forcibly reminded of an exclamation made by Gen. [Alfred] Sully, many years ago, on this spot: "This is hell with the fire out."[75]

We struck the Missouri River last Friday [July 30] at this, the Cheyenne [River] Agency, two hundred and seventy-five miles (by land) above Yankton. This reservation extends eighty miles on the river and west to the Black Hills. Here nine thousand Indians, all included in different bands of the "Great Sioux Nation," live under the supervision of Major Henry W. Bingham, their agent, who has been here three years. I shall have more to say of the affairs here in my next letter and will only mention in this that a council was held here to-day, at which the head men and chiefs of all the bands were present and not one word or complaint against the agent or any of his employees was heard. This is very unusual. I have heard complaints and excuses since I have been in the Indian country almost constantly. Here the Indians are wild enough for anything, no doubt. Some of them do not appear with any trace of civilization in their dress or manner. I know that they are remarkably free of speech, for one of them yesterday told a white man that he had a mind to strip him of his boots and clothing and lead him home naked, but for their agent they had only words of kindness and respect. White

Bull, their orator, said to-day that his father (meaning Major Bingham) was not a large man but he was one of the best men he had ever known.[76]

The council held to-day was eminently satisfactory. The Indians here will all attend the grand council, and they are favorably disposed towards the Great Father and the "white chiefs" that he has sent out.

The commissioners leave to-morrow for Standing Rock Agency, one hundred and twenty miles up the river. They will all pass through Omaha on their way to the grand council. I am watching for a boat, and shall leave homeward bound, by the first opportunity.

H. S.

[*Omaha Daily Herald*, Friday, August 13, 1875]

[August 3, 1875 – Homer Stull, from Cheyenne River Agency, Dakota Territory]

The Indian Problem

Cheyenne River Agency, D. T., [Tuesday] August 3

To the Editor of *The Herald*

In my last letter I mentioned the council held here between the four commissioners, who are preparing the way for a purchase treaty for the Black Hills and the Big Horn country and the head men of the nine thousand Indians living on this reservation. This is a great event here (I have just heard a Miniconjou, who came to attend the council, say that the white man has not seen his face for twenty-three years) and I presume a full report would be of interest to your readers. The talk, if carefully noticed, throws light upon more than one phase of the complicated Indian problem that is pressing upon the public attention.

What shall be done with these Indians? is a question which the white people of this country can well afford to study. The Sioux (they call themselves Dakotas) number thirty-five thousand; they are brave, intelligent, and war-like. I do not believe that the tax-paying citizens of the United States will long consent to support these Indians in idleness. The contrast between the white man on the border who works for his daily bread and the Indian who stalks about in absolute idleness with no care on earth but to wait for ration day, is too great to last. This subject has been a matter of almost daily discussion with the commissioners and "*The Herald* man" since we have been in the Indian country. Mr. Hinman, the chairman of the commission, has lived fifteen years among the Sioux as an eminently successful missionary of the Episcopal Church. He speaks their language like a native, is familiar with their modes and thought and, as we have often had occasion to observe, possesses their confidence. All the bands seem to be acquainted with him, and they are constantly coming with friendly greetings and to ask his advice.

The Miniconjous, Two Kettles, Sans Arcs and Black Feet were represented in the council by a considerable number of Indians, among others by the following chiefs and head men, viz: Spotted Bear, White Bull, Bull Eagle, Duck, Burnt Face, Charger, Rattling Rib, Little No Heart, Black Tomahawk, Yellow Hawk, and White Ear.[77]

Mr. Hinman opened the council by explaining the object of the proposed treaty. He said,

"The present treaty with the Sioux is a bad one; when it was made the Indians did not understand it. The treaty provides that they were to receive clothing for thirty years and food for four years; the Indians believed that they were to receive food also for thirty years. The four years are now gone and for the last two years Congress has given them food gratuitously, but the members talk about it every winter and unless some new arrangement is made they will soon stop giving it to them. Again, there is not money enough provided in the old treaty to furnish clothing for the whole people. There are always old men and women and children who do not get any blankets, and if they only got the blankets that their Great Father gives them they would freeze to death. The treaty was made without consulting the people, and the money that Congress gives is not enough. In the winter a great many are naked. We wish to make a treaty that shall provide clothing for all the Sioux who will be ready to live like white people and educate their children.

"You know that your country here is not good for farming. A great many years your crops are burned up, grasshoppers sometimes destroy them and hail-storms ruin them in other seasons. We are satisfied you can never learn to live like men here, and support yourselves by cultivating the soil. But there is one thing you can do. People who live in a dry country like this have another way of obtaining a living; they have cattle and sheep and horses. We wish to make this treaty so that the Great Father shall provide all the Sioux who will listen to him, with cows so that they can raise cattle. You know how to take care of your ponies and you can [take] care of cows and sheep in the same way. If the Great Father provides for you ten years, each family may have a large herd. The buffalo are gone and the deer are fast disappearing. If you listen each man may soon eat his own beef and mutton.

"The American people cannot do all this for nothing. The Great Father wishes to buy some part of your country. All the American people told him that he must buy it. You know there is one thing the white people want, that they all work for. They do not go away off on the prairie to hunt; they do not go as far as the mountains to make war, but they go up to heaven and into the bowels of the earth to get money. Where there is money you cannot keep the white people away; you might as well try to keep grasshoppers out of your cornfield. The soldiers last year discovered that there was gold in the Black Hills. The white people have heard of this, it has been published in their newspapers, and although the Great Father has tried to keep them out of the Black Hills, they still keep going. They go in wagons, on horseback, and on foot; they go in winter and in summer; they go by day and by night; there are old men and young men, and lame men and all kinds of men there already. The Great Father has tried to keep them out. Next summer he cannot keep white men out of the Black Hills any more than you can prevent rain falling when the clouds are ready. Therefore he wants to buy the Black Hills and the Big Horn country or that part of your country that lies west of them and contains gold. In order that we may make a fair treaty, and that all may understand it, he wishes to have all the Dakotas (Sioux) together. The old treaty was made in two places and you never understood it.

"We have decided that this council shall be held at Red Cloud Agency, because there are twenty thousand Sioux who live there and at Spotted Tail, which is near there, and because it is a good country where there is plenty of water, grass, and wood, and because they are related to the northern Sioux and have sent out their relatives to bring them in. There is no wish to remove you from the river or to remove your agency; but we come in the name of the Great Father to invite and command your chief men to go to this council. In his name we now tell you that a council will be held there in thirty days. You will be provided with rations by your father. The chiefs at Red Cloud and Spotted Tail, and all the chief men, wished me to say that they will be glad to see you there, that if you come it will make their young men happy, and probably you will not have to go home barefooted.

"I will tell you again about the treaty that we wish to make in one word. We want to make you better off than you are and to put you on the road where you will be going ahead all the time instead of standing still. We shall return here from Standing Rock in nine days."

Fool Dog, a pilgrim from the Yanktonai, who had wandered up the river without knowing why, made a few remarks not worth relating, and then, after a pause, White Bull, chief of the Sans Arcs, rose to speak.[78] His tribe has a history that is so much in keeping with his appearance that it might answer for his personal biography. In a time long ago, when the war-like Dakotas had quarreled by themselves until the different bands had got handsomely by the ears, and the young busters were prancing about the prairie in proud expectations of a general shindy, a council was called. All the tribes appeared fully armed except White Bull's people who came without weapons, thereby giving notice that they held themselves able to take care of themselves without artificial aids. Their courage was applauded and they received the name "Sans Arcs"—without bows—that they have borne ever since.

White Bull is a handsome specimen of the wild Indian. He was dressed in a picturesque costume composed of skins of the mountain lion and his manner seemed to say, "You see who I am; who sent for you?"

He strode into the circle, shook hands with all the white men present, and said: "My young men standing around here wish me to speak a few words to you. Pray to the Great Spirit for your living and everything you have to do. I was raised in the country known as the Black Hills by the good will of the Great Spirit. I have always heard that the only way I would expect to live prosperously and have something to live on would be to hold on to my country. These young chiefs who went to Washington to see the Great Father brought us back very kind and good words, and I have sent these words out amongst our people.

"There was a time when the American people, through their soldiers, made a treaty on the west side of the Black Hills (at Fort Laramie) and the people have not lived up to it. The elements have been dead and the four winds have been dead since that treaty. I have always had an idea that I would like to live in peace and quietness with the whites, but it appears that I am to live with them only temporarily. I think about it frequently, whether I shall live in that way all the time or not, I cannot tell. I wish for another treaty that shall be better than the old one. I understand you are speaking my words to me now, the same as I wish it. These people have all heard what you have to say, and when you go away we will council and have a fair understanding among ourselves and give you an answer when you come back."
H. S.
[*Omaha Daily Herald*, Saturday, August 14, 1875]

[August 6, 1875 – Homer Stull, from Standing Rock Agency, Dakota Territory]

The Indians
Special Correspondence of *The Chicago Tribune*
Standing Rock Agency, Dak. Ter., [Friday] Aug. 6

The Sioux Commissioners arrived here yesterday, and held a council to-day in an Indian village 3 miles from the agency. All the Indian tribes residing in this reservation—the Yanktonai, Blackfeet, and Hunkpapa—were represented. Big Head, Two Bear, Wolf Necklace,

John Grass, Kill-Eagle, Slave, and Long Soldier were the principal chiefs and head-men present.[79]

There had been some apprehension that, these Indians having been omitted from the list of those invited to visit Washington last spring, they might offer some obstacle in the way of the proposed treaty. Happily, they are in a very friendly mood, and are generally disposed to sell the Black Hills. We have seen but few Indians who do not agree to this policy, and those who want to retain that country will certainly be in the minority; but it is quite likely there may be a wide difference of opinion as to the price to be demanded. Old Red Skirt, a Miniconjou chief, insists that he must not hear of selling the Black Hills in fifty years to come; but he appears to stand almost alone.[80] John Grass, one of the head chiefs of the Blackfeet, will accompany the commissioners to visit the Indians lower down on the Missouri, at Fort Thompson, Brule, and the Yankton Agency. The Indians here will almost immediately start for Red Cloud Agency, to attend the Grand Council to be held near there in the first days of next month. They will hunt on the way, and will find no lack of game. One party, which lately came in, say that they killed 748 antelope; and a band of Indians out six weeks killed 1,800. John Grass, the leader, himself killed 53.

Travelers who approach this place observe a bold promontory, and suppose that the agency derives its name from it. The true Standing Rock of the Indians is situated in a secluded place, 2 miles from the agency. It is a small granite bowlder, 2 feet high, and 20 inches in diameter at the base. The place is jealously guarded by the Indians, who regard this ugly stone with superstitious awe. They worship it, and at regular intervals bring offerings of food and water. Some believe it to be a petrified woman, and bring it female dress and ornaments. The face of the stone is nearly covered with strange hieroglyphics in paint, and a number of medicine-bags are suspended in the vicinity.

The Indians here appear prosperous and contented, and make no complaints to the commissioners against Col. [John] Burke, the agent.[81] They have been favored with a plentiful supply of rain, and their country appears to the best advantage. They have planted some corn, but the grasshoppers have done most of the harvesting.

S.

[*Chicago Daily Tribune*, Friday, August 20, 1875]

[August 8, 1875 – Homer Stull, from Cheyenne River Agency, Dakota Territory]

The Cheyenne Agency

Cheyenne River Agency, D.T., [Sunday] Aug. 8, 1875

William Fielder is the official interpreter at the agency and for the military post [Fort Bennett] adjoining it. He is a full-blooded white man, an American, who was taken to live among the Sioux when he was seven years of age, and has been with them ever since. He is intelligent and appears to be candid; he certainly possesses a fund of information concerning all that pertains to the life of the Indians and the situation in which they are placed scarcely equaled by any of his countrymen. He tells me that he spent many years with the Oglalas, Red Cloud's people, and that he is personally acquainted with nearly all the Indians there. He has seen them in camp, at their sun dance, and on other great occasions when they mustered all their strength, a hundred times, and he says that he knows there is not now, and there never has been, more than half as many Indians there as are reported present and for whom the government provides rations. The pretended recounting of the Indians was a humbug so plain that not even the half-breed interpreters there pretend to excuse or defend it. He says also that the government is issuing rations to far more Brules, Spotted Tail's people, than have existed in the present generation.

I learn from another source that these Indians have a chronic disposition to cheat in the count, and that they consider that they have been so often swindled by white men that they feel perfectly justified in so doing. In a former treaty it was provided that each Sioux should receive $20 in cash as a part of his annuity. Frauds so gross and palpable were attempted that military officers penned up the Indians in a corral and paid each $20 as he came out through a line of sentries. Of course this stopped the extensive borrowing of children and transferring of members of one family to another.[82] The hostility of the Indians at Red Cloud to any attempt to count them will be remembered by *Herald* readers, and, considering all the facts in the case that are accessible to an outsider, it is not at all probable that a correct census was ever had.[83]

"This civilizing Indians is fine, very fine," said an army officer to me yesterday. "Maj. Bingham is the Indian's friend; he helps him to build a house. The Indian and his forefathers have, for many centuries at least, been accustomed to out-door life. Shut him up in a house and he and his family get sick and soon die. I wish all the Indians had houses."

I find that Dr. Cravens, the agency physician, is called upon to administer advice or medicine to from fifteen to twenty ailing Indians daily, and this he says, is not so many applications as would be made by an equal number of white people.[84] The sanitary report of this agency for the month of June 1875, states that the number of Indians belonging to the agency and entitled to treatment was 7,586; number treated 145; restored, 68; died 16; number of births, 18. During the month five Indians died of consumption, four of scrofula, three of whooping cough; three of dysentery and one of diarrhoea.

These figures are doubtless as correct as any that could be obtained, but they do not present the whole truth for this reason: the Indian's worst foe, when he attempts to subject himself to the influences of civilization, is consumption or scrofula, which I understand to be also [crease in paper] thing and when he finds that he is sick, beyond recovery, he is likely to go away to some lonely spot where he can die attended only by the Great Spirit. Many deaths occur that are never reported. On the other hand, when a birth occurs the fact is made known at once, the new comer is duly entered on the agency books, and an extra ration drawn.

I recently asked a man who ought to know, what the effect of living in houses was upon the Sioux. He replied,

"They don't do it much."

"I was told that two hundred and fifty log houses had been built on this reservation for Indians and that most all the work had been done by the Indians themselves."

"That is true, but don't you notice that each log house has a tepee close by it? Look when you are riding in the camps and villages. See if the family is not living in the tepee."

"What, then, is the house used for?"

"It is good to keep horses in."

"But can they live comfortably in tepees in winter? I suppose they would prefer log houses then?"

"They don't. Their tepees are warm enough, as warm as they are accustomed to. And a great advantage is that they are ventilated at the top. Build a log cabin for an Indian family and if they live in it at all, they pack into it like sardines in a box, the man very likely to have three wives, all have young children and, when he has anything to eat, it is quite probable that six, eight, or a dozen of his friends will stay with him and feast and smoke several days and nights until it is all gone. Of course, under such circumstances, the air in the little cabin gets very bad, and it is no wonder that the family prefer the tepees. There is another reason why this is so. Indians are very filthy in their habits, anyplace they live soon gets fearfully dirty, and it is easier for them to move than to clean up."

Another gentleman who has lived many years tells me that they really are not so far advanced as they were before the massacre in Minnesota.[85] Then they lived in substantial brick houses and gave more signs of civilization than they ever have since. He has witnessed the career of several agents, civil and military, and has always heard and read most encouraging reports of progress. Let no reader suppose that my informant is one of the wicked "men of the country" who regards all attempts at improving the Indian as a huge joke.[86] He says that if you read the reports of Indian agents you see that great improvements are made in the way of farming. The sixteenth part of an acre is quite enough for an Indian's "farm." What is planted there is seldom hoed or otherwise cultivated. He did once know an Indian whose heart was *big asta*, a desire to cultivate the soil. He worked a few hours one day and came back the next morning very sad. His neighbors had called him a woman and his warrior spirit drooped at the insinuation. Sometimes an Indian really does a little work in cutting hay, but if the "father" gives him a mower, some Frenchman owns it before the next season.

These squaw men are the curse of all agencies; everybody acquainted with the Indian country agrees to that. They are a low class of white men who long ago bid farewell to honest work, and by marrying Indian women, and living with the tribe they acquire all the cunning of the savage without possessing his redeeming qualities. They have considerable influence with the Indians, and always endeavor to plant themselves firmly between the government and the tribes. The treaty of 1868 was made with the squaw men; the Indians never understood its provisions and it has been the cause of no end of trouble.

I was once present when another Indian agent advised Dr. Saville to get rid of the squaw men at Red Cloud. He said that they were married to Indian women who had treaty rights, and he did not see how he could do it. Major Bingham, the agent here, succeeded almost entirely at the first effort, and this was the way he managed. Soon after he came here, now three years ago, he posted a notice to all whom it concerned that white men not married to Indian women would not be allowed to live with them on the reservation. A considerable number of weddings was the result. Old sinners who had been living with squaws since the palmy days of the American Fur Company considered their rations endangered and virtuously resolved to marry. Dusky women, mothers of whole broods of frisky half-breeds, stood up in faded finery brought from St. Louis long before Iowa or Nebraska had a settlement, except those at widely separated military posts, to join hands with men in their shirt sleeves who answered the missionary's questions in broken French.

This done, the squaw men felt quite virtuous and regular. They were then greatly astonished to find that they could draw no rations from the new agent. "The man," said Major Bingham, "is the head of the family, the United States government is under no obligation to provide for your

78

wife, you must do that yourself." Finding that the rule that so sadly affected their food supply was inflexible, the squaw men took down their tepees and moved away.

Among the missionaries sent to this region was a devoted Catholic priest, who was filled with the true missionary spirit. He went to a camp north of this place, built a neat chapel, and labored long and faithfully with the Indians there. They were good listeners, and he poured into their ears, the old story, so dear to the Christian world, of man's fallen and sinful condition, of the blessed atonement and redeeming love. Many of the Indians appeared interested, though they were [not] at all demonstrative and had little to say. The good father proposed that a number should be baptized. They agreed to the proposition, provided that he would pay them well for the operation. He came back down the river, saying that he was satisfied that the time had not come when he at least could do good among them.

I was yesterday in Maj. Bingham's office when Bull Eagle, a young chief of the Miniconjous, came in.[87] He has a round and manly face, with large generous eyes and a look that is a sight draft on every man's friendship and confidence. He brought the interpreter with him and after he had seated himself and gone through with the usual handshaking and how-ing with Maj. Bingham and *The Herald* representative he said:

"I have come to ask a favor and I am afraid my father will make an argument."

Maj. Bingham – "Nothing pleases me so much as to grant favors when I can. What do you want?"

Bull Eagle – "I would like to give a feast to all the Indians at the agency and want extra rations."

Maj. Bingham – "I have heard that you want to have a sun dance. Is that the feast you mean?"

Bull Eagle – "We never interfere with the white man's religion; we want him to do the same by us."

Maj. Bingham – "Two years ago I issued rations for a sun dance and the Great Father censured me for it. He does not approve of that manner of worshiping the Great Spirit, nor does the church through whose influence I was sent here.[88] I do not interfere with your religion. If you insist in holding a sun dance after you have drawn rations next Wednesday, or any other time, I shall not try to hold you. I only say that the government does not approve it and I cannot give you rations for that purpose."

Bull Eagle – "I expect this will come to a fight yet. I wish you would take your rations and all the white men with you and leave the country. (To me). Write down the river and to the Great Father saying that Maj. Bingham is coming with all his people and all the rations together. I do not want them in my country."

Maj. Bingham – "All the Indians do not think so; they want me to stay and give them the food the Great Father has sent, and so will you when you think about it. If I was to go away now Bull Eagle would go about with a bad heart and cry because his father had left him."

Bull Eagle – "I would never cry for such a father. I have no father and I didn't want any. I want my country and that the white man should stay out of it. The white man has lied to me about the Black Hills; he has no business there. My interests and my friends are still in the hostile camp and I think I will go there. I do not belong here."

Two of Bull Eagle's men sitting in the adjoining room, where they heard what was said, came in afterwards and regretted that he had talked such bad words to his father. It is especially unfortunate, they say, at this time, because he is going to dance the sun dance—an act of most solemn worship to the Great Spirit—and when an Indian does that his heart must be free from all bad feeling towards any one.

Another Indian, of a different tribe, came to Major Bingham yesterday and said, "When my father sees me sharpen my knife he must not think it is meant for him. I have listened to wise men and I like to live at the agency. The first thing I think of every morning is how many days it is to ration day."

H. S.

[*Omaha Daily Herald*, Monday, August 16, 1875]

[August 9, 1875 – Anonymous, from Custer's Gulch, Black Hills, Dakota Territory]

The Black Hills

(From a Special Correspondent of *The Tribune*)

Black Hills Expedition, Custer's Gulch, Dakota, [Monday] Aug. 9

Gen. [George] Crook had suggested the 10th of August as the day when the miners should all meet in this gulch.[89] Desiring to know what action would be taken I came hither this morning. It was a fortunate move, as Major [E. A.] Howard and a number of Indian chiefs had arrived last night from their agency, on a tour of inspection, to calculate what damage had been done to their country by the miners.[90] Col. [Frederick] Benteen 3d [Seventh] Cavalry, with his company, was found here, having been sent from Fort Lincoln, on the Missouri River, in the Department of Dakota.[91] The Indian chiefs here are Spotted Tail, White Wash, Slim Thunder, Big Tongue, Blue Tomahawk, Indian John, Blue Teeth, Medicine Bear, and his wife Rose, Walking Eagle, Bear's Ghost, Long Face, and Yellow Breast.

Spotted Tail is perhaps the most noted Indian now on the plains. He has been in his time a bitter enemy of the whites. Now he is a diplomat, preferring peace to war, and by his careful management has perfect control of his band. In 1868 at Fort Laramie no one, white or red, who took part in the great council held there, spoke more forcibly or showed a clearer head for the business in hand than this wily Indian. The government was represented by Gens. [William T.] Sherman and [William S.] Harney, Gov. [J. A.] Campbell, and Messrs. [Felix R.] Brunot, [John B.] Sanborn, and others.[92] Spotted Tail said to them: "Choose peace or war; feed us or fight us. My friends, let me tell you flour and coffee will be cheaper than blood and powder." Gen. Sherman, before replying, asked Gens. [Alfred H.] Terry and [Christopher C.] Augur, commanding the Departments of Dakota and Platte, "What will it take to make war in your departments, gentlemen?" Gen. Augur said, "15,000 men and $50,000,000;" Gen. Terry replied, "the same." These enormous figures led Gen. Sherman to choose peace.

In Gen. Harney's time at Fort Laramie, after the Ash Hollow fight, where he gave the Sioux a terrible defeat, a mail party was murdered. The general sent word to the guilty band and demanded that the murderers should be given up. His alternative was that "not a lodge should have an Indian left to keep the squaws in order." In four days Spotted Tail and three comrades went to the post, reported themselves as guilty, and "ready to die for their tribe." President [Franklin] Pierce, after keeping them in confinement for over a year, released them.[93]

I was introduced to Spotted Tail. Major Howard detailed his interpreter, and Spotted Tail sat down to have a talk with me. He knows perfectly well what an "interview" means.

Correspondent – "What do you think about the miners being here?"

Spotted Tail – "We are wronged. The Great Father's promises are broken. This land is not bought yet. It belongs to us still. We are to have a council soon about it. This was never thought of."

Correspondent – "White men are fond of gold, and it is hard to keep them from hunting for it."

Spotted Tail – "It is stealing. If this country belonged to the whites and Indians wanted to get gold, they would have to buy it. Whites are different; they come and take it."

Correspondent – "How much will the Indians ask for the Hills?"

Spotted Tail smiled as a horse jockey might when asked a price. Finally he said, "A great deal."

Correspondent – "Will there be a war with the northern Indians?"

Spotted Tail – "I can't tell anything about it. I don't want to go to war on either side. I want to be at peace. The Indians are all angry (their hearts are bad) because the miners are in this country."

In a former interview with Red Dog, a chief accompanying the commissioners, I took occasion to say that the horses lately stolen from Laramie Plains by Indians belonged to the Hon. W. D. Kelley, explaining that Mr. Kelley was a congressman, and had been a friend to the Indians, and that Red Dog and the other chiefs should try and recover this herd, to which he assented. He wished to have Mr. Kelley come to the big council to be held in September, on Chadron Creek.[94] I suggested the same idea to Spotted Tail, but the old fellow only shook his head and said, "We can tell about the horses when we know where they are and who stole them."

Spotted Tail was taken to see the operation of gold mining. He wished to know how it was done and to get a specimen. Mr. Harrison's sluices were visited, and three men worked vigorously for an hour, and then the dirt was "panned out," but no "color" could be seen in the pan. Spotted Tail shook his head and grunted. He evidently meant to say: "Played out; the boys have put up a job."

Spotted Tail made a speech to a mass meeting of miners last night, in which he scolded them roundly for coming in here. It was rather an imprudent thing, for more than one hand itched to take out a pistol. Whether or not the old fellow was conscious of the danger there might be in stirring these men up was not indicated by word or look. Someone laughed in derision at his claim for damages. He said: "White men laugh while I talk; if a squaw did that while a white man were talking in my camp she would be whipped."

There is no doubt that the Indians are willing to sell the Black Hills, but whether their price, which I understand to be $7,000,000 will be paid is another thing. If this sum will buy the Big Horn country, and with it a lasting peace, the bargain would be a good one.

Quitting Major Howard's tent, I visited the miners' camp, or rather a part of it. While I was asking a few questions an eager and excited crowd gathered around. All the miners in the gulch were there. It seemed a favorable opportunity to anticipate the meeting of to-morrow, and thereby gain one mail for *The Tribune*.

The meeting will be called to order at 10 a.m. The object is to follow out the suggestion of Gen. Crook that they meet in this gulch "and make such regulations as may seem to them best whereby each may be protected from the loss of the labor already expended on their mineral locations." Resolutions to this effect will be adopted, and the time for representation will be fixed between the 1st to the 15th of May, 1876.

This is hardly necessary, however, as each mining district has already adopted its own law on this point. Some have agreed that if a man be not on his claim 60 days after the ratification of the treaty by Congress the claim will be open for relocation by other persons. Probably there will be a resolution adopted thanking Gen. Crook, Col. Dodge, the officers and the soldiers for their treatment of the miners. The number of the miners remaining here will be reduced to-morrow. Many of them, availing themselves of Gen. Crook's permission, will accompany Major Burt's train, which will leave this creek to-morrow morning early for Fort Laramie, returning for supplies. They tell me that the feeling is quite unanimous in regard to going by the 15th. There are a few, they say, who will be so foolish as to hide; but if they do elude the military now they cannot work their claims. There is a lively contest going on, as I take notes, over the future town to be built here. Nine men staked off a town, intending to give all the miners a lot, but desiring to do a land office business, they reserved all the corner lots for themselves. Here was an affront to popular rights. An indignation meeting has decided that the town lots shall be thrown open to "the boys," every one having a "fair shake" and the first choice being decided by lot. Its name may be Custer, which is popular justice, they say; not in those words but in these:

"That ____ Secesh wants to call this 'ere town Stonewall! Eny how, wont it be a log town? Isn't that enough? Haven't I seed Custer! Don't he wear his ha'r long like California Joe? He's one of the boys."

I think the town will be called Custer.[95] Col. Dodge, Surgeon [George] Jacquette, and Lt. Morris N. Foote came over from Rapid Creek, arriving a few hours after I did. The colonel will personally superintend the evacuation of the Hills until the arrival of Capt. [Edwin] Pollock with his command. The latter is expected about the 18th.[96] Col. Benteen, who is here accompanied by Lieuts. [Francis] Gibson, [Charles] Derudio, and [William T.] Craycroft and Dr. Burns, comes from the Department of Dakota to arrest the miners. He suspended the execution of his orders after learning from Gen. Crook what had already been done, and that Aug. 15 was the last day.[97]

Mr. Jenney has been told by Col. Dodge that no miners hired by him before the proclamation was issued will be permitted to stay. The plans of exploration are likely to be changed somewhat. If would not be surprising if the last of September found the expedition knocking at the gates of Fort Laramie.

[Undetermined author][98]

[*New York Tribune*, Thursday, August 19, 1875]

[August 16, 1875 – Homer Stull, from Yankton, Dakota Territory]
Commissioners
Special Correspondence of *The Chicago Tribune*
Yankton, Dak. Ter., [Monday] Aug. 16

The Hon. A. A. Comingo, of Independence, Mo., and the Hon. William H. Ashby, of Beatrice, Neb., two of the commissioners appointed to treat with the Sioux for the purchase of the Black Hills, arrived here this evening from the Indian country, on the steamer *E. H. Durfee*, accompanied by your correspondent. Three of the commissioners—including all in the field except Mr. Ashby, who was sick—left Cheyenne River Agency on Friday last, and drove to Fort Thompson, 100 miles distant, arriving there on Saturday at 2 p.m. It was their plan to meet the Indians at Fort Thompson, and those at Brule, which is 9 miles distant, in joint council, and thus finish their business so as to be ready to take the steamer *Durfee* on her return from Bismarck. They telegraphed from Fort Sully, and a messenger was sent to the Indians at Brule in ample time, but the chiefs there answered that, if the white chiefs wanted to see them, they must come to their agency. Mr. Hinman and Mr. Collins, the chairman and secretary of the commission, accordingly went to appease the offended dignity of the Brules.[99]

All the members of the commission are expected to meet at the Grand Central Hotel, in Omaha, on the 25th inst., leave on the following day for Cheyenne, and proceed thence, by way of Fort Laramie, to Red Cloud, near which the Grand Council is to be held on the 1st of next month. The government will furnish transportation by the Union Pacific to Cheyenne; a line of stages runs to Fort Laramie, and Dr. Daniels, Indian inspector, who acts as quartermaster to the commission, will have conveyances in readiness there. It is expected that 20,000 Indians will attend the council, and it will probably last a month. I predict that a great majority of the Indians will be found in favor of selling the Black Hills and Big Horn country, but that they will demand a higher compensation than the commissioners will feel authorized to give. The squaw-men and half-breeds would prevent the sale if possible; failing in that, they will insist on a sufficient price to make the Sioux, including of course their noble selves, independent for all time to come.

The treaty of 1868 was made with squaw-men; the Indians never understood its most important provisions. They believed, and still insist, that they were to receive both food and clothing for thirty years, while the treaty provides for clothing for thirty years, and food for only four years. It is time now to see that this mistake is not repeated. The squaw-men are Frenchmen who have been many years with the tribes;

they have abandoned the habits of the white man long ago, and they are bitterly hostile to the Government.

S.

[*Chicago Daily Tribune*, Friday, August 20, 1875]

[August 19, 1875 – Omaha, Nebraska]

Mr. Homer Stull, city editor of *The Herald*, returned from the Black Hills country yesterday, after an absence of nearly two months, very much improved in health and general "tone." He occupied yesterday with relating reminiscences of wild adventure to scores of friends who called upon him, and will drop back into the old journalistic groove to-day.

[*Omaha Daily Herald*, Thursday, August 19, 1875]

[August 26, 1875 – Omaha, Nebraska]

The Black Hills Indian Commission and Council

The Indian Commissioners were concentrating at military and newspaper headquarters for this part of the West yesterday, and we had the pleasure of meeting several of them whom we had not met before, among others, Col. Comingo and Mr. Beauvais of Missouri, and General Lawrence of Rhode Island. Senator Allison of Iowa and Gen. Terry will probably be on hand to-day for the forward movement and final charge on the red men for the peaceable capture of the Black Hills. These distinguished gentlemen will be glad to know that they are to be followed upon their important mission by the approving and supporting moral influences of the only paper in America which the better class of Indians are bound to respect, and of which those who wrong and rob these remnants of an expiring race of men have any real fear.

The council with the Sioux will mark an important event in the history of our Indian relations and the progress of the frontier. Upon its results depends the issue of peace or war with the red men. For it is a part of the beauty of what somebody has perpetrated the bitter sarcasm of calling "our Christian civilization" to obtain the property and override the rights of all races in the country except the almighty and ever-lasting Negro race, by force, when it cannot be done by peaceful means. If the Sioux refuse to part with their country on terms the white man dictates, then will come Gen. Crook's bayonets and bullets, answering to the declaration the general made to a *New York Herald* reporter, "The government has to whip the Sioux * * * The sooner it is done, the better."

We confess to serious apprehensions for the result of the coming council. Rumors have already reached us that after Hinman, Comingo,

Collins, and Ashby left Standing Rock Agency, the Missouri River Indians held a council and resolved to neither sell the Black Hills nor to attend the council near Red Cloud's home. We may properly discredit this report, as we do, and yet the view of Mr. Beauvais expressed to us yesterday, is not without force. It is that the government made a mistake in not ordering the whole commission into the field of preliminary negotiations and dividing their labors between the Missouri River Indians and those in the regions of Red Cloud and Spotted Tail agencies. The four gentlemen who performed such hard and important service did not have time to make the Missouri River tribes fully appreciate what was wanted of them. To make a satisfactory treaty requires that the Indians concerned in the sale of the Black Hills region shall be present at the Grand Council *en masse* to consider and ratify it. Indians are Democrats in politics, and, with them, as with us, the voice of the people is the voice of the Great Spirit. Representative Indians, few in number, cannot negotiate treaties for whole tribes. There is almost as much jealousy and rival ambitions among Indians as there is among political leaders in Indiana and Ohio for the presidency. Senator Allison will not understand this until Capt. Ashby or Mr. Beauvais tells him all about it. The case is not so clear, the way is not so plain as many hope, to success in the coming Grand Council, and yet we have serious fear that it will be a failure.[100]

[*Omaha Daily Herald*, Thursday, August 26, 1875]

[August 26, 1875 – Omaha, Nebraska]

The Frontier

The Sioux Commission Will Leave This City To-Day to Enlarge its Boundaries

Pioneer Talk of the Very Early Days

Nearly all the members of the commission appointed by the president to negotiate a treaty with the Sioux for the purchase of the Black Hills met at the Grand Central Hotel in this city yesterday, according to the plan published several days ago in *The Herald*. Col. A. Comingo of Independence, Mo., Mr. John S. Collins of Omaha, the secretary of the commission, and Capt. W. H. Ashby of Beatrice were present to represent the members of the commission who were directed to visit the Indian tribes. Gen. A. G. Lawrence of Rhode Island, and Col. G. P. Beauvais of St. Louis, members of the commission, are also here and Rev. S. D. Hinman, chairman of the commission and Senator Allison of Iowa will arrive this morning. Gen. Terry, also a member, has telegraphed that he cannot come to-day, but will follow us in a few days.

The commissioners will go west by the Union Pacific express train this forenoon, leave the railroad at Cheyenne, and proceed to Red Cloud Agency by way of Fort Laramie.

A *Herald* representative yesterday called upon Col. Beauvais, whose name he often heard while in the Indian country, and learned from him some interesting facts concerning the early life of the white men on the frontier.[101]

Reporter – "You must have been here when there was no Omaha?"

Col. Beauvais – "Yes, we used to make our camps near this place. I have been here when there was not a house here. I recollect when this was winter quarters for the Mormons. We stopped to trade about this point in 1849 or 50."

Reporter – "When did the fur company go out of business?"

Col. Beauvais – "The Chouteau company sold out to the northern company about the year 1833. I went up the River first in 1858 [*sic*], hired to the old company as a voyageur, and stayed with them 21 years.[102] I was then only 17 years of age."

Reporter – "Did you find the Indians friendly?"

Col. Beauvais – "Yes, sir, very friendly; much more so than they are now. I have been among them six months at a time, entirely alone."

Reporter – "I saw old Joe Merrivale on the frontier and he told me about it."

Col. Beauvais – "I know him very well, but I was ahead of him. Bissonette, Richard, and others came in after me."

Reporter – "What did you trade to the Indians in those days?"

Col. Beauvais – "Mostly alcohol. When they were going to drink they would organize and detail two or three of their soldiers who would not drink and who would guard the white men to see that they should not get hurt. And they would do it. I never knew but one white man to be hurt by an Indian in liquor and that was young Joe Richard who was stabbed by accident. One Indian reached for another Indian and struck Richard in the shoulder."[103]

Reporter – "I have been told that Indian trading was more profitable in those days than it is now."

Col. Beauvais – "Oh, yes. The Indian then had plenty of buffalo. It was his life; he was not in want, and he did not beg. Now, when you have bought a robe the Indian will beg of you so that you have to give away much more."

Reporter – "From your knowledge of the Indian, what do you think are the prospects of success of your commission in negotiating the treaty for the purchase of the Black Hills?"

Col. Beauvais – "I would rather not speak of that now. I will tell you all about it when I return."
[*Omaha Daily Herald*, Thursday, August 26, 1875]

[August 28, 1875 – Omaha, Nebraska]

Mr. Al. Swalm, of the *Fort Dodge Messenger*, arrived yesterday on his way to attend the council of the Sioux Commission with the Indians. He is at the Grand Central.[104]
[*Omaha Daily Herald*, Saturday, August 28, 1875]

[August 29, 1875 – Omaha, Nebraska]

Commissioner Ashby has started for the Grand Council. He tried to get a special car for his own personal use, but finally consented to travel with his colleagues. This was very considerate and condescending in Commissioner Ashby. As an Indian treaty negotiator, Mr. Ashby holds about the same relation to the rest of the commissioners that a whale does to the pollywog.[105]
[*Omaha Daily Herald*, Sunday, August 29, 1875]

[August 29, 1875 – Sioux City, Iowa]

The Noble Sioux

Dr. J. J. Saville, agent for the Red Cloud Indians, who is at present visiting his family in this city, is of the opinion that the approaching grand Indian council, for the ceding of the Black Hills to the government, will be a protracted and tedious affair. The council will not get together before the middle of September, if then. The river tribes will not reach the Agency before the 10th of that month, and they will be obliged to hold a ten days' pow-wow after their arrival in order to get themselves in shape for participation in the big talk.

A few bands of Sioux have declined the invitation to take part in the September council, together with the entire hostile camp under the command of the noted Hunkpapa chief, Sitting Bull, who claims the Yellowstone country as his empire. This action of the hostiles has enraged the "good Indians" at the Red Cloud and Spotted Tail agencies, and they intend to declare war upon these obstreperous reds at the close of the council, which it is thought will be sometime during the latter part of October. If these "good Indians" succeed in subduing old Sitting Bull and his warriors, they will be entitled to an extra allowance of annuities for life. Old Set is a terror of every inhabitant in the country between Fort Berthold and the Rocky Mountains. He is not the Sitting Bull who visited Washington last spring. Not by any means. He is made of different stuff and belongs to a different brand. Nothing could induce him to visit the haunts of the whites, with whom he has sworn to be at war to the end of his life, and we reckon, from what we know of the old scalper, that the "good Indians" will have a hard and bloody job in bringing him to terms. The report that the Indians will demand $7,000,000 for their rights in the Black Hills, Dr. Saville assures us, is nothing but the idle talk of the "squaw men." The Indians will ask for an annuity to extend twenty-five or thirty years, and the only point of contention between the commissioners and the aborigines will be the amount of this yearly annuity.

[*Sioux City Daily Journal*, Sunday, August 29, 1875]

---

[1] J. W. Daniels, agent at Red Cloud 1871-73, was now an inspector for the Bureau of Indian Affairs. He accompanied the Lakota delegation on its return from Washington D. C. to make sure the agreement was finalized. The delegates had refused to sign it when they were in the national capital. Although the agreement was signed at the two Nebraska agencies on June 23, it did not include Red Cloud's signature and Olson concluded the government did not ask him to sign as part of an effort to undercut his authority among his people. Olson, *Red Cloud*, 185-86, 188.

[2] The investigating commission did not include everyone mentioned in Stull's letter. The members were Fletcher, West Virginia Cong. Charles J. Faulkner, Benjamin Harris of Massachusetts, Sen. Timothy O. Howe of Wisconsin, and Prof. George W. Atherton of Rutgers University. Olson, *Red Cloud*, 190. George Lane may have been considered for the commission because he was a prominent New York financier and vice-president of the New York Chamber of Commerce. George Wilson, comp., *Portrait Gallery of the Chamber of Commerce of the State of New York* (New York: Press of the Chamber of Commerce, 1890), 57-59.

[3] The activities of this commission and its investigation of John J. Saville, who had replaced Daniels as Red Cloud agent, is covered by Olson, *Red Cloud*, 189-98, and also by the *Report of the Special Commission*. An article that analyzes the situation at Red Cloud Agency and the work of the investigating commission is Robert H. Keller, Jr., "Episcopal Reformers and Affairs at Red Cloud Agency, 1870-1876," *Nebraska History* 68 (Fall 1987): 116-26.

[4] William A. Carter had been post trader at Fort Bridger in 1857-58 and by 1867 had become involved in locating mining claims in the South Pass vicinity. He was appointed postmaster and probate judge in Green River County, Utah Territory (later Wyoming Territory), among other public offices. By the 1870s he had become engaged in the cattle business. Lawrence M. Woods, *Wyoming Biographies* (Worland, WY: High Plains Pub. Co., 1991), 55-56.

[5] John A. Creighton, brother of transcontinental telegraph builder Edward Creighton, freighted to the Montana gold fields in 1863 and operated a grocery business in Virginia City until 1868. Evidently he came into possession of a large gold nugget during that time. J. Sterling Morton, succeeded by Albert Watkins, *Illustrated History of Nebraska*, 3 vols. (Lincoln: 1905-13). 1:630.

[6] Gilbert H. Collins, brother of Fort Laramie post trader and commission secretary John S. Collins, was in partnership with his brother in a well-known Omaha saddlery and harness shop and also in the post tradership. Ibid., 1: 623-24.

[7] B. L. Ford announced the construction of his new Inter-Ocean Hotel in February 1875, which was completed later that year. *Cheyenne Daily Leader*, Feb. 16, 1875. George C. Leighton would open his new Metropolitan Hotel on Oct. 4. *Cheyenne Daily Leader*, Sept. 28, 1875. Livery stable owner J. C. Abney also had the mail contract from Cheyenne to the Spotted Tail Agency and to Fort Laramie. By 1876 he would begin carrying passengers to the Black Hills. Agnes Wright Spring, *The Cheyenne and Black Hills Stage and Express Routes* (Glendale, CA: Arthur H. Clark Co., 1949), 45, 49-50, 57, 79.

[8] The "peaceable Indians" were the Two Kettle, Sans Arc, Miniconjou, and Sihasapa at the Cheyenne River Agency; the Lower Yanktonai and Lower Brulé at the Crow Creek Agency; the Lower and Upper Yanktonai, Hunkpapa, and Sihasapa at the Standing Rock Agency; the Oglala, Northern Cheyenne, and Northern Arapaho at Red Cloud Agency; and the Brulé at Spotted Tail Agency. The first three agencies were located on the Missouri River. The "wild northern Indians" were from the same bands, principally Hunkpapa, Miniconjou, Sans Arc, and Oglala, followed Sitting Bull, Crazy Horse, and other leaders, and sometimes visited the agencies but never intended to settle down there until all the game was gone. See Bray, *Crazy Horse*, 172-90, passim.

[9] John "Portugee" Phillips was the miner who carried news of the so-called "Fetterman Massacre" near Fort Phil Kearny from that post to Fort Laramie in late December 1866. He later gave up mining in favor of ranching. Douglas C. McChristian, *Fort Laramie: Military Bastion of the High Plains* (Norman, OK: Arthur H. Clark Co., 2009), 286-87. John M. Thayer, colonel of the First Nebraska Infantry at the onset of the Civil War, later Union brigadier general and elected one of Nebraska's first two U.S. Senators in 1866, was appointed territorial governor of Wyoming by President Ulysses S. Grant in 1875. Morton-Watkins, *Illustrated History*, 1: 528.

[10] A letter from Ed Smith and Jesse Potts, dated Custer's Gulch, June 19, 1875, had been published in the *Cheyenne Daily Leader* on June 29, 1875.

[11] Sanders had briefly been a civilian employee of the Dodge-Jenney Black Hills exploring expedition, which used both wagons and pack trains. "General" Myers was Maj. William Myers of the quartermaster's department, who

had received brevet rank of brigadier general of volunteers during the Civil War. Francis B. Heitman's *Historical Register and Dictionary of the U.S. Army* (Washington, DC: GPO, 1903) 1:740. Evidently Myers had been involved in organizing the pack train for Colonel Dodge's expedition.

[12] Harney City was a townsite laid out near the stockade erected by John Gordon's party of prospectors during the winter of 1874-75. The townsite and stockade were located about three miles east of present Custer. Parker, *Gold in the Black Hills*, 33, 72n.

[13] Sanders meant Crow Peak, which lies northwest of the modern town of Spearfish, South Dakota, rather than Crow Butte, southeast of Crawford, Nebraska. Both landmarks' names are attributed to skirmishes between the Lakota and the Crow. Crow Butte in Nebraska was named for an 1849 fight between the Brulé and some Crow raiding horses from James Bordeaux's nearby trading post that served the Brulés. See James A. Hanson and LaRee Wyatt, "The Battle of Crow Butte," *Museum of the Fur Trade Quarterly* 45 (Fall/Winter 2009).

[14] Louis Richard ("Reshaw") the son of John Richard Sr. and the brother of John Richard Jr., had gone to Washington, D.C. in the spring 1875 as an interpreter with the Red Cloud and Spotted Tail delegations. He would later interpret for the Grand Council and serve as a scout with General Crook during the Sioux War of 1876-77. He is frequently mentioned in Jensen, ed., *Voices of the American West, Vol. 1: The Indian Interviews,* and *Vol 2: The Soldier and Settler Interviews of Eli S. Ricker* (Lincoln: University of Nebraska Press, 2005)

[15] Probably Lt. John J. O'Brien, Fourth U.S. Infantry, then stationed at Fort Laramie. Heitman, *Historical Register*, 755; see also "Roster" in *Cheyenne Daily Leader*, July 20, 1875.

[16] Stull may be referring to an episode that occurred in 1873. On Apr. 26, Col. John Smith at Fort Laramie sent a telegram to Dept. of the Platte headquarters in Omaha to the effect that A. Cooper, the "mail carrier from White River" had been brought to the post the previous evening suffering from six gunshot wounds inflicted by "Miniconjou Indians." Although the Red Cloud Agency had not yet been relocated from its North Platte River site to the White River, the Spotted Tail Agency (then known as Whetstone Agency) was already on White River, necessitating courier service from there to the nearest telegraph office at Fort Laramie. Department of the Platte, Letters Received, 1866-1878, on file at Fort Laramie National Historic Site, courtesy of Sandra K. Lowry.

[17] This comment refers to the provision of the 1868 Fort Laramie Treaty that declared the region north of the North Platte River and east of the Bighorn Mountains to be unceded Indian territory.

[18] The trip mentioned was likely for the return to the agencies of the Lakota leaders who had gone to Washington in May and June to meet with government officials.

[19] Some Southern Cheyenne and Arapaho had fled to join their northern kinsmen in the aftermath of the Red River War of 1874-75 on the southern Plains. A party of Cheyenne was nearly wiped out in an April 23, 1875, fight on Sappa Creek in Kansas. The most recent study of this episode is John H. Monnett, *Massacre at Cheyenne Hole: Lieutenant Austin Henely and the Sappa Creek Controversy* (Niwot, CO: University Press of Colorado, 1999). Gen. John Pope commanded the army's Department of the Missouri at this time.

[20] On June 20 the *Cheyenne Daily Leader* reported that Capt. John Mix had been sent from Fort Laramie with two cavalry companies after Indians who had stolen 250 horses on the Laramie plains. Mix found only a trail that indicated the horses had been driven north to the Powder River country.

[21] Saville had been agent since August 1873.

[22] Red Dog was from the Oyuhpe band of Oglala, married to Red Cloud's sister, and often served as Red Cloud's spokesman. Bray, *Crazy Horse*, 76-77.

[23] John W. Dear was one of two licensed traders at the Red Cloud Agency. Thomas R. Buecker, "Red Cloud Agency Traders," *Museum of the Fur Trade Quarterly* 30 (1994): 4-14.

[24] Black Bear and Pawnee Killer were Southern Oglala who had become affiliated with Spotted Tail's Brulé by 1870-71. Black Bear moved to Red Cloud Agency in 1871. Kingsley M. Bray, "Spotted Tail and the Treaty of 1868," *Nebraska History* 83 (Spring 2002): 32, and personal communication from Kingsley M. Bray.

[25] Mexican José Merrivale frequently served as a scout and interpreter, including as a guide for Dodge in the Black Hills. Kime, *Black Hills Journals*, 12-13 and n 20.

[26] Dr. John L. Mills, a native of Auburn, New York, graduated from the University of Michigan in 1860 and became the agency physician in March, 1875. Mills to E. A. Howard, Mar. 20, 1875, Letters Received by the Commissioner of Indian Affairs, Spotted Tail Agency, 1875-76, National Archives and Records Administration, Microcopy 234, roll 840 (hereafter Spotted Tail Agency Letters). He witnessed the signing of the agreement ceding hunting rights in Nebraska. *ARCIA, 1875*, 681. Later he accompanied the sub-commission and Indian delegates to the Black Hills. Kime, *Black Hills Journals*, 166n208.

[27] Nicholas Janis, a Missouri native of French descent, had a varied career in the West including employment by the American Fur Company, guide for military expeditions, and employee/interpreter at Red Cloud Agency. He mar-

ried Red Cloud's niece about 1851. Although he was frequently at the agencies on White River, he also resided part of the time at the Old Red Cloud Agency on the North Platte River just west of today's Nebraska-Wyoming state line, where correspondent John T. Bell encountered him when en route to the Grand Council. See Bell's Sept. 3, 1875, letter. By the mid-1880s Janis had a ranch on White River about twenty miles from the town of Chadron, Nebraska. Eli S. Ricker interviewed his wife. See Jensen, ed., *Voices of the American West: The Indian Interviews*, 367-68; Janet LeCompte, "Antoine Janis," in vol. 8, *The Mountain Men and the Fur Trade of the Far West*, ed. LeRoy R. Hafen (Glendale, CA: Arthur H. Clark Co., 1971), and *Chadron Democrat*, Oct. 1, 1885.

[28] The Red Cloud and Spotted Tail agencies were not within the boundaries of the reservation as established by the 1868 treaty.

[29] Camp Sheridan, first sited half a mile south of Spotted Tail's Beaver Creek Agency in September 1874, was relocated in May 1875 about a mile north of the agency. Here, permanent construction commenced, which would have been underway when the sub-commission arrived in July. Paul L. Hedren, "Camp Sheridan, Nebraska: The Uncommonly Quiet Post on Beaver Creek," *Nebraska History* 91 (Summer 2010): 80-101.

[30] On July 7, 1875, Reverend Hinman alerted the commissioner of Indian affairs that it would be difficult if not impossible to hold the Grand Council on the Missouri River. The chiefs and headmen at Red Cloud and Spotted Tail agencies argued first that the lands proposed to be ceded "lie in this vicinity." Moreover, they stated that "the Missouri River tribes are mere colonies and they the parent stock, and that it would therefore be more becoming for the colonies to come to them." Hinman to CIA, July 7, 1875, Spotted Tail Agency Letters.

[31] From about 1871 to 1877 Joseph Bissonette operated an independent trading post about a mile northwest of the Bordeaux Trading Post, the latter the site of today's Museum of the Fur Trade, three miles east of Chadron. Charles E. Hanson, Jr., "Joseph Bissonette's Last Trading Post," *Museum of the Fur Trade Quarterly* 16 (Fall 1980): 2-4.

[32] Remnants of the military wagon road between Camp Robinson and Camp Sheridan, later extended to the Pine Ridge Agency in Dakota Territory, survive today in present Dawes and Sheridan counties, Nebraska.

[33] The reference is to where the military road crossed Bordeaux Creek near Bissonette's post.

[34] Selah is a Hebrew word that in today's parlance means "unknown."

[35] John Bridgman operated a ranch near the military road between the two agencies and west of the present village of Whitney, Nebraska. Apparently he

had belonged to one of the "Galvanized Yankee" regiments sent west during the closing months of the Civil War. Having married an Oglala woman, he spoke the language and served on occasion as an interpreter and also as assistant farmer at Red Cloud Agency. In early January 1875 Capt. Guy V. Henry's detail of the Third U.S. Cavalry was caught in a blizzard while returning from the Black Hills, where it had gone to evict miners. The command was saved when it stumbled upon Bridgman's Ranch, where the men took refuge. Henry survived injuries from frostbite only to be severely wounded at the Battle of the Rosebud on June 17, 1876. Nevertheless he continued his army career rising to the rank of major general before his death in 1899. See Thomas R. Buecker, "'The Men Behaved Splendidly': Guy V. Henry's Famous Cavalry Rides." *Nebraska History* 78 (Summer 1997): 54-63.

[36] William Garnett, who accompanied the 1875 delegation as interpreter, identifies "High Lance" as a member of the delegation. Jensen, ed., *Voices of the American West: The Indian Interviews*, 82. Tall Lance was also one of the Oglala who would meet with the Red Cloud Agency investigating commission. Olson, *Red Cloud*, 192-93.

[37] Anson Mills, then in command at Camp Sheridan, gives the origin of this raid as being several weeks earlier while the chiefs and headmen were in Washington, D.C. During the annual Sun Dance, young men from the Oglala and Brulé organized a war party to raid the Pawnee, Ponca, and Omaha. Mills said that after the chiefs had come home, "When Spotted Tail heard of it he was very angry and sent a message for those belonging to his band in the party to return." Mills testimony in *Report of the Special Commission*, 497. The Ponca reservation was located in present Knox and Boyd counties, Nebraska, though that area in 1875 was part of Dakota Territory and had been included (inadvertently, it is assumed) in the Great Sioux Reservation designated by the 1868 Fort Laramie Treaty. This error prompted even more Lakota raids on the hapless Ponca than before. The Brulé attacked the Ponca Agency on July 6, 1875. Jerome A. Greene, *Fort Randall on the Missouri, 1856-1892* (Pierre: South Dakota State Historical Society Press, 2005), 121.

Apparently the encounter with the soldiers took place as the Brulé were returning from the raid. The Little White River flows generally east through present Bennett County, South Dakota, before turning northeast in western Todd County (the Rosebud Sioux Reservation). It joins the White River south of Murdo, South Dakota. Red Cloud Agency trader J. W. Dear reported the incident and said it took place "at a point 140 miles southeast of Spotted Tail," which would place it in Nebraska. *Cheyenne Daily Leader*, July 17, 1875.

[38] Capt. Anson Mills, Third U.S. Cavalry, commanded Camp Sheridan during the post's relocation and "permanent" construction. Hedren, "Camp Sheridan," 83-84.

[39] The reference is to an Oct. 23, 1874, incident at Red Cloud Agency when Indians resisted Agent Saville's attempt to erect a pole to fly the U.S. flag. The Oglala Sitting Bull and others helped to prevent an outbreak of violence. Thomas R. Buecker, *Fort Robinson and the American West, 1874-1899* (Lincoln: Nebraska State Historical Society, 1999), 36-38.

[40] Brothers John H. and James W. Bosler of Carlisle, Pennsylvania, had the government contract to supply beef to the Nebraska agencies. The cattle were purchased from Texas trail drives and herded along the North Platte River until a certain quantity was requested to be driven to the agencies. There the cattle were weighed and receipted before issue on the hoof to the Indians. John H. Bosler's testimony appears in the *Report of the Special Commission*. James W. Bosler described the beef contracting process in a letter appearing in the *Carlisle (Pa.) Herald*, July 2, 1875, and reprinted in the *Omaha Daily Herald*, Aug. 7, 1875.

[41] Baptiste Good, a Brulé also known as "Brown Hat," is noted for his winter count, referenced in Garrick Mallery, "On the Pictographs of the North American Indians," *Fourth Annual Report of the Bureau of American Ethnology, 1882-83* (Washington, DC: Smithsonian Institution,1886), 127-29.

[42] Article 10 authorized a suit of clothing, or the materials to make it, annually for each Indian on the reservation for a period of thirty years. The same article authorized the issue of one pound of meat and one pound of flour daily for each Indian above the age of four years for a period of four years. The text of the treaty appears as an appendix in Olson, *Red Cloud*, 346-47.

[43] This is Chadron Creek, flowing north just west of the present town of Chadron to its confluence with the White River. The apparent agreement by the sub-commission that the council would be held there would lead to much wrangling and delay when the full commission in September claimed that Chadron Creek was never the intended council site and blamed the Indians for that misconception.

[44] The delegation consisted of one hundred men, led by Young Man Afraid of His Horse and the mixed-blood Louis Richard. It reached Crazy Horse's village in early August. The envoys had returned to Red Cloud Agency by August 16. Bray, *Crazy Horse*, 188-90.

[45] Capt. James Egan, Second U.S. Cavalry, Heitman, *Historical Register*, 399. Capt. William H. Jordan, Ninth U.S. Infantry, supervised the construction of Camp Robinson near the Red Cloud Agency and commanded the post at this time. Buecker, *Fort Robinson and the American West,* 43, 47.

[46] The party would have been following the road connecting the two agencies, which had been used to haul both military and agency supplies for a year and was, therefore, already well traveled.

[47] The "Old Spotted Tail Agency" here refers to a site about ten miles northeast of Chadron on White River near the mouth of Beaver Creek. Then known as Whetstone Agency, Spotted Tail's Brulé were there in 1873-74. When troops were sent to the Nebraska agencies in March 1874, a military camp overlooked the agency until September, when both the troops and the Brulé were relocated to the Spotted Tail Agency/Camp Sheridan sites on Beaver Creek.

[48] No Flesh was a leading man of the Brulé. Thomas Powers, *The Killing of Crazy Horse* (New York: Alfred A. Knopf, 2010), 104.

[49] Red Dog had been included in delegations visiting Washington, D.C. in 1870 and 1872. Olson, *Red Cloud*, 97, 150-51.

[50] Francis C. Boucher, of French Canadian ancestry, had married one of Spotted Tail's daughters and lived with the Brulé, often serving as an interpreter, as he was doing here with the sub-commission. Beginning about 1872 Boucher ran James Bordeaux's old trading post (present site of the Museum of the Fur Trade near Chadron) periodically before being put out of business by the army in 1876, having been accused of selling arms and ammunition to the so-called "hostile" Indians during the Sioux War. Charles E. Hanson, Jr. and Veronica Sue Walters, "The Early Fur Trade in Northwestern Nebraska," *Nebraska History* 57 (Fall 1976): 311-12.

[51] This was the U.S. Springfield rifle, a single-shot breechloader in .45/70 caliber, which had a long firing pin extending through the "trapdoor" breechblock, hence the appellation of "needle gun."

[52] Lt. Col. Luther P. Bradley, Ninth U.S. Infantry, commanded at Fort Laramie and later at Fort Robinson. Heitman, *Historical Register*, 239; Buecker, *Fort Robinson and the American West*, 97. When the letters attribute higher rank to officers mentioned, it is likely based on brevet ranks awarded during the Civil War.

[53] Also called "Buffalo Gap."

[54] This would have been the stockade established by the John Gordon party of miners in the winter of 1874-75 east of the modern town of Custer. Kime, *Black Hills Journals*, 4. 87.

[55] In August 1874 Hinman had explored the southern Black Hills as part of a commission charged with finding a new site or sites for the Red Cloud and Spotted Tail agencies. Anderson, "Samuel D. Hinman and the Opening of the Black Hills,"524-26. While Hinman was chairman of the 1875 sub-commission, Sen. William B. Allison chaired the full commission.

[56] Lane was one of the two military doctors with the Dodge expedition. Kime, *Black Hills Journals*, 58n58.

[57] Camp Harney was the Dodge/Jenney expedition's first "permanent" camp within the Black Hills, about four hundred yards from the Gordon stockade. This was the expedition's base camp from June 14 to July 18. Ibid., 87, and map, "Itinerary, the Black Hills Expedition, 1875," 242-43. Homer Stull gives the names of the ten Indian delegates who accompanied the sub-commission in his Aug. 2 letter below.

[58] Lane here means the Cheyenne River Agency where Miniconjou, Sans Arc, Sihasapa, and Upper Yanktonai Sioux resided.

[59] When the Red Cloud and Spotted Tail agencies were established on the White River in northwestern Nebraska, the Nebraska/Dakota Territory boundary had not yet been surveyed, leading to the erroneous assumption by some (but clearly not by Lane) that the agencies were located on the Sioux Reservation.

[60] H. Bishop and Charles Long were members of the John Gordon party of prospectors, the first to enter the Black Hills in December 1874. The party built the Gordon stockade in which they spent the winter and in March 1875 laid out a nearby townsite christened "Harney City." Annie D. Tallent, *The Black Hills: Or, the Last Hunting Grounds of the Dakotahs*, 2d. Ed. (Sioux Falls. SD: Brevet Press, 1974), 18, 50, 61.

[61] This was likely W. Harrison, whom Dodge encountered several times and who was later delegated to remain to guard the claims after Gen. George Crook ordered the miners to leave the Black Hills by August 15. Kime, *Black Hills Journals*, 167n212. The "mining laws of the Cheyenne Mining District . . . Near Custer, Black Hills, D. T., Adopted June 11, 1875" with the signatures of thirty-four miners, including W. Harrison and W. Trainor (probably the "Mr. Tainer" mentioned later in this letter) are found as Appendix I in Parker, *Gold in the Black Hills*. A John Harrison, who was en route to the Black Hills, sent a letter published in the *Cheyenne Daily Leader* on June 26, 1875.

[62] A rocker was used for placer mining where water was limited. It was a shallow wooden trough about four feet long, supported on curved rockers so it could be shaken. The upper end contained a box with a perforated sheet metal floor, while transverse wooden strips and carpeting were placed at the lower end. A small amount of water applied to gravel in the upper box washed out small nuggets and dust when the rocker was shaken and the gold was captured by the strips and carpeting. Parker, *Gold in the Black Hills*, 57.

[63] William H. Hare, Episcopal Bishop of Niobrara, oversaw the Indian agencies in Dakota Territory assigned to the Protestant Episcopal Church under President Grant's "Peace Policy" that enlisted religious denominations to reform Indian affairs. Hare had nominated John J. Saville for the Red Cloud Agency post. Following initial charges of fraud connected with the Red Cloud Agency, Hare had served on a commission that inspected the agency in February 1874 and exonerated Saville. Keller, "Episcopal Reformers and Affairs at

Red Cloud Agency," 117, 121. Kime, *Black Hills Journals*, 6n8 credits Jenney's mentor, geologist J. S. Newberry, for nominating Jenney for the job.

[64] Moses "California Joe" Milner, a well-known scout and frontiersman, had been hired by Colonel Dodge as a packer, but later became a guide when the skills of José Merrivale were found wanting. Milner was murdered by Tom Newcomb at Fort Robinson on Oct. 29, 1876. Kime, *Black Hills Journals*, 22-23; Thomas R. Buecker, *Fort Robinson and the American Century, 1900-1948* (Lincoln: Nebraska State Historical Society, 2002), 195n34.

[65] Bear Butte, a noted landmark and Native sacred site, is just east of Sturgis, South Dakota.

[66] Inyan Kara is an igneous protrusion left by erosion of the surrounding sedimentary material. It is ca. 6,368 feet above sea level. Mabel Brown, comp., "The Wyoming Portion of the Custer Expedition of 1874 to Explore the Black Hills," *Annals of Wyoming* 46 (Fall 1974): 271-74. Bear Lodge is today's Devils Tower National Monument, also an igneous protrusion or "plug" and also a Native sacred site located northwest of Sundance, Wyoming.

[67] Capt. Andrew S. Burt, Ninth U.S. Infantry, left the Dodge/Jenney Expedition on Sept. 3 to cover the council near Red Cloud Agency for the *New York Tribune*. Kime, *Black Hills Journals*, 8n13, 198. His career is treated in Merrill J. Mattes, *Indians, Infants, and Infantry: Andrew and Elizabeth Burt on the Frontier* (Denver: Old West Publishing Co., 1960).

[68] This could be Thomas McClaren, who had gone into the Black Hills in December 1874 with the Gordon party. He and Charles [James?] Blackwell had left the Hills in February 1875, probably to get supplies. McClaren was then described as "a practical miner and has mined in Montana." The men proclaimed their intention to return to the Black Hills. *Cheyenne Daily Leader*, Mar. 16, 1875; Parker, *Gold in the Black Hills*, 34.

[69] Although the investigating commission found no solid evidence that Saville had committed fraud or had otherwise failed to carry out his difficult job as Red Cloud agent to the best of his ability, the commission concluded that he lacked the necessary temperament and administrative skill and should be removed. Saville subsequently resigned. Keller, "Episcopal Reformers and Affairs at Red Cloud Agency," 123-24.

[70] The temporary post was actually established near the Gordon stockade/Custer City in the fall of 1875 under command of Capt. Edwin Pollack of the Ninth U.S. Infantry. It was named Camp Collins. The garrison included Capt. Guy V. Henry's Company D of the Third Cavalry. Companies A, H, I, and K of the Third Cavalry were part of the military escort for the Jenney scientific party in the Black Hills. The companies had been detached from Fort McPherson in the spring of 1875. Parker, *Gold in the Black Hills*, 70-71; Kime, *Black Hills Journals*, 43n31; Fort McPherson Post Returns, 1875, Re-

turns from U.S. Military Posts, Records of the Adjutant General's Office, RG 94, NARA, microfilm at the NSHS.

[71] This was Dodge's "Camp Crook," occupied from July 21 to July 28. Kime, *Black Hills Journals*, 143 and map, 242-43.

[72] Lt. John F. Trout, Twenty-third U.S. Infantry, in December 1874 had been assigned by then Dept. of the Platte commander Gen. E. O. C. Ord to take charge of distributing relief supplies to Nebraskans suffering from the grasshopper plague of the previous summer. Gary D. Olson, "Relief for Nebraska Grasshopper Victims: The Official Journal of Lieutenant Theodore E. True," *Nebraska History* 48 (Summer 1967): 123-24.

[73] Ring Thunder is probably the correct name of the Brulé delegate here identified as Round Thunder. "Report of the Sioux Commission," *ARCIA, 1876*, 352. Blue Horse was an Oglala chief of the Loafer band and a brother of Big Mouth, who had been killed by Spotted Tail in 1869. Personal communication from Kingsley M. Bray.

[74] Dodge's own version of this conference substantially conforms to how Stull described it. Kime, *Black Hills Journals*, 146.

[75] The locale prompting Stull's observation was likely near the confluence of today's Rapid Creek and the Cheyenne River near Badlands National Park. The quote attributed to Gen. Alfred Sully applies to the Little Missouri River badlands in present North Dakota, through which he led an expedition in 1864. That expedition did not pass through the Black Hills region. The quote evidently does not appear in any of Sully's official reports or correspondence, but can be found in David L. Kingsbury, "Sully's Expedition against the Sioux in 1864," *Collections of the Minnesota Historical Society* 8 (1898): 457.

[76] White Bull was a Sans Arc headman at Cheyenne River Agency, not to be confused with the more famous Miniconjou of the same name who fought with Crazy Horse at the Rosebud and Little Bighorn and surrendered with Crazy Horse's band at Camp Robinson in 1877. For the latter, see Thomas R. Buecker and R. Eli Paul, eds., *The Crazy Horse Surrender Ledger* (Lincoln: Nebraska State Historical Society, 1994), 158. In 1876 the band of White Bull, the Sans Arc, was consolidated with that of Sans Arc head chief Crow Feather, indicating a family connection. Personal communication from Kingsley M. Bray.

[77] Dodge encountered a delegation from the Cheyenne River Agency, including Black Tomahawk, on Oct. 5, 1875, when Dodge and his party were proceeding to Camp Sheridan and the Indians were heading home from the Grand Council. Kime, *Black Hills Journals*, 335-36. Most of these men signed the 1876 Manypenny agreement to surrender the Black Hills at Cheyenne River Agency on Oct. 16, 1876. They included Spotted Bear and Rattling Ribs (Two Kettle), White Bull, Charger, and Yellow Hawk (Sans Arc), Duck, Little No

Heart, and Yellow Hawk (Miniconjou). "Report of the Sioux Commission," *ARCIA, 1876*, 354-55. Bull Eagle was a Miniconjou headman mainly resident at Cheyenne River through the 1870s but with important links to non-treaty Lakota. Burnt Face was a Sans Arc headman, whose followers settled at Cheyenne River Agency in 1868. Personal communication from Kingsley M. Bray.

[78] Fool Dog, a Lower Yanktonai, was at the Standing Rock Agency on Oct. 11, 1876, where he signed the Manypenny agreement, "Report of the Sioux Commission," *ARCIA*, 1876, 353.

[79] Big Head and Wolf Necklace were Upper Yanktonai; Two Bears was a Lower Yanktonai head chief who led the Standing Rock Agency delegation to the Black Hills Council with fellow chiefs Running Antelope (Hunkpapa) and John Grass, Sihasapa (Blackfoot). Long Soldier was a Hunkpapa. "Report of the Sioux Commission," *ARCIA, 1876*, 353-54, and personal communication from Kingsley M. Bray. Kill Eagle, also a Sihasapa, was at the Little Bighorn fight. Powers, *Killing of Crazy Horse*, 299, 323. Biographical information on John Grass appears in Josephine Waggoner, *Witness: A Lakota Historian's Strong Heart Song of the Lakotas*, ed. Emily Levine (Lincoln: University of Nebraska Press, 2013), 321-23. The *Cheyenne Daily Leader*, May 17, 1876, reported that Slave, "a Standing Rock agency chief" and three other Indians had been killed recently in a fight with miners going into the Black Hills via the route from Yankton.

[80] Old Red Skirt, Miniconjou headman, whose band had settled at Cheyenne River Agency in the winter of 1874-75 due to game failure in the hunting grounds. He fled the agency in 1876 when the army was confiscating arms and ponies and later surrendered to Gen. Nelson Miles on the Yellowstone and interned as a hostage pending the surrender of his followers. He subsequently returned to Cheyenne River Agency. Personal communication from Kingsley M. Bray.

[81] John Burke had been agent since May 1875. *ARCIA, 1875*.

[82] Apparently this is Stull's misconception of Article Ten of the 1868 treaty, which authorized an appropriation of ten dollars annually for thirty years for each Indian who continued to "roam and hunt" and twenty dollars annually for each Indian who "engages in farming," the appropriation to be expended by the Secretary of the Interior to purchase goods that "the condition and necessities of the Indians may indicate to be proper." Article Ten did not provide for direct cash payments to individual Indians.

[83] Stull refers here to Agent Saville's November 1873 effort to take a census of Indians at Red Cloud Agency, an effort that the Indians strenuously resisted. Buecker, *Fort Robinson and the American West*, 5.

[84] Perhaps J. E. Cravens, who succeeded Bingham as agent at Cheyenne River Agency. *ARCIA, 1877*.

[85] Meaning the 1862 uprising of the Santee in southwestern Minnesota.

[86] In other words, whites who lived among the Indians, commonly known as "squaw men."

[87] See n. 78.

[88] Bingham's agency was assigned to the Episcopal Church under Grant's Peace Policy. Keller, "Episcopal Reformers and Affairs at Red Cloud Agency," 118.

[89] Newly appointed Dept. of the Platte commander George Crook arrived in the Black Hills on July 28 and he and Colonel Dodge drafted a proclamation ordering the miners to leave by August 15. The miners were encouraged to hold a meeting in advance to draft rules to secure their claims pending the expected future opening of the Black Hills. The meeting was set for August 10. Kime, *Black Hills Journals*, 8, 163n206. The proclamation appears as Appendix II in Parker, *Gold in the Black Hills*.

[90] Agent Howard of the Spotted Tail Agency reported that he, Spotted Tail, Doctor Mills, Reverend Cleveland, and twelve Indians left the agency on Aug. 5 and returned on Aug. 8. Howard said "The Indians expressed themselves as well pleased with the steps taken by the Govt. to prevent the whites from invading their country until after the treaty is made." He was referring to Gen. George Crook's visit to the Black Hills, and his proclamation ordering all miners to leave by Aug. 15. Howard to CIA, Aug. 14, 1875, Spotted Tail Agency Letters.

[91] Capt. Frederick W. Benteen of the Seventh U.S. Cavalry, who had been ordered from Fort Randall by Dept. of Dakota commander Gen. Alfred H. Terry. Greene, *Fort Randall*, 117; Kime, *Black Hills Journals*, 165n207.

[92] The members of the Peace Commission for the 1868 Fort Laramie treaty were Generals William. T. Sherman, Christopher C. Augur, William S. Harney, Alfred. H. Terry, and John B. Sanborn; the civilian members were Sen. J. B. Henderson of Missouri, S. S. Tappan of Colorado, and Commissioner of Indian Affairs N. G. Taylor. Campbell and Brunot were not members. Olson, *Red Cloud*, 59, 74.

[93] On Sept. 3, 1855, Harney's troops destroyed a Brulé village under Little Thunder on Blue Water Creek in Nebraska, retaliation for the killing of Lt. John Grattan and his detail near Fort Laramie in August 1854 and for the attack on a government mail party in November 1854, in which Spotted Tail was involved. Spotted Tail was imprisoned at Fort Leavenworth during the winter of 1855-56. Merrill J. Mattes, "Little Thunder's Disaster," chap. 10 in *The Great Platte River Road* (Lincoln: Nebraska State Historical Society, 1969), particularly 313, 328.

[94] William Darrah Kelley was a Pennsylvania congressman who evidently had invested in Wyoming ranching.

[95] At the August 10 miners' meeting, the name "Custer City" was chosen. Kime, *Black Hills Journals*, 166-67.

[96] Lt. Morris C. Foote, Ninth Infantry, and Surg. George P. Jaquette were in Dodge's command. Capt. Edwin Pollack, Ninth Infantry, had accompanied Crook to the Black Hills and was to establish a military post near the Gordon Stockade that would be named Camp Collins. Kime, *Black Hills Journals*, 44n36, 58n58, 151n182, 152n183.

[97] Lt. Charles C. De Rudio, Lt. Francis Marion Gibson, and Lt. William T. Craycroft of the Seventh U. S. Cavalry had accompanied Benteen to the Black Hills. Heitman, *Historical Register*, 337, 369, 453; Kime, *Black Hills Journals*, 166n209.

[98] Although Capt. Andrew Burt sent dispatches to the *New York Tribune* from the Black Hills and subsequently during the September council at Red Cloud Agency, it is unlikely that he was the author of this letter. The author mentions that "Major Burt's train" will leave the Black Hills the next day for Fort Laramie. Nor is it likely that Burt would misspell fellow officer Frederick Benteen's name as "Burtine" as the published letter had it, or credit him as being an officer in the Third rather than in the Seventh U.S. Cavalry. Kime in *Black Hills Journals*, 199n251, indicates that persons other than the "regular" correspondents sent letters to the newspapers, including Valentine T. McGillycuddy, who served as a topographer on Jenney's staff.

[99] The agencies for the Lower Yanktonai and Lower Brulé were Crow Creek (Fort Thompson) on the east side of the Missouri River and the Lower Brulé sub-agency on the west side, soon to be known as "White River Agency" with its own agent. *ARCIA, 1875*, 740.

[100] This editorial was likely by George W. Miller, founder of the *Omaha Herald* in 1865, a leading Nebraska Democrat and, as he demonstrated during the Civil War, no supporter of emancipation or of civil rights for the former slaves. As this editorial and other *Herald* editorial commentary at the conclusion of the council reveals, Miller was much more sympathetic to Indians.

[101] The reporter's reference to his having been in the Indian country suggests that it was Homer Stull who interviewed Beauvais.

[102] According to Charles E. Hanson, Jr., who wrote Beauvais's biography for the *Mountain Men and the Fur Trade* series, the latter first ascended the Missouri aboard the steamboat *Yellow Stone* in 1831. When John Jacob Astor retired in 1834, the Western Department of the old American Fur Company headed by Pierre Chouteau Jr. became Pratte, Chouteau, and Company. Beauvais had wide experience in the western fur trade before establishing a road

ranche near Fort Laramie in 1853 and another at the crossing of the South Platte in 1859. He took a Lakota wife during this time, though he had also married in St. Louis. After suffering heavy property losses during the Indian war of 1864-65, Beauvais essentially retired to St. Louis before being called upon to serve on the Black Hills Commission. He died Nov. 15, 1878. Hanson, "Geminien P. Beauvais" in vol. 7, *Mountain Men and the Fur Trade* (1969), 35-43; Louise Barry, ed., *The Beginning of the West: Annals of the Kansas Gateway to the American West, 1540-1854* (Topeka: Kansas State Historical Society, 1972), 275.

[103] Joseph Richard was the brother of John Baptiste Richard. Nothing more is known of the incident Beauvais described. Joseph Richard and his brother were partners in a Denver store during the gold rush years of 1858-64, where Joseph died in the latter year. John Dishon McDermott, "John Baptiste Richard" in vol. 2, *Mountain Men and the Fur Trade* (1965), 288, 300-1.

[104] Twenty-nine-year-old Albert Swalm learned the newspaper trade with his parents and served in the Thirty-third Iowa Volunteer Infantry during the Civil War. Afterwards, he ran newspapers in Grand Junction and Jefferson, Iowa, and was an employee of the Iowa legislature. On June 4, 1874, with his wife Pauline, Swalm purchased the *Fort Dodge Messenger*. His obituary is silent about how he came to know commission chairman Sen. William B. Allison, though it was likely in the arena of Iowa Republican politics. Swalm died Aug. 24, 1922. *Annals of Iowa* 14 (July 1924): 398-99.

[105] As the *Omaha Herald* implies, William H. Ashby was certainly the most obscure member of the commission, with no known qualifications in Indian affairs. A Missouri native, he had been a captain in the Confederate army and wounded at Vicksburg. After the war he practiced law in Nebraska City for several years before moving to Beatrice in 1869. There he continued his law practice and also was part owner of a newspaper. What prompted his appointment to the Black Hills commission is unknown. Hugh J. Dobbs, *History of Gage County, Nebraska* (Lincoln: Western Publishing and Engraving Co., 1918), 330-31.

Red Cloud Agency in 1876. NSHS RG2095-80

Commission member Geminien P.
Beauvais. NSHS RG2411-482

U.S. Senator William B. Allison of
Iowa chaired the Black Hills Com-
mission. Courtesy of Paul Hedren,
Omaha

Oglala and Brulé leaders from the Nebraska agencies were photographed in Omaha on May 14, 1875, while on their way to Washington, D.C. to meet with government officials. They visited Julius Meyer's "Indian Wigwam" curio store during their stop in the city. Standing, l. to r.: Meyer; Red Cloud, Oglala. Seated, l. to r.: Sitting Bull, Oglala; Swift Bear, Brulé; Spotted Tail, Brulé. **NSHS RG2246-8a**

Indians and interpreters in the Black Hills, July 1875. *Omaha Herald* correspondent Homer Stull accompanied the sub-commission and the ten-member delegation from Red Cloud and Spotted Tail agencies that traveled through the Black Hills en route to the Missouri River agencies. Calamity Peak, northeast of the modern town of Custer, forms the backdrop in this image. The man in the center is probably Red Dog, one of the delegation's leaders. The man on the right may be Francis C. Boucher, Spotted Tail's son-in-law. A correspondent at the September council described him as "a portly Frenchman." Albert E. Guerin, Jennewein Collection, Dakota Wesleyan University, Mitchell, South Dakota

Red Dog, Oglala orator, often served as Red
Cloud's spokesman. NSHS RG2955-13

Red Dog's village southeast of Red Cloud Agency.
Crow Butte is visible in the distance at extreme left.
NSHS RG2955-48

Part 2

Palavering, Prognosticating, and Procrastinating: September 1 – 19, 1875

ॐ

John T. Bell, representing the *Omaha Herald*, and Charles Collins, hired by the *Omaha Bee*, traveled to the Red Cloud Agency, as did the government commissioners, by taking the Union Pacific to Cheyenne and then proceeding overland via Fort Laramie. Commission employee Albert Swalm of the *Fort Dodge (Iowa) Messenger* and correspondent for the *Chicago Tribune* accompanied the commissioners.[1] Reuben Davenport of the *New York Herald* and Capt. Andrew Burt, who sent dispatches to the *New York Tribune*, reached Red Cloud Agency a few days after the other correspondents, having spent the summer with the Jenney-Dodge Expedition in the Black Hills. The authorship of occasional dispatches from the council to the *Cheyenne Daily Leader* and the *Sioux City Journal* is not always clear. Several signed "D" may have originated with Red Cloud Agency trader John W. Dear.

[September 1, 1875 – John T. Bell, from Cheyenne, Wyoming Territory]
Cheyenne
From our Special Correspondent
Cheyenne, W.T., [Wednesday] September 1, 1875
    The special commission sent out to treat with the Sioux for the relinquishment of whatever right the latter may have to the Black Hills country, left this place yesterday morning for Red Cloud Agency, distant one hundred and sixty miles by the "cut-off," but thirty miles farther by way of Fort Laramie, which is the route taken by the commission for some reason best known to themselves.[2]

The party consisted of the following named: Senator [Timothy O.] Howe, of Wisconsin, Senator Allison, of Iowa, Rev. S. D. Hinman, of Santee Agency, A. Comingo, Independence Mo., W. H. Ashby, Beatrice, Neb., H. W. Bingham, Cheyenne [River] Agency, G. P. Beauvais, St. Louis, J. S. Collins, Omaha, Evan T. Howe, Wisconsin, J. E. Allison, Dubuque, Iowa, Albert Swalm, Fort Dodge, Iowa, and Jas. R. Porter, Omaha.[3] The transportation for the outfit was furnished by W. M. Ward of this place, and consisted of nearly a dozen vehicles, a portion of which were comfortable double carriages.[4] The expedition will reach Fort Laramie this evening and Red Cloud Saturday night, in the immediate vicinity of which it is proposed to hold the council. The commissioners expect to be absent twenty days, which will allow twelve days for said talk, which would seem to be enough for even an Indian outfit.

It is thought the council will be attended by 25,000 Indians. Maj. John Burke, agent at Standing Rock, came in yesterday and he says that one thousand of Uncle Sam's wards under his care are on their way, having left Standing Rock last week. There is a great deal of jealousy and bad feeling among the Indians, and a satisfactory arrangement cannot be effected with them except by the exercise of great care and prudence. When they left Cheyenne the members of the commission had not agreed on any definite plan of action, but they were advised by old residents here to not offer the Indians any sum of money whatever for their rights in the Black Hills, but to bind the government for a considerable term of years to the issuing of rations to all the Sioux tribes under a similar system to that now followed, and also to provide them with farming implements, seed and building material sufficient to get them started in agricultural pursuits. These are understood to be the views entertained by Hinman and Beavais and the long experience of these gentlemen in the Indian country and familiarity with the Indian character will give weight to any suggestions they may make.

The cattle business of this country is immense and is constantly increasing. In coming up from Omaha yesterday I made the acquaintance of Mr. D. H. Snyder of Austin, Texas, who has been in the cattle trade along the line of the U.P. since 1870.[5] He says that in shipping cattle from Cheyenne to Chicago it is the custom of cattle men to feed their stock in pens at North Platte, Council Bluffs, and Clinton, Iowa, stopping over at each place from eighteen to twenty-four hours. He says the accommodations at the Bluffs are the worst on the run, and that cattle dealers generally would much prefer stopping over at Omaha, if suitable accommodations could be had there, as this business, though large, is but in its infancy as yet. Common business prudence would dictate that steps should be taken now to secure a portion of the profits thereof to Omaha. The Saratoga bottoms would be an excellent locality for stock yards, and fame and fortune await the men who will take hold of this enterprise.[6]

The Cheyenne cattle dealers are jubilant over the speck of railroad war which has appeared on the horizon. The Rock Island road has cut down its rates to Chicago from this point five dollars per car, and before this reaches the eye of *The Herald* readers, the Northwestern and Burlington companies will, in all probability, have cut down another V, making a reduction in the present rates of $10 per car.

[James M.] Pattee, erstwhile of Omaha, and extensively known to the residents of that locality, is now established at Laramie City, where he is doing a rushing business in the lottery way. He is reported to be in receipt of an income from this source of $1,000 per week, and is consequently deeply interested in perpetuating the existence, upon the Wyoming statute books of the gambler's license law which was passed in 1869, and by virtue of which he is allowed to follow his profitable pursuits. The proposition to repeal this law is to be the bone of contention in this winter's session of the territorial legislature. The *Leader* of this city is taking strong position in favor of the repeal, while on the other hand the said Pattee has signified his intention of spending several thousand dollars to prevent it. The law is certainly very questionable and could have been passed only in a country where gamblers and desperadoes predominated, as was the case in this territory in 1869.[7]

Cheyenne runs a brace of daily news papers, the *Leader* established in 1867 edited and owned by Mr. H. Glafcke and the *News* owned by Benton & Fisher (the former a Fremont boy) and edited by W. P. Carroll, a lawyer of the place, who is evidently very new to the editorial harness.[8] Both papers are doing a fine advertising business and have a greater demand for job work than they are able to supply.

I leave for Red Cloud to-morrow in company with Mr. G. H. Jewett, the trader at Spotted Tail.

J. T. B.

[*Omaha Daily Herald*, Friday, September 3, 1875]

[September 2, 1875 – Omaha, Nebraska]
Ashby—*The Herald*, and the Indian Council

"Ever since Indian Commissioner Ashby declined to aid the *Omaha Herald* in sending a reporter to the Indian Council at the government's expense, he forfeited all claims for the admiration and adulation of that enterprising sheet – *Omaha Bee*"

Long before the reporter business was ever mentioned or thought of, we paid our respects to the ponderous Ashby, and so far as his having "declined to aid *The Omaha Herald* in sending a reporter to the Indian Council," that eminent and able Indian negotiator came to the Editor of *The Herald* and volunteered his invaluable services in that behalf. Mr. Commissioner Ashby could not have prevented *The Herald*'s reporter from going to the council in the employ of the commission if one at Laramie had not been already engaged, but he was never permitted the honor to "decline" "aid" which was never asked at his hands. He volunteered that "aid" which was not considered worth having, and then sneaked off, if we may credit the *Bee*, to give it to another.

The Herald prefers to send its own reporters to Indian councils, as it has done, and it was only at the urgent solicitation of prominent members of the commission, including the insufferable squirt, Ashby, that Mr. Homer Stull's name was mentioned in that connection.[9]

The Herald has its own reporter at the Red Cloud Council, and it did not have to "catch a ride" on that point through Mr. Charles Collins of the *Sioux City Times*, who agrees with nine-tenths of the journalists and readers in the West in declaring that *The Herald*'s special correspondence from the Black Hills was the best ever printed.
[*Omaha Daily Herald*, Thursday, September 2, 1875]

[September 3, 1875 – John T. Bell, from Old Red Cloud Agency, Wyoming Territory]

The Sioux Country
Old Red Cloud Agency, Eighty-Nine Miles North of Cheyenne, [Friday] Sept. 3, 1875
From our Special Correspondent

At 11 a.m. yesterday, *The Herald* correspondent left Cheyenne for the scene of the grand council in company with Charley Collins of the *Sioux City Times* and Mr. Jewett, trader at Spotted Tail. Our means of conveyance consisted of a span of horses and a two-seated open buggy. Eighteen miles out we stopped for dinner at the ranch of Lane and Sturgis, where we were furnished with a passable meal, dished up by a young fellow who said he was thoroughly disgusted with life in this country and desirous of getting a "situation" elsewhere.[10]

At 9 p.m. we reached a comfortable home-like place owned and run by Mrs. John T. Freel, whose husband was killed last December by a man whom he had just discharged from his service. The killing occurred within sight of the ranch and the murderer is now confined in the Cheyenne jail, his trial being set for next November. At this place we were provided with a well cooked supper and breakfast, consisting of hot biscuit, butter, syrup, fried chicken, bacon, fried potatoes, pickles, coffee, tea, and milk. The ranch is situated on a fine stream called Horse Creek, forty-five miles from Cheyenne, which stream we have crossed four times in our journey to-day.[11]

Leaving Mrs. Freel's at 6 a.m. to-day, we reached "Patsey's" about ten o'clock. This ranche is situated near a splendid spring and is called Hawk Spring Ranche. The proprietor, familiarly known as "Patsey," lives entirely alone, but the dinner he got up for us would have done credit to a professional cook. Patsey is an ex-newspaper man and has worked on various papers from Pittsburg to San Francisco. He told us that the correspondent of the *New York Herald*, who was with the Jenney expedition, [Davenport] was very much disgusted because he didn't find fried chickens and eggs on the table, whereupon Patsey expressed his regrets and assured him that the next time he came that way he would furnish him with an abundance of chicken and eggs, and also pie and poundcake.

The Hawk Spring ranche is situated in an immense cattle range and from his cabin door Patsey pointed out Creighton's main camp, or rather the butte near which it is located. He said there were at least 45,000 head of cattle feeding on that range, and soon after leaving the ranch we passed several groups of cattle bearing the Creighton brand, all of which were as sleek and fat as seals. The cattle are allowed to follow the promptings of their own sweet will and roam over the country unmolested by herders until the season for the annual counting and branding comes round.[12]

The country thus far is not of a very attractive character. For half a dozen miles out of Cheyenne we had fine gravelly roads. Then we encountered stretches where the sand predominated, with an occasional mile or so of good traveling. The ground is covered with buffalo and gramma grass a few inches in height and here and there, along Pole and Horse Creeks, we found small patches of meadow. We have not met a team until late this afternoon, since leaving Cheyenne, just before reaching this ranch we passed half a dozen ox teams engaged in hauling hay to Fort Laramie.

Old Red Cloud, our present quarters, was abandoned about two years ago and the agency removed 80 miles still further north. The buildings are made of sod and are now occupied by Nick Janis, a Frenchman, who has been in this country since 1849. He has served the government repeatedly as an interpreter, in which capacity he has made frequent visits to Washington. He is enrolled as a member of Red Cloud's band of Sioux and draws his regular rations and supplies of clothing, tobacco, etc., when at the agency. He has very comfortable and commodious quarters here, on the north bank of the North Platte, and is doing finely at the ranching business. He is a tall, heavy set man, being six feet high and will weigh about two hundred pounds. He has all the characteristics of a Frenchman, speaks English with a very slight accent, and can rattle off half a dozen different Indian dialects blindfolded and with one hand tied behind him.[13]

Janis thinks Saville is an honest man, and that the only reason the Indians do not get first class supplies is because Uncle Sam don't pay first class prices. He says Marsh is a humbug and that [William] Welsh is a crotechetty [sic] old fellow.[14] He has spent several weeks in the company of both of these latter-day reformers and says that when he met Marsh in Washington recently and the professor attempted to interview him on the ration business, he refused to talk to him. He says that in making a treaty with the Sioux, the commission should go slow, but he thinks a week's talk will be sufficient. He is going to Red Cloud day after to-morrow and will be present at the council. He will object strongly to the government giving the Indians money for the Black Hills, for he says if they were given money the agencies would soon swarm with thieves and gamblers who would soon "absorb" all the Indians' wealth.

Last fall a young Sioux girl was induced to marry against her own wishes. She had long loved a young man of the tribe, but the latter was not considered by the "stern parents" as a desirable match and the girl had been ordered to give him up. After the marriage took place the young wife became so sick that she refused food and in a few days thereafter was confined to her bed. Late one evening, she ceased to breathe and was buried after the Indian fashion on an elevated pole platform, the face being left uncovered according to a request previously made by the unhappy wife. The deceased was supplied with the articles of food which are always furnished in such cases for the use of the deceased in the journey to the spirit land, and for an hour or so the bereaved young husband sat upon the burial platform mourning for the departed one. That night the camp was moved, as is the custom of the Indians after a death has occurred in the tribe, and the next day the husband returned to resume his mourning, but was astonished to find that the corpse had been removed and with it the store of provisions left upon the platform. An excited search followed, which resulted in the discovery that the girl had shammed death in pursuance with a plot made with her lover and that the two were then on their way to the Missouri River country as fast as their ponies could carry them. At the present writing the adventurous pair are living in the vicinity of the old Whetstone Agency happy and contented.

If any of *The Herald* readers doubts the foregoing narrative, and will address me at once, I will forward the papers in the case by return mail.

To-morrow, at an early hour, our party resumes its journey, expecting to travel the 80 miles between this ranche and Red Cloud in twenty-eight hours. It will be a dreary drive, as there is not a sign of civilization on the entire route.

J. T. B.

[*Omaha Daily Herald*, Friday, September 10, 1875]

[September 6, 1875 – John T. Bell, from Red Cloud Agency, Nebraska]

Among the Sioux

From Our Special Correspondent

Red Cloud Agency, Neb., [Monday] Sept. 6, 1875

The team which conveyed our little party of three from Cheyenne to this place was a remarkably willing one—the off horse being willing to do all the work and the near one being perfectly willing he should. The result was the former played out yesterday, compelling us to lay over several hours on the Niobrara River in order for him to get rested up. We expected to reach Red Cloud by 10 a.m. yesterday, but in consequence of this unanimity of sentiment on the part of our team, did not arrive until 6 p.m.

The road from Janis to Red Cloud is entirely devoid of attraction. For the first forty-five miles it passes over a dead level of sand, with but one stream of water in the entire distance and that a very small one. This forty-five miles we traveled Saturday, the 4th, reaching the Niobrara at 7 p.m. Here we found a beautiful stream of cold water, about ten feet in width at the ford and running over a gravel bottom. Along this stream we found an abundance of excellent pasturage which our horses evidently appreciated—especially the philosophical bay whose post of duty was on the near side. During the day we had seen but one human being besides ourselves, and he was a mail carrier whom we had met soon after leaving Nick Janis' ranche that morning. As the next white man's habitation was at Red Cloud—thirty-five miles distant—we went into camp upon reaching the Niobrara, lariating one of our horses and turning the other loose.

At 3 a.m. yesterday we hitched up and drove on expecting to reach the head of White Earth River, twenty-five miles distant by seven o'clock, there feed our team and drive the remaining ten miles in a couple of hours. But our plan was not carried out for we discovered after driving until we saw day light appearing that our team had been fagged out by the forty-five miles of sand we had traversed the day before and needed more rest. We were still on the Niobrara and so turned out of the road, turned our horses loose again, spread our blankets, and slept until nearly ten o'clock, when we resumed our journey. Fortunately we soon struck better roads and from that we made better time.

After traveling ten miles we ascended a high ridge and there saw for the first time Crow Butte, near which Red Cloud is situated, distant twenty miles, though it did not appear to be more than eight miles, such is the wonderful clearness of the atmosphere in this country.[15] Twenty miles out we reached a range of hills which forms the divide between the Niobrara and White earth Rivers, which range is about one hundred miles in length and is covered with a scattering growth of pines, while along the White River bottom is found considerable elm, box elder, and willow.[16] Some ten miles out from the agency we came upon an extensive Indian camp, with a fine herd of ponies—numbering at least one thousand—feeding upon the hill sides and valleys in the vicinity. From this on we passed small camps of Indians until we reached the agency, upon arriving at which we found the commission very comfortably quartered in the house Dr. Saville, the agent, had built for his own use, while inside the stockade was a row of half a dozen wall tents, to one of which Collins, of the *Sioux City Times* and *The Herald* ambassador were assigned, the remainder being occupied by Maj. Burke of the Standing Rock Agency, Maj. Bingham of the Cheyenne [River] Agency, [Robert] Lines, the official stenographer of the commission, Swalm, assistant secretary, Allison, a nephew of Senator Allison, and other attaches of the commission.

Senator Howe, who joined the commission at Cheyenne, having come up from Denver for that purpose, left here yesterday on his return east in consequence of a telegram from Washington requesting him to be present at that point with the investigating commission of which Gov. [Thomas C.] Fletcher is chairman, of Missouri, and which is about to close its labors.[17] Senator Howe had been accompanied by his niece, Miss Grace Howe, who left Cheyenne last Tuesday with the intention of remaining with the party and attending the grand council, but upon arriving at Fort Laramie she concluded to stop there until the commission returned, probably having seen enough of this desolate region after a two day's experience.

There are about ten thousand Indians encamped within a few miles of this agency and others are constantly arriving, a large proportion of which are being stopped at Spotted Tail Agency by the wily old savage, from whom the agency takes its name. Spot is extremely desirous of having the council held near his camp, and the quarrel between himself and Red Cloud on this point may be the means of delaying the council somewhat.

"Is this business likely to occupy more than two weeks' time"? I inquired of a member of the commission this morning.

"It is likely to last more than two weeks," was the reply, "and what is more, it is not likely to result in anything."

Per contra, Major Burke, of Standing Rock Agency, tells me the Indians are very anxious to effect the proposed treaty, and that as the commission are equally solicitous on that point, he thinks the council will result satisfactorily to both parties and without much waste of time. However, as *The Herald* has frequently had occasion to remark, the average Indian is preeminently a person of leisure and not disposed to rush things. Colonel Beauvais says he is going to do all he can to bring matters to a focus within the next two weeks.

J. T. B.

[*Omaha Daily Herald*, Sunday, September 12, 1875]

[September 7, 1875 – Charles Collins, from Red Cloud Agency, Nebraska]

The Black Hills

(Correspondence of the *Bee*)

Red Cloud Agency [Tuesday] Sept. 7 [1875]

The commission appointed by the President to treat with the Sioux Indians for the purchase of the Black Hills, arrived here on Saturday last, and have been holding secret councils among themselves since that time. From what we are able to glean of their doings, it is apparent that their work so far is only preliminary to their anticipated grand council, which, it is hoped, they will soon be able to obtain with the Indians now here and arriving. In order to conciliate old Spotted Tail, chief of the Brule Sioux, the commissioners had agreed to hold the council at a point called Chadron Creek, midway between this and the Spotted Tail Agency, but having comfortable quarters here, they have finally prevailed on all the head men of the various tribes, excepting Spotted Tail, to consent to a change of council ground to a point within six miles of this agency, known as Crow Buttes. The commissioners affect a great deal of wisdom by being very guarded and reserved in their conversation. They apparently believe they have a very responsible duty to fulfill. The commission to treat with the Indians for the purchase of the Black Hills, is composed of Senator W. B. Allison, of Iowa, president of the commission; Senator P. Howe, of Wisconsin; Hon. A. Comingo, of Independence, Mo., ex-member of congress from a Missouri district; Rev. S. D. Hinman, Episcopal minister of Yankton Agency and who has likewise supervisory control of the Episcopal Indian missions for the Sioux nation; G. P. Beauvais, of St. Louis, formerly a well known Indian trader; General A. G. Lawrence, of Newport, R.I., and Hon. W. H. Ashby, a prominent Nebraska lawyer, whose home is at Beatrice, in your state; J. S. Collins, post trader at Fort Laramie, is secretary to the commission.

There are at present something over 25,000 Indians here to attend the council to make a new treaty with the whites. The Indians here, with a few exceptions, represent every tribe and band of any importance that are in any way interested in the ceding of the Black Hills. Major H. W. Bingham, Indian agent at Cheyenne [River] Agency, is here with 6,000 of his Indians. They represent the Sans Arcs, Two Kettle and Black Feet bands. Col. John Burke, formerly of Omaha, but now Indian agent at Standing Rock Agency on the Missouri River, has between three and four thousand of his Indians here. The latter represent the Upper and Lower Yanktonais, Hunkpapas and Black Feet tribes. This agency (Red Cloud) claims to have 14,000 Indians on its feed roll under charge of that now somewhat famous chief Red Cloud. Spotted Tail's Agency will swell the Indian council by 8,000 more, with several wild minor bands and tribes to hear from; so the outlook promises such a gathering of Indians to ratify a treaty as has never been collected at any previous time for any purpose. Runners have just arrived from the camp of Sitting Bull, who is recognized as chief of all the wild Indian bands who have heretofore refused either to make or recognize treaty obligations. These runners represent that almost one-half of Sitting Bulls' Indians will attend the council. The conjectures as to the success in making a treaty are various, many of the old Indian men and interpreters claiming that the Indians have got such an exaggerated idea of the wealth of the Black Hills, and the desire manifested by the whites to obtain it, that they will ask and hold out for a fabulous price to cede it to the government, while the commissioners believe that they can force the Indians into making a treaty by threatening in case they refuse, to have Congress cut off the appropriations which has for the past two years supplied them with food. The terms of the treaty of 1868 was only to cover a period of four years in food and thirty years in annuity goods. For the last two years Congress has been making special Indian appropriations to supply them with food; and speaking of food reminds me that there is many a poor family would like to be a government ward. Here is the daily allowance issued to every Indian, old and young, by the government. Three pounds of fresh beef for twenty-seven days in the month, the remaining days they get one pound of pork, half-pound of flour, four pounds of sugar for each 100 rations, with a liberal allowance of beans, salt, tobacco, saleratus, soap, etc. and all the axes, plows, wagons, harness, stones, nails, hardware and carpenter's tools they desire, and if they show any disposition to cultivate the soil, they are furnished with cattle or horses.[18]

Red Cloud, who lives within eight miles of the agency, has up to the present failed to put in an appearance here, notwithstanding the fact that previous to the arrival of the commission he was here the greater portion of his time.

Old Spotted Tail says he will not attend the council unless it is held at Chadron Creek, but it is believed he will be brought to terms before negotiations are commenced. Just now the commissioners are awaiting the arrival of General Terry, one of their number, who is expected here in a few days. Senator Howe left here on Sunday for Washington, in answer to a request of the president. Dr. Saville, the agent at this place, has not yet returned from his eastern visit.

The Marsh charges are looked upon as the work of parties who desire to affect a change in the brook of Indian contractors and agents at present ending this end of the Indian business; but of course all such theories must be taken with due allowance for the interest that everyone who lives here feels in the agent and the agency.

There are here and at Cheyenne, Fort Laramie, Sidney, and scattered through and about this country hundreds of miners awaiting the consummation of the forthcoming treaty, when they will make a grand rush for the Black Hills. Everyone, from the highest to the lowest, all classes and grades, that I have met with in this country is affected and afflicted with the Black Hills fever. If the Hills were opened tomorrow I doubt whether a sufficiency of white employees could be retained to run the agencies and do the citizen work at the military posts. Hereabouts the fever is all-prevading [sic].

Col. John D. Burke leaves this morning to bring up his Indians, who are camped about fifty miles from here, to this agency, to attend the council. Major Bingham has also sent for his. Red Cloud's Indians are camped in this neighborhood, while Spotted Tail can have his Indians here in two days from the time they commence moving. The outlook don't look to promise anything practical for one or more weeks. Indians think and act very slowly. They have no idea of time, and place no value on it. Camp Robinson, located one and a half miles southwest of here, is garrisoned by six companies of troops, two of cavalry and four of infantry. The cavalry is made up of Company K, 2nd Cavalry, under Captain James Egan, and Company H, 3rd Regiment under command of Captain Guy Henry. The infantry is made up of four companies of the Ninth Infantry; the post is in command of Major Jordan, captain of A company, 9th Regiment. Mr. J. W. Dear is the licensed post trader here. He is an old resident of Omaha, and is universally esteemed. He is meeting with a well merited business success. He also keeps the restaurant here, where meals are served that are not surpassed, both as to quality and variety, by any hotel we have been a guest of west of the Missouri. Frank Yates also keeps a trading post here and is doing a successful business.

In my next I will give you the progress of the council, post and agency gossip, and other matters that it is hoped will be of interest to *Bee* readers.

Charles Collins

[*Omaha Daily Bee*, Monday, September 13, 1875]

[September 7, 1875 – John T. Bell, from Red Cloud Agency, Nebraska]

The Grand Council

From our Special Correspondent

Red Cloud Agency, Neb. [Tuesday] Sept. 7, 1875

An Indian ought to be a happy creature, at least those who are protégés of the government. He has nothing in the world to do but draw his regular rations which consist of the following: Three pounds of beef per day for twenty-seven days in the month, with one pound of pork per day for the remainder; half a pound daily of flour; four pounds of coffee and eight of sugar for each hundred rations; four pounds of beans to the hundred rations with saleratus, salt, tobacco, soap, candles, etc. in abundance. In addition to the foregoing they are provided with axes hoes, plows, wagons, oxen, harrows, stoves, and a score of other things of that character, and when they wish to build houses, are furnished with all the necessaries and have the services of government carpenters free of charge. When he wants to go out hunting or fishing he does so, but is not compelled to in order to sustain himself, as every member of his family, big and little, is furnished with rations in the same generous fashion as himself. But he is a trifling, lazy, "shiftless" dog, and when he is induced to build a house at Uncle Sam's expense, and fit it up with the necessary furniture with means drawn from the same free purse, he invariably shakes it at the approach of cold weather and takes to the woods, where he stretches his tepee and, turning his pony to browse on the boughs of trees, spends the winter in very comfortable fashion.

The foregoing applies with especial force to the Sioux, and the result of such excessive kindnesses on the part of the government is that the frontier Indians have become very high toned and impudent and now that they are being sued, as it were, for a surrender of the Black Hills country, all the young men of the tribe are putting on airs and entertaining a desire on their part to retain their quasi ownership of the section of country about which so much has been said and written of late, and to "clean out" the white man if the latter dare to enter the Black Hills. Of course this talk amounts to nothing, as the young bucks are all under the control of the old men, many of whom have been to Washington and have thus gained a better idea of the numbers of the white race.

Old Red Cloud has had a fit of the sulks ever since the arrival of the commission, and up to the present writing has not yet put in an appearance at any of the informal talks which have been held at the agency during the past two days. Spotted Tail was here last Saturday—the day the commissioners arrived—and was in excellent spirits, but "you can't most always tell" by an Indian's manner what his intentions are. For instance, all the Missouri river Indians, who were visited by the commission this summer, appeared to be perfectly satisfied with the proposition to surrender the Black Hills country to the whites, but Major Burke, agent at Standing Rock, says that after the commission left the Indians held meetings among themselves at which a great deal of dissatisfaction was expressed, and many of them declared they would never consent to the proposed treaty.

Two hundred lodges of northern Indians came in to-day, making a delegation of some sixteen hundred. Eight thousand left the Cheyenne and Standing Rock agencies two weeks ago and are expected in daily. There have been consultations held with various small squads since the arrival of the commission, but they were all of an informal character and without result.

The Indians generally are well armed, several thousand of them sporting Henry rifles, which they have bought of the whites. All of the camps are surrounded with droves of ponies. The Indians are well dressed and sleek-looking, from which fact it is apparent they are not stinted in the supplies furnished them by the government, notwithstanding the popular belief that the majority of their agents are adepts at stealing. They are well supplied with canvas lodges, and these have gradually taken the place of the skin lodges used by the Indian in his wild state.

This agency is well secured in case an assault should be made by the red skins. It is entirely surrounded by a heavy plank stockade, all the gates being provided with chains and locks, but notwithstanding this security, a young man by the name of Frank Appleton, brother-in-law to Dr. Saville, was shot dead inside the stockade one night several months since by a Cheyenne, who clambered over by means of a pole resting against the top of the stockade, and who succeeded in making his escape.[19] The reason for the shooting is shrouded in mystery, but it is generally supposed it was a case of jealousy. It was the duty of the night watchman to have given the alarm in time to have prevented the murder, but as that official is compelled to go about on crutches in consequence of having had both feet frozen so badly last winter as to necessitate the amputation of those useful members, he cannot be held to a strict accountability.

The lumber used here is furnished by a steam mill on White river about half a mile below the stockade. On the same stream, about a mile above, is another steam mill owned and run by the government, from which is procured the lumber and building material used at Camp Robinson.

There is a great difficulty in getting hay in this country. That used at Fort Laramie costs the government from fourteen to seventeen dollars per ton, and that used at Fort Russell, near Cheyenne, is hauled from the North Platte—a distance of one hundred miles. The contractor this year gets but fourteen dollars per ton, hence he will not accumulate a fortune from the profits of this job.

Dr. Saville, the agent at this point, has not yet returned from his reconnoitering expedition to "the states," though he is expected hourly. He left Omaha last Tuesday but stopped off at Kearny Junction. He is said to be a very sensitive man and it is reported that he will resign his official position no matter what may be the result of that investigation. It would be a pity for his resignation to be accepted, for the reason that it is decidedly refreshing to refer to one Indian agent by a title other than "major," for in that connection it is major this, and major that, though it would probably be safe enough to say that not more than one in five of them knows enough of military matters to distinguish between a redan and an abatis, for instance, or could tell on which side to dig the ditch in throwing up an embankment. With this superabundance of majors about him, one can really imagine himself down South surrounded by the "pomp and circumstance" of ante-bellum days.

The following prominent chiefs have reached the agency: Sioux—Red Cloud, Red Dog, Little Wound, Man-That-Is-Afraid-Of-His-Horse, Conquered Bear, Black Bear, Red Leaf, Pawnee Killer, White Cow Killer, Yellow Hair, and No Water. Cheyennes—Roman Nose, Little Wolf, Turkey Leg, Calf-Skin Shirt. Arapahoes—Black Coal, Six Wings, Sharp Nose, and Many-A-Bear. William Rowland is present as interpreter for the Cheyennes and Arapahoes and Billy Garnett as interpreter for the Sioux. Major Howard came in late last night.[20]

Major Burke, of the Standing Rock agency, went out in the direction of Spotted Tail this morning for the purpose of bringing in the Missouri River Indians, with a view of holding the council at this point. With these and the Indians belonging to this agency, there will be a majority of the Indians concentrated there and the probability is the big talk will take place near Red Cloud.

J. T. B.

[*Omaha Daily Herald*, Tuesday, September 14, 1875]

[September 7, 1875 – Albert Swalm, from Red Cloud Agency, Nebraska]

Among the Indians

Editorial Correspondence of *The Messenger*

Red Cloud Agency, [Tuesday] Sept. 7, '75

The two hundred miles of country between Cheyenne and Red Cloud Agency is composed almost entirely of sand and gravel, the only exceptions to the rule being the valleys of the Chugwater, Rawhide, Niobrara, and White Earth Rivers. The valleys of the first two are exceedingly beautiful, and contain the finest vegetation seen on the route. Several good ranches are found in the first, while the others are held in the Sioux Reservation and therefore not open to settlement. The uplands are covered with the nutritious buffalo grass—with great patches of cactus and prickly pears. It is excellent for grazing purposes, but it would take considerable money to make me claim ownership of it all. Innumerable prairie dogs, owls and rattlesnakes are its only inhabitants that we discovered, and we found these in social intercourse, the three being seen together at the opening of the dog house. Along the valleys, away from the traveled road, we found deer and antelope, but not plentiful. While in camp on the Rawhide, in company with Captain Ashby of the commission, we galloped up the valley some ten miles, and found a country of the most lovely description, the sides of the valley being high buttes of a soft sandstone, covered with a brushy growth of pine and cedar. We found volunteer stalks of corn three feet high—something very strange in this almost rainless section. But, of course, the influence of the stream that meandered through the valley, gave enough dew to nourish the corn mentioned. Deer are plentiful in the upper end of this valley, and very fat. But as many of the more sulky Sioux have their tepees there it is not considered safe to be found fooling around there. We continued our gallop until darkness made hunting impossible, when we turned back and got into camp about ten o'clock at night, tired and hungry enough to demolish a vast amount of palatable hash. Long drives have to be made for water—from 18 to 30 miles between these "rivers." None of them is as large as the Lizard, near our city, but the water is very clear, and as it comes from the melted snows of the mountains, it is quite cool and excellent for drink. The value of good water makes itself manifest here to man and beast, and cannot be over-estimated. The agency is located on the White Earth, some 20 miles from its head and down the valley of which the road leads. It was formerly the camp ground of Crows and Cheyennes, and several battles have been fought there. We found many bones of defunct braves whitened by the suns and storms of many years, while the antlers of the deer, elk and antelope could be picked up in great plenty. Good fish are caught in the river and many strange petrifactions jut out from the high banks. From these rambling notes you may be able to gain something—so at least I hope.

Camp Robinson, one of the new military posts, is situated about one mile up the valley, near a famous spring. The quarters are all good, and Dr. [Curtis E.] Munn, a former surgeon of the Potomac army, has about completed a very large and comfortable hospital built of logs, but plastered inside.[21] The post has a saw mill in connection, and as pine timber is plenty, there is no starvation for lumber. The quarters of the officers are made exceedingly comfortable and well they should be, for the sake of their families.[22] The comforts of civilization are not plenty, and those that they have are appreciated to their full value. We have received many kindly courtesies from them, and only such as were prompted by our apparent needs.

The climate is very fine, the air pure and bracing. Beef can be hung up in the open air for four or five days with the mercury among the 80's. I would not tell this item did I not see this thing tried on near our own quarters. And the beef here, by the way, such as we have [been] served, is the best I have eaten for years, fairly scooping anything for juiciness and tenderness that our own prairies can produce. That's about all the good I can say for the country.

We arrived here on Saturday last, and since cleaning up after our long and dusty ride, have been the recipients of many visits from the chiefs and head men. Spotted Tail, one of the wisest Indians of the Sioux nation, and of the whole country, called with Swinging Bear [Swift Bear] and had a pow-wow about the council, he wanting it down on Chadron Creek, and the commissioners desiring it here at the agency on account of the comfortable arrangements now provided, while below nothing save bad water and the hot sun is found. After a pleasant interchange of remarks the chiefs concluded to go home and will be back soon again [I am] convinced. Red Cloud has not yet come in, waiting for a call first from some of the Commission. Sitting Bull, Little Wound, Yellow Hair, and some dozen others have come in and said the usual "How! Ka lo!"—which is "how are you friend." Blue Horse, another man of much influence, called in a nearly naked condition. His heart was bad, as one of his grandchildren had been scalded to death. He was a friend to the whites, and wanted some clothing and food in order that he might go out alone and mourn according to Indian Hoyle.[23] These Indians are very economical in their habits—on some things. For instance, a steer was issued to a batch of lodges yesterday and he was soon a dead bullock. The Indians carefully saved all the entrails, and last night had a grand feast, in which the aforesaid entrails formed the grand and only dish—just as they were when doing duty for the Texan bovine! Then they kept up a fearful hellabaloo until about two o'clock a.m. when death did not end their career, as we devoutly hoped, but they dumped down in their tepee for a sleep. Every lodge has a regular nest of young papooses, from the one in swaddling clothes up. None are good looking; the women are fearfully ugly; some of the men really have handsome bearing, being tall, shapely and apparently intelligent. The women, of course, do all the drudgery—positively all of it, and just now I see a great two hundred pound buck passing, carrying a colored umbrella to shield himself from the sun, while his squaw follows, loaded with a babe on her back and the others following, quarreling over a bone got from the cook. Such is life in some of its phases among the Sioux. The Arapahoes are the worst of all Indians. About eighty lodges of them are camped near here. The women of the tribe are all prostitutes, under the management of their loving husbands and fathers and brothers. It is a veritable Sodom, and disease is rapidly destroying the whole tribe. Blindness, scrofula, and such diseases are fearfully prevalent, and the half breed mixture that appears quite plentiful does not improve the morale of the camp. In fact, an Arapahoe camp is about as near hell itself as is possible to imagine on earth. Still, we feed and maintain these cut-throats in idleness and their orgies, and talk about making men and women of worth out of them without making them learn the hard and wearisome lesson of labor. There are now about one thousand lodges in sight of the agency, from the butte that rears its ugly head just across the river.[24] Thousands of fine horses are being grazed on the hills, and the streets about the agency are generally filled with the red men seeking some of the *olaco hebee*—the treaty-makers—and to say *How! ka lo!* They are the greatest gossips in the world, and each one is anxious to impress one with his great importance and influence, and the necessity of having him around when the grand council occurs. Then, they act just like the small politicians of civilization. The followers of Young-Man-Afraid-of-His-Horses are sure that Spotted Tail is an old fool, and Red Cloud a very poor stick, and vice versa. Any one who has been called to see the Great Father at Washington is a big man and generally insists upon the white man getting up in his presence and shaking hands. They all hate soap and Bibles and value highly all manner of nonsensical trinkets. Thus, this morning I saw a great greasy buck trade a dried beef hide, worth $4, for a small trunk, not larger than 10x12. But I must close—the disgust created by an observation of Indians as they are in nature compels me to drop my pen and go out among hills, where possibly I may find a pine not ornamented with an Indian grave or a hill not covered with their fluttering rags and bits of tobacco offered as a sacrifice to their god whose good pleasure they want for some deviltry.

S.

[*Fort Dodge Messenger*, Thursday, September 16, 1875]

[September 7, 1875 – Capt. Andrew S. Burt, from Red Cloud Agency, Nebraska]

The Grand Council with the Sioux

(By Telegraph to *The Tribune*)

Red Cloud Agency, [Tuesday] Sept. 7, via Fort Laramie, Sept. 10

The council for the sale of the Black Hills and Big Horn country will probably begin its work on the 9th. Since the arrival of the commissioners, on the 4th, efforts have been made to begin work at once, but disputes between rival factions as to where the council shall be held has delayed matters. The commissioners, seeing no termination to the dispute, have ordered Major Howard to bring Spotted Tail and his Indians here. This chief has caused all the trouble, wanting the council near his agency. The 2,500 [Indians] collected from the Missouri and the Big Horn represent the most varied and largest interests ever made the subject of a council in this western country.

Your correspondent, to be here, has just arrived from Camp Transfer of the Black Hills expedition, making a ride of about 200 miles on horseback, over a difficult and dangerous country, accompanied by three soldiers and Mr. Davenport.[25] The great interest in the sale of the Black Hills and Big Horn Mountains warrants the effort. No doubt a sale will be effected, but at what price cannot be approximated. Red Dog says, "It is his country, and the miners must pay for the gold they have taken out and for the damage done." The council will last many days, interspersed with dances by the Omahas, Foxes, and other exercises of different tribes.[26]

The Miniconjous, the Bad Faces, and the Sans-Arcs, fierce tribes of the north, are more subdued than ever known.[27] They are no longer in the ascendancy. Hunger has turned them. They will eat government beef, poor as it is. The last 50 miles of my ride was over a route swarming with these red Arabs. Many stopped us for talk, all eager for news of Kea-Sap at the Black Hills, seeing us coming from there. They were the interviewers. Crazy-In-The-Lodge dragged your correspondent into his Tee-Pee, to have the news all to himself, to the disgust of the assembled crowds of warriors and squaws. He wanted to get some idea what price to ask in the coming council. Not being retained as attorney, and also moderate in my views, my information was not particularly satisfactory.[28]

The Black Hills expedition is at Camp Transfer, trying to make its way north with a train to the Bear Lodge butte [Devil's Tower]. Possibly it may not affect this. Work will have to be done with pack animals for transportation. There are no new gold discoveries. In fact it is thought that the expedition has reached the boundary of the gold land, and gone beyond the sandstone. The expedition will start soon on the homeward march. Possibly it may come this way through the Mauvaises Terres [badlands] to collect fossils and bones.

[Unsigned]

[*New York Tribune*, Saturday, September 11, 1875]

[September 8, 1875 – Capt. Andrew S. Burt, from Red Cloud Agency, Nebraska]

The Great Council for Their Sale

(From a Special Correspondent of *The Tribune*)

Crow Butte Council, Red Cloud Agency, Neb., [Wednesday] Sept. 8

The Black Hills Exploring Expedition having almost completed its labors, in fact having accomplished its important work, naturally the interest of Eastern people will tend toward the negotiations for buying the land from the Indians. I reached this place yesterday after a tiresome ride of 200 miles on horseback through the Indian country, and across the Mauvaise Terres. Judging by a short conversation with the gentlemen of the commission, the work to be done will take a long time. The varied interests to be considered have delayed the holding of the council several days. It may be a week before the grand pow-wow will begin. The members of the commission, I feel assured, are thoroughly in earnest, and are workers; no delay will arise from neglect of their duties. The following is a complete list of the commission: Senator Allison, Chairman; the Hon. A. Comingo, the Rev S. D. Hinman, Mr. G. P. Beauvais, Mr. W. H. Ashby, Mr. A. G. Lawrence, Mr. J. S. Collins, Secretary. Absent – Senator Howe, Gen. A. H. Terry, U.S.A..

Declined – Bishop E. R. Ames, Judge F. W. Palmer. Senator Howe will probably not take part in the council.

The treaty-making in years past has taught the Indians to expect much circumlocution, arising not from tact and diplomacy, but an unreadiness to come to the point. The Indians are wily diplomatists and talk against time when necessary, but they always know what their wants are. At any time in a negotiation their ultimatum could be given. On the other hand our commissioners have seemed not to know what they could or would agree to accept. This hesitation can be partly explained in the fact that treaty-making is by no means a general business; it is not taught in academies. These savages, on the other hand, begin the work at an early age, and it may be said making and breaking treaties among different tribes has been a pastime of their youth and an innocent resource of their old age. With no reflections on their sincerity and good faith, this could almost be taken literally. If we may judge from their conduct in treaties with the United States Government, it must be acknowledged to be so. But unfortunately the whites have invariably set the example in treaty-breaking. Such a statement seems unwarranted. The facts will sustain it, however, I believe. Said a gentleman yesterday to one of these commissioners, in a private conversation, "I assert it as an incontrovertible fact, and I appeal to Dr. Hinman to corroborate me, that there has never been a treaty made with the Indians but is to-day unfulfilled." In 1866, for example, Col. H. B. Carrington (now a retired officer teaching school somewhere in Indiana, I am informed, should he be needed to confirm this statement) was sent to the Powder River country with a column of troops to build posts there.[29] At that time negotiations were pending which ultimately led to the abandonment of what was then known as the Powder River route to Montana. That no treaty had actually been made does not alter the case, for it was understood that the Indians had a right to barter the right of way through the country. This was a meaner species of bad faith than if the treaty which ultimately went into effect had been signed. It was a shot at the sentinels during a flag of truce. It is pleasant to know, however, that the government representatives were not aware of the merits of the case nor responsible in any way, excepting perhaps that if they had entered a protest it would have been a record for them on the side of justice. That this was not done arose, perhaps, as much from ignorance as anything else; in fact, that is a general fault. This seems strange when it is known that men served on treaty commissions who ought to have known all about the Indians, their history, habits, and rights. It may have been true that a certain amount of carelessness has crept into these negotiations. This may be explained partly by the fact that commissioners heretofore have not been fully informed of their powers, nor had sufficiently explicit instructions, nor known, as I have said, how far they could agree to this or that, that they were empowered to do. In my opinion nothing of this kind will mar or retard the work of the present commission. These gentlemen seem to have taken pains to inform themselves, and where a doubt has arisen, an immediate consultation has been held as to the rule in former treaty commissions. Their instructions, though somewhat obscure and impracticable, are an improvement on those usually issued. As they are an important outline of the treaty negotiation, I will give a few of them. Indian Commissioner [Edward P.] Smith uses the following language:[30]

"You have been appointed by the Hon. Secretary of the interior, under the direction of the President, as member of the Commission to negotiate with the Sioux Indians relative to the procurement of a cession by them of such portion of that country known as the Black Hills, between the north and south forks of the Big Cheyenne, as the President may determine to be desirable for the Government to purchase for mining purposes. And a relinquishment of their right to that portion of Wyoming known as the Big Horn Mountains, and lying west of a line running from the point where the Niobrara River Crosses the east line of Wyoming to the Tongue River. Said line to keep distant of the last not less than 50 miles from each of the Forts known as Fetterman, Reno, and Kearney, [Fort Phil Kearny] and also of the necessary right of way through their country to reach the portion ceded. By reference to the treaty of 1868 made with these Indians, Sections 2 and 16, copy of which is herewith furnished, you will be informed as to the nature and extent of the respective claims of the Sioux to these tracts of country. That portion of the Black Hills country which lies within the boundaries of Dakota is without dispute a part of their permanent reservation. The country mentioned as Wyoming, as described in the 16th section of the treaty above referred to, is a portion of 'unceded territory.' To this the Indians have no claim except for hunting purposes and the exclusion of other people. By reference to a map of this country, inclosed herewith, you will observe that the cession of the Black Hills and the relinquishment of the Big Horn country leaves a considerable tract between these two cessions still within the claim of the Indians, as defined in the 16th section. This region, especially along the Powder River, is known as the Sioux hunting-ground for buffaloes, and is intended still to be preserved to them for that purpose, a passage to it being left open on the north of the north fork of the Cheyenne, as well as on the south of the south fork. In negotiating with these ignorant and almost helpless people, you will keep in mind the fact that you represent them and their interests not less than those of the Government, and are commissioned to secure the best interests of both parties as far as practicable."

The land for which the negotiation is made is not well known. Involving as they do a curious and important feature in the history of our country, I have given the subject of the rights of the Indians more space than would be otherwise warrantable. Remember we are buying in one sense what we already possess; we are purchasing land within our own territory, made ours by the deeds of the Pilgrim Fathers and beyond discussion. We are buying the right of way across our own cow lot. But if this be the golden milking time, and when, too, it is to feed and clothe, however poorly, a race forsaken seemingly by God's providence, buy I say, be the price any amount within reach of the people's purse. The Powder River country is a pleasant land, a part of which contains the Big Horn Mountains. It is an ambiguous term, without giving one a clearly defined idea of its geographical location. It lies west of the Powder River from its source in the Big Horn Mountains, the point where it empties its waters into those of the Yellowstone; thence along the Big Horn Mountains, following their general direction north and west until the Big Horn River is reached; thence along the east bank of the Big Horn River, north, to its confluence with the Yellowstone; whilst the Yellowstone itself, from the mouth of the Big Horn to that of Powder River, is the general east and west line on the north.

The first precise knowledge of this interesting region was obtained after its occupation by troops under Col. Carrington before spoken of. It will only be necessary to mention that part from Fort Phil Kearny to Fort C. F. Smith, and more particularly that about the latter post on the Big Horn River. The reader will remember that it is of these mountains that Gens. [William T.] Sherman and [Philip] Sheridan speak positively as to their containing gold and silver in paying quantities. The writer himself spent some time there, and can say he believes it will prove a rich and permanent mining country. I have not made so strong a statement as that about the Black Hills.

In the spring of 1866 the general government, at the solicitation of several persons representing the mining interests of Montana, determined to open a wagon-road from old Fort Kearny in the then Territory of Nebraska by way of Fort Laramie through the Powder River country to the mining settlements in south-eastern Montana.

How the country was occupied for two years, and then abandoned by treaty stipulation with the Indians, is already known. Little has been written, however, about its beautiful scenery and natural advantages, its fine climate and valuable resources.

The streams flowing from the mountains through to the Yellowstone River into which they all empty, water a land wherein cereals may be raised; thus, like Colorado and Montana, having a backbone of agricultural resources to warrant settlement and improvement, should the mines fail to prove rich. If the agricultural resources, too, should be found lacking, the grazing is as fine as ever a cattle man could wish. The day is not far distant when it will become a serious question where these vast herds can find stamping ground. The hay fields are numerous. This fact will attract sheep men, who must lay up fodder to feed the animals during the winter; and sheep, not like cattle, must have sheds and be provided for at least during stormy weather. These considerations make the purchase of this region desirable. It will be seen, however, that the commission are instructed to negotiate for only a strip of 50 miles lying along the base of the mountains, and the right of way through the approaches. The government has received mistaken information or there has been a fatal oversight. Why should the government deliberately provide for itself another Nebraska trouble: It is but now that the Sioux rights in this state have been purchased—the present reservation, which is in Nebraska, is excepted in this statement—at what cost of time patience and money few know.[31] It is utter folly to leave open so vexed a question, when no such favorable opportunity may ever occur again to extinguish forever all claims on the country, excepting such as may be held for the permanent reservations. The oft-repeated and little understood "hunting ground" term of Mr. Cooper is the block thrown in to bar the way to a final adjustment of the ownership of this country, which can be made satisfactorily to both parties.[32] There is no "hunting ground along the Powder River" now, and I question whether it ever has been much of a pasture for buffaloes. Do not confound the locality. "Along the Powder River" is the term. The testimony of Lewis and Clark is against the theory; old trappers say so. "Jim" Bridger, who was with Sir George Gore—the latter being in the West expressly to hunt—only guided the party along its margin or outskirts.[33] And now what has brought the wild Miniconjous and Wazhazhas to terms? Why have they who ever scorned the idea of a treaty, come in to attend this council? Starvation! There is game in the country. Where? North, and particularly "along the Powder River." Old Gray Head [Gray Hair?] has made the statement here this summer that he could find no buffaloes there, and that they were all across the Big Horn in the Crow country. He and his band camped for days starving in sight of game across the swollen and impassable river. The same report is made by the Indians from the Pumpkin Buttes.[34] With these facts in their possession, why need the commission point the way to the Indians for making future claims? It would be a kindness to them to buy now what will be stolen perhaps; for should a mining people congregate, and ultimately make a lodgment because of abundant gold and silver in the mountains, in less than five years the Indians could make no claim on a preemption backed by a rifle. The government would not, perhaps could not, give protection. Has it done so in Colorado with the Utes?[35]

It will be enough that the Indians may make the point on which to dispute, without the commission's leading up to it. There are factions in all the bands, more especially, of course, among the northern ones, who may excuse themselves from further attendance at the council, or leave the question open out of their bad faith. It is possible some may withdraw when this matter comes up, making it a pretext to do what is in their minds now; that is, to make war. Be the decision of the Indians what it may, it will be a comfort to know that Major Gen. George Crook commands this department—a man who never gave up the pursuit of faithless Indians, the chase being to the death or complete submission in word and act to the laws of the land; the securing of perfect safety for life and property of citizens exposed to such marauders; a man, be it said, who never broke faith with faithful red men.

Will the Indians be ready to sell? Who can tell? Indian ways are inscrutable. What one of them thinks in the morning, a good meal, a passing bird, or any chance omen may change before the sun sets. Their best men are not free from prejudice and superstition. Perhaps the one or two infidels, of whom Red Cloud is one, may be free from such influences; but then what one of them is a free agent in act. Some [none?] of the so-called chiefs rule; they are at the bidding of the Indian "soldiers." Spotted Tail, perhaps the wisest of their men and the most able, has repeatedly been compelled to yield to the orders of his lieutenant, Two Strike. Red Cloud, Red Dog, Sitting Bull, Man-Afraid-of-his-Horses, Rocky Bear and others have told me they are willing to sell. What their price will be is not known. When asked, they have replied in Crow language (I do not understand Sioux) "A-hook baht-sahst;" or in English, "A great deal." I predict it will be anywhere up to $50,000,000. As they have but little knowledge of dollars, it must be inferred that they get their promptings from white men. Said a shrewd observer to me this morning:

"You are wrong about the squaw men putting the Indians up to asking a big price for the Hills. That pie is cut by the Indian Ring. I know men calculating now, in a business way, on handling 'their share of those millions.'"

The United States soldiers are particularly requested not to come to the council The Indians have expressed themselves to that effect, and even the company (Major Vroom's 3d Cavalry) which has escorted the commission thus far is not camped at the agency where the commissioners are staying.[36] This is interpreted as a demand that perfect faith must be shown. It is to be hoped it is not trusting to a straw. Once or twice commissioners have been grandly trusting, and the result has been a somewhat painful climax. There are said to be not less than 25,000 warriors present.[37] There has been no time to verify these figures; possibly it cannot be done. There has been no record kept of arrivals, and the various bands are camped in a circle of not less than 50 miles. Mr. Collins, secretary to the commission, has no official information, or, more properly, exact data to judge by, but places the number as given above by approximation. I have no doubt of the correctness of the estimate. When a list can be prepared I will forward it.

Such a gathering has never been seen west of the Missouri; perhaps the same numbers, but not so varied a representation. It will be seen by reference to Commissioner Smith's letter of instruction that six different agencies will be represented and in addition about 5,000 Indians will be present who have never attended a council with the whites. It seems impossible that a stormy debate can be avoided, and should a few determined ones start the ball, a puzzling question presents itself; where would it stop rolling? If all the Oglalas, Red Cloud's band, who are to be the guard, could be trusted to fight, would they be able to restore order? Then there are bitter animosities to help on a fight once begun. Spotted Tail and his people, and the river Sioux are discontented over the choice of place at which the council is to be held. They would not be very strong backers of the commissioners. Our soldiers are particularly requested to be kept away.

It is far from my purpose to create a sensation by exaggeration. I speak only of a possibility but yet one which can be considered as such. The Modoc massacre is not so long gone by that it is forgotten.[38] A mere handful of Indians perpetrated that deed. But the number, however small, is not the point. It is to what a condition of bloody purpose savages may work themselves and to what desperate undertaking, and how faithfully it may be performed.

[Unsigned]

[*New York Tribune*, Tuesday, September 21, 1875]

[September 9, 1875 – John T. Bell, from Red Cloud Agency, Nebraska]

The Black Hills Business

From our Special Correspondent

Red Cloud Agency, Neb., [Thursday] Sept. 9, 1875

It is a fact not generally known to the whites that Old-Man-Afraid-of-his-Horses, and not Red Cloud, is in reality head chief of the Oglala Sioux. When the treaty of 68 was made the former was the recognized chief while Red Cloud was in command of the soldiery of the tribe. He refused to attend the council and in order to pacify him Man-Afraid-of-his-Horses "abdicated" in his favor on condition that the treaty he had just made with the whites on behalf of his tribe should be strictly observed by Red Cloud, and hence the latter has been recognized by the government, since that time, as the head man of the Oglalas, and in this capacity has made numerous visits to Washington. He has had but little influence with the Indians, however, they refusing to give up their allegiance to Man-Afraid-of-his-Horses, who is a man of some 65 years of age, and of superior intelligence, being also a firm friend of the whites. Meanwhile, a son of the latter has been growing up and he is to-day the most influential and popular man in the tribe, next to his father, notwithstanding the fact that all negotiations with the Oglalas, on the part of the government, are conducted with Red Cloud. Yesterday these three Indians visited the commissioners for the first time since the arrival of the latter, and then they did so in pursuance of special invitation sent them the day before.

They filed into the room in which the commissioners were seated, followed by nine old men of the tribe and about a dozen young braves, the party squatting flat down on the floor, with the exception of Red Cloud, who was given an arm chair in which to deposit his kingly person. He wore a pair of handsomely beaded moccasins, a pair of leggings, white shirt, black vest and dress coat, and a black felt hat which he carefully deposited on the floor between his feet. He is about forty-five years of age, with a low forehead surmounted by a heavy growth of hair, one side of which was braided up with strips of red flannel.

Old-Man-Afraid-of-his-Horses took his seat on the floor on Red Cloud's right, and never opened his mouth except to eject huge volumes of smoke from the same when the pipe which the party were smoking reached him in its regular rounds. He bore evidences of age, but appeared to be in excellent health. He was attired in full Indian costume. His hair grew thick upon his head and hung down over his shoulders in wild profusion.

To the left of Red Cloud sat Young-Man-Afraid-of-his-Horses—a bright-looking, intelligent fellow about 25 years of age, apparently.[39] He was dressed in full Indian costume with the addition of a low-crowned white felt hat ornamented with a turkey feather. He paid the strictest attention to all that was said and carefully watched the half breed boy who acted as interpreter. He had just returned from the tour he had made among the northern Indians at the request of the commissioners who were here last summer, for the purpose of inducing them to attend the council, and for which service he was promised 100 American horses, which are to be divided among the fifty Indians forming his party, and which horses have not yet been delivered by the government.

The pow-wow began by Senator Allison, chairman of the commission, directing the interpreter to tell Red Cloud and his men that the commissioners were glad to see them, which information was received with grunts of approval, after which Red Cloud remarked that Spotted Tail had been talking about having the council held on Chadron Creek, but that his Indians wanted it held on White Clay Creek, six miles from Red Cloud Agency.

Allison (to the interpreter) – "Tell him we think we have found a suitable place near Crow Butte" (about eight miles from the agency).

Interpreter (after stating it in Sioux) – "Red Cloud says he has sent some of his young men out to bring the Indians to the mouth of White Clay Creek, near Crow Butte, and he thinks it will be a good place to hold the council."

Allison – "Ask him if he has made preparations to take care of these Indians hospitably."

Interpreter – "He says most of them have seen white men and there will be no trouble."

Hinman – "Tell him Col. Beauvais and myself will go down to Crow Butte tomorrow and select a place for the council."

Interpreter – "He says 'good,' 'good.'"

Allison – "Tell him that is all we want to say to him today."

Interpreter – "Red Cloud says he wants to say something for Young-Man-Afraid-of-his-Horses. He says he sent him away to bring the wild Indians in and that he was promised good horses by the commissioners and that he wants gentle horses."

Allison – "Tell him this will require more time. We can't get the horses at Cheyenne or anywhere this side of the Missouri River. We expect to get the horses and give them to them." (Cries of "How," "How.")

Interpreter – "He says that is all right and that he will want more beef for these people who have just come in."

Allison – "Say to him we will give an order for as much additional beef as he will want, provided he will always give us three days notice. Ask him if there is anything further."

Interpreter – "He says that is all he has got to say and if there is any other that has got anything to say he can say it."

Allison – "Tell him we are ready to hear it."

Cries of "How," "How!" and grunts of satisfaction on the part of the Indians, after which Young-Man-Afraid-of-his-Horses indulged in a bit of oratory couched in purest Oglala.

Interpreter – "Young-Man-Afraid-of-his-Horses says he wants to get the horses Mr. Hinman promised him before the council is held."

Hinman – "Tell him we sent a message to Washington about those horses at that time and there has been some misunderstanding about it. We want to get them good horses, and we guarantee they will receive them, but it will take at least a month to get them into the country and we can't wait. Ask them if that is satisfactory to them."

The translation of this explanation, by the interpreter, was followed by a moment or two of profound silence, and then the Indians engaged in an earnest and somewhat excited conversation among themselves, the interpreter joining in on his own account, and then remarked in English that Young-Man-Afraid-of-his-Horses said the horses had been promised to him and that he wanted them.

Hinman – "Tell him he has been gone all summer on this business and so have we, and have just got back."

To this, Young-Man-Afraid-of-his-Horses responded: "How!" and then devoted several moments to an industrious puffing of the pipe, which had been just handed him by Red Cloud.

The interpreter – "Red Cloud says the Indians think the horses are nearby."

Hinman – "Tell him the Great Father had ordered the horses bought at Cheyenne and afterwards changed his mind because he found he could not get good ones there."

Interpreter – "Red Cloud says he has told these Indians that the horses should be bought east of the Missouri River where there are good horses. There is nothing but bronchos here and he don't want them. Young-Man-Afraid-of-his-Horses wants the horses delivered before the commissioners leave."

Allison – "Tell him the horses will be delivered as soon as they can be procured but we can't fix the time."

Interpreter – "Red Cloud says he thinks it would be best to have the council inside the stockade and that if it is outside, the young children will be playing around your tents and trouble you."

Allison – "Tell him we are much obliged to him for his kindness, but that it is our intention to keep our camp here and come back to it every night while the council is being held."

Red Cloud then said he had some brave men who would take charge of the council tent and grounds, and with this the talk ended.

Three thousand extra head of cattle have been ordered here for the purpose of feeding the multitude.
J. T. B.
[*Omaha Daily Herald*, Friday, September 17, 1875]

[September 9, 1875 – Albert Swalm, from Red Cloud Agency, Nebraska]

The Indians
Special Correspondence of *The Chicago Tribune*
Red Cloud Agency, [Thursday] Sept. 9

The Sioux Indian Commission are now comfortably housed inside the stockade of the agency—the house of the agent, and wall-tents affording ample accommodations for all. The commission have formed a mess of their own, have their own cook and servants, and are entirely isolated and independent, save in the use of the house. Daily sessions are held in the morning for three hours, preparing the work for the Grand Council, and the commission would be ready for that event in a few hours, were the prospect good for an immediate gathering of the various tribes.

The place chosen by the commission for the holding of the council is at Crow Butte, about 6 miles east of Red Cloud Agency, where plenty of wood and water is found for the wants of the Indians, and which, at the same time, will allow the commission to retain their present quarters. Red Cloud and all his chiefs are heartily in favor of the Butte, and will carry most of the Indians with them. Spotted Tail, however, is determined to force the commissioners to Chadron Creek, 25 miles eastward, and has corralled nearly all the Missouri River Indians at his agency, where he holds them. Their agents are now with them, endeavoring to bring them around to an agreement to the Crow Butte place, with every prospect of success. Spotted Tail's obstinacy in this matter is easily traced to two things: first, to his jealousy of the Red Cloud people; and, secondly, to his being coaxed up to it by some white men of doubtful color. Old Spotty is a great fellow at bluff, but must yield in this case. The council will be held at Crow Butte, or not at all; for it would be utter foolishness to allow the noble old bluffer to drag the commission just where he pleased, and would be a virtual surrender to him in the more important matters of the treaty.[40]

A state visit was paid to the commission yesterday by Red Cloud, Young-Man-Afraid-of-his-Horses, American Horse, and some dozen other big men. Red Cloud is sharp and shrewd, and as diplomatic as any white chief could be. He came simply to assure the great chiefs of the commission that he was glad to see them, and that his soldiers would protect them from all harm, and that American Horse would command the sword of honor. All of which was duly acknowledged with many "Hows"; after which the red diplomat called attention to the horse question.

This arises from the fact that the sub-commission sent out to make the preliminary arrangements with the several tribes found it impossible and dangerous to go to the wild Sioux, on Powder and Tongue Rivers, and arrange for the representation at the council. So Young Man, the hereditary chief of the Oglalas proposed, in the interest of peace, to take his best men and go to them some 400 miles, and do his best with them; for which service the sub-commission promised compensation in horses. The mission was successful, since 200 lodges of the wild Sioux are now camped on the White Earth. The Indian Department advertised for the horses, but then withdrew the advertisement. All this the Indians know, and hence many inquiries. In order to hold Young Man and the 400 or 500 lodges he leads, the promise was made that the horses should be furnished, as a matter of common honesty—an article somewhat scarce in this particular locality. With the pledge of Senator Allison Red Cloud seemed satisfied, and the party withdrew.

The wild Indians that Young Man succeeded in bringing in are indeed wild, many of them being entirely clad in skins and furs, and all of them carrying their arms at all times. You can scarcely approach one, save in the company of a more civilized Indian; and then you always find the wild individual nervously fingering a navy revolver or repeating rifle. Sitting Bull is the greatest chief among the wild ones, and he refuses to have anything to do with the council, and will make war to protect his rights in the country north of the Black Hills. He has about 200 lodges with him, and his men are well armed and mounted. He might be found a thorn in the side of the mining Black-Hillers next year.

Nearly one month ago, the proper department was apprised of the location of the council at Red Cloud Agency, and the immediate necessity of moving supplies forward from Sidney and Cheyenne. What is the condition of things here to-day? There is not one pound of flour here, nor has there been any issued here for the last thirty days. [Dwight J.] McCann, the contractor for the present year, has not delivered one pound on the new year, and there should have been thirty days' supply on hand July 1, 1875.[41] There is not one pound of corn that can be issued, and but a few pounds of tobacco. The Commissioner of Indian Affairs desires that the rations of flour, corn, and tobacco shall be ample; but none of the contractors are prodded up with the official prod to a performance of their duties. How the thousands of Indians are to be subsisted is a serious question to the commission, and not easily settled. It shows a management worthy of either a Napoleonic mind or that of our friend Damphool; and the unprejudiced reader may make his choice.

They have discovered a new way of doing things when the flour and corn rations are short. By order of the proper authorities, where such a state of things occurs, they increase the ration of beef to one and a half pounds per day. Thus, Bosler's numerous bulls are made to serve as corn and flour, and all at the regular contract price. Can it be that, because the margin on the flour-contract is small, the Ring sees more profit in trotting Bosler's beef to the front—and that, too, where scalawag steers are made to weigh the pounds that only belong to good cattle?[42] I don't pretend to fathom the business; but, to a man from the States, the thing looks decidedly as though a game was being played upon someone, and that it was not on Bosler. Of course, it is a good thing to make the Indian take beef in his'n all the time; the squaws are poor cooks, and their flap-jacks are very hard on poor Lo's digestion. It is purely for sanitary purposes that the flour is withheld. Another evidence of our kindly disposition to ye gentle savage.

So far as I can learn, there are no enthusiasts on the commission in regard to the purchase of the Black Hills country. The tall stories about the richness of the diggings fall upon leaden ears, for reliable information has been found that knocks all the glitter out of the mountains of gold we have heard so much about. The country is very good, in spots, for grazing purposes. It is too far north to ever make anything in the agricultural line, so far as it relates to the growth of grain, and, even this early in the fall season, ice half an inch thick forms in every part on quiet pools. There is a good supply of timber there, and good water. Some gold has been found, but not enough to pay for the labor of getting it. I have seen specimens to-day mined on Rapid Creek, but it took four men two days to get $2.75 in dust. Of course their apparatus was somewhat defective; but, trebling the find, nearly every common laborer in Chicago makes more clear money. I have also seen quartz, said to come from the Hills, that would assay $15,000 to the ton; but the fact that the man who found it entered the Hills one day, and brought his "find" out the next, places great discredit on the story. Then, the quartz presented has never, in any other mining district, been found short of a depth of from 40 to 1,000 feet. It is only one of the many "salting" processes adopted to create a great furor.

The capture of a man with 7 pounds of gold-dust going into the Hills is another evidence that fraud is being perpetrated by somebody interested in way-trading posts and the transportation business. There is nothing to warrant the claim of rich diggings in the Hills. There is some gold there, but more of it in the corn-fields of Illinois and Iowa. The reports of Prof. Jenney should be taken at their par-value. Dr. [Henry] Newton, a thorough geologist, with the Jenney party, is of the opinion that no gold in paying quantities will be found—that is to say, to correspond with the great cost of general and thorough mining.[43] Maj. Burt, who has just come in from the Hills, reports that, with six men, he worked two days, cleaned up twice, and got $1.50 the first time and 25 cents the second. These are sad and simple truths; and the organs that shriek for the great golden wealth said to be found there, can take as much comfort as possible out of them.[44] At last accounts, Prof. Jenney was in the northwestern part of the Hills, and nearly through with his work. Col. Dodge and command will leave in a few days for this agency and the railroad. At present, six miners are on French Creek, in charge of the property of the miners who were compelled to "git up and git." They are under the supervision of Capt. Pollock, who also has some twenty-four men under arrest, sent out by the Sioux City Transportation Company at the uniform rate of $15 per head, and no deadheads.[45]

What the Indians will ask will be a "stunner" to commence with. From $30,000,000 to $50,000,000 is being talked of by them, and a long treaty with it. Of course, they do not want that in cash; but they do want it in Bosler's beef, McCann's flour, and the usual shoddy goods furnished by the contractors. They will want a few millions as a bonus. What they will receive from the commission will not exceed $5,000,000 or $6,000,000; and if that much, it will be paid in annuities running through at least ten or fifteen years. We are now paying them about $1,500,000 annually; or it might be better said the contractors receive that much, while the Indian gets along as best he may on about one-half. To avert the expense of a war with them it would be about as well to pay the cost of it to Bosler & Co., and then we would be ahead in the saving of the lives of men and horses.

At the urgent request of Senator Allison, the Hon. T. O. Howe, senator from Wisconsin, was added to the commission at Cheyenne. Senator Howe came over—a long journey of five very dusty days' duration. He was appointed by the President; but, on the day following our arrival, a courier came from Laramie with a dispatch stating that the President was of the opinion that, as Senator Howe was a member of the Red Cloud Agency Investigating Committee, he could not act on the Treaty Commission. The Senator at once left for the States by way of Cheyenne.

When the council is to be held is hard to say. The preliminary one will occur early next week, but the general council will hardly take place before the 20th of September. Such are the slow-paced movements of the noble red. They have more time than anything else, and propose to delay everything to the fullest possible limit. There is no hurrying of them in a matter of this kind. With the jealousy of chiefs to contend with, the exalted notions of the Indians as to the price to be demanded, the utter absence of supplies, the work promises to be longer by many days than was anticipated, and the task one requiring the best judgment of the men composing the commission. The Iowa members are now hopeful of reaching home in time to vote—about the middle of October.

Dr. Saville, the agent here, in company with Mr. Bosler, the cattle-contractor, came in this afternoon from the south. The doctor's heart is very bad just now, to use the Indian lingo, and the report of the committee that recently went through him here will not make him feel any better. Mr. [J. D.] Terrill, of the Auditor's office for Indian Affairs, is also with the party, on a tour of official examination.[46]

Gen. Terry has not yet arrived, but is expected by Sunday.

Capt. [Azor H.] Nickerson and Lieut. [John G.] Bourke, of Gen. Crook's staff, left yesterday for Fort Fetterman.[47] Maj. [Andrew] Burt, of the Ninth Infantry, rode down from the Black Hills in less than ten days, in order to represent the *New York Tribune* at the pow-wow. Mr. Davenport, of the *Herald*, accompanied him. Davenport's heart is also very bad. An Indian found him riding a pony that had been stolen and taken to the Hills, where Davenport bought him. The Indian took the pony, and Davenport is looking for the seller with a navy revolver.

Louis Richard has been employed as one of the interpreters for the commission. He is a half-breed, and one of Prof. Marsh's witnesses, and, therefore, under the ban in this country among the regular residents.

The commandant of Camp Robinson, Maj. Jordan, and others, were entertained at the tables of the commission yesterday. The usual doings were had, with toasts and remarkably short responses.

[Unsigned]

[*Chicago Daily Tribune*, Monday, September 20, 1875]

[September 9, 1875 – "Mart," from Red Cloud Agency, Nebraska]
Letter from Red Cloud
From our Own Correspondent, Red Cloud Agency, [Thursday] September 9, 1875
Editor *Nebraskian*

I have just returned from Spotted Tail, and am both tired and disgusted—tired of waiting and disgusted with the dogged obstinacy of old Spot, who will not consent to hold the council, so far as he is concerned, at Red Cloud or Crow Buttes, six miles from here. He says that he was promised that the council should be held at Chadron Creek, mid-way between here and Spotted Tail. But the commissioners do not care to hold the council there on account of the want of accommodations at that point, and in case of trouble, would be too far removed from the protection of a fort. Probably the latter influences them more than ought else. They have not had experience enough with the Indians to feel entirely safe surrounded by twenty thousand or more of the stinking, savage and treacherous devils, and, considering their inexperience, we do not much blame them for their timidity. As yet no compromise has been reached between Spotted Tail and the commissioners, and it is our opinion that the council will have to be held between the two agencies, else Spot and his 8,000 subjects will have to be left out of the talk. This would not do, however, as in order for the council to amount to a rush it is necessary that all of the main chiefs figure in it, especially so important a personage as Spotted Narrative. The matter, no doubt, will be arranged in some way so that the giant intellects will clash in the course of a week. The commissioners are holding private meetings daily for the purpose of arranging the preliminaries of the "swap," and the Indians are doing the very same thing and in very much the same manner—very private, you know, and the amount of wisdom depicted in each "swapper's" face is actually distressing. The commissioners are thoughtful, silent and dignified, and the Indians will not be discounted by any such clap-trap nonsense. The reds are a set of wary diplomats and there is, perhaps, only one way to _____ means of "fire-water." But in this "swap" neither article will be used as a specialty and hence we may expect a magnificent display of diamond cut diamond.

One thing is a certainty, the Indians have an exaggerated opinion of the value of the Black Hills which they now believe to contain even greater wealth than that attributed to them by the poetic Custer. They say if there was not all of the wealth in the Hills now believed to exist there by the Indian, why does the white man run every risk in order to effect an entrance into them? When an attempt is made to explain [illegible] of mining [illegible] they give a very significant grunt and shake their heads. I have visited the head quarters of Major H. W. Bingham, of the Cheyenne [River] Agency, who has a band of 6,000 Indians from his agency, and Col. John D. Burke, of Standing Rock Agency, who has a band of 4,000 Indians from his agency. There are

15,000 belonging to this agency making in all now here 25,000 Indians without including Spot's band which numbers about 8,000 Indians.

Sitting Bull is recognized as chief of the wild tribes. There is reason to expect that one half of this class of Indians will be at the council, but Sitting Bull will not, probably, do anything towards encouraging his braves to put in an appearance. His stoical indifference to the object of the council is only equaled by his deep-seated love of white men's scalps; and an opportunity to harvest a score of these without endangering his own would be sufficient compensation to him for all of the interest he has in the Hills. There is some talk among the agents of trying to overcome the opposition of the Indians to ceding away their rights to the Hills by threatening to have Congress cut off their rations for the next year if they refuse to accept a fair price. The daily allowance of one Indian is as follows: Three pounds of beef for twenty-seven days in the month, and one pound of pork the remaining days, half-pound of flour, eight pounds of sugar, and four pounds of coffee for each one hundred rations, with a liberal ration of salt, tobacco, soap, saleratus, beans, etc. and axes and agricultural implements and hardware until you can't rest; and in case an Indian will cultivate the soil, he is furnished a team to do it.

A good many miners are scattered around the agency waiting for the treaty to open the Hills when they will pull out for the "diggins." The gold fever here is all-pervading and of the most virulent type.

The agents left the day before yesterday to bring in their bands of Indians, some of whom arrived to-day. An interesting time is expected. Agent Saville is doing his utmost to make all hands as comfortable as possible, under the circumstances. He is a first-class gentleman, and is esteemed a good agent, notwithstanding the Marsh charges, which are regarded here by many of the best and most sensible men about the agency as malicious as they are utterly futile.

Mart

[North Platte *Western Nebraskian*, Saturday, September 18, 1875]

[September 10, 1875 – John T. Bell, from Red Cloud Agency, Nebraska]

From Red Cloud

From Our Special Correspondent

Red Cloud Agency, Neb. [Friday] Sept. 10, 1875

To the Editor of *The Herald*

There is considerable difficulty experienced in sending off news matter from this place. The nearest telegraph station is at Fort Laramie, nearly one hundred miles distant and between that point and this there is no regular communication and even when a telegram is sent to the fort there is no knowing but what it will have to be sent from there to Cheyenne—a distance of another hundred miles—by mail, as the line between Laramie and Cheyenne is run by the government and it frequently happens that the wire is lying on the ground for a great portion of the way. There is a semi-weekly mail between Red Cloud and Cheyenne, leaving Fort Laramie some twenty miles to the westward, but five days time is occupied in reaching Cheyenne from this place and then if it arrives at Cheyenne after 2:30 p.m.—and I suppose it does—two days more elapse before a letter reaches Omaha. If a dispatch is sent from here by mail to be telegraphed from Cheyenne it is five days old by the time it is put in print. Under these circumstances it is quite likely that information sent the press in the shape of telegrams and letters, regarding the doings of the commissioners, will be somewhat mixed as to date by the time it reaches the eye of the reader.

Tuesday night a long haired young man giving the name of Davenport, and representing himself to be a correspondent of the *New York Herald*, came in from the Black Hills country on the outside of a broncho and in company with a military chap [Burt] who has been with Prof. Jenney this summer. He at once made inquires for shelter and remarking that he had had all he wanted of living in tents, asked Dear, the post trader, if he could furnish him with a "private apartment." Dear stared at the man in amazement, and then replied that as he was not running a Grand Central hotel, he could not, but that he could provide him with the same sleeping accommodations he himself enjoyed—that is a blanket and a buffalo robe and room enough on the floor to spread them out. A look of disgust passed athwart the countenance of the New Yorker—who was evidently new to western life and general style—and to cheer him up, Dear asked him to join him in a glass of sherry.

"Thank you, I will, sir," responded the *Herald* chap. "I'm very fond of sherry, but I never allow myself to drink anything stronger than wine of some sort."

Then that wicked trader, with malice aforethought handed the newcomer a demijohn and a glass of generous dimensions, whereupon the latter filled it nearly level and dashed off a glass of—raw whisky. He finally procured a place to lodge at the establishment of Mr. Frank Yates—who is also a trader at this agency—but as he did not make his appearance in our midst the next day, it was generally understood he was devoting his entire time and attention to the growing of a new coating to his tongue and the inside of his mouth.

Tuesday night we all went over to Camp Robinson, two miles west of this agency, and attended an excellent dramatic entertainment given by a company of amateurs connected with the post. The performance was given in a long log building, used as company quarters, from which the boys had removed the bunks and personal effects. This building was crowded, and as fifty cents per head was charged for admission, a handsome sum was realized.

A novel necklace is sported by an aborigine of this locality who has achieved a reputation as one of the most persistent and consistent loafers in the Sioux nation, and who is known to fame under the romantic appellation of "Old Blinky"—so called because of the absence of his left eye. Said necklace consists of a fine collection of finger bones, which he had clipped from vanquished enemies of the Crow nation in his younger and more industrious days.[48]

A remarkable similarity in personal appearance exists between Red Dog and Beecher, and this likeness is the more striking in that Red Dog is a born orator and very influential with his people. He has been a famous fighter but is now the firm friend of the whites, and is much more reliable in this connection than Red Cloud.[49]

Dr. Daniels, the former agent of the Sioux, has had charge of Red Cloud Agency during the absence of Dr. Saville, who has just returned from his visit to the east. Dr. Daniels has been closely connected with the management of the Indians in this country for a number of years and seems to be especially adapted to the business. He has carefully studied their manners, customs and habits, speaks their language, is kind and sympathetic in his nature, and has succeeded in thoroughly winning their confidence. It is to be regretted that he is not at the head of the Indian department at Washington, for if he were, the duties of the position would be attended to much more honestly and intelligently than they are now.

Capt. Nickerson and Lieutenant Bourke, of General Crook's staff, started on their return to Omaha to-day, after a week's sojourn in this vicinity. Capt. A. S. Burt of Co. H, Ninth Infantry, it is reported here, has just been court-martialed for having kept back Black Hills correspondence entrusted to him to mail, by a *New York Herald* correspondent, Burt being a correspondent of the *New York Tribune*. The result of the court martial has not yet been made public.[50]

Terrell of the treasury department, J. H. Bosler, the beef contractor whose name has figured prominently in connection with the recent investigation, Mrs. Bosler, Miss Bosler, Mrs. Terrell, and Mrs. Steele arrived here yesterday in company with Dr. Saville. Hon. [W. S.] Steele, delegate from Wyoming, and Judge [J. P.] Kidder, delegate from Dakota, are expected here to-day.[51]

The name of Dr. Saville has been published far and wide during the past three months, and *The Herald* readers may have a desire to learn "what manner of man he is," in personal appearance. He is an open-hearted, jolly sort of a person, about 45 years of age, his black hair and beard slightly tinged with grey, is stoop shouldered and looks like a well-to-do farmer. He has been a resident of Sioux City, Iowa, for eighteen years past, with the exception of a few years spent in Colorado.

J. T. B.

[*Omaha Daily Herald*, Saturday, September 18, 1875]

[September 10, 1875 – Charles Collins, from Red Cloud Agency, Nebraska]

The Indian Council

(Correspondence of the *Bee*, forwarded by Special Courier to Fort Laramie)

Red Cloud Agency, [Friday] Sept. 10

Editor *Bee*

The first preliminary council held with the Indians since our arrival here took place yesterday [*sic*, Wed. Sept. 8] at this agency, between the commissioners and Red Cloud and his chiefs. The object of the council was to obtain the views of Red Cloud's band as to the contemplated change in holding the forthcoming treaty council at a point on White Clay Creek, within six miles of this agency. The conversation was commenced by Senator Allison, who, as president of the commission, thanked Red Cloud and his associate chiefs for their prompt response to the request of the commissioners to be present at the present interview. President Allison then instructed the interpreter to ask Red Cloud whether or not he and his band (Red Cloud lives here and represents 14,000 Oglalas) would acquiesce in the determination of the commissioners in holding the grand council for the making of the forthcoming treaty at White Clay Creek (6 miles east of here), instead of Chadron Creek, which is the place originally agreed upon. Red Cloud and his associate chiefs, of course, readily agreed to the change, as it will give them greater prestige by the council being held and the treaty being made on his agency. Old Spotted Tail, chief of the Brule Sioux, which band of Indians, numbering 9,000, are located but a short distance from Chadron Creek, opposes the change, as it might likely have the effect of lowering him in the esteem of his tribe if he fails to hold the commissioners to their original agreement of Chadron Creek. Spotted Tail is one of the wiliest Indians and untutored politicians in the Sioux nation, and he had, on Tuesday last, succeeded in getting the

146

consent of all Indians from Missouri River agencies to oppose the changing of the council ground, but the different Indian agents, interpreters, and influential men have gone down among the dissatisfied, and have instructions to use every effort to [gain] their acquiescence in the change of base. As the commissioners hold all their sessions in secret we are not permitted to make positive statements as to their doings, but with reference to the change of location in holding the council, it is alleged that the commissioners thought it would be more pleasant to be within six miles of Camp Robinson and its seven companies of soldiers than like Sheridan at Winchester, when "twenty miles away."[52]

The commissioners move slowly, and the Indians are already complaining that the commissioners have been here a week and still have taken no steps toward commencing to make a treaty. The commissioners seldom or ever allow themselves to mingle with ordinary people, preferring to stand upon the assumed dignity which their position as Indian treaty commissioners is supposed to confer on them. Dr. Saville, Indian agent at this place, who has been absent in the east for several weeks, returned yesterday. During his absence Dr. J. W. Daniels, ex-Indian agent at this and other places, acted as agent here. The duties were very onerous, and it was fortunate alike for the commissioners and the Indians that he filled the position. He is universally admitted to be one of the most competent and upright officers that has ever been identified with the Indian department. There are two traders at this agency, one being Mr. J. W. Dear, an old resident of Omaha, and here as there, universally esteemed for his rare social and business qualifications. Mr. Dear runs the restaurant here and he carries a large stock of goods, and we are pleased to say is doing a flourishing business.

Frank Yates is the other agency trader. He is a very estimable young man, buys his goods of Omaha wholesale houses, and thus largely facilitates his opportunities in doing a large and lucrative trade.

To-morrow is issue and ration day, an account of which may be interesting to *Bee* readers.

C. Collins

[*Omaha Weekly Bee*, Wednesday, September 22, 1875]

[September 11, 1875 – Capt. Andrew S. Burt, from Red Cloud Agency, Nebraska]

Possible Trouble Ahead

(By Telegraph to *The Tribune*)

Crow Butte Council, [Saturday] Sept. 11, via Fort Laramie, Sept. 12

The Missouri River Indians, in charge of Messrs. Bingham and Burke, arrived last night, and had a talk with the commissioners this morning. Major Howard returned from his agency to-day, reporting that Spotted Tail has consented to attend the council, yielding to the positive orders of the commissioners. His opposition has influenced the Sioux soldiers to prevent the river Sioux from accepting Crow Butte as the place for the council. It was reported yesterday that they had driven the river Sioux back with clubs and bows when they attempted to move the lodges.

Spotted Tail, in private council with his people yesterday, announced his price as $6,000,000 for the Black Hills, or an annuity of $100 a year for grown people and $25 for squaws and children. Half of that would stick to the whites' hands. Good authority says that another price put on the Hills by the Indians was $50,000,000. Any such proposition will not be entertained by the commissioners. It is impossible to obtain the amount from the Indians themselves. In an interview with Red Cloud to-day, he was reticent. He said, "I am a big chief, and when I talk I want it in an open council and big crowd. No use talking now for fun. I don't sell a dollar twice."

Franklin Grouard, a Sandwich Islander, six years a prisoner among the northern Sioux, Sitting Bull's band, now with Sword, Red Cloud's head soldier, told me to-day that that chief and Crazy Horse would make war this fall. They refused to come in to the council under any consideration. A southern Cheyenne is said to have threatened to break up the council if he had to kill one of the commissioners.[53] I believe the story to be true, but there is no meaning to such a threat. It is only the idle boast of young bucks. Besides, Red Cloud has promised that his soldiers will be on guard. The Grand Council will probably open on Wednesday.

[Unsigned]

[*New York Tribune*, Monday, September 13, 1875]

[September 12, 1875 – John T. Bell, from Red Cloud Agency, Nebraska]

Red Cloud Agency

From Our Special Correspondent

Red Cloud Agency, Neb. [Sunday] Sept. 12, 1875

To the Editor of *The Herald*

Saturday a party of Missouri River Indians from Cheyenne [River] and Standing Rock agencies, came into the stockade. There were about seventy-five in the party, principally young men, and they were painted up and decorated in gorgeous style. The commissioners took position near the agency ware-house, and their visitors sat upon the ground in the form of a semi-circle around the commissioners. Louis Richard, a half-breed—and a regular subscriber of *The Herald*'s, by the way—acted as interpreter.

Crow Feather, a young bummer with his face painted a bright yellow, came forward, shook hands with all the whites and then taking position in front of Uncle Sam's representatives began the talk by saying the Indians wanted the grand council held on Chadron Creek, and he hoped the commission would move down there at once, to which Senator Allison replied, through the interpreter, that the commission was just going out to select a place near Crow Butte, and that the Indians would have to come there.[54]

Crow Feather – "When the Indians go to see the Great Father at Washington they go all the way. They do not meet him half way, but go all the way, and so we want you to come to us and not meet us half way."

Allison – "We have come a long way to your country. We are here as your friends but it is inconvenient for us to go to Chadron Creek. We propose to hold the council on White Earth Creek near Crow Butte, and you will have to come there. Arrangements have been made to issue rations from this point to all who attend the council."

Crow Feather – "We did not come here for any fun, but to do business, and we want you to move down to Chadron Creek." (Loud cries of "How! How!" on the part of the Indians).

With this, Crow Feather took his seat and Drag Stone, a middle aged individual, dressed in Indian attire, with the addition of a broad brimmed white hat, ornamented with eagle feathers, came to the fore, with the complaint that upon leaving home, twenty-one days rations had been issued his people and he was afraid they would starve to death, hence he wished an additional issue for seven days.[55]

To this the commission responded that that was a matter which he must arrange with his agent, as it was beyond their control, whereupon Drag changed the subject by remarking that when the whites speak together the side that had the most always won. Here the side that wanted the council held at Chadron Creek had the most and the weak side ought to give up. Then the wily old red skin suggested that the choice of a place for the council be left for Spotted Tail and Red Cloud to decide, said a good many of his young men were afraid to go to Crow Butte, as it was a "war butte," and closed by saying that Mr. Hinman had told the Missouri River Indians last summer the council would be held on Chadron Creek.[56]

Hinman replied that he had told them no such a thing, but had told them the council would be held at or near Red Cloud Agency, and that the Indians had allowed themselves to be mislead by Spotted Tail; that the commission did not propose to hold the council at Crow Butte, but at some place near there and that he did not think the soldiers he saw around (referring to the Indians then present) were afraid to go even to Crow Butte.

Little Black Coat was the next speaker on the part of the Indians. His face was painted red, and he had swinging to his neck a polished silver plate [gorget] as big as a soup tureen. He is head of the Black Feet tribe of Cheyennes.[57] He said Mr. Hinman had told them before leaving home that there was a creek between Red Cloud and Spotted Tail agencies and that on this creek the council would be held. They had come to that creek, found where the Sioux had stuck a stick, and had there encamped.

Mr. Hinman told him it was not where the Sioux stuck the stick, but where the commission had stuck one, that the council would be held, and then Black Coat said there was no grass for the Indians' ponies at Crow Butte, while at Ash Creek, thirteen miles from the agency, there was an abundance.

However, the commissioners were firm and insisted upon the council being held on White Clay Creek, six miles from the agency, and with this understanding the conference ended.

Saturday was the day for the issuing of beef at Red Cloud and 550 head were thus disposed of, being about 150 head in excess of the regular issue for ten days. The cattle were weighed on the hoof and then let out of the pen in which they were contained, by ones, twos, threes, fours, and fives, according to the number each sub chief was to receive, his name being called as the number of cattle he was entitled to was turned out. As the frightened animals crowded upon each other in the pen, arrows, which had been shot by juvenile Indians, were seen sticking in the bodies of perhaps one-third of them, and when a "ration" was allowed to pass out of the gate, the Indians, to whom they belonged, immediately started in pursuit, all mounted upon ponies and in this way each animal was chased down, sometimes running for twenty minutes with the Indians pouring arrows and revolver and rifle balls into him as he ran. Occasionally a terror stricken creature would dash toward the corral in his frantic endeavors to escape and then there would be a rapid scattering here and there of the hundreds of red skins who were seated upon their ponies waiting for their names to be called.

When a beef was finally killed in this horrible way, it was skinned and cut up by the squaws who would then carry the meat to the camp, while the bucks would take the skin to the agency traders where they received $3 each for the same, the sum of $1,700 being thus paid out to the Indians at this agency yesterday. As a general thing the carcasses are left upon the prairie where the animal was shot down, and a great deal of valuable food allowed to go to waste, for the reason that the Indians draw more rations than they can eat, although it is a well-known fact that an able-bodied Indian will eat as much as two white men.

In journeying about their camps Thursday, *The Herald* man saw great piles of flour and corn, especially in the tepees, though that was the last of the ten days for which they had drawn rations.

In consequence of being thus generously fed by the government, these Indians have given up the hunt almost entirely. One of our party here has been endeavoring to get a pair of moccasins made and has visited twenty-five tents for the purpose, being told by the occupants in every instance that they didn't have buckskin enough to make them. Last night, however, a piece of buckskin was procured at the cavalry camp, two miles from here, and furnished a squaw who is now at work upon the moccasins.

As we came to Red Cloud, not a day passed that we did not see antelope frequently, half a dozen together, but I think I am safe in asserting that five hundred pounds of antelope meat could not be found today in the entire camp of 14,000 Indians, who are fed at this agency, and yet, during the past eighteen months thousands of our own race have actually suffered for the necessities of life, though willing and eager to work, if work could only have been found for them.

Dr. Daniels, ex-Indian agent at this point, has general charge of the commission, providing them with transportation, etc. He is quartered here at present and has with [him] his son, a bright little fellow about ten years of age. The latter had been a little unwell and his father advised him to make his supper on a couple of steamed crackers. The little fellow fell to work with a relish, stopping after taking two or three mouthfuls to exclaim, "Pa, I believe this stuff's doin' me good a'ready."

The report in circulation here to the effect that Capt. Burt of the 9th Infantry had been court-martialed for suppressing correspondence intended for the *New York Herald* entrusted to his care, proves to be untrue. Such correspondence was entrusted to Burt to mail, and as it failed to come to hand on time, he was called upon for an explanation, which explanation I understand was accepted as being satisfactory.

A little Indian girl was accidentally shot just outside the stockade Saturday evening by an Indian who was flourishing his revolver around "permiskus like," the ball plowing a groove through her chin. The affair caused a terrible commotion among the squaws.

The commission is still waiting for things to turn up, with an exhibition of patience which can be accounted for only by the fact that they are each drawing $8 per day, with their solids and liquids thrown in.[58] Major Howard, of Spotted Tail Agency, has been vibrating between that point and this agency with considerable regularity, and we "outsiders" are given to understand that he is undoubtedly engaged in an endeavor to bring his Indians here so that the council may be held in this vicinity. It is barely possible the council will begin to-morrow and then again, it may not.

J. T. B.

[*Omaha Daily Herald*, Sunday, September 19, 1875]

[September 14, 1875 – Albert Swalm, from Red Cloud Agency, Nebraska]

The Indians

Red Cloud Agency, Neb. [Tuesday] Sept. 14

Yesterday the hills about the agency presented a gala appearance, the occasion being the issuance of rations to the Indians at this agency, to the number of about 12,000. At first only the old men, old women, and squaws came in, but toward noon the chiefs and warriors, splendidly mounted and armed, and dressed in the most gorgeous costumes, circled in a magnificent sweep to the grounds, and then commenced the grand show of jabber and horsemanship. Many of the warriors brought their favorite squaws with them, who, being favorites, of course had a monopoly of all the fine store clothes. They presented—that is, the favorites—an appearance quite romantic and fascinating, showing an independence of the use of soap that would scarcely be allowed in a belle of Prairie Avenue. Some of these dusky Cleopatras wore robes worth from two to five horses, the currency by which values are regulated among these Indians. Some of the warriors claimed as many as four wives, but the majority content themselves with two—one for work and the other as a sort of personal servant and mistress. Thus furnished, the poor Indian man has a particularly soft thing on this life.

Several Indians have commenced farming on the patches of bottom found on the creeks near here. The way the work is done is this. The squaws do the planting and cultivating entirely; the men eat the product, sell what they can for trinkets and personal ornaments, and that is about the extent of Indian farming here. Some of them have teams and wagons furnished them by the government, but even with this help the squaws do the hauling of the wood for the tepee, and where there is no team the same obedient, hard working females carry the wood on their backs, and this for long distances. Among the

Arapahoes [a] woman fares worse than among the Sioux. The latter people are far more virtuous, and death is the punishment for any straying into forbidden pastures, but the Arapahoes do not hesitate to make merchandise of their women, and that too, for almost anything, from a pup to a blanket. These are the worst Indians known, and rob and steal upon the slightest temptation. Venereal diseases, however, fortunately, are rapidly reducing this once powerful tribe to a mere handful, and now it is utterly impossible to find a thoroughly healthy man or woman, or even child, in the camp near here. Abortions and deaths therefrom are also terribly frequent. The Cheyennes are not much better, and other tribes look upon the Arapahoes as the natural bawdy house, and patronize them accordingly.

An observer of the occurrences of issue-day will see many things of interest. For instance, the squaws will take a load of 160 pounds on their backs and walk away with it with ease, their lord and master following along behind, with deep satisfaction depicted on his countenance at the prospect of a coming feast. But if the rations happen to be short, the squaw catches particular thunder, and she takes it quietly.

Yesterday I attended the issue of rations from the house. A register has been made of all the lodges belonging to the agency, aggregating a total population of over 13,000 persons. To every head of a lodge—or by agreement some man may act for a number combined—a ration ticket is issued calling for so many rations every seven days. On presentation there is issued coffee, sugar, beans, corn, bacon, and soap. Flour is an article of issue, but none has been given out here for over a month, on account of the delay by McCann, the contractor. The sugar and coffee are issued by actual weight—or were when your correspondent was present; the bacon was "lumped off" by a carver who "guessed" at the various amounts required—from 10 to 50 lbs. And the guess never seemed in favor of the Indian. Beans and corn were measured out in the common grocery scoop—five pounds of corn to each dip of the scoop, and about the same of beans. Of course such a way of issuing may be all right and thoroughly fair, but it didn't look so to one from the States. The articles issued were of excellent quality, the coffee being quite free from foreign substances, the sugar of fair color, and the other articles as good, if not better, than ever issued to the volunteer army. Some great improvements could and ought to be made in the issue of rations. In the one article of corn, a mill should be provided and the corn made into meal, and the flour ration abolished or commuted into hard bread. At every issue-day the hog-men and transportation people gather here and buy the whole sacks of corn that are issued at their own price. Yesterday over 5,000 pounds of corn were purchased at a nominal price by these men from the Indians, and more than double that quantity was bought by others, and wasted. The Indians use the corn made into hominy, and feed some to their ponies, but as the equines are not bred to it they do not eat it, save in extremity. The issue of flour is served exactly in the same way, and thousands of sacks are annually purchased by outsiders and thousands more wasted, and fed to horses. The Indian women do not know how to manipulate it so that it becomes a palatable article, and hard bread is highly relished by them. But to feed the Indians on an economical plan, saving to the people and more satisfactory to the Indians, is contrary to the rule of the ring, which is all-powerful in this western country.

The great day with the Indians and Bosler, the beef contractor, comes with the issue of beef. The Sioux Commission went down to-day to see this performance. The cattle were all "Texans," great heads and long horns, and had been weighed before the commission arrived. One beef is issued to about each squad of thirty-five persons, and as the name of the Indian is called the number of cattle required are driven out of the corral, when the big time for the Indians commences. For an hour or two previous to the issue the Indian boys had been shooting arrows into the cattle and cutting their tails off, so that they were in an active condition when turned out. Then a half-dozen well-mounted Indians slashed after the bovines with yells that were perfectly devilish, and the chase was continued over the plains, an occasional shot in the body of the animal making it skip out more lively until some dozen or twenty shots brought death to the tortured beast. With a thousand Indians in hot chase after the fleet-footed "Texans," with here a steer charging the hunters, others bellowing and moving with pain you have about as brutal a scene as our civilization can provide. At the Missouri River agencies this barbarous practice has been abolished, and the killing is all done in a corral and by a regular butcher and should have been enforced here long ago. Nothing is more demoralizing, or rather more detrimental to the advancement of the ways of civilization among the Indians, than the weekly occurrence of this hellish cruelty. But Dr. Saville claims that he would have much trouble on hand did he endeavor to do his own killing. Still, Maj. Bingham and others have done so and succeeded admirably.

The butchering process of the Indians is crude, and the hides are very much injured by cuts and bullet holes. The meat is cut from the bones and "jerked" direct without salting—the bones for the most part being left to the dogs and coyotes.[59] The larger entrails and stomach are considered choice delicacies, and I have just passed a group feeding on

154

raw tripe, with just enough of the "stuffing" sticking to it to give it a relish! Great is the stomach of the Indian!

The lot of cattle issued were small, save a few old stags—yet the official return will show that 379 were issued, and that the average weight was 973 pounds! Several gentlemen were present who had handled many beeves and they put the average of the lot, after a full half hour's examination, at not more than 650 pounds. A great many of the cattle were small cows and steers, 3 years old and under, and many of the cows were pregnant. This beef business has some beauties about it that even the venerable gentlemen on the boss Indian Commission don't fully understand. But farewell to the agency matters and now treaty news.

The commission have been out in a body and selected a high plateau about 5 miles east of the agency as the place for holding the council. A beautiful spring is found near it, and Crow Butte rears its ugly head about 1 mile to the southeast. The Oglalas have their camp near the ground selected, while the Brule Sioux will camp about 4 miles further east, on the White Clay Creek. The Missouri River Indians, comprising the Miniconjou, Hunkpapas, Yanktonais, Santees, and Lower Brules, will camp on White Earth River in convenient distance. The wild chaps from the north will camp near the Oglalas, while the Arapahoes and Cheyennes have found room for their camps north of the agency and west of Camp Robinson, 1 mile west of the agency. After much pow-wowing, the Brule bands, which were at, and of, Spotted Tail Agency, have concluded to move, but they still insist upon a change in the council ground, which will not be acceded to under any circumstances. The commission propose to occupy their present quarters, and have the council just where it is located, with no such foolishness as the gadding away 15 or 20 miles. The Standing Rock and Cheyenne River Agency Indians have made their call in state on the commission, and shot off their barbaric yawp for a change of ground. They heaved a good logical brick into the commission by stating this: "When we go to see the Great Father at Washington, do we stop at Baltimore and tell him to come out and see us?" This was very generally "how-how'd"—the Indian approval—and it put the chairman to his smartest taps to make such an answer as satisfied the Indians. Finally they asked for hard bread to enable them to consider the matter and the pow-wow closed.

Some of the more turbulent fellows, who have grown fat and saucy on Bosler's bulls, talk very big about what they propose doing, but [no] more than an outbreak, in which few would join, is anticipated, and the anticipation is mainly founded on Indian bluster.

As a sample of modesty and pudding of the above description, let me quote Red Dog, a great fat, jolly-faced chief of the Oglalas, who spoke the words given to the commission the other evening. They are here:

"The gentlemen of the commission are all men of high standing, great intelligence, and much influence, and I am the same. I have for four years been the friend of the President, and made him strong. Among the white people, men who own no land are not respected. I am the exclusive owner of the Black Hills myself, but I have sent out and brought in the different bands of Sioux, my poor relatives, and out of pity for them, I shall share with them the proceeds of the sale. I am rich and can afford it. Spotted Tail knows this. If I were not the leader of the great Sioux Nation I would go down and tell Spotted Tail that he must come here to hold council and he would do it. But it is not consistent with my position to go there. In 1868 I made a treaty with the President and had Spotted Tail made chief, as he now is. At that time I located the Indians on the Missouri River. Having done so much for the Indians, Spotted Tail was made jealous of me. I retired to the wilderness for a time. Afterward I went down to the Platte, and sent for Gen. Smith. He came. I took him with me to Washington, where I saw the President. Some time ago a man walked along the Missouri River and the people trembled. His name was Red Dog, and I am the man. A man walked along the banks of the Platte and the earth quaked; his name was Red Dog, and I am the man. Now, friends, can't you let me have a blanket for my poor, starving daughter?"

This is a sample of a great deal of talk shot at the commission at all times; brag that would have made a Falstaff hang his head in confusion. Red Dog failed to get a blanket, for the reason that Inspector Daniels had given a shawl a few days before, only to find out that it had been made the currency for the payment of a night's spree with a Cheyenne princess. Daniels even furnished a wagon, as it was between the agencies, to haul the old dog and his "take" along. But the best of inspectors are sometimes imposed upon by the innocent red man of the mountains.

Daily and almost hourly do the Indians change the rumors on the price to be asked for the Black Hills, the highest peaks of which just lift above the horizon on the north. None are less than $30,000,000 nor exceed $50,000,000. The leading men say that the Hills must be sold at some price for the army cannot keep them clear of miners, and if they go to war they will lose their rations. The logic of the Indian's stomach is irresistible and will prevail. The Hills will be bought out; no big bonus will be paid for them by the commission. They will conduct the matter on a safe business basis, and act as though they had to honor the debts from their own pockets.

One of the most perplexing duties attendant will be the securing of the routes by which entrance shall be lawful to the Black Hills. The nearest point by rail is from Pine Bluffs, Neb., on the Union Pacific road, that point being only about 190 miles. As to the route, I know nothing. Sidney is about 30 miles longer and is a good route, having water at convenient distances. Influences are at work among the Indians seeking to close all routes save those that come from the south, and the Indian is not short for arguments—kindly made up by disinterested white men. The trade that the coming emigration will bring will be immense, and hence the trading permits held along the southern route would be very rich bonanzas.

The eastern routes are the best for wagon trains, and my impression is that every section will be allowed a "fair shake," notwithstanding the efforts made in the other direction. The Indian Ring town of Cheyenne would make a very fat thing out of it could the eastern routes be corked up, but that is now beyond hope. If the treaty is made, the people of Iowa, Illinois, Wisconsin, and other states will have the privilege of going to the Hills with their wagons from the east, no odds whose trade it may hurt.

Spotted Tail is a very liberal sort of an Indian, and to the river Indians now with him he gave as presents 150 good ponies and slaughtered a great many fat dogs for the feasts. Being a liberal man, he wants a liberal price for the cession of the Black Hills and Big Horn country. He therefore thinks that the Great Father ought to set aside $30,000,000 in 5 per cents for thirty years and pay the interest annually in annuities to the Sioux tribes, and also to continue to be liberal in other supplies. The 5 per cents would yield $45,000,000 in the thirty years—a good sort of bonanza for the Ring to handle.

Turbulent Indians abound here. The council has brought out all the scalawags of the tribes, and they threaten to do much mischief. Last evening one of the young Oglalas deliberately shot into a small gathering of Indian girls, wounding one in the chin seriously. The cut-throat Cheyennes are the worst, and one has promised that he will kill one of the commissioners during the council, and then scoot for the wild bands north of the Black Hills. Indians as well as some other people are given to much boasting, and that is what ails some of these cut throats. All possible and proper precautions will be taken against the repetition of the Modoc affair. There is no danger whatever, however, as the Indians propose to furnish a grand guard from the two great bands to keep the peace and kill all who attempt an injury to the whites of the council.

These are the orders of the chief, American Horse. Maj. [Peter D.] Vroom, with a company of the First [Third] Cavalry, will act as escort for the commissioners. Gen. Bradley, commandant at Fort Laramie, will also be present, with Capt. [John] Mix's company of cavalry. In all, some seven companies will be near at hand, with two Gatling guns ready for action. They will not be needed, but readiness for use will not be amiss. Dog feasts, dances, and all the other amusements of the Indians are now in full blast every night, some of which I have had the pleasure of attending. Of them in the future.

[Unsigned]

[*Fort Dodge Messenger*, Thursday, September 30, 1875]

[September 12, 1875 – Reuben Davenport, from Red Cloud Agency, Nebraska]

The Grand Council

Red Cloud Indian Agency, Neb., [Sunday] Sept. 12, 1875

The gathering of red men on the White River for the Grand Council will be a more imposing and important spectacle than will probably ever be presented hereafter by the remnants of the early American race. In the language of their own chiefs, the Sioux Nation has not long to exist. It will soon become extinct. It is now stronger than ever since the Great Father took it absolutely under his guardianship and more capable for a brief period of perpetrating serious mischief upon the whites; but this power is ephemeral and would consume itself, leaving a whole people to perish if they continued to remain in a hostile attitude. But the savage is not far seeing, and the present occasion is one on which accidental circumstances might rouse in him the unreasoning and uncontrollable frenzy of murder and set the region west of the Missouri and east of the Rocky Mountains ablaze with the terrors of a barbarous war. The Sioux chiefs, with the exception of a few of the wiser and older of them, carry themselves with a good deal of arrogance and insolence. They have undoubtedly a feeling of sullen dissatisfaction, not conducive to a continuation of a solid peace. Sooner or later there must be a sound drubbing administered to the Sioux, unless, through the present negotiation, they imbibe a salutary idea of the overwhelming power of the whites. This can be given them through firm and authoritative conduct on the part of the commissioners if they so choose. If they assume such a bearing toward the chiefs to be assembled in council they can shorten the duration of the powwow by many days and will be able to secure a treaty just to both the government and Indians. The latter are nearly as weak as children in mental development, although they possess a shrewdness and a cunning which are sometimes very surprising.

They are extremely slow in reaching conclusions, and unless the course which is left them is plainly indicated to them they will consume several weeks and, perhaps months in long-drawn out discussion. The commissioners are empowered and directed in their formal instructions to act for the best interests of the Sioux as well as of the government and can, therefore, use any means to shape even the demands of the chiefs to conform with their views. This policy is the most sensible means of reaching a settlement of the troublesome question of the Black Hills as speedily as possible. If adopted, and the commissioners inform the Indians at once of what the government will do in their favor in return for the relinquishment of their hunting grounds, the council ought to complete the business within ten days from the opening.

There are, however, influences at work adverse to the success of this council. A very brilliant opportunity is presented for the pliant fingers of the Indian ring to draw from the public pockets a large roll of greenbacks. It is one of those rare chances when there is no great risk of detection.

The financial stupidity of the Indian has before made him an easy victim for official robbers. But it is not improbable that continued lessons in the futility of trusting the white man's alleged good will where there is a temptation to embezzle may have, at this late period, educated the Indian to a degree of intelligence sufficient to make him more guarded and watchful. Recent expressions of Red Cloud, Spotted Tail and Red Dog are significant. They do not expect ever to get all the money that they bargain for in exchange for the Black Hills. They are not so simple. Half of it, they say, will go into the pockets of white men.

It would be unjustifiable to make insinuations founded on mere presumption. Therefore I shall make merely certain true statements, which may be considered as significant when looked upon in the light of the past history of the "Indian Ring." The desirability, to the government, of the purchase of the Black Hills, was apparent over a year ago. It will be distinctly remembered that, according to correspondence from the Sioux country, the Indians were at that time well disposed to cede that portion of their reservation by treaty. Now there will evidently be much haggling and dispute. At that time they thought little of the Ke-Sapa [the Black Hills]. Some of the Indians belonging at the remote agencies on the Missouri depreciate the Black Hills, in conversation with white men, not having been imbued, as have those on the White River, with large ideas of their wealth. Striped Cloud, a northern Sioux, possessing much influence, told me on Saturday that he did not think there was any gold in the Black Hills. This gives the lie to Spotted Tail's statement that the existence of the *masa si* there has been known to the nation for a great many years.[60] The truth is that the exalted opinion of the Black Hills has been held by the Sioux only during the past year. It has owed its origin to the great ado made by the government about the value of the country, the failure of the military to prevent a rush of adventurers to the gold field, and the sending of a scientific expedition this summer to study its resources. The heads of the Indian Ring see in the future the inevitable result of buying their hunting ground from the Sioux. It will be their removal to the Indian Territory and management by officers of the army, under a system which will not admit of the perpetration of fraud quite so easily as heretofore. The strongest secret influences of the Interior Department were at first employed to prevent the sale of the Black Hills by the Indians; but it early dawned upon Mr. Delano that the occupation of the country by the whites, an irresistible influx of whom had already begun, was a foregone prophecy.[61]

The policy of the "Ring" was speedily metamorphosed. The restoration of the Indian Bureau to the War Department might not occur during this administration; the price of the Black Hills would probably touch the palms of the "Ring," which, it is pretty well known by this time, have a peculiar itching propensity. The government knew then sufficient from the results of Custer's expedition of the value of the Black Hills to have offered the Indians a price for them; the peculiar method of the "Indian Ring" was different. Mr. Jenney, an inexperienced young man, fresh from school, was sent out as chief of a scientific corps, with an escort of troops, to thoroughly explore the Black Hills. Before this step was taken a few hundred thousands could have purchased them. Now the compensation which the Indians expect for relinquishment of almost their last foothold of territory is among the millions. It is needless to point out that the expedition devised by the Interior Department has enhanced the price of the Hills and has piled up the difficulties which now confront the commissioners in the way of effecting a treaty.

To further this object—for such it seems to be—actual advice has been given to the Indians by one of their agents not to sell their country unless they secure an immense price. He has told them—and doubtless with a great deal of truth—that they will be egregious fools if they surrender so beautiful a region, almost all that they possess of country, and without "a local habitation" pass out of existence, as they surely must, finally becoming extinct and remembered only in name. If white men would always give to red men advice so sound as this there might be less shame in the record of their intercourse during the last two hundred years. But the motive in the present instance may not be so transparently pure as could be hoped by humanitarians. The retention of Ke-sapa by the Sioux means a continuation indefinitely of the fraudulent system of contracts and issues carried on at present at the agencies, and the skillful augmenting of the sum to be given to the Indian land owners means a richer harvest for government pilferers.

The commissioners intrusted with the negotiations with the Indians are, I believe, disposed to be liberal toward them, while at the same time they will trust more to their own sense of right and justice as representing both sides in the treaty, instead of to the slow moving intelligence with which they have to deal. Much useless "talk-a-heap" can be avoided. They will aim to compass that end by confining the discussion to the making of propositions to the chiefs and eliciting from them their assent or dissent. The members of the Commission are United States Senator William B. Allison, of Dubuque, Iowa; Brigadier General A. H. Terry, United States Army, commander of the Military Department of Dakota; General A. G. Lawrence, of Rhode Island; Rev. S. D. Hinman, missionary at the Santee Indian Agency, Nebraska; A. Comingo, of Independence, Mo.; W. H. Ashby, of Beatrice, Neb.; G. P. Beauvais, of St. Louis, Mo.; and John S. Collins, of Fort Laramie, Wyoming. Mr. Collins is secretary of this commission. General Terry has not yet arrived here, but will probably appear on Wednesday, as he has been heard from on his way. The commissioners were accompanied from Omaha, after their return from the agencies on the Missouri River, by Captain Nickerson and Lieutenant J. G. Bourke, aides-de-camp on the staff of the commander of the Department of the Platte. From Fort Laramie they were escorted to this agency by Major Vroom's cavalry, who are now encamped at Camp Robinson. It was anticipated that they would be stationed as a guard near the place of council. Red Cloud, however, approached the commissioners on the subject of their safety while among the Indians, and said that he did not wish that any soldiers should be at the council; he should feel in such a case that his good faith was doubted. He would arm his own young men and would place them as a guard where they could protect the commissioners. Mr. Allison, as chairman of the commission, in response, said that the Indians should comprehend that the commissioners came from the Great Father authorized and instructed to care for the good of the Indian as much as for that of the white man, and they had it just as much at heart.

One of Red Dog's speeches to the commission is so characteristic of Indian eloquence that if it were written in full it would be a literary curiosity. It was delivered before my arrival here, and I have only been able to obtain a few sentences. Red Dog is unquestionably the John Cochrane of the Dakotas.[62] He began his oration by alluding to his power as a chief; said it was he who had made the treaty of 1868 with Tonkasila (the Great Father), and he who had placed the Sioux on the Missouri River and on the Platte. If it were not beneath his dignity as the greatest man of his nation, he would go down to Sintigaliska (Spotted Tail) and tell him to come up here with his people to council, and he would come. He dare not disobey. But, because he was such a very great man, other chiefs had become jealous of him and had tried to keep him down. He had made Spotted Tail chief and had made Red Cloud chief, and if he commanded them to-morrow to give up their leadership, they would do it. After he had settled his nation in this country he had sent for General Smith and had taken him up to Washington with him. Now he had sent out and had brought in all of his people from the other agencies, because he wanted to be kind to his poor relations. He himself owned the Black Hills, exclusively, and all the country north of the Platte, and could sell it if he wished, but he was willing that others should have something to say about it. In conclusion, Red Dog said:

"There was a man walking upon the shores of the Missouri, and the nations trembled. That man was Red Dog. There was a man who was walking by the Platte and the earth shook. He was Red Dog. And there is a man who treads the banks of the White River and the tribes listen and obey, and he is Red Dog."

When Red Dog was first met by commissioner Ashby he was assured of the great pleasure the occasion afforded.

"I do not wonder," he replied, "that you should be glad to see so wise a man as I."

Red Dog, in reality, has not the full rank of a chief, but is a big medicine man. He holds the position of a much-talking politician, and has as little power. He is one of the three chiefs who led the Fort Phil Kearny massacre.[63]

Mr. S. D. Hinman, in private conversations with the Indians, is instructed by the Secretary of the Interior to interpret into English for the commission; in the more important councils, however, the Indians will be represented by an interpreter selected by themselves.

One of the most puzzling features of the present condition of the Sioux nation is its division into tribes, bands, and families. The names given to all these are significant but so numerous and the inter-relations of the different communities are so intricate as to bewilder the inquiring mind. The explanation of some of the names which they bear involves the history of part of the lifetime of the nation in the far distant past. Red Cloud (or, as it is in the Dakotah, Mocpea-Lutah) gives a meager outline of the tribe of which he is a great chief, Man-Afraid-Of-His-

Horses has, however, a much higher hereditary rank than he and may be considered a prince of the nation. The story is in a very few words. In the old, old time two brothers who were chiefs, holding joint authority in the same tribe, quarreled on the banks of the Missouri River. One threw dirt at the other, who called him tauntingly, "Dirt Thrower," and told him to take his followers and depart. "Dirt Thrower" or Oglala has been the name of each member of the tribe ever since. Formerly there were bands known as the Sioux of the Leaf, the Sioux of the Broad Leaf and the Sioux who Shoot in the Pine Tops. They have, however, blended with larger communities and the names now are obsolete. The Santee are the Leaf Indians; the Miniconjou Sioux are those of the Rippling Water; the Brule, of the Burnt Thigh; the Powboxas [Payabya], of the Cut Head; the Sans Arcs have no bows; the Ohenopas, of the Two Kettles; the Kiyuksas, cut off (from their tribe).[64] There are minor bands, whose names have all some reference to the initial facts of their history. The Arikarees, as is well known—now a tribe by themselves, although just on the verge of extinction—were an off shoot from the original Pawnees, when that once powerful nation met its severe reverses.

Major Burke, agent at Standing Rock, Dakota, brings here 2,000 Indians of the Upper and Lower Yanktonais and Hunkpapas or Black-feet tribes of Sioux. The principal chiefs accompanying him are Two Bear, Iron Horn, Bull's Ghost, Mad Bear, Running Antelope, Grass, and Slave. He says that before starting they felt very favorably in regard to the proposed sale of the Black Hills. Major Burke met with serious difficulties when he took charge of his agency owing to the administration of the previous occupant, but has his people apparently under better control than other Indian delegates I have seen. Major Bingham of the Cheyenne River Agency is accompanied by 3,000 chiefs, head warriors, and braves. The principal personages among them are Lone Horn of the North, Swan and Duck of the Miniconjous, Mandan and Rattling Rib of the Ohenopas, and Burnt Face and Crow Feather of the Sans Arcs.[65]

On Friday [Sat., Sept. 11] quite an imposing council occurred in the open air inside the stockade which encloses the offices of the agency and the storehouse. The commissioners were seated in the shade of a wall, side by side, and your correspondent perched upon a rough board laid upon some boxes immediately behind them. Several ladies now here formed a bright group of figures on one side. Major Burke, at the head of his charges, marched them in and presented them to the commissioners with an air of military discipline. The Miniconjou, Ohenopas, and Sans Arcs followed, led by Mr. Bingham. The chiefs numbered about forty, representing those who had not come and whom they had left in camp on Bordeaux Creek. They all sat themselves upon the ground, forming a quadrant, and, with great deliberation and dignity, began smoking their pipes. Grass was presented to the commissioners and shook hands. He wore a fur turban, the hair dyed yellow, a feather streaming behind, red leggings, and a blue mantle.

Commissioners – "We are glad to see you."

Red Face, a Cheyenne, with a hideous countenance, painted a deep crimson, shook hands.[66] The Indians in the quadrant had their faces variously embellished. Many were striped, others were laid out in blocks of different colors, like the townships on a county map; while still others had painted claws and feathers on their cheeks. All of them were armed with tomahawks and rifles, their belts full of cartridges, and supporting pistols and sheath knives, tobacco pouch and whetstone. One or two of the chiefs shielded themselves from the sun by carrying parti-colored umbrellas over their heads. A chief, who adorned his chin with dark green paint, wore proudly a cavalry hat with letters and figures on its front indicating the regiment and company to which the original wearer had belonged.

The commissioners – "Have you anything to say?"

Lone Horn of the North (who wore around his head a brilliant bandanna handkerchief) – "Good. In my camp there are seven different bands. They are not all here. I come now only to see my friends and to shake hands with all of them—the Cheyennes, Arapahoes, and Oglalas. I want to go to visit them, and I expect to get presents from them all. I am afterwards going back to Spotted Tail Agency to draw rations and to stay two or three days."

Crow Feather (who is distinguished by a red diagonal stripe across his face) followed Lone Horn in an earnest speech. He is rather an unpleasant looking Indian. He said that word had been sent around to all the Indians to go to one place to meet there for the Great Council. That place was Chadron Creek. He did not think that any Indians would go to another place.

The commissioners – "We propose to select the place for the council, and we wish the Indians to come to that place."

Crow Feather – "The Indians have all decided to meet at Chadron Creek and have sent for one another to come there. (From all the Indians, "Ugh!") When the Sioux went to the Great Father they did not stop halfway and then send for him to come to them. They went clear to his place, and you commissioners ought to do the same toward us."

Crow Feather observed a smile on the faces of some of the commissioners at the shrewdness of his last remark, and closed the discourse abruptly by saying, "I did not come here for fun, but to do my duty." He then strode off and seated himself with dignity.

Senator Allison, after a brief consultation among the commissioners, then said to the interpreter, Louis Richard:

"Tell them that we have come a long way to their country. We are their friends. (Ugh!) It is inconvenient for us to go as far as Chadron Creek to hold the council. We will go out as far as will be convenient from this point. We propose to have the council on Little White Clay Creek, near Crow Butte. That place will be just as convenient for them as Chadron Creek, and more so for us who have come a great distance. We are their friends, sent by the Great Father and sent for their good, which we desire. Chadron Creek is too far away; we cannot go there."

Drag Stone, an old chief with a gray beard, rose and came forward. After becoming satisfied on a question which had been disturbing his mind regarding rations, he said that he would like the commissioners to send for Spotted Tail and Red Cloud, and let them decide upon the place where they wanted the council to be held. Many of his young men were afraid to go to the Crow Buttes to talk, as they made bad luck in case of war.

Mr. Hinman replied through the interpreter. The commissioners had gone to the Missouri River, by direction of the President, to invite the Indians there to the council. They had told them that the council should be held at or near the Red Cloud Agency. The Indians started to come and now, before they have arrived here, they are trying to change the place of the council. The commissioners had selected it and the President had approved of it. Their colleagues had joined them and were unwilling to make a change. The place of the council was fixed and could not be changed. The President had not told the Indians to fix the place of the council but had told them. If these Indians would come to the council at all they must come to the place appointed and bring their families, and when they come here they will be fed. The commissioners did not propose to go to the Crow Buttes, but near them. He did not think that all the soldiers present were afraid of the Crow Buttes. (Smiles among the Indians.)

Little Black Foot, perspiring visibly through the thick pigment on his face, was next to speak. A lively conversation ensued, in which Little Black Foot received "the lie direct" from his brother of the black cloth, Mr. Hinman.

Little Black Foot – "You went to the Missouri River and told us of the council, and you said it would be at a creek between the Red Cloud and Spotted Tail agencies."

Mr. Hinman (to Richards) – "Tell him that we never said any such thing."

Little Black Foot (apparently somewhat confused) – "The Sioux told us so (Ugh) and stuck a stick in the ground to show us where to come."

Mr. Hinman – "You are not to come where the Sioux stick a stick, but you are to come where we stick a stick."

Little Black Foot – "At the place which the commissioners have picked out it is as bare as this ground. There is no grass."

Mr. Hinman – "We have not yet picked out any place."

Little Black Foot then said that there was a good place on Ash Creek, where he would like to encamp, and he was told to do so and come part of the way from there to meet the commissioners in council.

Burnt Face, second chief of the No Bows, said he was a good man, and then shook hands. The conclave then was broken up. Walking Shooter, a chief of the Hunkpapas, shook hands. He wears a white label on his hat with his name printed in English thereon. His appearance is eminently respectable.[67]

The delay of the council is altogether due to the impression, produced in some mysterious way among the Indians on the Missouri River and the Brules, that they were to meet on Chadron Creek. The commission deny any responsibility for the error, but it seems to have arisen from their asking Spotted Tail where the Indians would like to hold the council. Spotted Tail considered himself empowered to select the place and sent word to the other tribes and bands. When he found that the commissioners were going to choose a different locality, he objected to going there. Major Howard returned from his agency on Saturday evening and reported that Spotted Tail had consented to come to the place appointed.

A native of the Sandwich Islands came to this agency last winter from a northern band of Indians, carrying upon his lips a considerable story of his life and adventures. He had been living as a Sioux for six years under the chieftainship of Sitting Bull of the North, who is the terror of the ranchmen and herders north of the Platte River. Frank Grouard is the name given him by his mother, Louisa, who was a domestic in the household of Franklin Grouard, an Englishman, and a missionary of the Protestant Episcopal Church, residing at Tehyta [Tahiti]. Frank was born there, as well as a brother and a sister. He has the Mongol type of countenance, and dull, rather sleepy expression. The mother, Louisa, left her native land and came to California, bringing Frank with her, when he was still at an infantile age. From youth to manhood he experienced severe knocks without number. His last employment in a semi-civilized sphere was that of letter carrier between Helena, in Montana, and the mouth of the Musselshell Creek. He was chased here by Sitting Bull and his band, captured and robbed, and was doomed to death in its most horrible form, when the old chief interceded for his life. He became as one of the band, but never reached the dignity of a warrior. The Indians named him "The Standing Bear," but during four years they did not allow him to possess a horse or any arms. In that time he learned the Dakota tongue. Grouard was a young man, and shortly became enamored of a comely Sioux maiden and was married. He departed from Sitting Bull's camp last winter, and brought her with him to the White River country.[68]

Grouard accompanied Louis Richard and Man-Afraid-Of-His-Horses to the Rosebud Creek this summer to aid in securing the attendance of representatives of the wild bands at the council. He there talked over the proposed cession of the Black Hills to the government with the principal chief, Sitting Bull of the North. He has recounted to me the knowledge which he gained by his visit. The gist of it I have already sent you by telegraph. There is little to be added to that.

Sitting Bull declares that he will never come in to make a treaty with the whites. He merely desires to have traders sent to him. He says that he shall continue to fight the whites. He has about 120 lodges in the winter, but more in the spring. Many of his families move to the agencies to receive their subsistence during the cold months and return to his band as soon as the snow is gone and the grass springs up to afford their ponies forage. He says that he will get a great many men from the Oglala Sioux and the Arapahoes this fall and will make war along the Missouri River. This he will do when the leaves fall.

Crazy Horse was less communicative to the Standing Bear [Grouard]. He would not talk about the proposed treaty, but said that whatever Black Twin did in council with the whites would be right and he should approve it.[69] He now has only five lodges, but in the spring his camp numbers sixty. He is preparing to make a series of raids along the North Platte River this fall, expecting aid from the Southern Cheyennes. The Northern–known also as the wild Indians, under these two chiefs, with the adherents which they can gain from the Cheyennes and Arapahoes, can in the summer command 200 lodges. If they commit the depredations which they propose this winter, they are likely next summer, with a larger array of warriors, to seriously employ the attention of the troops stationed on the frontier.

A half-breed who came from the Fort Thompson Agency with White Ghost has been entertained as a guest by Spotted Tail at his lodge, for some days.[70] He says that Spotted Tail has given expression to some of his ideas about the gain of the Black Hills in private councils with his sub-chiefs. Spotted Tail has said that he cannot ask less than $6,000,000 and intimates that would be an exceedingly small price for the country. In his own phrase, it would, in his opinion, be "like taking three cents out of a dollar and puffing it in the wind." He does not expect to get more than half of what the government will agree to pay to his people after the white man has once touched it. The agents will steal much of it and one agent will initiate another who does not understand stealing into the mysteries of that art. He said that the agents now sell rations to the half-breeds and squaw men, which ought to be issued to them, and appropriate the proceeds. Spotted Tail further said: "I have been reared in this country, and the half-breeds are my kin. They have been deserted by their white fathers, who came among and married their mothers. I feel for them. They are helpless. I would care for them—the widows and the orphans. Their tears burn into my heart and their hunger is a great distress to Sintigaleska [Spotted Tail]. I want to give to the orphans half of the Black Hills, and the rest I will sell to the Great Father. It will be a home for them for a long time when I am gone, and, maybe when the Sioux as a race are extinct."

Spotted Tail said that he would like to receive for each of the old people of the nation an annuity of $100; and for the young men $25—like the Pottawatamies. He wanted to get these annuities for the Sioux until they should be extinct, which, he remarked, would not now be long. He did not believe in fighting any more. After they were gone, the half-breeds, as their heirs, would enjoy the fund.

Spotted Tail, in naming the above terms, evidently intends to ask $6,000,000 as a first payment to the Sioux and subsequently the annuities mentioned, until his nation shall pass away. This price is many times as large as that which he would have demanded one year ago. Too much significance should not be ascribed, however, to preliminary expressions of the Indians. Not until the council has actually opened can the sentiment of the majority be surmised. When that will occur no mortal can yet say; but it is probable that it will be before the close of this week. Red Cloud is very friendly and courteous, but refrains from giving an inkling of his position on the question of the treaty. A council of his tribe is being held to-night, of which I shall learn the incidents to-morrow. Spider, who is a brother of Red Cloud, absolutely refuses to indorse a sale of the Black Hills.[71]

[Unsigned]

[*New York Herald*, Wednesday, September 22, 1875]

[September 13, 1875 – Charles Collins, from Red Cloud Agency, Nebraska]
The Commissioners
(Special to the *Bee*)
Red Cloud Agency [Monday] Sept. 13, via Fort Laramie, Sept. 15

A rumor is currently credited to the effect that a Cheyenne Indian, from the northern camps, says he has to kill the commissioners. The latter are uneasy in consequence, and may delay the opening of the council, which was expected to commence Thursday [Sept. 9]. Nothing will be done until Gen. Terry arrives on Thursday. The Indians are reconciled to a change of council ground from Chadron Creek to within six miles of here. The Indians are becoming restless at the uncalled-for delay of the commissioners in not commencing the council.

Spotted Tail says he wants six millions, a suit of clothes for all the Indians, and an annual annuity for eighty years. He says that he expects by that time that the tribal Indians will become mixed with the whites or entirely obliterated. It is hoped cold weather will force the commissioners and Indians alike to practice brevity. Men versed in the Indian character express grave doubts, in the present condition and temper of the Indians whether any treaty can be made.

The country is flooded with men awaiting the action of the council, preparatory to entering the Black Hills.

It is feared that the Indian supplies will not hold out, caused by the Indian agents not having sufficient notification.

Delegates Kidder, of Dakota, and Steele, of Wyoming, arrived Friday; also J. H. Bosler and ladies. [J.] D. Terrill, of the second comptroller's office, supervising Indian agencies, and wife, arrived Saturday.
Charles Collins
[*Omaha Daily Bee*, Wednesday, September 15, 1875]

[September 14, 1875 – Anonymous, from Red Cloud Agency, Nebraska]
Special to the *Leader*
Red Cloud Agency
[Tuesday] September 14th, 1875

It having been finally determined to hold the council at the mouth of White Clay Creek, six miles northeast of this place, the Indians are all moving in this direction. The Missouri River Indians and Spotted Tail's band having left Spotted Tail Agency yesterday, are expected here to-night. The commission are now awaiting the arrival of Gen. Terry, from St. Paul, Minn., who is due here to-morrow. Senator Allison says that as Senator Howe has returned to Washington, he is unwilling to proceed with the negotiations until Gen. Terry arrives. A great many of the Indians are becoming dissatisfied at the delay, as those living at a great distance are desirous of returning home before cold weather sets in. The attaches of this agency are constantly besieged by the Indians with inquires as to the cause of the delay, and when the council will begin. The commission have been together three weeks now, and thus far have accomplished nothing beyond having informal talks with the Indians who have visited them, at none of which was there a word said about agreeing upon the day for the beginning of the council; consequently the Indians have been left in utter ignorance on that point.

On Saturday five hundred and fifty head of beef were issued to the Indians, and yesterday a large train loaded with supplies came in from Cheyenne.

Thus far no definite amount has been spoken of as the purchase price of the Black Hills country, and on this point the Indians are very anxious. They are perfectly willing to sell and will take whatever is offered them, as they say the white men are going to occupy that country anyway.

It is thought that the commission will not offer the Indians much money, but will provide for their sustenance for a long term of years, which arrangement would be preferable to all parties, as the government must support them anyway.

A large delegation of Missouri River Indians waited on the commissioners on last Saturday and expressed much dissatisfaction because the commission had not moved down to Chadron Creek, twenty-five miles from here, and half way to Spotted Tail Agency, as they said Rev. Mr. Hinman, one of the commissioners had told them last summer that the council would be held there. Spotted Tail presented them with one hundred and twenty horses with the understanding that they were to insist upon the council being held at Chadron Creek. Upon this occasion, their visit Saturday, Red Cloud's band also presented them with a large number of horses.

Judge Kidder, delegate to Congress from Dakota, and Col. Steele, delegate from Wyoming, are here, and expect to remain until after the close of the council. J. D. Terrill, of the Treasury Department, is also here, accompanied by his wife.

The number of Indians who will attend the council is estimated to be about twenty-five thousand. The camps extend a distance of about forty miles along the White Earth River and the bluffs in this vicinity are covered with their ponies, each head of a family owning, on an average, about fifty ponies. These are all in excellent condition, and the Indians themselves are well clothed and healthy looking.

An Indian girl was accidentally shot near the entrance to the agency stockade on Saturday night by an Indian, the ball grazing her chin.
[Unsigned]
[*Cheyenne Daily Leader*, Thursday, September 16, 1875]

[September 14, 1875 – Jimuel Briggs, from Red Cloud Agency, Nebraska]

From Red Cloud
Red Cloud Agency, Neb., [Tuesday] Sept. 14, 1875
Editor *Journal*

The work of the Sioux Indian treaty commission seems to be considerably more of a job than was first supposed, and though the commission has been in camp here a week but little has been done save in the preparatory department. There is great rivalry between the chiefs of the Oglalas and Brules—one represented by Red Cloud and the other by Spotted Tail—and when the council was appointed for this place, the Brules at once kicked up about it and refused to attend. Spotted Tail corralled the river Indians near his agency, and got them into the notion that the council must be held at Chadron Creek. They came to call on the commission and fight with jabber for their point, but the end of it all was that the commission went out about five miles to the east, where a fine spring forms a brook, and declared that to be the council ground and there it will be. It is located about one mile north of Crow Butte, on a high plateau and the peaks of the highest mountains in the Black Hills can just be seen above the horizon in the north.

The great Sioux nation is now nearly all here—that is within a radius of a good Iowa county. Spotted Tail, with about 8,000 men, is marching this way and will be in camp fifteen miles out by Tuesday. Fully twenty-five thousand Indians will be here, and the council will be the grandest gathering of the kind of the age, and its like is not possible to again occur. The Indians are all well mounted and well armed with the best of guns, but are in the most friendly disposition, especially just after the issue of rations.

The price that they will at first ask for the Black Hills is varying from fifteen to fifty millions, in all of which operations the hand of the disinterested white man is seen. What will be paid for them is a figure not definitely known outside of the commission, but you may be assured that no such figure as the gentle savage proposes. It is not thought the proper thing, however, to tear up the old treaty and nothing will be done save the purchase of the country desired—and that for a fair valuation, based on information received from authentic sources.

The most important question arising out of this treaty is the matter of routes of ingress into the Black Hills country. There is a great influence at work in favor of only southern outlets—by way of Sidney and Cheyenne. Persons acquainted with the internal working of matters in this section, in the way of trade permits, can perhaps see the gazelle frisking along. They ought to, for he is "bigger than a horse." But I am certain that all such dreams will be upset entirely, for there is no man on the commission, I think, so much of a tool of the ring as to fasten any such damnable iniquity on the people. The White River route is judged by all to be the best wagon route to be found, and that, as well as those coming in from the farther route, will be closely looked after. Senator Allison fully appreciates the importance of all having a fair show in this matter and will make his battle for it. There need be no fear of failure. The people of western Iowa, northeastern Nebraska and Dakota can take their wagons and go to the Hills—if anybody can. While it would be a great thing for the trading posts on the south, and a rough blow to break their monopoly, nevertheless it must be done, no odds who is made to squeal thereby. "A fair shake for all" is the idea entertained by the commission.

It is not probable that the grand council will be commenced before Friday next. Gen. Terry has not yet arrived here, but is expected on Thursday. Ten days or two weeks will be used up in the pow-wow, for there will be some knotty points to settle and where the hash and store clothes of the red man are concerned he is a hard customer to handle.

There are many turbulent young bucks around here. Last night one deliberately fired into a bevy of young Indian girls, wounding one severely under the chin. Another young buck, a Cheyenne, has made a threat that as soon as the commissioners go upon the council stand, he proposes to kill one of them. But the chief, American Horse, proposes to have a guard of Indian soldiers of many men and any offering to injure or insult the white men will be punished on the spot, death in the first case and a severe pounding in the latter. So you see we have lots of fun promised ahead, and possibly some life insurance man could make a good stake were he now here. There is no danger whatever, save at the hands of some of the worst desperadoes, and they are not numerous.

The valley in which this agency is located is the White Earth and is well wooded. In some places the Indian squaws have done a little planting, but it amounts to very little. The bucks are too dignified to labor, save at gambling or horse racing, while the squaws do all the work that is done. I know of no section where a ten-day shower of red-hot pitchforks would do more good than along here for about fifty miles. Of course, it would put an end to a good deal of stealing and a great many

Indians—and for the first there would be many hearts made to feel very bad, as the Indian expresses it.

Jimuel Briggs

[*Sioux City Daily Journal*, Tuesday, September 21, 1875]

[September 15, 1875 – John T. Bell, from Red Cloud Agency, Nebraska]

The Home of the Sioux

From Our Special Correspondent

Red Cloud Agency, Neb. [Wednesday], Sept. 15, 1875

To the Editor of *The Herald*

Half of September is gone and yet the grand council for consideration of propositions for the purchase of the Black Hills country, which was set for the 1st is a thing of the dim future. Yesterday it was said that the council would begin either Thursday or Friday. This morning the commissioners are talking about beginning it Friday or Saturday, and to-morrow they will probably tell us it will begin Saturday or Sunday. Gen. Terry is expected here to-day, and we outsiders are united in the earnest hope that he may prove to be a man of vim and energy, with no foolishness about him, and that he will promptly attend to the duties devolving upon him as a member of the commission without a further prolonging of this vexatious delay.

Meanwhile the time drags slowly. The semi-weekly mails bring us quite a supply of papers, but as we have little else to occupy ourselves with, the day following the arrival of the mail sees the contents exhausted, advertisements and all, and then we are out again. The latest papers we have had up to date were of last Tuesday's issue—a week ago today [*sic*]—and thus far they have been filled principally with the details of the failure of the Bank of California, which event occurred last month, and regarding which we had read all we cared to know before leaving home. However, hope has not entirely deserted our breasts, and we comfort ourselves with the reflection that next Friday's mail may bring us at least one paper in which the names of Ralston and Mills will not be mentioned, nor the bank of California even remotely referred to.[72]

Yesterday morning a healthy looking buck approached a tent in front of which a small party of us were sitting, and explained that he was an Oglala, that his wife was a Brule, that his two children which he had with him were half Oglala and half Brule, and that "consequently" he wished us to present him with a clean shirt and each of his children with a new suit of clothes. It was quite apparent that the articles in question were greatly needed, but yet we managed to resist his importunities, and the Indian finally walked away with a scowl of dissatisfaction perched upon his majestic brow.

A squaw dance was gotten up in front of the agency stockade yesterday morning. It was participated in by about twenty middle aged women belonging to first class Sioux families, under the leadership of an Amazonian "medicine woman" whose head was decorated with an immense structure composed of feathers two feet long, buckskin and bead work. The squaws were all picturesquely attired, some of the costumes worn being worth several hundred dollars, numberless small bells forming an important part of their "get up." These, together with a highly ornamented Indian drum, furnished the musical part of the entertainment, in conjunction with the infernally tiresome and monotonous "hi, yi, hi, yi," which the Indians call singing. The dancing was not of a very violent character, but consisted principally in a raising upon the toes simultaneously and then dropping the weight back upon the heels in like fashion, meanwhile keeping time to the rude music. The object of the dance was to secure contributions from the white people present, and in this they were quite successful, as enough groceries and dry goods had been piled up within the circle formed by the dancers by the time the entertainment closed to fill a coal cart.

One of the features of "aborigine" society here is the large number of young Indians who are "on the court," which fact is indicated by their wearing their blankets wrapped tightly about their persons and completely enclosing the face with the exception of coal-black, treacherous-looking eyes. They carry no weapons, usually go in couples, pay no attention whatever to what is going on around them, but occupy themselves with moving in and out among the hundreds of other Indians who congregate about the agency, closely watching the Indian girls, prepared to take advantage of an unguarded moment, suddenly throw their blanket around the latter and hug them and talk love to them in [a] very energetic and enthusiastic manner. The girls are supposed to make a considerable show of resistance when thus entrapped, but as a general thing, the resistance is all show.

Another feature of Indian life in these parts is the fact that perhaps one fifth of the Indians show traces of white blood flowing in their veins, notwithstanding the fact that these tribes have until within a few years past been waging fierce warfare against the whites. For half a century, or more, white men by the hundreds have been making their home in this country, some as agents and employees of various fur companies, others from a desire to forsake the restraints of civilization and others again have taken up with the life of the plains for the reason that an outraged law had declared their longer existence prejudicial to the safety and welfare of their fellows and had declared them outlaws. All these have adopted Indian ways and Indian views and a numerous progeny of tallow-colored descendents has resulted. Occasionally one sees here bright-eyed, well formed children and whose mothers were half breeds and fathers white men, but usually this mixture of the races has not been followed by beneficial results as the half breeds in most instances appear to have inherited the vices of both races and possess the virtues of neither. To be sure, there are exceptions to this rule, but they are rare indeed.

The white ladies who have contributed largely by their bright smiles and cheerful presence to relieve the monotony of our dull life at this agency for the past week, leave us to-day. The party consists of Mrs. J. H. Bosler, and Miss Gertrude Bosler of Carlisle, Pennsylvania, Mrs. J. D. Terrill of Washington city, and Mrs. Steele, the wife of the delegate from Wyoming. They arrived at Red Cloud about a week ago intending to remain to witness the grand council, but our easy-going commissioners have succeeded in wearing out their patience and they depart for Cheyenne this morning, accompanied by Mr. Bosler, Mr. Steele, and Mr. Terrill. They have kindly offered to take charge of all mail matter we may desire to send by them, and they will thereby be the means of placing this letter before the great army of readers who draw daily inspiration from the columns of *The Herald* several days sooner than would have been the case had it been forwarded by the regular mail.

Religious services were held last Sunday, Rev. S. D. Hinman and a brother clergyman from Spotted Tail Agency officiating.[73] They were well attended and unusually interesting. Mr. Will Dear, the popular trader at this agency, assumed leadership of the singing exercises with a reckless confidence characteristic of western men. He got along finely with the first line of the opening hymn, and would have closed the hymn with victory perched upon his banners, had not the discovery been made—as it was upon his tackling the second line—that he was endeavoring to dovetail a short metre hymn into a long metre time, and also that he had pitched the latter upon so high a key that no one not possessing ability to wrestle with "high C" could carry it. Then he wilted, and with his face the color of the red, red rose, backed out, whereupon the ladies whose names are mentioned above quietly stepped in—metaphorically speaking—and filled the long building in which the services were being held, with sounds of sweetest melody.

The indications are that this section of country is to be deluged with eloquence when the big talk finally begins, for it is reported that one hundred and thirty speeches are to be made by the Indians alone, that number of "chiefs" having already announced their intention to make speeches, with several of the more remote camps yet to hear from. And when it is remembered that several of the commissioners are remarkably tonguey chaps, the stoutest heart is appalled. Well, Crow Butte, eight miles eastward of this agency is a very high point, and in this connection it would prove a modern Mount Ararat.[74]

J. T. B.

[*Omaha Daily Herald*, Thursday, September 23, 1875]

[September 15, 1875 – Charles Collins, from Red Cloud Agency, Nebraska]

Red Cloud

(Correspondence of the *Bee*)

Red Cloud Agency, W. T. [Wednesday] Sept. 15, 1875

Editor *Bee*

Having already advised you by special couriers and telegraph of what is being done here by commissioners and Indians looking to the assembling of the council for treaty purposes. It is now definitely understood that the council ground is to be at White Clay Creek, six miles north of here, and that the opening pow-wow will commence on Friday next.

A painful rumor circulated here on Saturday evening to the effect that a Cheyenne brave, whose heart felt bad, had made the declaration that he would kill a commissioner. This news had a very demoralizing effect on the members of the commission sent here to make a treaty, and for that, and for the other reason that their colleague, General Terry, had not arrived, they have postponed the commencement of council until Friday next, 17th. Active efforts are being made to hunt up and reconcile that Cheyenne barbarian.

Large trains of supplies are daily arriving here to feed and feast the Indians while the making of the treaty continues. Spotted Tail says that the Indians will demand as a compensation for their interest in the Black Hills, six million dollars in cash, a suit of clothes for every Indian interested, and a guaranteed annuity sufficient to subsist them for eighty years. He claims that at the expiration of the time mentioned the Indians as a separate and independent race will have become obliterated. From this it will be observed that Spotted Tail, as well as the prominent men among the Indians, fully comprehend the situation and inevitable destiny of the red man.

Two wagons loaded with vegetables arrived here yesterday all the way from the Cache La Poudre, Greeley County, Colorado. The enterprising huxters soon sold out their loads, getting 12 ½ cents per pound for onions, 8 cents per pound for potatoes, the same for squash, and from 75c to $1.00 each for water melons.

The weather here is delightful, but it is hoped that it will soon turn cold, and thus drive both the commissioners and the Indians into expeditiously doing the work for which they have assembled here.

Mr. J. W. Dear, post-trader here, leaves this morning for your city to lay in his fall and winter stock. Your people cannot treat him too kindly. He is a gentleman of sterling worth, has a heart as big as an ox, a sense of humor as sharp and keen as a Damascus blade, and business qualities rarely vouchsafed to one of his years. He is justly rolling up wealth here, but that does not interfere with his unbounded hospitality.

There will be a big Indian dance to-night a short distance from the agency, in which several thousand Indians in all their paint and feathers will participate.

Among the arrivals here yesterday was the Viscount Lewisham, a young Englishman, who came to see the grand council.[75]

Major Howard, United States Indian agent at Spotted Tail Agency, is here arranging for the care of his Indians. He is very indignant at the letter which appeared in the *Bee* charging him with harsh and partizan treatment toward some half-breeds and squaw-men (white men living with squaws) whom he ordered off the reservation.[76]

Having taken particular pains to get at the fact in the case, I am fully confirmed in the belief that your correspondent knowingly misrepresented Agent Howard, and knowing that the *Bee* is as ready to rectify an error as it is to attack or expose a wrong, I take this opportunity of setting Major Howard right before your readers. Amongst the representatives of the press here is Mr. J. G. [T.] Bell, representing the *Omaha Herald*. Mr. Davenport of the *New York Herald*, in addition to many of the subalterns and attaches of the commissioner, correspond with papers in various parts of the country. Col. Burke, formerly in the book and stationery business in your city, is now Indian agent at Standing Rock Agency on the Missouri River. It is generally remarked here by the commissioners and outsiders that the colonel has got his Indians under better discipline than any other agent in the Indian department. His were the first Indians to agree to the change of council ground from Chadron Creek to White Clay.

At the conference between the Indians and the commissioners on Saturday last the commissioners squarely stated to the Indians that if a council was held at all it must be at White Clay (6 miles northeast of here). Spotted Tail and his tribe, who were the strongest opponents of changing the council ground from Chadron Creek to White Clay, finally consented to the change; so that on Friday next the groundwork of the most important Indian treaty ever made between the government and their wild protégés will be laid. How long it will take to bring the treaty to a close your deponent sayeth not.

C. C.

[*Omaha Daily Bee*, Monday, September 20, 1875]

[September 15, 1875 – Charles Collins, from Red Cloud Agency, Nebraska]

The Black Hills Treaty

(From our Special Correspondent)

Red Cloud Agency, Wyoming [Wednesday] Sept. 15, 1875

Appearances would now indicate that the long looked for and always postponed council between the Indians and the treaty commissioners may be indefinitely postponed or continued. Unless the commissioners appoint an early day upon which to meet the Indians in council, it is more than possible that the Indians who have come here from the Missouri River agencies will pack up and leave, disgusted. Those of the commissioners with whom we have conversed assign the flimsiest reasons for the unnecessary delay. It is our candid opinion that the commissioners are actuated by some imaginary dread. Whether it is a realization of their incompetency or a premonition of coming danger, we do not presume to know. Dr. Daniels who has charge of the commission leaves this morning for Cheyenne. He expresses the opinion that there will be no council held until his return as it will take him eight days to make the round trip. The outlook for immediately gratifying the *Bee* readers with the doings of the council are not encouraging. Yesterday morning the commissioners and other temporary residents at this agency were found with a squaw dance, which for a few minutes possessed the merit of novelty, but from its monotonous sameness soon lost its interest. The squaws to the number of seventy-five, form in a half-moon circle; four of the most distinguished of their number get in the centre and keep up a steady thud, thud on the head of a drum head of domestic manufacture; while the drumming is continued those inside and forming the circle keep up a low moaning hi-ha-he-yi, accompanying the voice by a slight bending of the knees, and in some instances making a visible jumping motion on their feet. While this is going on the medicine squaw dances or jumps around the circle with her feet close together and ringing a small bell all the time, making motions with their hands and body. If the council ever gets together, the proceedings, if ever published would be appalling to one who would be compelled to read them. One of the interpreters informs us that already nearly 150 of the chiefs and counselors or the different tribes have announced their intention of expounding their peculiar views on their rights and the duty of the government in the matter. The Indians are getting an exaggerated idea of the wealth of the Black Hills, and of their own importance—information that is daily being imparted to them by squaw men and others interested in keeping the present status of the Indians with the government unchanged.

J. T. [D.] Terrill, of the treasury department, who is now on a tour of the Indian agencies, looking into their management as an expert, leaves here to-morrow, and notwithstanding the public clamor raised about the mismanagement of this agency, he makes no secret in saying that under the circumstances and the peculiar surroundings, Dr. Saville has been a faithful, conscientious, and honest-intentioned public servant.

J. H. Bosler, wife and daughter leave this morning for San Francisco.

Charles Collins

[*Omaha Daily Bee*, Tuesday, September 21, 1875]

[September 15, 1875 – Reuben Davenport, from Red Cloud Agency, Nebraska]

Before the Council—A Savage Dance

Red Cloud Indian Agency, Nebraska, [Wednesday] Sept. 15, 1875

Brigadier General A. H. Terry, a member of the Treaty Commission, arrived here to-day, accompanied by General Luther P. Bradley, commandant of the Black Hills District, and Captain [Christian C.] Hewitt, aide-de-camp, and escorted by Company M, of the Second Cavalry, under Captain John Mix. General Bradley, soon after reaching Camp Robinson, wrote an order directing Major Mills, stationed at Camp Sheridan, near the Spotted Tail Agency, to move his company of cavalry to this point. The order is understood to be meant as a safeguard against possible treachery by the Indians. General Bradley, however, says that it is "merely to add to the ceremony of the council."

"Boots and saddles" were sounded at the post [Camp Robinson] to-day in consequence of a false alarm. A teamster came riding in with all possible speed, and announced that he had been attacked by Indians a short distance from the post, and had immediately mounted his led horse, left his wagon and team, and so escaped. Captain Egan was ordered out at the head of his company, but before he proceeded to the place indicated he met some Indians who gave a plausible explanation of what had occurred by saying that the shots which they fired were not aimed at the teamster and that they meant no harm. The story was credited and the cavalry returned to the post. General Bradley, however, has undoubtedly taken a wise course. At least two regiments of soldiers ought to be stationed at the council. If the young men are dissatisfied with the attitude of the commissioners an outbreak of war is not at all improbable. The burning of the agency buildings and the massacre of all the white men hereabouts would be among the first acts of the savages. The small force of military at Camp Robinson, numbering less than 500, would be utterly inadequate to cope with 30,000 well armed Indians. It would be an opportunity of inaugurating in what the Sioux would deem a glorious manner the red man's general war, so long pending and so long prophesied.

The commissioners show at the outset of their negotiation a lamentable tendency to vacillation. When they first reached the agencies on the White River and passed on northward to visit those on the Missouri they gave the Indians, whether intentionally or otherwise, at every point where they found them the impression that Chadron Creek had been appointed the place for the holding of the council. They returned to this agency to begin the great talk in the first week of September; but, as soon as they were here, announced to the Indians, who had come from a distance to the White River and camped on streams adjoining Chadron Creek, that the council would assemble thirty miles nearer to the Red Cloud Agency. At a talk with the Indians from the Standing Rock and Cheyenne River agencies, held here on Saturday, the commission informed the chiefs that a place had been selected by them on Little Clay Creek, near the Crow Buttes, to meet the Indians, and that they would not change their selection. To-day, however, Spotted Tail having brought his people as far as Ash Creek called upon the commissioners and made a speech to them full of his usual eloquence, setting forth the justness of his wish that the council should not be held further from his agency than from this. Red Dog replied to him in support of the selection already made by the commission. The latter answered Spotted Tail by agreeing to submit the question of the location of the council to him and Red Cloud and four of their chiefs. Great delay might have been avoided ere now had one course or the other been pursued by the commission—either to have adhered to their own choice or to have accepted that of the Indians.

The commission will date the beginning of the council on next Friday, the 17th, and if all is not then in readiness they will adjourn to another day. General Terry expresses a wish to shorten its duration as much as possible. The other members have the same disposition, but certainly do not understand very well the proper methods of diplomacy to employ with Indian chiefs.

There was some commotion in Red Cloud's village this morning. It is situated beyond a hill north of the agency, on a bend of the White

River. Preparations were making for the grand Omaha dance, which was to be given in honor of the commissioners. Yesterday was the appointed time for the ceremony; but a slight dash of rain dampened the ardor of the bucks, so that they deferred their coming until today. The great drum, heard afar off, gave early warning of their approach, and when they appeared on the brow of the hill, with the big medicine man and the head warrior of the society of Omahas at their head, with the banner of feathers held aloft and lances with human scalps attached pricking the air, the sight was imposing. The Omahas were on foot, but a great throng of braves, squaws, and boys all mounted, followed them, sometimes joining in the guttural music, keeping time to the heavy stroke of the huge drum and sometimes shouting with all the strength of their lungs. The costumes of the dedicated braves have already been often described, but as there is sometimes a variation in their performance I may mention again some portion of it. The body of brilliantly decorated warriors halted in front of the stockade and the gates were thrown open. They marched slowly in, with rhythm of step and solemn intonation. The first impression on the mind is that the ceremonial is of diabolical significance. Many of the figures look like devils just loosened from their infernal cages; others are purely grotesque. One of them apparently has the duties of a clown to perform. He does so with success. A circle was formed in the centre of the stockade, with a wide opening toward the house occupied by the commissioners, near which sat the medicine man upon his horse. He wore a huge war bonnet, decorated with long eagle feathers, and bore in his hand the banner of the Omahas, a long "medicine stick" fringed also with feathers. His body was nearly naked and painted a dull yellow. On the opposite side of the circle was a small inner ring, formed by the musicians sitting around the drum. Outside the circle at this point sat three or four young squaws, who sung treble in some of the refrains. One the left was stationed the head warrior, sitting stolidly upon a parti-colored pony. He wore a war bonnet similar to that of the medicine man, and carried in his hand a bright and gleaming sword. Moc-pea-lutah (Red Cloud) sat on the left of the circle of musicians. During all the ceremony, except when he joined in a part of the dance, he sat with his head on his hand, his long, heavy hair drooping over his cheeks and his face peculiarly sad. He wore none of the decorations of the order. Two little boys, brightly dressed, sat next to Red Cloud. They danced with the dancers.

It would be but a repetition of terms to attempt a full description of the ceremony. At first the exertions of the braves were very moderate and they seemed very slowly to imbibe the necessary enthusiasm and frenzy, but gradually their movements became livelier. An assistant of the medicine man, who was apparently master of ceremonies, walked around the circle, uttering incantations or reciting deeds in a loud, metallic voice. The one by one the braves rose from the circle and began a slow dance to the stroke of the big drum and the chanting of a chorus by all those seated. Parts were rendered quite beautiful by the sudden accession of the female voices. The deep, guttural bass also produced melody, impressive as it was dissimilar from that of the cultured order.

The corners of the open space in the stockade were crowded with Indian spectators, mounted and on foot. During the pauses in the dance some of the toothless old women, crouching in groups in the shade of the building, would set up a quivering refrain too piercing and unearthly to be agreeable.

A tall Indian mother, of shapely form and regular features, appeared at the opening of the ring, bearing in her arms her infant. She had wrapped about her and covering her head a long crimson shawl, and on her feet were blue moccasins, small and of pretty workmanship. The master of ceremonies conversed with her a few minutes in an undertone, and then, leading her into the circle, made a short speech. The drum was loudly beat, and a melody was chanted of more cheerful import than those preceding it. Then the braves arose and danced again. The squaws withdrew, and a horse was brought forward to be dedicated to the use of the infant Oglala, who had just been adopted from its mother's arms into the society of the Omahas. The medicine man touched the steed with a wand and he was led away. More dancing and intoning ensued. The chief warrior was led into the arena by the master of ceremonies, and recited a long list of his achievements, in which he had shown his bravery and cruelty to his enemies. Dancing followed and continued until the spectacle began to grow monotonous.

The most hideous looking of the painted braves was the clown. His body was a dark yellow and the lower half of his face a deep green. Behind he wore a tail of huge feathers, which were spread out fan shaped, and some of them decorated with blue and red ribbons. This portion of his embellishment looked as if it should properly belong to the American bird of freedom. His nude legs were grotesquely covered with figures of new moons, eagle beaks, and talons. He exaggerated the gestures of the dancers with a degree of humor unlooked for in an Indian. He was a living caricature.

When the commissioners were wearied of the spectacle they presented to the medicine man an order upon the trader for presents, and the Omahas departed. They afterward visited the trader's store and several white men's lodges, and marched home to their village at dusk to the sound of the drum. This evening there is considerable festive excitement in the tepees near the agency, and songs and the sound of the drum are heard intermittently.

Last evening Spotted Tail again called upon the commissioners and told them that he, accompanied by Two Strike and No Flesh, had called upon Red Cloud, Red Dog, and Young-Man-Afraid-of-His-Horses in the afternoon at that village and had tried to arrive at some agreement with them as to the place of the council. He proposed to the Oglala chiefs that it be held a short distance west of the Old Spotted Tail Agency, ten miles from this point.[77] They declined to listen to any such proposition. Red Cloud said that if the council took place on the prairie he wanted it to be on Horse Creek; otherwise he wanted it held in the stockade at the agency. Spotted Tail informed the commissioners that he desires them to confer with Red Cloud and Red Dog and try to induce them to become more reasonable. He said that if it was impossible for his Indians to come to the views of the Oglala chiefs there ought to be two separate councils. Spotted Tail concluded by saying that he could meet the commissioners wherever they wished.

The expedient of referring the question to a committee of six chiefs having failed, the commissioners, at ten o'clock last evening, decided to once more assume the reins and to choose the council seat themselves. They ignored their former selection of a spot near the Crow Buttes and rode out this morning in a different direction to find what they sought.

It will be remembered that some of the Sioux warriors have expressed a superstitious fear of holding a council in the vicinity of the Crow Buttes. They denominate them "war buttes," and seem to think them capable of an unlucky influence upon the fortunes of the Dakotas. Twenty years ago they roamed far south of the North Platte River and did not come further north than the Cohile in their hunts.[78] The Absaroki or Crows then possessed the northern portion of the country west of the Missouri and east of the Rocky Mountains, and were neighbors and enemies of the Sioux, as they still are, although driven by the latter into the Big Horn Mountains, which they now rightfully hold. On one occasion they came down upon the herds of the Sioux "like a wolf on the fold," and captured much of their stock, but were fiercely attacked by overwhelming numbers of the enemy and sustained for a long time a losing fight. They saw that if an escape was not effected they were all doomed to bite the dust. Night came and they retreated from the plain bordering the White River toward the tall bluffs on the south, and climbed up the sloping side to the summit of the larger of the Crow Buttes, also known as Dancer's Hill. It is a small space a few hundred yards in extent; but here for a time their bleeding and exhausted band held an advantage and fought with desperation. But the Sioux had the pass by which they had gone up the hill and guarded it closely. They could not retreat by the way they had come. On the second night, however, when their food was exhausted, they cut up their buffalo robes and tied strips of them firmly together. Each man lowered himself safely down the perpendicular side of the butte, on the north, which had been left unwatched by the Sioux. They left on the summit one of their dogs, which kept up a constant barking that deceived the enemy into the faith that they were still there. The surviving Crows got back to their own country. The disappointment of the Sioux was great. They have never forgotten it, and ascribe it to the ill luck of the place.[79]

The commission chose a spot on the banks of the White River, about six miles east of this agency, and two miles from the mouth of Little White Earth Creek.

This morning a score of chiefs, of the Upper Yanktonai tribe of Sioux, who, with their families, had just arrived here from the Standing Rock Agency, presented their respects to the commissioners and shook hands with all the white persons present. The principal of them are Mad Bear, Red Wolf, Bear Ribs, Red Horse, Yellow Robe, Cross Bear, Big Knees, and Big Head.[80] The commissioners expressed pleasure at seeing them and said that they would send word to all the Indians to-day that the council would begin on the White River on Saturday. The levee was then ended.

This council will probably be officially baptized, either as the "Crow Butte" or the "White River" Council. The question has not yet been settled. Either name would be sufficiently proper. None of the commissioners will yet express definitely an opinion upon the terms which they hope to make with the Indians. Senator Allison, the chairman, is in favor of giving only the value of the land comprised in the Black Hills, as a wild and unsettled country, less the cost to the government of surveys necessary for fixing boundaries and area. He says that after a certain sum has been given to the Indians immediately after the purchase, an annuity of from $120,000 to $200,000 may be paid to them for the period of thirty years. He also speaks of making some provision for the education of their children and the future encouragement of civilized pursuits. This is a mere outline of his views, but at present he will not divulge his ideas more fully. General A. H. Terry is disposed to conclude the negotiation with as much businesslike brevity as possible. Speaking comparatively of the differences of the present treaty making and of that of 1868, he considered the latter greater. The Indians were then in a great ferment, the Union Pacific Railroad was building, and the public had but shortly before been horrified by the Fort Phil Kearny massacre. The reader will remember that Red Cloud, Red Dog, and Red Leaf, three of the pet chiefs to participate in this council, were leaders in that terrible work. General Terry said there was hazard in the commission trusting themselves utterly to the good faith of the Indians, but did not apprehend any treachery on their part. He, however, thought it wise to go to the council at the beginning with a guard of 100 soldiers so that the Indians would become used to their presence and, if danger arose, the force could be increased without causing trouble. The difficulty in having troops in the neighborhood of the council tepee would be the protests of the Indians, on the ground that the commissioners doubted their good faith, and also that they would fear to set their own desires in the face of what might seem to be the coercive presence of the military. There was a danger that sullen dissatisfaction might result, defeating the object of the council and perhaps precipitating war upon the government. General Terry thought that the five companies of troops at Camp Robinson were sufficient to save the lives of the commissioners in case of an outbreak. This opinion, however, is not shared by many. Although General Terry is a military authority, he, doubtless, in his expressions, is anxious to deprecate all causes of apprehension. If the danger were ever so apparent the army is so small that it could not spare enough soldiers to meet the emergency.

American Horse, when recently visiting the commissioners, desired of them the honor to be permitted to organize his young men into a guard for the chiefs. As their consent would invite, by exciting the jeal-ously of other bands, the very clashing which ought to be avoided, it was withheld.

Mr. Ashby, who is a politician of Nebraska, seems to be impressed with the impossibility of moulding the Indian into anything other than what he is—an unredeemed savage. Mr. Comingo has a benevolent heart and devotes to the interests and the probable future of the Sioux nation much profound and conscientious study. He says he will not consent to pay the Indians an exorbitant price for their lands. Mr. Beauvais, of French birth and an old Indian trader, perfectly versed in the Dakota tongue, feels a fatherly sympathy for the children of the plain, and perhaps some natural instincts mingle with the impulses of a generous soul. He has lived a long time in intimate relationship with the Indians, and probably comprehends their character, wants, and necessities better than anyone else in the commission, excepting Mr. Hinman. His kindly pity and consideration for them is often shown. When a begging Indian intrudes himself in the council room, at the agency, where his presence is obnoxious, he will save the feelings of his inferior fellow creature by not permitting anyone else to dismiss him. He will take him aside, invent a plausible excuse, and acquaint him with it delicately, doubtless sending him away with only a large conceit of his own importance. Mr. Beauvais opposes making any proposal to the council, but favors waiting for the Indians to make up their minds and name the price. He condemns the weak course thus far pursued by the commission.

Mr. Hinman theorizes upon the advancement of the North American race. He believes in compelling the Indian to labor for his livelihood, issuing him supplies in proportion to his industry. He says that in selling the Black Hills the Dakotas are selling all that now remains to them, and as a friend to the Indian he evidently feels like encouraging them in demanding a price equal to their value. General Lawrence will be liberal in his ideas of the compensation due the Indians for relinquishing their hunting grounds.

The first step of the commission in the beginning of the council will be to lay before the chiefs, as representing the government, their proposition for the purchase of the desired territory. In it they will name a price. The Indians will then hold their private debates before further public counseling.

This evening the commission have held a late session, but did not reach any harmonious conclusion. A division in their views is developing, and from information received from some of the members, it is not improbable that there will be a permanent disagreement, and that if a treaty is consummated it will be signed by only a majority. The difference is understood to consist in the extent of concession to be made the Indians in regard to the amount of money to be paid for the Black Hills. The commissioners apprehend that an exorbitant price will be demanded of them. Some of them—the minority—will accept this as just. Their motives might prove of special interest if analyzed.[81] The other portion will stand firm upon a reasonable proposition, intended to be made at the beginning by the chief of the council. Tedious counter-propositions are expected from the Indians, and the effort to make a treaty may finally fail.

General Bradley, commanding the Black Hills military district, and Colonel Steele, delegate from Wyoming in Congress, will be present at the council. The Hon. Mr. Lee, son of Lord Lee of England, is also here.[82]

[Unsigned]

[*New York Herald*, Monday, September 27, 1875]

[September 16, 1875 – John T. Bell, from Red Cloud Agency, Nebraska]

The Black Hills Purchase

From our Special Correspondent

Red Cloud Agency, Neb., [Thursday] Sept. 16, 1875

To the Editor of *The Herald*

Gen. Terry arrived yesterday, and as the Indians themselves are getting very anxious for the council to take place, there is no reason why our easy-going commissioners whom Uncle Sam sent out to treat for the purchase of the Black Hills country should not proceed to business at once.

The slow movements of the commission have for ten days past been the subject of considerable joking. For instance, as a lot of us, consisting of Indian agents, newspaper correspondents and bummers sat down to supper last night at the mess-house run by Dear, the trader at this agency, and by whom we are all fed, with the exception of the members of the commission, who run a mess of their own, one of the party put off a most venerable joke by remarking, "I never miss a meal nor pay a cent," to which another responded, "I haven't paid a cent so far, neither, but I'm afraid these commissioners will finally wear my credit out," whereupon a third growled, "These commissioners are calculated to wear out anything, including the seats of their own trowsers." (Applause in the galleries.)

Yesterday Spotted Tail, Two Strike, Swift Bear, and several other Indians came up from Spotted Tail Agency, and held a little talk with the commissioners at which old Spot said the Missouri River Indians, who have all been encamped at Spotted Tail Agency for nearly two weeks, were getting very anxious to get home before cold weather comes, and that they wanted the council to come off as soon as possible. In order to conciliate Spotted Tail and to patch up a little difference which is supposed to exist between that mighty potentate and Red Cloud, the commissioners concluded to give up their own choice as to the place of holding the council, and therefore selected Spotted Tail, Two Strike, and Swift Bear as representatives of Spotted Tail Agency, and Red Cloud, Red Dog, and Young-Man-Afraid-of-his-Horses as representatives of Red Cloud Agency, to choose a site for the council, stipulating that it must be near for the commissioners to go out from this agency in the morning and return in the evening. During the talk Old-Man-Afraid-of-his-Horses had entered the room and when the "committee on grounds" was announced, Spotted Tail—who seems to be a joker, and whose eyes indicate mirthfulness well developed—turned to him with the remark, "There, you see your son is getting ahead of you," whereupon there was a general laugh among the Indians present at the old man's expense. The latter is the hereditary chief of the Sioux nation, but on account of his extreme age has allowed Spotted Tail and Red Cloud to usurp his prerogatives during half a dozen years past, but he has found his son, now about 25 years of age, a worthy successor, and the white men and half breeds here say that if he lives he will occupy the position his father has voluntarily surrendered, before many years have passed, to the discomfiture of both Spotted Tail and Red Cloud. He is a remarkably sensible young fellow, quick-witted and held in high esteem by the entire Sioux nation, his only drawback being a lack of that quality of which Red Dog possesses a super abundance—self esteem. The latter is an old romantic-looking individual who is constantly coming to the fore, is gassy and very evidently intends to figure very prominently in the coming council. He remarked the other day that if he could only read and write he would be a very smart man.

Two Bears, a leading man among the Yanktonai, of Standing Rock Agency, came up yesterday evening from the camp on Chadron Creek to which the Missouri River Indians have just removed from Spotted Tail Agency, accompanied by forty under chiefs of his tribe, the object of their visit being to propound to the commission these conundrums:

1. "Where are you going to hold the council?"

2. "When are you going to hold the council?"

Several of the members of the commission happened to be absent from the agency at the time of their visit, hence an answer to these very pertinent and common-sense interrogatories could not then be given them, but will be at a conference to be held to-day. No better evidence could be had of the fact that this commission is composed of a remarkable body of men than is found in this constant urging to "go ahead" on the part of the "party of the second part" in the proposed real estate dicker, for when any set of white men can tire out a body of Indians in a persistent "settin 'round," those white men have achieved distinction of no ordinary character.

Speaking of Two Bears, Maj. Burke, the agent at Standing Rock, tells me he is a very "big Injun" at home, that he lives in a comfortable house, owns a carriage and fine team, and that he will exert a commendable influence in the council.[83]

Mrs. Galpin, an Indian woman of much fame at Standing Rock, was also of the party, which accompanied Two Bears in his visit yesterday evening. She is a full blooded aborigine, does not speak a word of English, but has discarded Indian attire for that of her white sisters, and with the long black dress with voluminous hoops and black sun bonnet, which she wore last night, looks like a retired washwoman upon whom the world has constantly smiled through a considerable of years. She has been married to a white man by whom she had four daughters, all of whom were educated in the Catholic convent at St. Louis, speak French and English fluently, and are considered desirable "catches." That is, the three younger ones are, the eldest having married Capt. Harmon—an ex-army officer now engaged in business at St. Paul.[84] Mrs. Galpin is a sort of a trader at Standing Rock Agency, and in that capacity has accumulated considerable pelf.

An Omaha Dance was given inside the stockade yesterday afternoon by a party of 50 Sioux, bedecked in war-paint and feathers of the most gorgeous character. About half of them were entirely naked, barring a breech cloth of modest dimensions; those who were thus airily costumed having their bodies, legs, and arms painted all the hues of the rainbow. The dance itself was a wild, weird affair abounding in yells, violent gesticulations, and a recounting on the part of a portion of the participants of the number of scalps they had taken and ponies stolen, while just outside the ring formed by the dancers a pole was stuck in the ground with several scalps attached to the top thereof and fluttering gaily in the breezes. In the rear of the dancers and immediately opposite each other sat two braves on horses handsomely and richly dressed, and each wearing on his head a head dress of eagle's feathers of great length and beauty, with a tail of the same material dependant therefrom and reaching to within a few inches of the ground.

This dance was not all for show either, as it was made the occasion of presenting, with much pomp and ceremony, to a chief called Blue Horse, a large number of ponies, he having given away all his horses upon the recent death of his grandson, as is the custom among the Sioux. The presentations were made by individual members of the tribe, the horses being led out to the circle of dancers by squaws.

J. T. B.

[*Omaha Daily Herald*, Friday, September 24, 1875]

[September 17, 1875 – Charles Collins, from Red Cloud Agency, Nebraska]

Life among the Indians

(Special Correspondence of the *Bee*)

Red Cloud Agency, W. T., [Friday] Sept. 17, 1875

Editor *Bee*

The terrible monotony that seems to have overshadowed the treaty commissioners and all connected with them since their arrival here is beginning to assume a more hopeful aspect. General Terry, the only absent member of the commission, arrived here on Wednesday, and during the day large delegations of Indians, representing the heads of all the tribes who are to become parties to the treaty, paid their respects to and conferred with the commissioners, the most important visitor being Spotted Tail, chief of the Brule Sioux, and one of the most wily and prominent Indians on this continent.

Heretofore, since the arrival of the commissioners, all efforts to induce Spotted Tail to visit them had failed—the reasons assigned being that, learning the commissioners had decided to change the place of holding the council from Chadron Creek (midway between Spotted Tail and this agency) to a point within six miles of here, he became jealous and used every device and subterfuge known to an Indian to influence the Missouri River Indians to refuse to go into council unless the ground for the latter was held at Chadron Creek. He is jealous of the prestige it might give to Red Cloud to have the council held so near the latter's agency.

When the Missouri River Indians got within twenty miles of Spotted Tail's agency on their way to the council, they sent couriers out to welcome them, and on their arrival at Chadron Creek he made them a big feast and gave them 150 ponies. Red Cloud hearing of this, sent his head men to the camp of the strangers, invited them to a feast and went thirty better than Spotted Tail by presenting them with 180 ponies. This is considered an excellent stroke of strategic diplomacy on the part of Red Cloud. Spotted Tail is full of blarney as the most veritable of Irishmen. On visiting the commissioners he told them his heart was glad, that he was the white man's friend and that he was anxious to make a treaty, but that the Black Hills were very valuable and he expected the government to pay his people the full value. An attempt to get an expression from him, as to his estimate of their worth just then and there failed, but his agent at Spotted Tail Agency, Major Howard who accompanied old "Spot" into the Black Hills said that they would ask six millions in money, a suit of clothes for every Indian in the Sioux nation, ponies for the chiefs, and an annual annuity of food and clothing sufficient to sustain them for eighty years. Spotted Tail believed that at the expiration of the time mentioned, the Indians as a distinctive race will have run out.

Yesterday forenoon the Indian females of this agency (there is only one white lady residing here, Mrs. Frank Yates) favored the commissioners with a "squaw" dance, which consisted of about fifty dusky maidens, dressed up in all the finest toggery that an Indian female's wardrobe afforded. They ranged themselves in a circle, with their director and four companions to beat on a drum in the center. The dancing consisted in a visible attempt at a stiff jump with both limbs, the feet being kept close together. Some of the more demonstrative or enthusiastic among them would occasionally jump around the circle, making all kinds of gestures and motions, and bellowing out a monotonous and dreary-sounding guttural sound. This dance was kept up for about two hours.

In the afternoon about one hundred Indians, painted up in all the hues and in all the costumes imaginable, arrayed in all kinds of fantastic dresses (many of them having only a coat of paint) commended what is known among them as the "Omaha" dance, which, in most essentials, differed but little from that of the squaw dance. After dancing for an hour or more, each of the two leaders of the band, mounted on ponies and adorned with a bonnet of eagle feathers extending all around the head and reaching to the knees, were led into the middle of the ring formed by the dancers, and for half an hour each recounted his deeds of prowess, how many scalps he had taken, the manner of killing his enemies, and why he had killed them.

The most exaggerated ideal picture of a lot of savages fitting out for the war path, such as may sometimes be seen on illustrated covers of dime novels are tame compared with the actual appearance of these wards of the government. One of the most sickening sights we ever witnessed was on the occasion of issuing beef to the Indians of this agency on Saturday last. On the occasion referred to 550 beeves on the hoof were issued; the head man of each little band was issued from one to twenty beeves, according to the number of lodges he represented. About 3,000 mounted Indians surrounded the corral where the cattle were confined; as the names of the Indians were called out the gate of the corral was swung open and the requisite number of beef were let loose, and then commenced a most savagely exciting scene that pen or picture could depict.

As soon as the cattle gained an open space on the prairie the owners of squads of from two to twenty mounted on horses and armed with breech-loading rifles commenced a chase and running fire on the cattle. We have seen some of those Texan cattle having as many as a dozen rifle balls emptied into their quivering bodies before they fell. Sometimes a steer before falling would run, at the top of its speed, a distance of two or three, and even five miles, all the time receiving a steady fire from the savages that were following them up. Your readers can imagine, if they can, from one to two thousand wild Indians mounted and scattered over a high rolling prairie within an area of two miles, divided into parties of from one to ten persons, keeping up a steady fire into from one to two hundred infuriated Texan steers, divided into bunches of from one to ten cattle. To us it seemed like reviving all the excitement of the buffalo chase. It is universally considered that the method of issuing meat to the Indians has the very opposite from a civilizing influence on those whom it is claimed we are trying [to bring] within the pale of civilization, but the ways of Indians and Indian agents are, in this as in other cases, are beyond the comprehension of us "innocents abroad."

Charles Collins

P. S. – Just as the mail is closing, Red Cloud, chief of the Oglalas and head man of the Indians at this agency, has come in and informed the commissioners that he and his associate chiefs cannot agree with Spotted Tail and his chiefs as to the place of holding the council. They discussed the subject all of last night and this morning, not being able to agree, he and Spotted Tail were requested by the younger chiefs to leave the council tent—that they would settle it among themselves. Red Cloud now comes in and says that he and his tribe want the council ground for making the treaty to be within the stockade of this agency, and that they will not go anywhere else. Spotted Tail and all of the other Indians outside of Red Cloud and his friends agree to the ground selected yesterday by the commissioners. The latter have notified the Indians to meet them at the council grounds selected, regardless of the protests and, if need be, the absence of Red Cloud. There are many here conversant with Indian character who are not slow to proclaim that had the commissioners called a council, selected a council ground, and notified the Indians to attend it, immediately on their arrival here, the treaty might now have been made; but that the continued postponements, delays, and trifling ways displayed by the commissioners have robbed the latter of any dignity or prestige that their position might have conferred on them in the estimation of the Indians above all other races. The Indians admire and respect firmness, dignity, and unwavering resolutions, characteristic[s] which we regret to say we are unable to discover in any marked degree in a majority of those sent out here to make a treaty with the Sioux.

Hon. J. P. Kidder, congressional delegate of Dakota, who came here to look after the interests of his constituents in securing to the latter, through treaty stipulations, the requisite facilities for his constituents in the way of recognized route[s] to the Black Hills, leaves to-day for his home in Vermillion, Dakota, via Omaha.

Large numbers of Missouri River Indians who came here to participate in the council are leaving for their homes, fearing that cold weather might overtake them on their overland trip hope.

Messrs. Burke, of Standing Rock, and Bingham, of Cheyenne [River], agents for the Indians at the point mentioned, have just started for the camps of the Indians in the hopes of reconciling the dissatisfied Indians in their camp and inducing them to remain here until after the council.

The report circulated by malicious persons and published somewhat extensively to the effect that Captain Andy Burt, of the Ninth Infantry, and who has been acting as special correspondent of the *New York Tribune*, had been under court martial, at Cheyenne on the charge of using his position to detain the *New York Herald*'s correspondence from the Black Hills, to the advantage of the *Tribune*, is without the shadow of foundation, and [I] will gladly correct the slander.

C. C.

[*Omaha Daily Bee*, Thursday, September 23, 1875]

[September 17, 1875 – John T. Bell, from Red Cloud Agency, Nebraska]

Red Cloud Agency

Special Correspondence of *The Herald*

Red Cloud Agency, Neb. [Friday] Sept. 17, 1875

At the conference held by the commission to-day with Two Bears and his fellow chiefs of the Yanktonai, referred to in my letter of yesterday, the latter were informed—in answer to their inquiries as to when and where the council would be held—that they could not then be posted with regard to that matter until later in the day, when a courier would be sent to their camps with the desired information, whereupon they indulged in a general handshaking and a "How Kola" all around, and then mounted their ponies and rattled away across the prairies. These were an unusually fine-looking body of Indians, Two Bears closely resembling [former U.S. President] Andy Johnson in size, build, and general appearance.

Mention has been previously made by this correspondent of the fact that the selection of a council ground had been finally left to a committee consisting of six Indians. This committee skirmished around over the prairies Wednesday, wrangled over the matter all night the following night, and yesterday morning reported to the commission their inability to agree, thereupon the commissioners went out themselves and chose a site for the council a mile nearer Spotted Tail Agency than that they had already selected—making the distance from this point between six and seven miles. Here they will erect two hospital tents with a large fly in front of each, Red Cloud having stated that he will have guarded by a strong force of soldiers whatever tents the commission may wish to set up for council purposes.

It is the intention now to have the council begin to-morrow, and it is to be hoped that nothing may occur to change this intention on the part of the commissioners. Indeed, if there is a further postponement of the duties these officials were sent here to perform, they will have no Indians here to treat with excepting those connected with Red Cloud and Spotted Tail agencies. A number of lodges of Missouri River Indians started home yesterday and it is reported that a great many more will start to-day.

An Indian's idea of values is not a very definite one, and unless the commissioners have instructions from Washington as to the price to be paid for the Black Hills country, and begin the negotiations by making an offer themselves, some wild figures may be expected from the Indians as the price for which they are willing to sell. As few of them possesses sufficient mathematical ability to count a hundred, and financial transactions consist, in the main, of trading ponies for squaws, they cannot be expected to do otherwise than stumble when they come to deal with millions. Recently Dr. Saville proposed to Red Cloud the hiring by the government of a party of his soldiers, or young men, as a guard to the surveyors, who were running out the western boundary of Nebraska, to which proposition Red Cloud assented, whereupon Saville asked him how much a day he would want for his men. After considerable meditation over the inquiry, Red Cloud finally said he thought ten dollars per day, each, would be about right.

Of the $25,000 paid the Sioux last summer for the surrender of their right to hunt in Nebraska, $10,000 of the amount was paid them in wagons, horses, and cows, at their own request.[85] Not long since one of them asked the agent here, when they would get some more wagons and stock from the Great Father on account of this purchase. "You have already received all that is due you," was the reply. At this the Indian expressed great astonishment remarking that he expected at least fifty wagons as his share.

Day before yesterday the paymaster visited Camp Robinson, two miles from this agency, and distributed considerable wealth among the soldiers there stationed. The following night a couple of privates, belonging respectively to companies A and G of the 6th infantry "got up and got," without notifying any of their comrades as to where they proposed going.[86] Yesterday morning a detachment of cavalry started out to hunt them up with very favorable prospects of success. One cannot help sympathizing with the poor devils who have thus made a bold strike for liberty and the comforts of civilization, for a more lonely, desolate country in which to live certainly cannot be found this side of Alaska or the Siberian regions. In fact desertions from that portion of the army compelled to do duty on the plains are quite frequent, and in some instances the soldiers who thus abruptly sever their connection with the military succeed in making their escape, though the chances are strongly against them, owing principally to the openness of the country and the difficulty of procuring food away from the widely scattered settlements.

To-day Maj. [T. H.] Stanton, Capt. Egan and several other officers, together with a cavalry escort start on an expedition to the Bad Lands of Dakota in search of fossils.[87] Someone mentioned the fact as we gathered around our camp fire, whereupon one of our party—a man distinguished in the councils of the nation—exclaimed, "Well they needn't go so far in search of fossils for they can find what they want nearer home; let them just gather up the members of this Indian commission." And I blush for my race when I say that to this heartless and irreverent remark there was not a word of condemnation.

Cold weather is coming upon us, and a camp fire is now a very comfortable institution. This morning there are indications of snow, upon observing which, Maj. Burke, of Standing Rock Agency, remarked that if snow should come upon us now, his Indians would scatter like sheep in their anxiety to get home, as they dread crossing the open country between here and the Missouri River in stormy weather.

A sensible suggestion was made by General Lawrence, one of the commissioners, the other day, in connection with the extraordinary number of speeches it is reported the Indians propose making at the council, which was to the effect that all this might be avoided by the commission announcing at the outset that they could not listen to any but the leading men of the combined tribes, owing to their own exalted position. This proposition could not give offense to the Indians themselves, for if there is any one thing the latter are sticklers in regard to, it is "caste," the "lines" in Indian society being quite as clearly defined as among the whites if not more so, and they would really be highly pleased if the members of the commission should put themselves up on their "dignity" in conducting the negotiations. In one of the informal talks, held a few days since, Red Dog—that personification of conceit and self-importance—remarked, after some of the younger Indians had spoken their little piece, "You needn't write down what the young men say; just write down was is said by me and Red Cloud."

Just as the mail closes Red Cloud has made his appearance in the stockade declaring he would not attend the council if it was not held at this agency. He is a surly, bad-blooded old devil and has caused the commissioners constant trouble ever since their arrival here. Eight years ago he was the head soldier of the Sioux nation, and was the leader of about a thousand Indians who enticed about ninety soldiers out of Fort Phil. Kearny in 1866 and slaughtered them in cold blood. He is not half civilized, even yet, notwithstanding a very forbearing government has "condoned" his numerous and fearful crimes, and for seven years past has been feeding him and his people in the most generous manner, thereby relieving them of all necessity for exertion, besides transporting the old horse thief and murderer to Washington and all through the eastern states several times at enormous expense. It would be an excellent thing for both Indians and whites if a stray bullet should suddenly release the spirit of this vicious old red skin and send him to kingdom come.[88]

However, with regard to this last outbreak on his part, the commissioners say they will go on with the council business to-morrow as though nothing had occurred and if he sees fit to be present, all right, and if not, all right again.

Among the full blooded Indians here who talk English is a joker known to fame as "Old Ribs." As I write he is just telling the boys of a dance and feast he attended last night at which he says he ate two dogs, a pumpkin, a big dish of beans and ditto of corn. He extended a cordial invitation to his auditors to go to camp with him, where he says some of the remnants of the feast were left over, and that he will give them all the cold dog they can eat. This invitation was declined, however, courteously but firmly.

J. T. B.

[*Omaha Daily Herald*, Sunday, September 26, 1875]

[September 17, 1875 – Albert Swalm, from Red Cloud Agency, Nebraska]

The Indian Council

Special Correspondence of *The Chicago Tribune*

Red Cloud Agency, [Friday] Sept. 17, 1875

The commission hold daily sessions in perfecting the preliminary arrangements for the Grand Council, and but for the studied delay of Spotted Tail in failing to agree to a place for holding the council, much of the more important work of the commission would now be well on toward completion. An Indian is the biggest fool alive, measured by the standard of white civilization, and the arguments that would move even the most stubborn Briton fail utterly with such men as Spotted Tail— especially so when they are as smart and shrewd as the variegated caudal just mentioned. The trouble with the Indians has been the bitter jealousy that exists between the Oglalas and Brules—Red Cloud representing the one and Spotted Tail the other. No two political factions of one party could be more so. What the one agrees to the other is certain to object to, and thousands of Indians take up the rumpus just as the mob follows its chief in factional warfare among his whites. Thus, the council having been appointed at Red Cloud, which is the Oglala agency, the Brules oppose, and insist upon having it in the God-forsaken, barren plains near Chadron Creek, and to that end nearly one-half of the Sioux have been working. As has before been noted, Spotted Tail "sweetened" the river Indians with 150 ponies. Then Red Cloud got at them and gave in one lump 180 better ponies, which rather demoralized the efforts of the chief of Indian wire-workers Spotted Tail. The ways of civilization, you see, are fast making a sweep among the children of the plains—just as if some saintly Harlan or Dilworthy Pomeroy had given them lessons in the way of knowing how to "set 'em up."[89] Red Cloud's last gift rather broke Spot's combination, and on Wednesday he came, with a large retinue, to see about it.

After a long pow-wow, in which occurred the usual gush about how he loved the pale-faces, he waked up Red Dog, the Oglala chief, and the orator, par excellence, of the nation, who pinned Spotty down closely, and abruptly capped the climax with the proposition that the council be held at the mouth of Horse Creek, 40 miles below Fort Laramie.[90] Then the proposition of the commission was accepted that Red Cloud, Red Dog, and Young-Man-Afraid-of-his-Horses, for the one faction, and Spotted Tail, Two Strike, and Swift Bear, for the other, act as a conference committee and agree upon the place, it to be near enough to enable the commission to go and come from their present quarters to the ground morning and night. Thus the jabbering war rages, but must come now to a speedy end. It is the intention of the commission, if these chiefs do not agree, that they will set up the council tents at the place chosen, 6 miles east, invite in all who will come, and let the consequences that may arise fall upon those responsible. But there is very little danger of any bands absenting themselves, and one of the fullest councils ever held with the Sioux will occur.

Gen. Bradley, commanding the district, has made ample arrangements for the protection of the party. A guard of 100 cavalry, under the command of Capt. Egan, will attend daily. It is not considered dangerous, as the temper of the Indians never was better. If any of their bad young men are determined on having a crack at any of the commission, the whole of the army would be no protection. In case of trouble, Capt. Egan's cavalry, armed as they are with the best guns in the world, and kept well in hand, will be sufficient protection until the six companies at Camp Robinson can be brought on, with a battery of Gatling guns to aid them. The scalps of all are safe, save from the hand of the assassin.

The first meeting of the Indians and whites in general concert is set for Saturday morning at 10 o'clock. Nothing more will be done save to exchange compliments and generally mention the matter of business. It may be settled in a few days and it may take several weeks—the character of the red man is past finding out. They do not propose to have any mistakes occur, as they claim was the case with the treaty of 1868. Their prices will be exorbitant at first—that is the order of the Ring to its understrappers—and the Indian will have to be brought away from that point in council. Only that price what fair judgment will freely give will be paid, especially so since Gen. Terry thinks that a force of 800 men will effectually seal up the Hills to all encroachments from the whites. As I have previously intimated, the commission construe their instructions so as to not interfere with the general features of the Treaty of 1868, and take as their task the purchase of the Hills and the hunting-right of the Indians to the Big Horn Country. Anything else will be entirely subsidiary to these main propositions. This was not in accordance with the plan of the Ring, but its plans are not favored by the commission.

Yesterday the Oglalas gave a grand "Omaha Dance." In this dance many of the warriors appeared almost naked, and painted to a degree of hideousness that was startling. In this dance warriors display the scalps and other trophies of warfare, not excepting the bridles or tufts of the manes of horses stolen. They also relate their exploits, with sufficient exaggeration to make them very big men. It was a disgusting show, and ended only with the giving of rations to the bedaubed beggars. The squaws gave a similar performance in the morning, at which some magnificent costumes of bead-work were seen, made out of the whitest fawn-skins tanned. Some old women, above 80, kept up the noise and stiff-legged jump for hours.

Yesterday I saw and examined a highly-ornamented robe worn by a buck, the fringe of which was composed entirely of white women's hair, wavy, soft, and silken black, brown and auburn in its shades. Most of it came from the massacre of some emigrant families south of this a few years ago, the men having gone after antelope, leaving the train at the mercy of the savages. When the men returned—and they were absent only two hours—they found their women outraged and killed, and some of the children also. Some were carried off, but being hard pressed, they abandoned them to death by exposure. Another noble red man sports a necklace made of the nails and ends of fingers of whites killed. Nice, ain't it? Then Little Big Man, one of the wild northern chaps, the murderer of three Crow women and children, six in all, at one time, goes whistling about camp with a whistle made out of one of the bones of the forearm of a white woman killed in 1868. Another one has shown me a bunch of scalps taken from men killed while the Union Pacific was building, but he assures me that he loves the white man now very much, and we shook hands on it. This is a sample of the cases that could be cited in proof of the amiability, kindheartedness and all that sort of thing of the gentle individual now fed by the paternal government. A better day is dawning, thank God, and we can only hope for its more rapid dawn.

The personnel of the Sioux Indian Treaty Commission is certainly of a very excellent grade, and if chosen in the expectancy that the Indian Ring would find in them an aid to their schemes of plunder, by providing for an abominable treaty, a great mistake, fortunately for the people, has been made. The chairman, the Hon. W. B. Allison, of Iowa, is a man well known in American politics as one of steady growth and much promise. He represented the Third Iowa District in the Thirty-eighth, Thirty-ninth, and Fortieth Congresses, and took high rank as a hard thinker and practical worker, being an active member of the Ways and Means Committee. The late ex-Secretary Chase relied much upon him, and the most confidential relations existed between them. He was chosen senator from Iowa, after a long and very hotly-contested struggle with the clans of Harlan in 1862 [1872], and his time expires in 1879. [91] In the work of the commission his previous training evinces itself in the practical manner in which matters are presented and moved along. The trip and delaying work here, while removing him entirely from the campaign in Iowa for this year, gives him a fine opportunity to see how the Ring manages its robberies, and how best, as chairman of the Senate Indian-Affairs Committee, he can move measures of check and reform. In Senator Allison, during the next session, the Ring will find one of the most troublesome men in Congress, for he will have the advantage of having been an observer on the field where the grossest mismanagement has prevailed. There is hard luck ahead for those Indian patriots whose hearts throb with philanthropy for poor Lo, but whose hands reach out for the fat of the contracts. So let it be!

Another member of the commission who has had congressional experience is the Hon. Abram Comingo, of Missouri, who represented the Seventh and Eighth Missouri Districts in the Forty-second and Forty-third Congresses. He is 56 years old, and a man of practical common sense, with no inclination to do anything out of the way of honesty. His inactive patronymic must not be misconstrued, for he is a thorough Gough in his temperance practice, save when the mornings here are cold and frosty.[92] He resides at Independence, Mo., is a lawyer by profession, was a Union man during the whole of the late trouble, notwithstanding he owned slaves at the commencement. Born as he was, in Kentucky, he is well skilled in the game called "seven-up," a game which, of course, no *Tribune* correspondent understands, belonging as it does to the weak and wrecked elements of a vain world. But a jollier, more companionable gentleman is very hard to discover than the aforesaid Comingo.

Brigadier-General A. H. Terry, at the outbreak of the war, was a lawyer of high standing at New Haven, Conn. He entered the volunteer service, and won by meritorious service the promotion to major general. He commanded the expedition that captured Fort Fisher—one of the most brilliant engagements of the war. He ranks high as an officer, and his acquaintance with Indian matters and character make him an invaluable man for this work. To his acquaintance with these matters can be added an unspotted personal character, his good judgment as a lawyer, and the matter-of-fact way he has of doing things. He was a member of the commission of 1868 that gave us the treaty.

In the Fort Fisher engagement a brave young officer, then on Gen. Ames' staff, was wounded five times—in both arms, throat, and shoulder, causing the amputation of the left arm, and injuring his speech to a degree sometimes unpleasant. The officer was the present Gen. A. G. Lawrence, of Newport, R. I., member of the commission; and his meeting with the distinguished general [Terry] under whose orders he advanced to his mutilation, is the means of recalling many of the more pleasant reminiscences of the war. Gen. Lawrence was brevetted four times for bravery on the field, while on staff duty with Stahl, Martindale, W. F. Smith, and Ames.[93] He is a son of William Beach Lawrence, the eminent lawyer of New York, and author of a standard work on international law. Gen. L. is a student from the office of David Dudley Field, but has given only limited attention to his profession.[94] A graduate of Harvard, including its law department, with ten years' service as an attaché of the American Legation at Vienna, and Minister Resident, 1867-68 at Cost Rica, he is, of course, an intelligent man, and fills his position with great credit. He is not an enthusiast on the Black Hills question, and will favor only that which is fair for the people—the poor whites of the Ring are not in favor with the soldier Lawrence.[95]

Capt. W. H. Ashby, of Nebraska, is a fair representative of that class of western men, who are young in years, but endowed with an energy and go-ahead-ativeness that generally "knocks the persimmons" when it goes for the bush. Capt. Ashby was on the wrong side during the war, and carries five wounds as a certificate of that fact. He is most thoroughly reconstructed now, and is one of the strong men of the commission. He is quick to see into the movements of the Ringites, and as quick to act, in all cases, to their upsetting. The present opportunity of seeing the Indian elephant is not wasted, and the time will come when he will use his ammunition with good effect. The game is plenty, and as Ashby is a good shot, with either a gun or pen, the prospect of finding scalps in his tepee is promising. But few young men in his state stand as strong as he in the good will of the people, and his standing has been gained deservedly by his action as a citizen and a worker in politics.

Col. G. P. Beauvais, of St. Louis, is the farther [father?] in years of the commission, measuring them by sixty summers, for the winter of time has touched him but lightly. He is an old Indian trader, having entered the service of the American Fur Company as early as 1833, continuing in their employ for twenty years, when, in 1853, he started out on his own venture. He speaks fluently—English, French, Spanish, Mexican, Sioux, and the sign language of the Plains Indians. He was in the Black Hills country as early as 1842, and in his long career has bought over 200,000 buffalo robes, besides at least one half that number of other furs. His experiences with the tribes in those early days are interesting to a high degree, and furnish the groundwork for a volume hardly to be excelled in its line. Col. Beauvais is of French extraction, purely, well educated, and known by thousands of the Indians, who gave him the title of "Big Belly," on account of that rotundity so well becoming the reputable years of 60. His acquaintance with the Indians is a valuable aid to the work in hand, and his sound business knowledge forbids any extravagant notions about the proposed purchase. He was one of the 1868 commission.

The Rev. Samuel D. Hinman, the missionary among the Santee Sioux for the past fifteen years, has done a work in that line that is creditable in the highest degree. When he first went to his work he found the Indians very far from being pet lambs, as the New Ulm massacre in Minnesota proved. After the war and the transfer of the Santees to Dakota, 30 miles above Yankton, and on the Missouri River, effective work commenced. The tribe was one of the wildest, now they own their land—each man having 80 acres; the Indians all live in comfortable houses, built by themselves. They pay by labor for all the aid they receive from the government. Three Episcopal Churches and one Congregational Church have been built, and are all well attended. The pulpits of two of the first named are filled by native preachers. Boarding-schools for both sexes have been built and successfully operated, together with day schools. Isolation of the children from their parents is necessary to the success of educational efforts. It was found that, unless the women were made to learn the ways of civilized housekeeping, the progress of the men was delayed to a great degree, hence the Indian girls are trained in all the work that appertains to the home, and the girls are in great demand. Where they go you find decently-kept homes. The marriage relation is sacredly respected; all marriages are solemnized in church; many of these men will assume the rights of full citizenship soon; they do good farming; are honest, and all in all the Santees are the witnesses of the most successful effort at Indian civilization we can show. And the credit of this belongs to the efforts and works of Mr. Hinman—surely a monument that will prove as lasting as it is honorable. All the Sioux know him more or less, and "Hina-man" is very much in demand at commission headquarters of the Indians. Connected with nearly all the commissions that have treated with the Sioux for the last decade, he has always proven himself the friend of the Indian, and a competent, worthy personage at all times.[96]

John S. Collins, secretary, is one of the young and enterprising businessmen of Omaha, where he is engaged in a large business with his brothers. About three years ago he was appointed by the President as post warden [trader] at Fort Laramie, which position he now holds. In an early day the fathers of President Grant and Mr. Collins were engaged in the leather business together at Galena, Ill.—hence there has arisen from boyhood a personal friendship between "the boys." The President and Mr. Collins made a joint visit to the polls in 1860, casting their first ballots together for Stephen A. Douglas for President. Mr. C. was one of the first to call the President's attention to the Black Hills complication, and was designated by him to discover the temper of the Indians touching their sale, and has been active in the work of getting them into council from the first, being one of the party of commissioners—Messrs. Comingo, Ashby, and Hinman—that went through the Indian country during the summer, securing the attendance of the entire nation, save the warlike bands under Sitting Bull of the North.

Robert B. Lines, of Washington, D. C., is stenographer of the outfit, and was one of the commissioners of last year, securing the hunting right from the Indians south of the Platte.[97]

[Unsigned]

[*Chicago Daily Tribune*, Saturday, September 25, 1875]

[September 17, 1875 – "Mart," from Red Cloud Agency, Nebraska]
Red Cloud Letter
From our own Correspondent, Red Cloud, [Friday] Sept. 17, 1875
Editor *Nebraskian*

I informed you in my letter last week that the question of location as to where the council should be held was under discussion with no apparent signs of a conclusion being reached for some time. I am glad to say that the commissioners finally saw the necessity of being firm with the naturally obstinate reds, and told them emphatically that a certain point was determined upon, and that unless the Indians agreed to it, and that right off, no council would be held at all. This had the desired effect of bringing Old Spot and the other mulish chiefs to time, and White Clay, six miles northeast of here, was agreed upon as the ground which should become historic from having been the scene of the greatest pow-wow ever held on this continent. And truly it is an important affair. There is no longer any doubt as to the vast gold deposits in the Black Hills, and the eye of the entire country is upon them; and thousands of intelligent and enterprising men are waiting with chafing impatience for the doors to the Ophir of the western world to swing back and let them in. When the obstacle in their way is fully removed, it is confidently believed the rush to the new mines will be without a precedent, so immense will it be. The Indians seem to have an approximate idea of the real interest at stake, and are disposed to act very independently, and some of them very insolently, and the graver and more dignified nod their heads and grunt very significantly when a price for the hills is broached. They have not allowed themselves to canvass that feature of the business in hand to any considerable extent. But have gone far enough to foreshadow something of what will be the cost of gold and merchandise to Uncle Samuel in order to possess from his children this coveted country. Some of the leading men have said that probably six millions in ready cash, a suit of clothes for each Indian having a finger in the pie, and a well assured annuity for said Indians during a period of eighty years. This sounds pretty big and would no doubt be considered decidedly cheeky coming from any other source than from an Indian chief. Having set their hearts upon a price, it will in all probability be found almost impossible to induce them to change. However, nothing definite can be stated until the council gets on further into the work of unraveling this somewhat complex problem.

The clearer headed chiefs astonish us with cool philosophy about the extermination of their race. They talk about it as deliberately and as intelligently as if inspired by the Fates. The idea is fixed in their minds so firmly that they can even locate the time when it will have been consummated. They therefore say that they want a guaranteed annuity sufficient to meet their actual necessities of food and clothing for eighty years against which time their national cake will be dough.

We are having the most beautiful weather, and the commissioners and correspondents, and visitors enjoy it, the only drawback to the sublimest contentment being the delay, and a painful rumor that a Cheyenne brave had taken an oath before the gods that he would take the life of a commissioner. The name of the highly romantic savage is not known, but the chiefs have promised to find out the young man and dissuade him from his tragic purpose. Quite a sensation was produced by this rumor; and it is highly amusing to observe how exceeding cautious the commissioners are in the "goings out and comings in." I do not blame them at all; for, a senator's life, a doctor of divinity's scalp, a political demagogue's blood, or an editor's carcass are not things to be fooled away on the caprice of a stinking Indian. Yet, I do not anticipate that we shall be called upon to attend the funeral of any of these dignitaries from that cause. Rather it is possible that some one of the commissioners will die of over-eating, so extraordinary have become their appetites under the stimulus of this sort of life in so salubrious a climate.

The attaches of this post are large-hearted and courteous men, and have allowed no opportunity to pass unimproved to render our sojourn most enjoyable. We shall not forget the kindnesses of Agent Saville, and post trader J. W. Dear. One thing cannot be disputed—however much may be said to the disparagement of Indian agents and Indian traders on account of their supposed money making proclivities—and that is, they are unstinted in their generous hospitalities. Visitors and all are treated with the utmost civility, and entertained in the very best manner possible under the circumstances.

It is hard to say just how long the work in hand will occupy the attention of the council, but we shall keep you posted as fully as possible.
Mart
[North Platte *Western Nebraskian*, Saturday, September 25, 1875]

[September 17, 1875 – "D" (John W. Dear?), from Red Cloud Agency, Nebraska]

Special to the *Leader*
Red Cloud Agency
[Friday] Sept. 17th, 1875

We are still upon the ragged edge of uncertainty in relation to a successful termination of the Indian council. The Indians have been pulling against each other in reference to the place of holding it. Red Cloud wants it here, and Spotted Tail wants it held on Chadron Creek about half way between the two agencies. Yesterday the commissioners selected council grounds near the mouth of White Clay River, about six miles from this agency; and it is now expected that the council will begin to-morrow (Saturday) morning; and that it will continue for a week or ten days.

The Indians seem to be well disposed towards treating for the sale of the desired country, and it looks now as if the success of the negotiations depended entirely upon the commission and the temper, firmness and fairness with which they make their propositions. Those best acquainted with the Indians do not agree in opinion as to the probable result of the negotiations; but the general opinion is that success or failure rests entirely with the commission.

Delegations are present from the following agencies on or near the Missouri River: Cheyenne River, Standing Rock, Santee, Camp Thompson, or Crow Creek, Yankton, Lower Brule. The two agencies of Red Cloud and Spotted Tail are well represented, as are many of the Sioux bands in the Powder River country. The Cheyennes and Arapahoe tribes are also represented. It is estimated that there are now within fifteen miles of this agency from 20,000 to 25,000 Indians encamped. The Missouri River Indians are anxious to have the council proceeded with speedily, in order that they may return home before the bad weather sets in.

Maj. Stanton left this morning for the military post at Spotted Tail.

D.

[*Cheyenne Daily Leader*, Wednesday, September 22, 1875]

[September 18, 1875 – John T. Bell, from Red Cloud Agency, Nebraska]

From Red Cloud

From Our Special Correspondent

Red Cloud Agency, Neb., [Saturday] Sept. 18 1875

To the Editor of *The Herald*

Those who desire to reach the Black Hills country via Red Cloud and Spotted Tail agencies—and the majority will go by the way of those points for some time to come, doubtless—will do well to leave the Union Pacific at Sidney instead of Cheyenne. The distance between these stations is about one hundred miles and as Spotted Tail is almost due north of Sidney, it is quite evident that in reaching the former, via Cheyenne, that a hundred miles is traveled over twice. In addition to the advantage of having a shorter route by leaving the railroad at Sidney, the fifty miles of sand between the Platte River and the Niobrara, which he is compelled to travel over if he takes the Cheyenne route, the Sidney route being first-class, with a saving in distance of at least forty-five miles between Sidney and Spotted Tail. The fact that Cheyenne is the junction of the Union Pacific and Kansas Pacific, and that at that point are located the government depots of supplies for the various posts and agencies of this country has given it an undue prominence as an outfitting point. By examination of the map it can readily be seen that Sidney is much nearer Red Cloud and Spotted Tail than is Cheyenne, and when it is known that the road is a superior one in every respect, it will certainly become the popular route for the roads in this country, but the Sidney route had facilities equal to any other in that respect.

Mr. Will Dear, erstwhile of Omaha, where he was connected with the well-known establishment of Megath, Whitney & Co., is trader at this point and is one of the most popular men in this country. He keeps a fine stock of goods which he disposes of at moderate figures for this country, and entertains the passing trader at his restaurant with a bill of fare which would do credit to a first class hotel. His treatment of our party has been of such a character during our stay at Red Cloud as to make a warm personal friend of every member thereof.

"You don't seem to recognize me," remarked a man connected with the Red Cloud Agency the other night after indulging in some general conversation with the occupants of the tent set apart for the use of the newspaper scribes accompanying the commission.

"Well, no, I do not, though I know I've seen you somewhere," responded the party addressed.

"I'm the man that killed a nigger at Sioux City about two years ago," explained the other. And so he was. At the time of its occurrence the killing had created considerable excitement but as the trial disclosed the fact that the negro was the aggressor, being armed with a revolver and on the search for the man in question with the avowed intention of taking his life at the time he met his own death, the white man was promptly acquitted by the jury trying the case, and upon being released, he drifted out to this country where he has resided ever since.

The Indians here are well supplied with horses, especially the Sioux. I am told that each head of a family has some fifty to sixty, while Old-Man-Afraid-of-his-Horses is the owner in fee simple of one hundred head. There is no demand for stock of this kind here and in addition to the natural increase, the Indian adds to his equine wealth as the average office-holder increased his possessions, i.e. by stealing. Then, too, the matrimonial business enlarges his herd of ponies in case he is fortunate enough to number several daughters among his household, as they are always disposed of at so many ponies per head. Old Spot has two marriageable daughters at this time upon each of whom he places what is considered in this country a pretty steep value as he will not let either marry unless he is given twenty horses as a sort of compensation for the tender solicitude and fatherly care he has bestowed upon her. Unless he reduces his price, it is quite probable that he will be under the necessity of providing his daughters with the odds and ends so dear to the feminine heart, for some time to come yet, as a very good article in the squaw line can be purchased for from four to eight horses. While on this tender and sentimental subject, I will remark that the squaw men whom several Indian agents endeavored to drive from their respective agencies, are likely to remain. In fact the majority of white men living in this country, outside of the military, are married to squaws, and in several instances are raising families in which the copper color predominates. As one marries the whole family in marrying a squaw, it is rather an expensive and troublesome business, but then there is nothing like getting used to a thing. Yesterday I was present when a white man connected with this agency was talking to a good looking half breed woman in her native tongue and [I] took occasion to observe that she was rather handsome, to which remark he gruntingly assented. I learned afterwards that the woman was his wife.

A lazy life is that led by the attaches of these agencies, equaled only by that of the Indians themselves. An hour ago one of them remarked that all he cared to do was to lean against a wall and think, "And I'm not willing to do that much," responded an honest by-stander, "for to do that requires something of an exertion."

In refreshing contrast to this inertia is the wonderful vitality of Collins of the Sioux City Times—otherwise the "Wild Irishman"—who occupies a tent with *The Herald* man, and who at this moment is wandering about among the tents explaining that he wants a drink of water, but is glad he can't find one as his failure to get it furnished him something to do—gave him an object in life.

The Indians here have nothing to "swap," generally speaking, with the exception of the skins taken from the beeves issued by the agents and which they killed themselves. These they usually sell for about three dollars each, to the post traders, taking the amount in trade. There is game to be found in considerable quantities in certain localities over which these Indians roam, but they are so infernally lazy that they will not go out and shoot it, the rations issued by our confiding and badly victimized Uncle Sam being quite enough to support them.

There has been nothing said in this letter thus far regarding the grand council, for the reason that there has been nothing to say. Major Bingham, of Cheyenne Agency, Major Howard, of Spotted Tail, and Major Burke, of Standing Rock, all went out to Spotted Tail yesterday and are not expected back until the last of the week. Meanwhile the commission is "waiting for something to turn up."

J. T. B.

[*Omaha Daily Herald*, Wednesday, September 22, 1875]

[September 18, 1875 – Capt. Andrew S. Burt, from Red Cloud Agency, Nebraska]

The Black Hills

(By Telegraph to *The Tribune*)

Red Cloud Agency, [Saturday] Sept. 18, via Fort Laramie, Sept. 20

The place of holding the Grand Council has been changed four times, also the day of opening. It seems finally arranged at last for Monday, six miles from here, on White River. Red Cloud, at the head of the Oglala band, has been the disturbing element. They became reconciled through the leadership of Red Dog and Young Man Afraid of his Horses. Gens. Terry and Bradley arrived Wednesday. Their counsels seem to have decided that a military force shall be present at the treaty. This will be explained to the Indians, if the question comes up, by saying that the general and his companion have a right to a guard of escort and a camp. The guard will be Col. Mills's company of the 3d Cavalry, Capt. Egan's of the 2d Cavalry, and Lieut. [James M.] Stembell with a guard from the 9th Infantry.[98]

[Unsigned]

[*New York Tribune*, September 21, 1875]

[September 19, 1875 – Charles Collins, from Red Cloud Agency, Nebraska]

West

(By Special Courier)

Red Cloud Agency, [Sunday] Sept. 19, via Fort Laramie, Sept. 21

The council that was to have met Saturday was postponed until to-morrow. The council ground is eight miles east of here. Ten of the Missouri River Indians are greatly dissatisfied. Two parties of Black Hillers, one of them of Sioux City, were captured and brought here yesterday. They say the weather is cold in the hills, and that troops are scouring the hills for miners. Outlook indicates no treaty, as the Indians are led to believe they can get whatever they ask, through vacillation and lack of Indian character displayed by the commissioners.

Mr. Bell, of the *Herald*, returns to Omaha to-morrow.

Gen. Terry says they will make a treaty in one week, but the Indians have an exaggerated idea of what the government will do—some say $50,000,000.

The weather is cold, and many distant Indians are leaving.
Charles Collins
[*Omaha Daily Bee*, Wednesday, September 22, 1875]

[September 19, 1875 – Reuben Davenport, from Red Cloud Agency, Nebraska]

Preparations for the Great Talk
Red Cloud Agency, [Sunday] Sept. 19, 1875, via Fort Laramie, Wy., Sept. 21, 1875

Blue Horse, of the Bad Faces, came to-day to tell the commission that Crazy Horse was on his way to the council, but it is hardly believed. The Kiyuksas held a council all last night, and there was much discord. It is feared that the agreement of yesterday will fall through. I visited Red Cloud's and Man-Afraid-Of-His-Horses villages to-day. There has been a big feast, and a council was in session. To-day the commission divided on the main question of the value of the hills. The minority wish to pay the Indians annually for a stated time only the amount of the present yearly appropriation for the Sioux. The majority would be more generous. Allison, Hinman, Beauvais, and Terry are in the majority.

The valley is whitened by lodges. Red Cloud on Thursday came to pay a visit to your correspondent, and with much dignity demanded compensation from him for his invasion of the Black Hills and sojourn there during the summer. He granted time for deliberation to the correspondent. An attempt was made on Saturday to issue poor tobacco to the Missouri River Indians but they would not accept it. The commission will take samples east as evidence of fraud.
[Unsigned]
[*New York Herald*, Wednesday, September 22, 1875]

---

[1] The *Fort Dodge Messenger* on Oct. 28, 1875, noted Swalm's return from the council. "During his absence Mr. S. was commissioned as the special correspondent of the *Chicago Tribune* and a portion of the time for the *New York Tribune*—sufficient work to keep him busy when not engaged in his clerical duties." At least four identical letters from the council appeared in both papers, though with different publication dates.

[2] The "cut-off" was the more direct route leading northeastward from Cheyenne that passed near the modern Wyoming localities of La Grange and Hawk Springs to the site of the Old Red Cloud Agency on the North Platte River just west of the Wyoming-Nebraska state line. The commissioners followed the

longer route via Fort Laramie, which was the same route the sub-commission used to reach Red Cloud Agency earlier that summer.

[3] Evan Howe and J. T. Allison were relatives of Senators Howe and Allison and were probably serving as their aides. Porter was probably James R. Porter, who had engaged in overland freighting from Plattsmouth, Nebraska, during the 1860s. He was said to have been at Fort Phil Kearny during the Wagon Box fight of 1867, where Porter apparently had contracts to supply the fort. He lived in Omaha during the 1870s and settled at Haigler, Nebraska, in the early 1880s, where he died Mar. 5, 1911. Lincoln, *Nebraska State Journal*, Mar. 12, 1911; Benkelman, Nebraska, *News-Chronicle*, Mar. 10, 1911. Porter's role with respect to the 1875 commission is unknown.

[4] William M. Ward was a liveryman and promoter who later became superintendent of the northern division of the Cheyenne to Deadwood stage line after the Black Hills were opened. Spring, *Cheyenne-Black Hills Stage Routes*, 249.

[5] During his testimony before the Red Cloud Agency investigating commission, Snyder said he had been driving Texas cattle north since 1868. By the mid-1870s his trail herds averaged two thousand head. Cattlemen such as Snyder preferred to sell their cattle to other parties holding the beef contracts for Indian agencies. This was partly so "we can go back to Texas and invest in more cattle." Another reason was that Snyder once had an Indian agency contract and never got paid when the government appropriation ran out. *Report of the Special Commission* 3:577-80.

[6] Although a stockyard was established at Omaha in 1878, it soon moved across the Missouri River to Council Bluffs. The Union Stockyards Company at Omaha was eventually established in 1883.

[7] James M. Pattee operated lotteries in Omaha in 1872 and 1873 before the city council put a stop to them. He then moved to Laramie and began a similar scam in March 1875 under Wyoming's liberal lottery law, flooding the nation with circulars advertising tickets for a dollar and promising monthly drawings for a first prize of fifty thousand dollars. The profits realized by the Laramie newspapers for printing the circulars stifled any interest they may have had had in crusading against the scheme. No drawings were ever held, and Congress in 1876 made it a felony to use the U.S. mails to swindle the public. Woods, *Wyoming Biographies*, 150-51; T. A. Larson, *History of Wyoming*, 2d ed. (Lincoln: University of Nebraska Press, 1978), 115-16

[8] The masthead of the *Cheyenne Daily News*, Jan. 20, 1875, lists William E. Benton and T. Joe. Fisher as owners.

[9] Stull had just returned to his job as the *Herald*'s city editor after covering the travels of the sub-commission.

[10] Thomas Sturgis came to Wyoming in 1872 and partnered with William C. Lane in the cattle business. Sturgis later became secretary of the Wyoming Stock Growers Association and also had interests in mining, banking, and railroads. Woods, *Wyoming Biographies*, 177-78.

[11] George Woodruff was the man indicted for the murder of John Freel. *Cheyenne Daily Leader*, May 27, 1875. J. H. Triggs, *History of Cheyenne and Northern Wyoming . . .* (Omaha: Herald Publishing House, 1876), lists the ranch of "J. Friel & Bro." on Horse Creek.

[12] Edward and John Creighton's extensive open- range ranch was in the vicinity of the range of bluffs in present western Nebraska comprising Scotts Bluff and the Wildcat Hills lying to the south. The unidentified "butte" where the "main camp" was located must have been one of the several prominent bluffs in the vicinity.

[13] For Old Red Cloud Agency and Nick Janis, see Pt. 1, n.27.

[14] Philadelphia merchant William Welsh had formerly headed the civilian Board of Indian Commissions. He was highly critical of the government's Indian policy. Olson, *Red Cloud*, 105n, 191.

[15] The noted landmark lies just southeast of the town of Crawford and the sites of Red Cloud Agency and modern Fort Robinson State Park. For its history, see "The Battle of Crow Butte" issue of the *Museum of the Fur Trade Quarterly* previously cited.

[16] The "range" is the Pine Ridge escarpment in northwestern Nebraska below which, to the north, lies the White River valley.

[17] U.S. Senator Timothy O. Howe of Wisconsin had been reassigned to serve on the Red Cloud Agency Investigating Commission, chaired by former Missouri governor Thomas C. Fletcher. Olson, *Red Cloud*, 190.

[18] The 1868 Fort Laramie Treaty provided that each Indian over the age of four was to receive one pound of meat and one pound of flour daily for four years, although the government was continuing to supply rations as Collins notes.

[19] Appleton was Saville's nephew, the son of Saville's brother-in-law Amos Appleton. It was a Miniconjou from one of the non-agency bands that mortally wounded Appleton on Feb. 9, 1874. Buecker, *Fort Robinson and the American West*, 6-7, 213n22. Bray, *Crazy Horse*, 175, identifies him as Kicking Bear, a cousin to Crazy Horse.

[20] Rowland, a Kentucky native, had a long career on the frontier. Married to a Cheyenne woman, he was a principal interpreter for the Cheyenne and Arapaho. William Garnett credited Rowland as being one of the best "sign talkers," who provided much information to William Philo Clark for the latter's book on Indian sign language. He was said to have died Oct. 6, 1906, on the North-

ern Cheyenne Reservation at Lame Deer, Montana. Jensen, ed., *Voices of the American West: The Indian Interviews*, 104, 391n.42. Garnett, the offspring of army officer Richard Garnett, stationed at Fort Laramie before the Civil War, and a Lakota woman, served both as an interpreter and army scout. He was among the keenest observers and most reliable informants of events connected with Red Cloud Agency and the Sioux War of 1876-77. An interview with Garnett by E. S. Ricker appears in Jensen, cited above.

[21] For the establishment of Camp Robinson, see Buecker, *Fort Robinson and the American West*. 62, which notes that the post hospital was completed in November 1875.

[22] These officers' quarters, built of adobe brick and covered with wooden siding, still stand at Fort Robinson State Park and are now used as tourist cabins. They are the only remaining original buildings from Camp Robinson's early years.

[23] An Oglala, one of the so-called "Laramie Loafers" who went to Washington, D. C. with the Red Cloud delegation in 1872. Olson, *Red Cloud*, 37, 150.

[24] This group of buttes lying just to the north and west of the sites of Red Cloud Agency and Camp Robinson are known today as the "Red Cloud Buttes."

[25] Camp Transfer was in today's Wyoming, southeast of Inyan Kara mountain. Kime, *Black Hills Journals*, map, 242-43. Burt and Davenport left there on Sept. 3.

[26] He means dances and ceremonies by specific Lakota warrior societies. See Bray, *Crazy Horse*, 433n17.

[27] The Bad Faces were a band of the Oglala. Many of the Bad Faces had followed Red Cloud in adopting agency life, while others had allied with the non-agency groups.

[28] A Brulé from Spotted Tail Agency and a prominent *akicita* (warrior policeman). Personal communication from Kingsley M. Bray.

[29] Carrington's Eighteenth U.S. Infantry constructed Fort Phil Kearny at the base of the Bighorn Mountains in 1866 to guard the Bozeman Trail to the Montana gold mines.

[30] Edward P. Smith, a minister and former agent to the Chippewa, served as commissioner of Indian affairs from 1873 to 1875. Olson, *Red Cloud*, 156, 248.

[31] Referring to the Indians' recent cession of the right to hunt in Nebraska that was authorized by the 1868 Fort Laramie Treaty. Burt's "present reservation" means the two Nebraska agencies, which were not on the actual reservation as defined by the treaty.

[32] Probably James Fenimore Cooper, whose novels reference Indian "hunting grounds."

[33] Gore was an English "sportsman" who spent two years laying waste to western game in 1854-55. Dan Thrapp, *Encyclopedia of Frontier Biography*, 3 vols. (Lincoln: University of Nebraska Press, 1991) 2:574.

[34] Buffalo were scarce in the Lakota Powder River domain in 1874 and only marginally more abundant in 1875, enhancing the attraction of agency rations. Bray, *Crazy Horse*, 178, 184. The Pumpkin Buttes are near the historic Bozeman Trail and southwest of present Wright, Wyoming.

[35] After the Ute concluded a treaty with the government in 1868 establishing their reservation in Colorado, gold was discovered within its boundaries and miners flooded in. As with the Fort Laramie Treaty with the Lakota, the government was supposed to keep the miners out. Instead, President Grant sent Felix Brunot, chairman of the Board of Indian Commissioners, to make a new agreement with the Ute. Although Ute Chief Ouray did not want to surrender reservation land, he was convinced that it was futile to resist the government. In 1873 he signed the Brunot Agreement ceding about a quarter of the 1868 reservation (ca. 6,000 sq. miles). J. Donald Hughes, *American Indians in Colorado*, 2d ed. (Boulder, CO: Pruett Publishing Co., 1987), 64-65.

[36] Capt. Peter D. Vroom. Heitman, *Historical Register*, 990.

[37] Certainly there were not that many warriors, if even that many Indians altogether, including men, women, and children.

[38] Gen. Edward R. S. Canby was killed by Modoc Indians in California on Apr. 11, 1873, during a negotiating session to end the so-called "Modoc War." Thrapp, *Encyclopedia of Frontier Biography*, 1:219.

[39] Joseph Agonito, "Young Man Afraid of His Horses: The Reservation Years," *Nebraska History* 79 (Fall 1998): 116, calculated that Young Man Afraid was born in 1836, making him about thirty-eight at the time of the council. He died in 1893 at age fifty-six.

[40] It should not be forgotten that earlier the sub-commission had given Spotted Tail and others the distinct impression that Chadron Creek was the preferred council site.

[41] The Red Cloud Agency Investigating Commission concluded that agency freighting contractor Dwight J. McCann was guilty of fraud and recommended his removal. He continued in his position for more than two years, however, before being convicted of stealing supplies for the Crows and Blackfeet on another contract. His conviction on this charge was set aside during a retrial in 1880. Olson, *Red Cloud*, 195, 197.

[42] During his testimony for the Red Cloud Agency investigating commission, Texas cattleman Seth Mabry described "scalawags" as cattle that "had lived their time out and got old and rough, they do not get fat at all, they are raw-boned, big, ugly steers."*Report of the Special Commission*, 2:528.

[43] Henry Newton was the assistant geologist with the Black Hills expedition of 1875. Kime, *Black Hills Journals*, 49n45.

[44] As Watson Parker notes, the gold rush of 1875 to 1877 relied upon placer mining, which could be done by hand labor. Extracting gold from hard rock ores required capital and equipment to make it pay. Gold continued to be mined in the Black Hills to varying degrees until 2001, when the Homestake Mine at Lead shut down. Since 1877 when the government took the Black Hills from the Sioux Reservation, ranching, logging, and tourism have been more significant to the region's economy than gold mining. *Gold in the Black Hills*, ix-xi, 200-2.

[45] At about this time Capt. Edwin Pollack, Co. E, Ninth U.S. Infantry, commanded Camp Collins, a temporary post near Custer City in the Black Hills. His assignment was to arrest miners entering the hills illegally. Pollack's troops were withdrawn and the post abandoned in mid-November 1875 when the government stopped enforcing the ban on whites entering the region. Parker, *Gold in the Black Hills*, 70-71.The Sioux City Transportation Company had organized several wagon trains bound for the Black Hills, one of which led by Fred Evans and John Gordon was halted by the army on the Niobrara River near present Gordon, Nebraska, in May 1875, the members arrested, and the wagons burned. Gordon was later granted a writ of habeas corpus and released on grounds that the army had exceeded its authority because the party had been in Nebraska and not on the Sioux Reservation. Ibid., 36.

[46] J. D. Terrill was head of the Indian division in the second comptroller's office, U.S. Department of the Treasury. Ben: Perley Poore, comp., *Congressional Directory*, 3d ed., 47th Cong., 1st sess. (Washington, DC: GPO, 1882), 110.

[47] Capt. Azor H. Nickerson, Twenty-third U.S. Infantry, and 2d Lt. John G. Bourke, Third U.S. Cavalry. Kime, *Black Hills Journals*, 42n29.

[48] John G. Bourke, in "The Medicine Men of the Apache," *Ninth Annual Report of the Bureau of American Ethnology, 1887-88*, (Washington, DC: Smithsonian Institution, 1892), 480-82 and Plate IV, discussed and illustrated a necklace of human fingers captured in the army's Nov. 25, 1876, attack on Dull Knife's Cheyenne village. The necklace belonged to High [or Tall] Wolf, who tried to reclaim it after his 1877 surrender at Red Cloud Agency. The necklace Bell describes here evidently consisted of finger bones only, unlike the High Wolf necklace, on which the fingers themselves had been preserved.

[49] The reference is to Rev. Henry Ward Beecher, who had been on trial for adultery in New York until July 2, when a hung jury resulted in dismissal of the case. Kime, *Black Hills Journals*, 129n159.

[50] Dodge mentions this incident when Burt was suspected of tampering with Davenport's package of letters being carried to Fort Laramie because Burt was a correspondent for a rival newspaper. Dodge concluded that a drunken enlisted man in Burt's detachment had removed the letters from the package meant for special delivery and put them with the regular mail. Kime, *Black Hills Journals*, 111-15, 117. In a subsequent letter from Red Cloud Agency, Bell set the record straight about Burt's innocence.

[51] Steele and Kidder were non-voting delegates who represented their respective territories in the U.S. House of Representatives.

[52] A line from "Sheridan's Ride," a poem by Thomas Buchanan Read, about the Oct. 19, 1864, Civil War Battle of Cedar Creek in the Shenandoah Valley of Virginia.

[53] Although this and subsequent letters attribute the threat to a Southern Cheyenne, one Ed. Welch who had been at Red Cloud Agency at the time credits it to Little Big Man, who later disrupted the council session on Sept. 23. North Platte *Western Nebraskian*, Oct. 2, 1875.

[54] A Sans Arc chief, who inherited a dynastic name. His father was Sans Arc chief from the 1820s until his death in 1858, when the name and leadership role passed to an older brother, who died young. This Crow Feather assumed them in 1870-71. Personal communication from Kingsley M. Bray.

[55] This was a Two Kettle headman from the powerful Four Bears family. He attended the 1851 Horse Creek treaty council. Personal communication from Kingsley M. Bray.

[56] The Lakota still recalled the 1849 skirmish or "Battle of Crow Butte" with the Crows, who had run off horses from James Bordeaux's trading post.

[57] Meaning the Sihasapa (Blackfoot) band of Lakota at the Cheyenne River Agency. "Little Black Coat" is the correspondent's error. The correct name is Little Blackfoot, headman of the Sihasapa band that located at the Cheyenne River Agency in 1868. He is correctly identified in Davenport's Sept. 12 letter that follows.

[58] The "solids and liquids" remark was apparently the correspondents' way of saying the commissioners were being rationed at the government's expense in addition to their salary of $8 per day. Commissioners who were already on the government payroll, such as General Terry, did not receive the per diem. Anderson, "Samuel D. Hinman and the Opening of the Black Hills," 529; *ARCIA, 1875*, 687.

[59] Not all of the skeletal remains of the slaughtered cattle were left to go to waste. In 1876 a Cheyenne hide dealer named F. L. Sigel contracted with teamsters hauling supplies to the Nebraska agencies to salvage the horns of the Texas cattle. On June 20 and June 27, 1876, the *Daily Leader* reported that 100,000 pounds of horns had been received from the agencies and Sigel had contracted for an additional 100,000 pounds. The horns could be used to make buttons and combs.

[60] Striped Cloud was a Sihasapa from the Cheyenne River Agency, who signed the Manypenny Agreement in 1876. "Report of the Sioux Commission," *ARCIA, 1876*, 354. G. P. Beauvais claimed to have received gold from some Brulé in 1858. Parker, *Gold in the Black Hills*, Chap. 1, evaluates the stories of early gold discoveries in the Black Hills, including those said to have been made by Indians.

[61] Secretary of the Interior Columbus Delano, whose resignation was accepted by President Grant on Sept. 22, 1875. Olson, *Red Cloud*, 196-97.

[62] This reference is probably to John Cochrane of New York, a congressman, Civil War general, state attorney general, and supporter of Horace Greeley's presidential bid as a Liberal Republican in 1872.

[63] While Kingsley Bray, *Crazy Horse*, 136, credits Red Dog as "one of the strategic architects of the Bozeman Trail War victory," the plan leading to the so called "Fetterman Massacre" at Fort Phil Kearny was devised by Red Cloud, High Backbone, and Crazy Horse, ibid., 96-99.

[64] It would appear that Davenport here has conflated the seven main divisions of the Tetons with some of the bands within those divisions.

[65] Lone Horn of the North was Miniconjou head chief. From 1868 to 1874 he had moved between the hunting grounds and the agencies, but settled permanently at his people's home agency, Cheyenne River, at the beginning of 1875. He strove to keep on the agenda plans proposed by Bishop Hare's 1874 commission to establish a new agency near the Black Hills, but the idea became moot with the outbreak of the gold rush. Lone Horn became alienated from the Black Hills Council and the Oglala-sponsored "seven generations plan" as the price to sell the Black Hills. Lone Horn left the council abruptly on Sept. 29, 1875, and was said to have died of a broken heart a few months later over the loss of the Black Hills. Personal communication from Kingsley M. Bray.

[66] A resident of the Cheyenne River Agency, rather than a Cheyenne Indian.

[67] A Hunkpapa headman, resident at Standing Rock Agency, also known as Belly Fat. Personal communication from Kingsley M. Bray.

[68] John S. Gray's article, "Frank Grouard: Kanaka Scout or Mulatto Renegade?" in the *Chicago Westerners Brand Book* 16 (Oct. 1959), traces Grouard's ancestry, which has been a subject of dispute among historians.

[69] A sometime rival of Crazy Horse, Black Twin was an Oglala shirt-wearer during the early 1870s. Although he joined with Crazy Horse to resist white intrusions and reservation life, by 1875 Black Twin had begun to consider opening negotiations with reservation leaders and the whites. His unexpected death during the winter of 1875-76 removed his potential moderating influence on Crazy Horse and the non-treaty Oglala. Bray, *Crazy Horse*, 194.

[70] White Ghost was Lower Yanktonai chief at the Crow Creek Agency, who signed the Manypenny Agreement in 1876. "Report of the Sioux Commission," *ARCIA, 1876*, 355.

[71] Spider played a role in negotiations to close the Bozeman Trail forts in 1867. He was present in the Camp Robinson adjutant's office when Crazy Horse died on Sept. 5, 1877. Bray, *Crazy Horse*, 115, 388.

[72] The Bank of California in San Francisco, founded by William C. Ralston and other prominent businessmen including Darius Ogden Mills, failed in late August 1875. Ralston was forced to resign as president and the next day, he drowned while swimming in the ocean, whether a suicide or accident being undetermined. Given the nation's precarious financial situation in the aftermath of the Panic of 1873, the bank's failure was national news.

[73] The second clergyman was likely Rev, William. J. Cleveland who, with his wife and Misses Mary J. Leigh and Sophia Pendleton, had gone to Spotted Tail Agency in June to establish a mission school. *Cheyenne Daily Leader*, June 14, 1875.

[74] The prospect of a "deluge" of speechmaking at the council inspired Bell to liken Crow Butte to the mountain in eastern Turkey, upon which Noah's Ark is said to have come to rest after the biblical flood.

[75] This was William H. Legge, born 1851, who became the 6th Earl of Dartmouth upon his father's death in 1891. While his father held the title as the 5th Earl of Dartmouth, the son was styled Viscount Lewisham. https://en./Wikipedia.org/wiki/William Legge, 6th Earl of Dartmouth, accessed Nov. 6, 2015.

[76] On June 3, 1875, Howard sent a letter to the commissioner of Indian affairs asking for authority to remove several white "squaw men" from the Spotted Tail Agency. The parties named were "constantly making disturbance and trouble," and they "use the influence they have with the Indians to breed discontent and trouble." Spotted Tail Agency Letters. The Aug. 31, 1875, issue of the *Omaha Bee* published a letter by "Graph" that included an interview with John Bigler. He and other "squaw men" at the agency had accused Howard of fraud in issuing Indian supplies which, said Bigler, was why they were being ordered away. On January 1, 1875, Agent Howard had conducted a census of "White men and Half Breeds living at Spotted Tail Agency" that tallied 68 men, 63 women, 113 boys, and 137 girls.

[77] This "Old Spotted Tail Agency," one of several locations occupied by Spotted Tail's Brulé before the final Beaver Creek site was selected, was just west of the modern village of Whitney, Nebraska, in 1871-72. The agency was then called Whetstone Agency.

[78] Whether the word "cohile" is as Davenport rendered it in his original letter or whether it results from a typesetting error is unknown. Efforts to determine its meaning from the context have not been successful.

[79] This is the essential story of the 1849 "Battle of Crow Butte." See *Museum of the Fur Trade Quarterly* 45 (Fall/Winter 2009).

[80] The list of signatories to the 1876 Manypenny agreement identify some of these men as follows: Mad Bear, Lower Yanktonai; Bear Ribs, Hunkpapa; Red Horse, Sihasapa; Big Head, Upper Yanktonai, all from Standing Rock. Yellow Robe was an Upper Yanktonai from Cheyenne River, and Cross Bear was a Hunkpapa, who later fled to Canada with Sitting Bull, according to Waggoner, *Witness*, 302-3, 683n.1.

[81] This may be an inference that some commission members were sympathetic to the alleged "Indian Ring," if not actually thought to be part of it.

[82] This is likely an erroneous identification for William Legge, Viscount Lewisham, whom Charles Collins mentions in his Sept. 15, 1875, letter.

[83] For Two Bears, see Pt. 1, n. 80.

[84] Probably William Harmon of Minnesota, who served in that state's volunteers during the Civil War and later won appointment to the regular army. Heitman, *Historical Register*, 501.

[85] On Aug. 6, 1875, the *Cheyenne Daily Leader* reported that local blacksmith and wagon dealer John Nealon had sent twenty-three Studebaker wagons to the Spotted Tail Agency, which included "a number of fine spring carriages, supplied each with two seats." These may have been some of the wagons mentioned in fulfillment of the agreement to cede the Nebraska hunting rights. Some of the correspondents mentioned Spotted Tail arriving at sessions of the council in such a conveyance.

[86] No companies of the Sixth U.S. Infantry were at Camp Robinson. The deserters would have been from the Ninth Infantry. Buecker, *Fort Robinson and the American West*, 201.

[87] Maj. T. H. Stanton was the U.S. Army paymaster who had come from Cheyenne to pay the troops at Camp Robinson. See "Roster" in *Cheyenne Daily Leader*, Sept. 20, 1875; Heitman, *Historical Register*, 916.

[88] Red Cloud died an old man in 1909.

[89] Perhaps referring to former U.S. Sen. James Harlan of Iowa, who had been secretary of the interior in 1865-66. "Senator Dilworthy" was a character in an 1873 Mark Twain novel, *The Gilded Age*. Dilworthy was based on the real-life Kansas U.S. Sen. Samuel Pomeroy. www.bioguide.congress.gov and www.senate.gov/reference, accessed 9-23-11.

[90] This had been the site of the 1851 Fort Laramie Treaty council.

[91] Allison had served in Congress from Iowa from 1863-71, and his position on the House Ways and Means Committee would have been his connection to Secretary of the Treasury Salmon P. Chase of Abraham Lincoln's cabinet. In 1872 Allison won election to the Senate over his Republican rival, former Secretary of the Interior James Harlan. David Hudson, Marvin Bergman, and Loren N. Horton, eds., *The Biographical Dictionary of Iowa* (Iowa City: University of Iowa Press, 2008), 15.

[92] John B. Gough (1817-86) became famous for his forty-year campaign against drinking.

[93] The reference is likely to Julius Stahel, John H. Martindale, William Farrar Smith, and Adelbert Ames, all Union army officers during the Civil War.

[94] Field was a prominent New York attorney.

[95] Albert Gallatin Lawrence attained the rank of brigadier general of volunteers during the Civil War. Heitman, *Historical Register*, 618

[96] For a review of the accusations that later damaged Hinman's career, see Anne Beiser Allen, "Scandal in Niobrara: The Controversial Career of Rev. Samuel D. Hinman," *Nebraska History* 90 (Fall 2009): 114-29.

[97] Lines had also served with Hinman in 1874 during the survey for a new site or sites for the Red Cloud and Spotted Tail agencies. Anderson, "Samuel D. Hinman and the Opening of the Black Hills," 524-25.

[98] Second Lt. James M. Stembel. Heitman, *Historical Register*, 920.

Commission member Rev. Samuel D. Hinman. Smithsonian Institution

John T. Bell, the *Omaha Herald's* correspondent at the Black Hills Council. NSHS RG2411-384a

Andrew S. Burt, then a captain in the Ninth U.S. Infantry, was the *New York Tribune's* correspondent at the council. This later photograph was taken after his promotion to lieutenant colonel, Seventh U.S. Infantry. Little Bighorn Battlefield National Monument, National Park Service

Little Big Man, an Oglala, led the delegation of non-agency Lakota to the council. NSHS RG2955-25

V. M. Bromley's engraving, "Driving Cattle into a Corral, Nebraska," depicted a beef issue at Red Cloud Agency. *Illustrated London News*, August 21, 1875. NSHS collections 10930-4

TELEGRAPHIC.

MIDNIGHT.

WEST.

The Black Hills Treaty— Preposterous demand of the Indians.

The Indian Council breaks up without accomplishing anything·

(Special to the Bee.)

RED CLOUD AGENCY, Sept. 29. }
VIA SIDNEY, Sept. 30. }

The commissioners submitted a proposition for treaty to the Indians on Wednesday, the text of which, I already sent you. It will not be accepted by the Indians, and the commissioners are prepared to return home and submit report. The following is the summary of what the Indians demand, in payment for the Black Hills : 6 yoke of oxen and wagons; 1 span of horses and wagon; Live Stock; Furniture, etc; and annuities of subsistance annually for 600 years. They also demand the appointment of agents and employees and removal of troops from all agencies on the reservations, and the removal of the Catholic clergy as religious instructors ; only one road into the hills via Bismarck ; the extension of the reservation to the middle of the Platte river in Nebraska, and an utter refusal to part with the Powder river and Big Horn country.

Their demands are considered preposterously unseasonable by the commissioners. The commissioners return Saturday.

CHARLES COLLINS.

Correspondent Charles Collins's report of the council's failure appeared in the *Omaha Daily Bee*, October 1, 1875.

223

Oglala leaders and interpreters who were part of a delegation from the Nebraska agencies that met with President Rutherford B. Hayes in Washington, D. C. on September 27-28, 1877. They went to discuss the government's plan to relocate the agencies from Nebraska to the Missouri River in Dakota Territory, as provided by the 1876 Black Hills Agreement. Most of the individuals pictured here also participated in the 1875 Black Hills Council. Standing, l. to r.: He Dog, Little Wound, American Horse, Little Big Man, Young Man Afraid of his Horse, Sword. Seated, l. to r.: Yellow Bear, José Merivale, William Garnett, Leon Pallady, Three Bears. NSHS RG2095-78

Part 3

Getting Down to Business:
September 20 – 27, 1875

❧

S eptember 20, 1875 – John T. Bell, from Red Cloud Agency,
Nebraska]
The Pow-Wow Opens
Special Correspondence of *The Herald*
Red Cloud Agency, Neb. [Monday] Sept. 20, 1875

The council for the proposed purchase of the Black Hills country
opened to-day. The commissioners left the agency at 10 a.m. with Capt.
Egan's company K, 2nd Cavalry, as an escort. The taking of an escort
had been a subject of very serious consideration as it was feared the
Indians might object to this seeming want of confidence, and a distrust
of their peaceful disposition on the part of the whites and consequently
refuse to attend the council. Even after arriving upon the site selected
for the council, it appeared as though there might have been a mistake
made in taking the escort, for not an Indian was to be seen in any direction, though we had passed through camps containing hundreds of
lodges on our way out. The absence of red skins caused Col.
Comingo—who is the funny man of the commission—to remark to
Gen. Terry:

"Terry, you're accustomed to estimating immense assemblages,
how many Indians do you say are present?" whereupon there was a
general laugh.

However the council tent was erected, a fly stretched in front of it
for the use of the commission, and directly in front of it and a few feet
distant another for Indians, and by the time these preparations had been
completed, several hundred Indians had arrived. Then the commissioners waited for Red Cloud to put in an appearance, but soon a courier

arrived with a message from that distinguished personage to the effect that all Indians belonging to his tribe should return at once to the agency as he proposed to hold his council there. It was noticed, however, that but few Indians obeyed this summons and as Old-Man-Afraid-of-his-Horses and Young-Man-Afraid-of-his-Horses—who are the real chiefs of the Oglalas—remained, the commission determined to go on with the council and at 1 p.m. invited the Indians present to seat themselves as conveniently as possible in front of the council tent and then the pow-wow began, Spotted Tail occupying a central position among the Indians with the two above named chiefs of the Oglalas, and Blue Horse on his left, and Two Bears, the principal chief of the Yanktonais on his right. In addition to these there were present some two hundred under chiefs of the various bands of Sioux, Cheyennes, and Arapahoes.

Louis Richard had previously been selected by the commissioners as their interpreter and at the request of Man-Afraid-of-his-Horses, he served in the same capacity for the Oglalas. The Upper Brules selected Wm. Quigley, the Lower Brules chose Alex Zephier, and the Yanktonais John Bruguier.[1]

The business of selecting interpreters having been attended to, Red Dog, who had also persisted in remaining away up to this time, crowded his way among the Indians and sat down in front of Spotted Tail, turning his back to the commissioners.

Senator Allison then addressed the Indians, announcing in substance (the speech in full has been telegraphed to *The Herald*) the desire of the government to "lease" the Black Hills country and to purchase a certain tract of the Big Horn country (already described in *The Herald*). As each of these propositions were made known, the Indians indulged in a burst of hearty laughter, especially when it was suggested that after the whites had dug all the gold "and all other minerals" in the Black Hills country, that country should be returned to them to dispose of as they chose, as they evidently thought that after the white man gets fairly located in the section referred to, it would be a very difficult matter to get him out.

At the conclusion of the speech of Senator Allison Red Dog arose and addressed the commissioners, saying: "There is a good many different tribes here and it will take us about seven days to make up our minds on this. That's all we have got to say."

This was a remarkably short speech for Red Dog—as he is one of the biggest "blows" west of the Missouri River—this fact strengthened the suspicion that he was in league with Red Cloud to break up the council. His remarks were greeted with cries of "how," "how," by the Indians. The Blue Horse announced that the Indians would hold a council this evening among themselves; with that the majority of them gathered their blankets around them and started off, Spotted Tail, Old-Man-Afraid-of-his-Horses and his son keeping their seats.

A rapid consultation was held by the commissioners ending in an announcement that they would expect to meet all the Indians again at the same place at 10 o'clock to-morrow morning, and with this the council closed, the commissioners returning to the agency and the Indians to their camps.

Spotted Tail has a very keen sense of the ridiculous and is known in this vicinity as a first-class joker. As we were driving back to the agency after the talk, the four-horse ambulance conveying the newspaper men overtook a light spring wagon in which Spotted Tail was seated; whereupon the latter called out, "I would like to get your mules to haul wood this winter and return them in the spring," thus making a sly drive at the proposition he had just listened to relative to the Black Hills country, and which joke was fully appreciated by the occupants of the ambulance.

The commissioners are thoroughly disgusted at the sullenness and mulish obstinacy Red Cloud has constantly exhibited since their arrival at the agency, and in consequence of their experience of to-day, are seriously considering a suggestion made to the effect that that self-important individual be deposed by them as the recognized chief of the Oglalas and the son of Man-Afraid-of-his-Horses be made chief in his stead. The latter is the hereditary head of the tribe and is yet in possession of their confidence and respect, and it would be generally satisfactory if his son were recognized by the Great Father as their chief, Red Cloud having been made chief by the commissioners who perfected the treaty of 1868. I understand, however, that Red Cloud has signified his intention to be present to-morrow.

We had been led to suppose that when the council opened the Indians would be decorated with a profusion of paint, feathers, ribbons, etc., but this was not the case, as they appeared very plainly attired, Spotted Tail himself being dressed, principally, in an old blue blanket and a white hat, both of which he kept on during the talk, in the course of which he had nothing to say to anyone.

The fact is the opening of the council has been a very flat affair, but the business may become more lively and interesting as it progresses. Let us hope so.

J. T. B.

[*Omaha Daily Herald*, Tuesday, September 28, 1875]

[September 20, 1875 – "D," from Red Cloud Agency, Nebraska]
Communicated
Red Cloud Agency, Neb. [Monday] Sept. 20, 1875
Editor *Leader*

After many delays, disappointments and vexations the first grand council took place to-day on White Earth River, about seven miles from this agency. The council was to have commenced on Saturday, but the Indians were not ready, and at 10 a.m. to-day, the appointed hour, not many were on hand, but they straggled in after some time, so that at about 12 m. the "pow-wow" commenced, although Red Cloud and some other "head devils" did not condescend to appear. Old Spot was on hand, as were also the representative men of the Missouri River agencies. The commission made a mistake at the start in their proposition, which is disgusting nonsense—they want to lease the Black Hills until the gold is all exhausted— when the country is to revert to the Indians, for men of sense to make such a proposition, as if the whites could be got out if once in possession. The proposition also embraced the purchase of the hunting rights, & c., in a large part of Wyoming, that is, leaving the Indians all east of a line drawn from the northwest corner of Nebraska to the Yellowstone River, which will give us the Big Horn and Powder River country, and the old road to Montana [the Bozeman Trail]. It is impossible to tell by to-day's proceedings what the prospects of success are, but we hope for the best and hope to finish this week. We are to have another talk to-morrow, which may develop something. Am afraid the commission is not made of stuff to deal with the Indians. All the "wretches" seem to think they know more about things than Dr. Daniels and such men. The Indians seem in good temper and will, I hope, make a treaty.
D.
[*Cheyenne Daily Leader*, Saturday, September 25, 1875]

[September 21, 1875 – John T. Bell, from Red Cloud Agency, Nebraska]
They Take a Rest
Special Correspondence of *The Herald*
Red Cloud Agency, Neb. [Tuesday] Sept. 21, 1875

Contrary to expectations, no council was held to-day, notwithstanding the fact that it was arranged with the Indians yesterday afternoon to return and renew negotiations at 10 o'clock this morning. This is the day on which beef is issued here, and I understand that the holding of the council was postponed until to-morrow for that reason. I do not get this officially, however. In fact, the newspaper men here get nothing officially, the members of the commission all being "non-communicants" in the matter of news. We understand there was a consultation held by the commissioners upon the arrival of the representatives of the press, whereat it was suggested that the proper thing to do was to furnish the latter with a tent, invite them to be present at all the informal talks held with the Indians, and, in short, extend them all facilities possible for obtaining information. To this suggestion, however, objection was made by certain members of the commission, solely because *The Herald* [had] occasion to make reference, editorially, to one of the commissioners in a manner which was not as complimentary as it might have been, perhaps.[2] The objectors carried their point and the result was the newspaper men have been studiously ignored by the commission from the day they reached Red Cloud, and whatever information they have found relative to the doings of that body, up to the present writing, they are under no obligations to the commissioners for.

The proposition to lease the Black Hills meets with universal disapproval from the Indians, their agents, and the attaches of this agency, and it is not at all probable that it will be accepted by the noble red men. The "squaw men" are also opposed to the proposition and whatever influence they may have with the Indians will be exerted in favor of a sale outright of the Black Hills country. The Indians are convinced that the white men will take possession of the Black Hills and trouble between themselves and the whites is anticipated even if they do sell whatever rights they may have to that country.

It is against the law for anyone to bring whisky upon an Indian reservation, and a very wise law this is for if there is any one thing an Indian has a passion for it is whisky, and when he gets it he is perfectly unmanageable and would kill his best friend. The agents are very careful with regard to this matter, as their own lives are endangered by a transgression of this law, but in spite of their efforts whisky is occasionally smuggled in. A few days since a Mexican brought some to this agency and Sunday night half a dozen drunken Indians made times exceedingly lively in this vicinity.

"How Are You Dad?" questioned a hearty looking young half breed one day last week, as he grasped one of the commissioners by the hand. The latter gazed for a moment at the young fellow and then returned his salutation, as a look of recognition shot athwart the official countenance. The young man is a resident at Spotted Tail Agency where he has a brother and three sisters. He came down on their behalf and his own for the express purpose of seeing their mutual father and conveying to him expressions of their filial regard, though they had not seen him for a number of years. It was emphatically a case of "though lost to sight, to mem'ry dear," and the scene was heartily enjoyed by the by-standers.[3]

We have a couple of young Englishmen here who are skirmishing around the country on a pleasure trip. They had met Gen. Lawrence, one of the commissioners, back east, I believe; at any rate, the latter received a letter from one of them asking him to designate a list of articles for him to procure at Omaha, preparatory to coming to Red Cloud. To this the general responded: "Get a demijohn of whisky and fill your trunk with cigars. You can procure a pack of cards out here."

Sunday a party of six Black Hillers arrived here, accompanied by a squad of cavalry, having been brought out by force. The six were found in company with twenty-one others, who went to Fort Laramie instead of coming here, they being allowed their choice between the two points. The entire party had come from Sioux City and were seven weeks in reaching the Black Hills, which fact is certainly a reflection upon that route.

Mr. G. H. [Gilbert H.] Collins, of Omaha, is expected here to-day from Fort Laramie.

J. T. B.

[*Omaha Daily Herald*, Wednesday, September 29, 1875]

[September 21, 1875 – Reuben Davenport, from Red Cloud Agency, Nebraska]

The Black Hills

The Great Council Ground on White River, Neb., [Tuesday] Sept. 21, 1875

Yesterday the Grand Council of the commissioners of the President and the Sioux nation of Indians was opened. This step has been achieved, however, after a series of delays which has, at times, seemed to presage an ultimate failure of all efforts to form a treaty. Some persons even, who have witnessed the proceedings of the commission during the past two weeks, intimate a doubt of their sincerity in seeking the purchase of the country defined by the Secretary of the Interior in his instructions to them. One, and perhaps two, of the gentlemen of the commission, with a few other intelligent men not deluded into a belief in the enormous value of the Black Hills, look upon their purchase as unnecessary to the public weal, and if it were not their duty as it is the object of their appointment, they would not favor the cession of the country to the government at all.

They are, consequently, very lukewarm negotiators. Their private opinion of the value of the land to be treated for is undoubtedly shared by the greater proportion of the reading public. They represent a powerful and healthful sentiment that is due to the truthful information given only by the independent press regarding the Black Hills. But the majority of the commission are anxious to consummate a written agreement with the Indians, and that as soon as possible. The course pursued thus far, however, has not been expeditious of the business in hand. Each delay granted to the inharmonious chiefs who have been jealously quarreling over petty issues has bred other delays, and this negative order of events might have continued for a year, had not a very little firmness displayed itself at last in members of the commission. Spotted Tail was the first cause of delay. He protested against the selection of the council ground so much nearer Red Cloud's village than to his, and insisted upon the first understanding being carried out, namely: that the council should be held on Chadron Creek. The commissioners one day sent word to him that he must come to a place selected by them, on a certain day, if he wished to join in the council. As the time approached Spotted Tail had made no appearance. The commission consulted; the opening day of the council was changed. They feared the secession of too large a body of representative chiefs, and waited. On another day it was still further postponed, and last Saturday was named as the date of the opening. The commission then, in deference to Red Cloud, abandoned the spot near Crow Buttes, first chosen, and named one on the White River, at the mouth of Little White Clay Creek. Once more the commissioners yielded to the barbarians. Red Cloud, grown sulky and arrogant, in consequence of the deference now shown to Spotted Tail, said he would not go where the latter wished and that the council ought to be held only in the stockade at the agency. A committee of Brules, Spotted Tail, No Flesh, and Two Strike called upon him, Sword, and American Horse to offer the olive branch and to form an agreement, but they met with a cold reception. Red Cloud would not listen.

After hearing of the result of their last diplomatic effort the commissioners evolved a policy which would have proven more profitable if adopted at the onset. They determined to ignore Red Cloud in fixing the location of the council. The opinion of Young Man Afraid of his Horses was sought. He undoubtedly has the greatest influence in the Sioux nation, excepting Spotted Tail, and also has the hereditary right to power. He was not unfavorable to the place pointed out by Spotted Tail, and on Saturday morning the commission, accompanied by several Oglala chiefs, among whom was Red Dog, Sword, and Spider, met Spotted Tail and his sub-chiefs, who, with their people, were in the act of moving up from their camps on Chadron Creek to pitch them nearer the council ground. The meeting was held on the summit of a large knoll, east of the Little White Clay Creek, overlooking the river bottom and the plain for miles.

None of the Brules or Minnconjous were present when the commission arrived there. The wind was blowing and it was bitterly cold. However, horsemen soon began to appear in the east, and soon the braves of the whole Brule tribe were seen winding, in a black sinuous column across the plain, with the squaws, children, and tepees behind them. Spotted Tail and Crazy in the Lodge came in a wagon, which had springs and was drawn by two ponies, driven by a needy-looking Indian attired in vests, pantaloons, a linen duster, and a hat, who sat on the front seat. Spotted Tail is clearly not adverse to symbols of state, although his personal taste is simple. His bearing was fine and noble, and he greeted the commissioners with an unconscious assumption of equality in his manner, which few other Indians displayed.

When a few more chiefs, belonging to the Missouri River reservations had arrived, a brief pow-wow was held by the commissioners and Indians, and the latter then retired to consult among themselves. Spotted Tail pointed out a spot near the river marked by an old and enormous cottonwood tree, and described it as the best situation for the grand tepee.[4] He had come so far to conciliate the Oglalas that he thought himself entitled to the concession of being allowed to designate the actual council ground. After some deliberation the chiefs present consented to the proposition; but neither Red Cloud nor Young Man Afraid of his Horses, who could overrule all other of the Oglala chiefs, were there. The gathering was about to disperse in uncertainty whether the agreement should be final, when Young Man Afraid of his Horses came. He is not tall or unusual in appearance, and his face has simply an aspect of intelligence, not of thoughtfulness of sagacity. His attire was plain, and his only mark of distinction is a certain expression of authority, resolve, and courage in his truly aboriginal countenance. Since he has it in his power to become, when he likes, the principal chief of the Sioux nation, his modesty in remaining what he is, is remarkable. It may be viewed as an evidence of the sterling nature of his good qualities. When the young chief heard the proposition made by Spotted Tail he approved it, and the preliminary trouble was felt to be over at last. Red Cloud was made a monument of discontent by his cool treatment, but it has long been known that he has not complete control of the Oglalas, and if he now incurs their displeasure by his jealous obstinacy it may prove a fortunate opportunity for them to depose him and bestow upon Man Afraid of his Horses his present authority. The latter, it is said, is very well disposed toward the whites, although a young man and full of ambition.

The Indians shook hands very cordially all around, and many of them accompanied the commissioners back to the agency.

Sunday [Sept. 19] was very quiet. The peculiar virtue of the day, in the estimation of the whites, seems to be recognized by the Sioux, although not respected, for they usually remain at their camps and indulge in feasts and gambling. Your correspondent rode to the village of the Oglalas in the afternoon and found the principal men in council, in a large tepee. They had been deliberating on the question of parting with their country. He could not enter, as it was, of course, private; nor could he learn what chiefs were engaged, as he could speak very little Dakota. In the centre of the camp were the remnants of a great dog feast, scattered on the ground, with stew pans and cups which had been blackened over the fire. A circle of squaws, squatting upon the ground surrounded them, they evidently having searched for dainty morsels before removing the ruins of former canine pets. The Indian thinks much of his dogs, and it is singular that he will eat them. Red Cloud was absent from his tepee and probably in the council; but one of his wives offered to bring him to see his guest, but was not permitted. One of his comely daughters, with her lips unwashed since a recent meal, was present. Such neglect of appearance is not, however, in Indian society considered a detriment to the peculiar style of beauty. Each nation proclaims its own the prettiest women. A white man, however, completely overcomes an Indian damsel by complimenting her on her face. As your correspondent left the village he saw a group of Indian youth playing at hoop and sticks for wagers. They bet their beaded belts, moccasins and other ornaments on the issue of the game. A very disreputable old buck, when he beheld a white man, walked away from the group, enunciating in loud and scolding tones a denunciatory harangue. In the evening a dozen drunken savages, believed to belong to the Wazhazha band, attempted to force the door of Mr. Frank Yates' store, and loudly threatened the inmates with massacre and scalping if they were not admitted. Such occurrences, it is stated, are not unfrequent here.

How the Indians get whisky or *minnewaka* is a mystery; but there is probably some lack of vigilance, which permits the violation of the regulation of the Interior Department. It should be most strictly enforced, for no enemy could be more dreadful to face than the *minnewaka* incarnate in a Sioux brave. This is one reason why the residence of white men among Indians, who marry among them and live as they do, is most pernicious. They are principally Frenchmen and Mexicans, and they reap a profitable reward from smuggling whiskey into the Indian reservations and selling it for money and ponies. The present council, which has drawn so many large bands to this point, will attract more of those scoundrels, and it is not improbable that any clashing which may occur between white men and Indians will be caused by them. They, besides supplying them with the drink that will excite a murderous frenzy, instigate them to do what they can to injure the government and to be extortionate in their demands. The Wazhazha band receives much of the whiskey brought in, and they are the most doubtful of the Sioux in times of apprehension.

They are headed by Little Wound, who is not the best of Indians. He is not half so good as those who repose in buffalo robes, suspended on airy platforms, on the summit of the knolls about here. His quiescence, in the event of trouble, cannot be counted on half so confidently. Last winter he started from the agency with his young men, mounted on their war ponies, seeking the war path, and threatened slaughter and robbery on the Platte River. It was young Sitting Bull who turned him back—the same who saved the life of Dr. Saville at the time of the attempted raising of a flagstaff in the stockade. Little Wound deserves to be looked upon with suspicion, and his band and the Cheyennes are the only sources from which any trouble may be feared.[5]

General L. P. Bradley undoubtedly came here for the purpose of studying the situation and providing for its military necessities. A courier was sent to Camp Robinson, [Sheridan] near the Spotted Tail Agency with an order for Colonel Mills' company to march here at once. Colonel Mills took command of his own and Captain Egan's companies of cavalry, which yesterday formed the escort of the commission. Fifteen infantrymen of the Ninth regiment form a guard which will camp upon the council ground until the council closes. They are commanded by Lieutenant Stemble.

When the commissioners reached the council ground there were no Indians there; but a crowd had gathered where the meeting of Saturday had taken place, and several groups were stationed on neighboring knolls, apparently merely for observation. The wagons containing the canvas and poles for erecting the grand tepee arrived, and the fifteen guardsmen consumed an hour in performing that labor. By that time Sintigaliska [Spotted Tail] had arrived, driven up from his camp by his coachman, and accompanied by No Flesh, his lieutenant in authority, Two Strike, and Crazy-in-the Lodge. Spotted Tail wore the air of a statesman and displayed immediately a statesman's tact and adroitness. He was clad in blue pantaloons, blanket and shirt, and a black hat similar in form to the Quaker pattern. No ornament was visible upon the great chief. He advanced toward the commissioners with a peculiar, courteous smile, which could not have been surpassed by any modern politician, and a noble gait, and exchanged greetings with them with ease and affability. He then remarked, with a broadening of the smile, pointing with his hand: "I want you to have fixed two stakes in the ground here, one there and one here, so that the Oglalas can only come so far; this country is mine henceforth from this point to Spotted Tail Agency, since I have come so far to meet them."

The commissioners and Spotted Tail joined in a laugh; but there was some doubt, expressed in good English, whether the politic chief was really in jest or in earnest.

Representative Oglala, Miniconjou, Yanktonai, Kiyuksa, Wazhazha, and Cheyenne chiefs at length being present, they were all seated in crescent form opposite the commissioners, who formed another crescent, completing a circle. Over all was stretched a broad canopy, at one end of which was a large, open tent. The principal chiefs there, whom I have not yet mentioned were: Young and Old Man-Afraid-Of-His Horses, Blue Horse, Red Leaf, High Wolf, Slow Bull, Young Sitting Bull, Face, Black Bear, Little Wound, Lone Horn, Striped Cloud, Running Antelope, Swift Bear, American Horse, and Wolf Necklace. The issue of rations at the agency had deterred many of the chiefs from attending. Senator Allison, president of the commission, said that they would assume that all of the representative men were there and proceed.

The council, as it sat thus, in the centre of a great plain, the Sioux's own country, was an imposing picture. The first row of Indians in the circle sat on the ground, and behind them rose a series of dusky faces, the last rank standing up. Spotted Tail sat, sedate and watchful, second from the front. He rose in height over his neighbors, and was regarded by many eyes, even among the Indians of other tribes of Sioux. Old-Man-Afraid-of-his-Horses wore, as usual, a brilliantly colored handkerchief on his head and a sable blanket. After the Indians had chosen their interpreters—John Brughier, Alexander Zephier, and John Quigley—who came forth and stood in the ring, President Allison announced to them that Louis Richard would render the English into the Sioux for their understanding.

Senator Allison then rose and began his address, on behalf of the commission, to the Indians. It was interpreted, sentence by sentence, by Louis; but it was noticeable that Messrs. Hinman and Beauvais, both of whom comprehend the Sioux, found it necessary to make frequent corrections. It is well known that Louis Richard is not the best interpreter in this country. His knowledge of the English language is very imperfect. His influence with the Indians, however, is great, and this fact induced the commissioners to overlook his known deficiency. As one of the greatest troubles, after the making of treaties with Indians, has been their ignorance of what stipulations they had signed. The employment of competent interpreters is of much importance, and whether the commission have acted wisely in this matter or not remains to be seen. The address of Senator Allison, already given to the public, contained something which even startled the Indians. It is needless to say that this was the form of the direct proposition to negotiate for the possession of the Black Hills and Big Horn Mountains. There were a few low mouthed comments among the red auditors as they listened to the expressions of good will and good faith addressed to them, but when the comprehended that they were asked to loan their country instead of selling it, they were led by Spotted Tail in a hearty laugh. In most of them it was probably caused by the mere novelty of the idea, but Spotted Tail saw more quickly and clearly.

Before the speech was finished Red Dog came into the circle, in a perspiration, having just arrived, and sat on the ground. He had come under instructions of Red Cloud, and a subsequent fact showed that he wished to terminate the council for that day. Red Cloud was keen enough to see that while he was absent from the council it would not be well for him that any reply should be made by any of his brother chiefs to the proposition of the white men. Red Dog had hastened to do his errand. He said:

"There have come here a good many tribes to be of the council. It will take seven days for us to study in our minds about this, and we will now hold a council among ourselves."

At a signal the Oglala and some other chiefs hastened to retire. Spotted Tail and his friends did not move. The interpreter for the commission called for the Indians to wait and some complied. They were then asked to meet the commission again in the morning, to consult with them.

Spotted Tail asked Dr. Saville, jestingly, how he would like to loan him a team of mules on the terms proposed by the commissioners.

Last night at a late session, the commission, having learned that the Indians desired to consult among themselves to-day, determined to omit a session of the general council. To-morrow, however, the pow-wow will be resumed.

As far as can be learned the Indians do not like the proposition to borrow the country belonging to them. They have sufficient cunning and suspicion to look upon it as an attempt to deceive them as to what they will really be surrendering if they agree to it, in order to lessen their demands for compensation. Even to the white man's intellect, this seems a most plausible charge. But I am fully assured that the commission in their proposition mean only good faith and honesty. They have singularly, however, and of course, inadvertently, fallen into an old method of cheating the poor savage, forgetting that they subject themselves to severe and justifiable criticism. They certainly well know that, by the changeless law of destiny, the Black Hills are the white man's to-day, and that when once in full possession they will never be driven out. The word "borrow" is, then, farcical in its connection. On the other hand the ostensible friends of the Indian will be secretly pleased at the form of the proposition. Those of them who are here, officially, of course, will endeavor to influence the Indians to favor its peculiar feature. The "Indian Ring" could desire no better promise of future nutriment. But if ever the Indians under any new treaty could receive what the government will pledge to them without passing through dishonest hands, a method of disposing of their country more to their advantage could not be devised. They will, however, fail to discern the fact, and may be expected to deny the loan of the Black Hills.

The measure propounded to them would perpetuate to them a strong claim upon the government for means of support. As long as white men inhabited the country belonging to them, the government would be bound to pay them the annual rental; and if, finally, it should desire to absolutely purchase their right of property, it would be obliged to give what they might then demand. If the land should be settled by white people, the lease, according to the terms proposed, would not expire until a purchase was made, because it would be impossible, without resorting to a barbarity like the removal of the Jews from their country, to return the possession of it to the Sioux.

Colonel Comingo said to-night: "I am ashamed of that proposition." Senator Allison confessed some of its weak points.

There was an extraordinarily large issue of cattle to the Indians to-day. All of the strange Indians will be fed here. Six hundred and forty beeves were killed and probably 200 more will share their fate to-morrow. The Cheyennes could not be supplied, and went home to their village in a sullen mood. One of them who was willing to accept one of the forty beeves remaining in the corral, but which would not supply the whole band, was set upon by the young men and beaten fiercely with their quirts or riding whips, until he put his pony at full speed and escaped from them.

Senator Allison has written the following letter to the Commissioner of Indian Affairs in reference to the feeding of the visiting Indians at this agency during the Grand Council. It contradicts an erroneous dispatch of the Associated Press sent from this point on September 11:

Red Cloud Agency, [Tuesday] Sept. 21, 1875

Sir: The Sioux Commission arrived here on the 4th day of September. We were unable to secure the opening of the Grand Council until yesterday, the 20th. The place of the council is eight miles distant from the Red Cloud Agency. This makes it necessary that for a time—probably ten days—all rations to the Indians must be issued from this agency. We have requested the agent here to issue all rations necessary to the visiting Indians, in accordance with your instructions, and charge to the other agencies the amount so issued, and have also asked him to notify you of each issue, so that you may be able to order other rations here to replace the rations so issued and withhold them from the agencies from which the visiting Indians come. We suggest that this should be looked after carefully, in order to avoid any excuse for a deficiency here, which would result in a demand for a deficiency bill next winter. We have carefully avoided incurring any extra expenses on account of the holding of the council, except some small items absolutely necessary, and have not ordered the issue of any extra rations. We are thus particular in giving you information, as an Associated Press dispatch of date September 11 stated that "the commission have promised the Indians extra provisions and have sent for 3,000 head of cattle additional." Every word of this dispatch is untrue, as the very contrary of this has been suggested by the commission, that no extra provisions be issued, but that the ordinary rations be issued carefully and promptly, as we understand that the same contractor furnishes beef for all these agencies, and the visiting Indians can receive their ordinary supplies here as well as at their agencies respectively.

The following is a list of visiting Indians as far as we can ascertain from the agents:

Cheyenne [River] Agency, Major Bingham, agent	3,000
Standing Rock Agency, Mr. Burke, agent	1,000
Santee Sioux	50
Fort Thompson Indians	30
Lower Yankton	80
Lower Brule	300
Indians attached to no agency	30[6]

Yours, very truly

W. B. Allison

Chairman of Sioux Commission

The Hon. E. P. Smith, Commissioner of Indian Affairs."

[Unsigned]

[*New York Herald*, Wednesday, October 6, 1875]

[September 22, 1875 – Albert Swalm, from Red Cloud Agency, Nebraska]

Earlier Talks

Special Correspondence of *The Chicago Tribune*

Red Cloud Agency, [Wednesday] Sept. 22

The result of the first day's meeting with the Indians in Grand Council you have had fully by telegraph, ending abruptly by the hasty withdrawal of all the red parties to the treaty. Since then they have held councils in all the tribes, some of them continuing for ten consecutive hours—the plan of leasing the Black Hills country finding earnest advocates and most bitter opposers. In considering the subject in general the commission were apprised of the fact that about the only decent country [within?] 150,000 square miles of reservation was the Black Hills country. All the rest is either "bad lands"—entirely desolate, high, dry and unprotected table-lands—or narrow valleys along the creeks and rivers that cross the reservation. None of these lands, save a few acres in the valleys, can ever be successfully cultivated. Hence, if ever the Indian is to be lifted from indolence and wretched degradation, some suitable place must be provided for him where he can take up the work of agriculture. The commission have no faith in the exaggerated gold stories told about the Black Hills. Some gold has been found there, but not to exceed $200 worth, all told, so far as can be satisfactorily traced. For the purposes of mining, the country will not be needed long; and when that need is over, the commission propose that the Indians shall re-enter the territory and use it as may be best. Being valueless for mining—at least so considered in the general sense—the commission does not feel warranted in buying it as an agricultural country, when millions of acres of far richer soil, under skies more favorable, are yet open to the hunter for homesteads and pre-emptions. The agents of the Indians all approve of the plan of leasing—knowing well that the time must come when the Indian must lay aside his blanket, in which he is forever wrapped, and labor like the whites; and, when that good day does crowd them from their indolence and unthrift, they want them to have a home a few degrees better than the present, barren, uninviting desert that barely affords grazing for their herds of ponies. Whether the plan will be adopted by the Indians is hard to determine; there are so many vexed divisions among them that a general agreement seems improbable.

If the plan of lease fails, the commission will then try to buy, when failure to do so is almost certain, by reason of the exorbitant price which will be demanded and not given. The Ring and its understrappers have coached the Indians to a fine degree, and have been aided in their efforts by a large number of persons who have claims on account of Indian depredations committed from three to ten years ago. As one Indian told your correspondent, the Indians want to pay all their debts by Black Hills drafts, and hence will agree to the admission of many claims, to be paid out of the proceeds of the sale. So far as justice is concerned, the claims are all good; the losses occurred, and should be paid; but just now they are made a stumbling block and operate as one of the causes that may bring failure.

The Indians desire peace, and will not do anything sufficient to cut them off from their regular supplies. Should the Hills remain as their property, they will make it decidedly lively for the miners who may go in, or attempt to. Thousands of the best arms the country affords are found in the hands of the Indians, including the improved breech-loading Springfield gun, army pattern; and they have now, within 20 miles of the agency, not less than forty thousand horses, some of which are exceedingly fine, and the whole average good. Therefore, if the gold-seeker bucks against the Sioux, and they are not cowards, they will have some of the loveliest fighting all along the valley of the White Earth and confluents. The Indians propose to have their price for the Hills, or will give the most active and effective assistance to the military in keeping out all intruders.

Senator Allison has prepared and sent to the Commissioner of Indian Affairs the following letter, which will, perhaps, prove a check of some Ring measures indicated in the dispatch about the 5,000 [3,000] extra head of cattle: [The Allison letter in all its essential respects appears above in Reuben Davenport's Sept. 21, 1875, letter and has not been repeated here. Ed.]

[Unsigned]

[*Chicago Daily Tribune*, Friday, October 1, 1875]

[September 22, 1875 – Capt. Andrew S. Burt, from Red Cloud Agency, Nebraska]

Crow Butte Council

(By Telegraph to *The Tribune*)

Crow Butte Council, [Wednesday] Sept. 22, via Fort Laramie, W. T., Sept. 23

The commissioners met on the council grounds this morning. There were only a few Indians present. Since the proposition to lease the hills, made on Monday, bitter dissensions have arisen among the chiefs, who have been in council day and night. Some do not want to sell. Others favor a lease. Others are willing to sell, but at exorbitant figures. To-day Spotted Tail did not meet the commission. He and his men were in council and could not come. The Hunkpapa, Miniconjou, Cheyenne, Arapahoe, Black Feet, and Oglala chiefs were on the ground, but did not go into the council. The last four tribes had a long consultation on the question of unity, at which Red Dog, Red Cloud, and others spoke. The conclusion reached was that they must counsel more together. To-night a great feast is being given in the Oglala camp. Much is expected from it. Spotted Tail's men are divided. Red Cloud and Young Man Afraid of his Horses hold their bands as a unit. The Miniconjous are divided, but the rest generally favor a lease. The young Crow [sic] Indians make the most opposition, threatening war if a lease is made. The prospect to-night is not favorable to any treaty because of jealousies between the whites. If the plan of leasing the Black Hills country fails, the commission will propose buying at a fair rate, not to exceed $5,000,000, paid in annuities, and charged to the General Support account with these Indians.

The commission will go to the council ground several more mornings. Then, if this fool's play continues, the camp will be removed to the agency, and the council will be held there, or not at all. The want of presents for the Indians, which never occurred before, is a serious detriment now. The commission has no power from Commissioner Smith to give anything.
[Unsigned]
[*New York Tribune*, Friday, September 24, 1875]

[September 23, 1875 – John T. Bell, from Red Cloud Agency, Nebraska]

Later. Thrilling Description of the Scene of the Threatened Outbreak at the Grand Council
Special Correspondence of *The Herald*
Red Cloud Agency, Neb. [Thursday] Sept. 23, 1875

Two thousand Indians, representing the various tribes of the whole Sioux nation, met in council to-day. They were gaily dressed and curiously painted. A number of the wild Wazhazhas brought in by "Young-Man-Afraid" attracted no little attention, not so much from a profusion of dress, as from a profusion of paint and an absence of dress.[7]

Colonel Mills and Captain Egan, each commanding a company of cavalry, rested in line in rear of the tent flies, under which sat the commission. At least 1,500 of the 2,000 Indians were armed, and a majority of them mounted. The Standing Rock Indians (John Burke of Omaha, agent) rode within 20 yards of the commissioners. The chairman requested Mr. Burke to have them dismount. He returned with the answer: "They refuse to dismount as they expect trouble and want their horses near them." The Indians all declined the invitation of the commission to be seated under the canvas.

Red Cloud came from the right, half way to the commissioners' tent, where he was met by Spotted Tail. Red Cloud wore, as usual, a slouch hat, a blanket and instead of pantaloons, red cloth leggings trimmed with brass bells. Spotted Tail was gaily decked in buckskin shirt and leggings trimmed with ermine wrought with porcupine quills and hung with locks of hair, acknowledged by all to be the most elegant and gorgeous dress on the ground. They shook hands and quietly squatted on the grass; all the leading Indian chiefs immediately assembled with Spotted Tail and Red Cloud.

At this moment, a death-like silence prevailed. While the commission were ignorant of an explosion resembling that of nitro-glycerine about them, it was afterwards known that both Red Cloud and Spotted Tail went to the council ground with the belief that if either attempted to speak he would be shot. The Oglalas feared Spotted Tail's influence and his control of the council, and were determined to kill him if he attempted speaking. The same could be said of Red Cloud and his men. Meanwhile, "Little Big Man," the leader of the 200 lodges of Wazhazhas was busily engaged in picking his half naked men from the crowd and placing them behind the cavalry.

The half breed squaw men were warned by the Indians to go away from the crowd as trouble was near at hand. They stood not upon the order of going, but went. "Young-Man-Afraid," who sat in the crowd quietly smoking a red-stone pipe, his quiet eye taking in the situation at a glance, summoned Sitting Bull to him. Immediately after, Sitting Bull whispered to an Indian by his side, "There will be trouble here and I will kill the first Indian that fires a shot. You stand by and watch me." He then directed "Young-Man-Afraid's" soldiers to displace "Little Big Man's" men and guard the white soldiers. This did not occupy the space of time we are writing it, and "Little Big Man" steals away and seats himself with three half-naked wild ones on a hill near by.

About this time a signal smoke was seen doubtless intended to call the Indians from the villages. An Indian began haranguing the Indians for bringing their arms into a council of peace. "Bull Eagle," a Miniconjou, replied, "The whites brought their soldiers armed first, and we came with arms last."

While it is almost incredulous to believe that the diplomatic move of Red Cloud and Spotted Tail joining their people without an attempt to speak in council prevented an outbreak that would doubtless have ended in the killing of all the commission, not as a fact that the spleen would have been directed to the commissioners, but that the jealousy of the tribes might have provoked a conflict between each other. No one will deny, and it is equally certain that, once begun, the commissioners would have suffered, and possibly all [would] have been killed. We can learn nothing of the plan or policy of the commission, but it is understood that no more chances are to be taken by the commission where trouble is anticipated.

[Unsigned]

[*Omaha Daily Herald*, Wednesday, September 29, 1875]

[September 23, 1875 – Albert Swalm, from Red Cloud Agency, Nebraska]

The Projected Massacre

Special Correspondence of *The Chicago Tribune*

Red Cloud Agency, [Thursday] Sept. 23

The safety of the entire Sioux Commission rested to-day, for a few moments, on the coolness and good judgment of one Indian chief, and the promptness of his aides in carrying out his orders. What might have been a repetition of the Modoc Massacre was happily averted, and possibly turned to profit. This was the third day of the council in session, and was attended by all the tribes. At the first council all the principal chiefs but Red Cloud were present, and they took the seats near to those of the commission. They were all very friendly, and seemed in an excellent mood for the work. At the second council a postponement was made on account of the absence of the Brules—Spotted Tail being their great chief. They were in council on the subject of the treaty, and therefore could not come. But they promised to be on hand at the next, and they were, in full force and feather. Spotted Tail to-day looked more like one of the romantic red chiefs that we only read of in Fennimore Cooper's works, than any man among the thousands present, and was in his usual amiable mood. The first tribes to reach the ground were the Oglalas, headed by Red Cloud and Young-Man-Afraid-of-his-Horses. They came in bands of tens, twenties, and fifties, nearly all armed, and all well mounted. They took up a position on the right of the council tents, the younger and more turbulent portion swinging lower down on the right toward the brush on the banks of the White Earth. The Cheyennes and Arapahoes came in, in the same manner, and these three tribes joined the circle that was started some 70 feet away from the awning that had been erected in front of the tents. About 200 chiefs, headmen, and head-soldiers, formed that portion of the circle on the right. The Hunkpapas, Miniconjous, Two-Kettles, Blackfeet, Sans Arcs, and others, formed the other half of the circle; but between the ends, in the centre, there was a vacant space of more than 100 feet. Just outside of the circle, and directly in front of the commissioners, was gathered a crowd of about 300 painted warriors, the most of whom were young men and very violent. The Hunkpapas, on coming into line in the circle, asked permission to remain mounted, and gave as their reason that some of the young men proposed to do great mischief, hence they wanted to be ready for anything that might turn up—and also to leave the field. The commission requested them to dismount; some did, but the majority remained mounted, with their guns in hand.

At no time could any of the Indians be got to fill up the strange vacancy in the council ring just in front of the commission, neither could any of the leading chiefs be induced to take the seats specially provided for them immediately in front of the commission. The seats were covered with an awning that drooped to the front—that is, toward the outer Indians. This awning was removed by request of the Indians, so that they could see the commission better—to use their own excuse for it. At about 2 o'clock, Bull Eagle, a Miniconjou, took up the remarks of American Horse, who had called attention to the fact that the whites were not accustomed to being surrounded by men with arms in their hands, and that it would look better if they were left outside of the circle. Bull Eagle called out loudly that the whites had been the first to bring soldiers on the field, and that they must abide by the result. American Horse, who is an Oglala, retorted that Bull Eagle was a fool, and must shut up or he would make him.

The irate Miniconjou then withdrew, and was now seen conversing with Little Big Man, one of the wild Wazhazhas of the North—the owner of one of the most fiendish faces in the whole gathering, and whose record is one of blood and brutality. Not long after, these nobles of the plains were found sneaking among the young men, being generally and unnecessarily very active. It should be remembered that many of the young men of all the bands, save some of the river tribes, are bitterly opposed to making any disposal whatever of the Black Hills, and, in the slang of the street, may be set down as very much "on their ear" about the steps proposed by their chiefs and head-men. Having threatened mischief, they were ready to fall in at the first opportunity, which they did to the number of over 200. Save the right flank of the cavalry force in attendance—Capt. Eagan's and Capt. Mills' companies of the Second, under the command of the latter—was covered by Indians, and the number increased every moment so that, in a few minutes, more than half the force was heavily covered by Winchester, Sharps, and Remington rifles, at not more than ten to fifteen paces. Mills' company was on the right, and completely double-covered. They were becoming altogether too thick for Egan, when he complained, and an interpreter was sent out to order them back. They only doubled up on Mills. Things were becoming "scary" at this time. The cavalry boys "stood to horse" with carbines in hand, while the commission held its seats as though nothing was occurring, yet showing a proper degree of uneasy interest in the matter.

Meanwhile the young chief, Young-Man-Afraid-of-his-Horses, had observed the movements of the discontented reprobates and, calling his lieutenant, he gave the order that his band should at once move on the Indians in the rear; and, as he is very popular with the people, his men were at hand, and in a minute were dashing their horses in among the hostiles and crowded them out into the field to the extreme right, and then formed on the flank, and held the ground until the council closed. Meanwhile the Young-Man was smoking his pipe as contentedly as though in his own tepee and, after the council closed, acted as rear-guard with his men for the commission to the agency. Previous to the move of Young-Man, nearly all the half-breeds near the tent, and some of the interpreters, had received warning from friends and relatives to clear away from the tent, as there was great danger. They did so, and left the whites unwarned. After the matter was over, those of Young-Man's men who turned out to "save the right" were most bitterly abused by those who had held the plan for a general massacre.

All the cavalry-men were to be shot down at the first fire, the horses stampeded, and then the commission were to get particular Jerusalem from that vacant space in front, which was held by Little Big Man and his crowd. To the promptness of Young Man and his men can be attributed the prevention of a massacre that would have been as complete as it would have been treacherous. In addition to the warning, proof is found in the fact that an unusually large number of shells for the breech-loaders were sold yesterday by the traders; that the bands who had camped near the road leading to the council-ground moved 2 miles away in the morning; and also, that a further band of 300 warriors, armed cap-a-pie, were discovered in a canon near-by, who were supposed to be there to make an attack on the agency, and to prevent the troops from Camp Robinson from going out to the council-camp, 8 miles below, after the fight should have commenced. A thousand facts known here all point to a corroboration of a plan for the massacre of the whole outfit by the young men under the lead of the wild devils of the North. The threat was made by them that they would kill the first man who spoke for the treaty; and no man was brave enough, save White Bull of the Sans Arcs, and he only incidentally, to say a word in favor of the sale of the country. The only commissioners proper to treat with such a gang are Gatling guns, with a Crook to manage them.

At a late hour last night the Hunkpapas moved their camp away from the neighborhood of Spotted Tail's and chose one easily defended. These Indians have favored business action all the time, hence, have been made the mark of jealousy and hatred by the young discontents. Their agent, Maj. Burke, of the Standing Rock Agency, leaves to-day for home, and the tribe starts in the morning.

In a condition of things that calls for the aid of Indian soldiery to avert a calamity, it is hardly probable that treaty-making will be very much of a success. The commission will hold another council to-morrow, when Young Man, American Horse, and Sitting Bull, who is now in charge of camp, will see that the hostiles are effectually squelched.

[Unsigned]

[*Chicago Daily Tribune*, Friday, October 1, 1875]

[This identical letter appears in *The Fort Dodge Messenger*, Thursday, Oct. 7, 1875, under the title, "The Indian Raid on the Commissioners. A Narrow Escape"]

[September 23, 1875 – "D," from Red Cloud Agency, Nebraska]

Red Cloud Agency

[Thursday] September 23d, 1875

Editor *Leader*

Nothing accomplished as yet. We held a council yesterday and to-day. Yesterday Spotted Tail failed to appear, so nothing was done. To-day all were on hand, and when the Indians were notified that the commission were ready, the Indians of Standing Rock Agency rode up and refused to dismount, saying they feared trouble and wanted to remain mounted.

"Little Big Man" came to the ground naked, threatening to kill a white man. A lot of the hostile young bucks got behind the cavalry and loaded their rifles and things looked a little mixed. Sitting Bull, to whom the President presented a rifle this spring, stepped into the circle with his gun in one hand and war club in the other and said "he would kill the first Indian who fired a shot." I cannot tell you all the little incidents, but it looked dubious for a time; fortunately, however, passing off all right, by the Indians breaking up the council and refusing to talk. There will be no talk to-morrow, but the Indians have promised to talk with the commissioners on Saturday. We cannot tell what the prospects are for a treaty. The Missouri River Indians are all ready to sell, so it is said, and Spotted Tail's people are also; but the Red Cloud Indians are divided, and it is hard to tell how the thing may turn, as the merest trifle may set the whole work at naught. The Standing Rock Indians are disgusted and start for home Saturday. They say they will not stay here any longer, but will agree to any treaty the others will make. There were from twelve to fifteen hundred Indians at the council to-day, in all their fixings, etc.

D.

[*Cheyenne Daily Leader*, Wednesday, September 29, 1875]

[September 24, 1875 – Charles Collins, from Red Cloud Agency, Nebraska]

West

(Special to the *Bee*)

Red Cloud Agency [Friday] Sept. 24, via Fort Laramie, Sept. 26

On Tuesday [Monday] the council adjourned on account of Red Cloud's absence. Wednesday adjourned on account of Spotted Tail's absence. To-day [yesterday] met five thousand chiefs and the head men of all tribes were present. After waiting until two o'clock Red Cloud and party appeared, and held a parley. Little Big Man chief of the wild Sioux rode around outside the circle of Indians and commissioners. The Indians [from] Standing Rock when requested to dismount and go into council refused, and said there was danger. Young Man afraid of his Horses requested to station guards of friendly Indians in the rear of the soldiers. The commission detailed soldiers and Indians to watch Little Big Man and his party, who threatened to kill the commissioners at one time. Great alarm prevailed. Twenty head chiefs went into council afterward, and said they would not meet the commissioners for two days.

Major Burke's Indians, of Standing Rock Agency, return home tomorrow. They authorize him to act as their agent in the treaty.

Things look squally; more troops coming.

Charles Collins

[*Omaha Daily Bee*, Monday, September 27, 1875]

[September 24, 1875 – Charles Collins, from Red Cloud Agency, Nebraska]

Red Cloud

(Correspondence of the *Bee*)

Red Cloud Agency, [Friday] Sept. 24

Editor *Bee*

Another week wasted in meaningless "talks" with the Indians, without an apparent gleam of hope in consummating a treaty. My last letter gave you the proceedings of the treaty council up to the 21st. At the conclusion of Monday's proceedings, the Indians notified the commissioners that as the next day (Tuesday) was issue day—the day the agent gives them beeves—they could not meet the commissioners. On Wednesday the commissioners were promptly on the ground at 10 a.m. They displayed their patience by remaining around the council until 2 o'clock, when a courier from Spotted Tail announced to them that as a relative of that renowned chief was sick, he could not favor the commissioners; so they again adjourned until Thursday [Sept. 23]. Promptly to time the commissioners were on the ground, but, as usual, no Indians put in an appearance until noon, when Col. Burke's Indians, belonging to Standing Rock Agency, on the Missouri River, dressed up in their noticeably gorgeous costumes, rode up, saluted their agent, and retired to await the further action of the council. Next came Major Bingham's Indians, from Cheyenne [River] Agency. They were followed by the Brules, Spotted Tail's tribe. At 2 o'clock p.m., Red Cloud, chief of the Oglalas, appeared, riding in a wagon driven by his son-in-law, Nick Janis, a well known Frenchman of the plains. The wagon on either side was flanked by large bands of mounted followers of Red Cloud. When it was ascertained that all the tribes were represented, the commissioners, through their interpreter, informed the Indians that they were ready to open the council, and now commenced the most interesting sight and subsequent exciting scenes we have ever witnessed. The council fronted to the east one hundred feet in front, and in a semicircle, the different tribes, on foot and horseback, ranged themselves. The Standing Rock Indians, mounted, took a position on the east flank of the semicircle, and right here was the first intimation we had of danger. Major Burke, their agent, said his Indians were all ready to go into council. Senator Allison suggested that they get off their horses and come closer, so they might hear the proceedings better. Major Burke said his Indians had expressed a desire to remain on horseback during the session of the council. When pressed for the reason of this somewhat singular conduct, the major said that his Indians apprehended some trouble, and wished to remain on horseback. While this parley was going on, all the other tribes, to the number of four or five thousand, had selected their positions [in] an open space of thirty or forty feet in front of the commissioners, but was vacant on the north and extending towards the east near the Oglalas and the Brules and extending west and north near the tribes from Standing Rock and Cheyenne agencies; toward the north-west were large parties of hostiles. All at once it was discovered that a complete circle (except the few feet fronting the commissioners) was formed around the commissioners and the two companies of cavalry were spread out in the rear in single file for a distance of several hundred feet. It was noticed that Little-Man-Afraid-of-his-Horses [Little Big Man] belonging to the untamed northern or wild Sioux, was riding around the circle, in front of the commissioners, naked and mounted on an elegant charger. He had, buckled around his waist, a belt filled with cartridges, while in his hand he carried a Winchester rifle. He was accompanied by his brother, another well known desperado named Sivure [Sioux] Jim and two other Indians.[8] While this peculiar state of affairs was occupying the attention of the council, Red Cloud, chief of the Oglalas was seen to rise up from the semi-circle to the right of the commissioners and walk over to the open space toward the east, simultaneously with this movement Spotted Tail, dressed in the most gorgeous fashion and realizing more fully than ever, fancy pictured him in our minds eye, the ideal Indian, so graphically described in Fennimore Cooper's works. The two chiefs met in the open space made by the semi-circle in front of the commissioners, they approached within two feet of each other, spoke a few words, and then squatted on the ground. Next came Red Dog, the orator of the Oglalas, and Red Cloud's man Friday, finally chief after chief joined the circle, until forty Indians had ranged themselves in the circle, the interpreters said they had gone into council. At this time rapid messages were passing between the commissioners and the military officers. It was noticed that every cavalry man was covered by from one to three Indians in their rear, to say nothing of the large numbers lying around promiscuously in the grass and willow patches skirting the White River in the rear of the commissioners and council. It was then noticed that Little-Big-Man had rode out on the prairie about a quarter of a mile. A squad mounted on horseback, rode around in the rear of the Indians, singing a melancholy Indian dirge, which we were informed by the interpreters was a supplication for bad Indians to harm no one. The moment was critical. Not a single white man of that little group composed of commissioners, interpreters, and military officers but fully realized that a singe accidental discharge of a fire-arm would precipitate a fight in which the odds were so uneven against the whites that it would be greater than a miracle if one of them should escape. At this critical moment Dr. J. J. Saville, the Indian agent here, sent word to "Young-Man-Afraid-of-His-Horses" (real chief of the Oglalas) to have his Indian soldiers remove the wild northern Sioux and other equally wild young Indians who were armed and mounted in rear of the cavalry. The chief referred to gave the order to his soldier crier (the Indians have regular soldiers and police, as well as police systems) to have the obnoxious Indians change position. A breath of relief was experienced from the knowledge that this source of danger was removed. It afterwards transpired that a cavalry orderly and two cavalrymen were detailed to watch Little Big Man, and on his making the first motion to fire his rifle, to shoot him down; half a dozen of well-disposed Indians were also out on a similar mission, so that no matter where these few hostiles went they saw they were tracked. Red Dog finally got up from the circle of chiefs and said that they wanted two days to counsel among themselves. To this White Bull, a chief of the Cheyenne Agency, said that his associates had come a long way to attend the council; that Spotted Tail and Red Cloud had purposely been delaying and frustrating the council; that his friends were now going to leave the council and go home; he said that his people had come here to make a treaty, but they found so much dissension among the Oglalas and the Brules that they were disgusted; that so far the council proceedings had been mere child's play, and that now the commissioners could come and make a treaty with his people after they had got through here. At this moment Grass and Two Bears, chiefs of the Standing Rock Agency Indians, were introduced to the commissioners by their agent, Colonel Burke (an old resident of Omaha). They said they were going home and that they had confidence in their agent, and designated him to make a treaty in their name. Senator Allison again asked them if they realized the power they thus placed in the hands of their agent. They said they did. Senator Allison, in behalf of the commissioners, allowed them to leave for their homes. The commissioners closed the council and adjourned until Saturday.

It was reported last evening that 300 mounted warriors were found secreted about two miles northeast of this agency, and it is believed that in case of an outbreak at the council, they would have shown fight to any troops that might have come to reinforce those at the council. Last night a series of signals were arranged between Gen. Terry of the commission, who is stopping here, and the officers of Camp Robinson, one and a half miles distant.

There is a terrible state of excitement, conjectures and speculation, as to whether this was a real or imaginary scare; also to the possible results of the commission. There are agencies to [at] work not realized by the commissioners, which will go far toward frustrating the making of a treaty. While the commission is composed of men of an average intelligence, it noticeably lacks the very essentials necessary to the success of its mission, but as the mail bag is being closed, I will have to reserve other news for my next letter.

Charles Collins

[*Omaha Daily Bee*, Wednesday, September 29, 1875]

[September 23, 1875 – Capt. Andrew S. Burt, from Red Cloud Agency, Nebraska]
A Plot to Massacre the Black Hills Commission.
(By Telegraph to *The Tribune*)
Red Cloud Agency, Neb., [Thursday] Sept. 24 [23], via Fort Laramie, Sept. 25

This has been an important day with the Black Hills Commission. The occurrence of an outbreak was only prevented by the coolness of the Oglala Chief Young-Man-Afraid-of-his-Horse. About 1 o'clock Red Cloud with the Oglala bands came to the council grounds. Spotted Tail and his bands, the Hunkpapas, Miniconjous, and other river Indians, soon followed. While waiting for the usual preliminaries to be settled, the Hunkpapas sent in word that they would attend the council but would not dismount, giving as a reason that some of the discontented Oglalas and Cheyennes proposed to open fire on the commission, and break up the council. The Hunkpapas, being peacefully inclined, wanted to be out of harm's way. Soon after it was discovered that about 200 of the worst Indians, well armed and mounted on their best horses, had crossed White Earth River in rear of the cavalry, and had slipped by their right flank, until nearly the whole line of the cavalry was well covered by the Indians' rifles, one or two Indians with Winchester rifles to each man.

Young-Man-Afraid-of-his-Horses discovered the situation at a glance, and quietly ordered his own soldiers to clear the undergrowth of all Indians behind the troops and the commission. His lieutenant at once moved, and over two hundred Indians by actual count were made to march to the front. It was a very critical juncture, and to Young-Man-Afraid-of-his-Horses is the credit due of having prevented the possible slaughter of some of the commissioners. After the Indians had been removed, the band of Young-Man-Afraid-of-his-Horses was joined to the right flank of the cavalry here, which was extended in the shape of a V, with the chief's men next to the river. Young-Man-Afraid-of-his-Horses gave orders to kill any Indians caught aiming at the commission or doing anything to bring on a contest with other tribes. Big-Little-Man and his gang from the North, who were all present, each well mounted, and naked save a robe, were also constantly covered by the rifles of friendly Indians.

After affairs had quieted down, the leading chiefs of the Sioux, headed by Red Cloud and Spotted Tail, came into the center of the circle made by the Indians for consultation. The chiefs differed on the matter of leasing the Black Hills country to the government. The Brules and Oglalas wanted more time. White Bull of the Sans Arcs made a speech, reproaching the Indians at the council with foolishness, and informing them that all the river Indians would go home on Saturday. The council then broke up, some of the Indians manifesting the worst of feeling, especially those who were driven out of ambush.

The commission will hold no council with the Indians to-morrow, but will meet them on Saturday. The prospects to-night are against making any treaty. The Indians are divided by the jealousy of factions, and will not accept the lease plan. They will probably offer to sell, at any sum from $40,000,000 to $70,000,000 which the commission will not pay. The general opinion in and out of the commission is, that no treaty will be made.

I have just had an interview with one of the soldiers of Young-Man-Afraid-of-his-Horses. He says the Indians who were bent on mischief to-day are mostly young men from the Cheyenne, Arapahoe, and Oglala nations. They did not want the chiefs to consider any plan for disposing of the Hills, and had said in their council that they would do something to make them desist. Young-Man-Afraid-of-his-Horses replied that he would kill every man who dared to fire at a white man or the Indians, and he did think that they would not come to the ground this morning. The chief now guarantees perfect safety to all. Every one of his soldiers has been put in fighting trim, and Sitting Bull, one of his head men, is in charge of the council camp. No danger is apprehended now. As further proof of the intended massacre, half-breeds and interpreters were warned by Indian relatives and friends to keep out of the council tent and to leave the ground. Most of them did so. Big-Little-Man also threatened to shoot down any chief who should speak in favor of disposing of the Black Hills, and he so told Spotted Tail, who did not speak.

[Unsigned]

[*New York Tribune*, Monday, September 27, 1875]

[September 24, 1875 – Reuben Davenport, from Red Cloud Agency, Nebraska]

The Black Hills

Red Cloud Indian Agency, Neb., [Friday] Sept. 24, 1875

The annals of human horrors might have gained a new and bloody chapter yesterday, had a signal been given. The Grand Council for the perpetuation of peace between the white people and the Sioux nation by the purchase of the Black Hills and the Big Horn Mountains would in a moment have become a scene of massacre unparalleled since that of Fort Phil Kearny.[9] It scarcely needs further demonstration that the making of a treaty at present will be most difficult, and is, perhaps, even impossible. Stumbling blocks have gradually filled the way since Lieutenant Colonel Dodge's expedition was sent into the Black Hills, and the commissioners, in the manner in which they have conducted the preliminary negotiations, as I have shown in a previous letter, have been far from mitigating the jealousies between tribes and chiefs, but have rather engendered fresh feeling of discontent. The two commissioners who are thoroughly acquainted with the Indian character—Messrs. Hinman and Beauvais—ought to have been able to have prevented this, but they did not. Beauvais is, indeed, disgusted with the modern method of treating with the Indians, and says that if a great feast had been made for all the chiefs and an immense pile of blankets and other presents had been placed in the middle of the council circle, they would have come to terms long ago. But this has not been done, and the experience of yesterday is the result of estimating the intelligence of the Indian too high and of expecting him to treat and bargain in the abstract. His mode of doing business is otherwise. He requires some evidence of his promised compensation to be visible and within his reach before his native enthusiasm for a trade is aroused. He is by nature a barterer, and a prompt one too, but all his transactions are performed with tangible values and seldom with mere promises, unless they emanate from him only. The commissioners have excited in him suspicion of a fraud intended, in making such a proposition as that of borrowing or leasing the Black Hills and Big Horn Mountains, instead of buying them outright, in accordance with the idea with which the chiefs were impressed when they went to Washington last spring. The speech of President Allison on Monday was a great surprise to all the Indians. Whenever they had talked heretofore with the commissioners the words used had been, "to buy the Black Hills." Without questioning the honesty of the commission it cannot fail to be apparent that to a dull intellect there would seem in this change of purpose a deep design to deceive. The motive would be in lessening the estimate of the councilmen of the value of what they would be relinquishing. Many of their chiefs are shrewd enough to discern so much but, unfortunately, cannot see further. The commissioners cannot be accused of insincere dealing, because they are all gentlemen of too much sagacity to stop where the Indian would and imagine that the acceptance of such a proposition would be more to the pecuniary advantage of the government than to him.

The feeling among the Indians inimical to the acceptance of a reasonable price for their lands has been mainly caused and nurtured by the miserable class of creatures called "squaw men" who, by all the machinations in their power, are and have been endeavoring to exaggerate in their minds the value of the gold region sought after. Spotted Tail has a son-in-law, a portly Frenchman [Francis Boucher], and Red Cloud's daughters are married to Nick Janis and Todd Randall.[10] These men have strong influence with the chiefs and their people, are sought after by them for advice, and in reality, if a treaty is made, will be the makers of it on the part of the Oglalas and Brules. Fielding [William Fielder], an interpreter, is of equal importance among the Missouri River Sioux. To serve private interests such men as these incite the Indians to any course which suits them and too often succeed in their purposes. They have considerable control over the Sioux with whom they reside. It is often used to embarrass the agents and is now employed to thwart the plans of the commission. Their influence is so powerful that orders for them to leave the Indian reservation forthwith have been time after time rescinded almost under compulsion of their red skin constituents.[11]

Another and more imminently dangerous element, however, to create trouble in council and lodge, are the northern Indians, whom the sub-commission, with the aid of Louis Richard, induced to attend the treaty-making. It would have been wiser to have allowed these wild warriors, who have never before been at an agency, to remain where they have hitherto roamed. Having never pretended to behave themselves, their right to the consideration of the government is very small. Little Big Man, their chief, has been a devil of discord in every council held by the Indians in their villages. He has argued, threatened and cursed to induce the Cheyennes and Oglala and Brule Sioux to withdraw from treating with the whites. The young men of the first would require little persuasion to put them in readiness for any devilment. Southern Cheyennes are still among them and still bitterly hostile to the whites. One of them, a week ago, was breathing bloody threats through the camps, which it is now certain were not altogether without significance. He had made a vow to shoot a commissioner in the council, and there were a sufficient number of young bucks in a similar mood to wipe out the whole of the delegation from Tonka-Sila.[12] Little Big Man abided many days at the village of Young-Man-Afraid-of-His-Horses. The young Oglalas are easily excitable, and do not like the peaceful pace of Red Cloud, nor, indeed, the stoic policy of Young-Man-Afraid-of-His-Horses. They envy and hate Sitting Bull, head soldier, and they are ready to do war or murder on their own responsibility. Little Big Man was also received by the Wazhazha and Kiykusa bands, and on the evening before the talk of yesterday was at the camp of Sintigeliska [Spotted Tail], engaged in an earnest council with the great chief. So earnest was it that it gradually grew confused and discourteous, and

Spotted Tail and Little Big Man exhausted Dakota invective upon each other. Little Big Man went from the council fire swearing away the life of Sintigeliska, who answered him that he had but once to die. Little Big Man threatened him with annihilation if he came to the general council. His anger knew no bounds because Spotted Tail would not relinquish his position in favor of ceding the Black Hills. For a week the young men in all the bands had not been in a happy frame of mind, and had warned their elders, when they were gathered to smoke the calumet and talk, to "heed the young men!" Even some of Spotted Tail's braves had joined in this cry.

Slight rumors, ugly in purport, had come to the agency during Wednesday, and in the evening not a red man was to be seen lounging about, as was usual, but all was still and deserted. Not so in the tepees, however. Impending trouble was continuously discussed, and there were close councils of the young men as well as of the old.

The commission on Tuesday [Thursday] morning started at a seasonable hour, with the escort of 120 cavalrymen for the council tree. Every soldier carried his carbine loaded. There was undoubted apprehension in all minds of an uncertain danger. Its importance or exact phase was unknown. The council ground was reached long before there were any Indians there, except the soldiers of Sitting Bull—fifty in number—who were on guard to secure the chairs, benches, and tables left in the tepee. The sun blazed hotly and there was no breeze to cool the air. Indians were grouped on the knolls and single horsemen were observed at a distance galloping through hollows, appearing and disappearing. Patience is a virtue with which the commission have shown an intimate acquaintance, much to their credit, as the savages are superlative in vexatious delays. They sat under the canopy and talked, and finally ate lunch in the tent before a single Indian came to shake hands with them. The ground was covered by a fine dust which the slightest movement caused to rise in penetrating clouds. The question discussed was the abandonment of the negotiation unless the Indians came forward and gave them some decisive response to their late proposition. Much discouragement was expressed by certain commissioners.

At noon No Flesh and a few Brules arrived, and soon after Spotted Tail came with all his sub-chiefs and warriors. They dismounted from their horses at a little distance and sat down to smoke and converse. From that moment dusky horsemen continued to appear over the eastern horizon, most of them in close rank. After the Brules, the Yanktonais and Hunkpapas appeared. Most of them were unarmed. They dismounted near the bank of the river, where they secured their ponies and then advanced toward the canopy, led by their prophetess and real chieftainess, Mrs. Galpin, a civilized and educated Indian lady, celebrated along the Missouri River as the widow of Galpin, formerly a trader at Standing Rock and a companion of Father de Smet in his dangerous visit to the camps of the wild and cruel tribes then living in the north. The Flat Heads were the principal of these and at length became tractable Christians and good Roman Catholics.

The Indians' cheiftainess, Mrs. Galpin a few years ago possessed a wonderful influence over all the Dakotas on the Missouri, and they evidently are guided by her at present. She is of matronly appearance and modest and timid in manner. Her features are of the Roman type and very refined and benevolent in expression. Her complexion is of a rich olive tint, her eyes darkly brown and her long and luxuriant black hair is slightly tinged with gray. She at present wears mourning attire, and there is nothing in her dress or countenance indicating the Indian. She commands the utmost respect among both whites and Indians, and her example and benevolent efforts in the cause of the advancement of her race are of great and undoubted public service.[13]

When these Indians were drawn up on the east side of the council ground, Mrs. Galpin standing at their front, carrying a sunshade over her bare head, Spotted Tail rose from his seat in the midst of his chiefs and came forward toward the commissioners, who were grouped under the canopy. His tread was stately and his mien noble. He stood before them a fine type of barbarian manhood. They had never seen him before in his costume of state, which he now wore. It consisted of leggings, striped with red and gold, and a jacket, richly embroidered with beads in which yellow, green, and white were harmoniously blended; and over all was a finely woven blanket, parti-colored in red, green, and white. In his hair, which was dressed in true Indian style, he wore two brilliantly tinted eagle feathers. It could be seen that, while the heart of the great chief was as firm as a rock and un-touched by fear, he felt a grave consciousness of the uncertain issue of that day's gathering. There was a paleness and a set expression in his face as he approached; but it immediately vanished when he grasped the hands of the white chiefs and greeted them with a true and brave smile. Spotted Tail knew at that moment that he might be standing in the midst of life that soon would be transformed into death; that the menace of Little Big Man was not made idly. By the time that Spotted Tail had exchanged greetings with all the whites present the Indians from the Standing Rock Agency had moved up closer to the commissioners and sat motionless on their horses, with guns supported with the right thigh and hand.

Looking across the plain to the west long ranks of Indians were seen, just crossing the verge of the horizon and riding down the long slope toward the council tree. It seemed as if there would be no cessation of the successive emerging of line after line of armed warriors to view. So well did they preserve the order which they have learned to imitate from the white soldiery that it looked as if a brigade of cavalry was approaching. The air was filled with their choruses. Their guttural voices, richly blending, sounded very melodiously. As these dense ranks advanced it was seen that each man bore a rifle, polished to a shining cleanliness, and was attired so loosely that all of his clothing could be cast off in an instant. They rode their ponies with nothing on their backs but blankets. Each soldier band formed a separate line of battle, and thus they closed into the circle on the west and south, Young-Man-Afraid-of-His-Horses at the head of the Oglalas, and the Cheyennes, under Little Wolf, massing in their rear to the number of 200.

The armed array of nearly all the Indians made an unpleasant impression on the commissioners. The chiefs and braves from the Standing Rock Agency, known to be very friendly in disposition and most completely under control, were asked why they remained mounted in council. Their reply was:

"We are afraid there will be trouble in this council, and if there is we want to have our horses near us. We would like to remain mounted."

The commissioners, after a moment's consultation, sent reply by an interpreter that, if they desired it, they could stay on their horses. Many of the Hunkpapas, Yanktonais, Brules, and Oglalas dismounted and sat on the earth, on the inner side of the circle. Young-Man-Afraid-of-His-Horses sat thus among his warriors, his father being on his right hand.

A silence reigned and the immense assemblage seemed almost inanimate. Directly in front of the commissioners, outside the circle, Little Big Man, in perfect nudity and painted appropriately, sat upon a splendid gray charger, probably once taken from a white man, with his scalp. Around him were a few of his young men, in scanty attire.

Little Big Man is of small stature, but finely formed, the well rounded muscles bulging from his limbs and indicating great strength. In his dark skin he looked like a bronze statue of some ancient gladiator. His hair is long and sable, his head small and round, and his features very regular for those of an Indian. His eyes gleam very wickedly below a low brow, and seem at times to have a look of madness and demonic cruelty. On the left, two other savages were observed to be naked, one of them wearing over his shoulders a checkered tablecloth. His name is White Robe.[14] The other was seated on a magnificent black pony, and both were painted in readiness to do battle. Spotted Tail's people were grouped on this side, and No Flesh regarded the naked Indians with watchful scrutiny. Young-Man-Afraid-of-His-Horses, although his face never lost its stolidity, kept his eyes fixed upon Little Big Man while he quietly smoked.

To say that the scene was brilliant and impressive is very little. The costumes of the chiefs were varied and conspicuous. Every Indian had a bunch of feathers tied in his hair. Their guns and pistols had been polished so that they shone brightly in the sun. The vast ring of savage warriors and chiefs in dense array was a noble sight, but suggestive enough of possibilities to thrill the stoutest breast. The cavalry had been posted in the same position as on the first day of the council.

The silence was broken by a crier, a venerable Indian with good lungs, who secured attention and indicated the commencement of business. Then about 100 chiefs came forward and shook hands with the commissioners, who smiled and responded to their "How! how! Cola!" with patient resignation. The principal of these chiefs were Conquering Bear, Black Bear, and Yellow Hair, Oglalas; Little Black Foot of the Blackfeet Sioux; White Bear of the Yanktonais; White Bull [Sans Arc], Turkey Legs, a renegade Cheyenne; Calfskin Shirt, Oglala; Red Cloud, Slow Bull, Miniconjou; Pawnee Killer, Kiyuksa; Wolf Nicoleus [Necklace] and Running Antelope. The last said that he desired the concluding council to be held then, as he and his people desired to go home. White Bear brought his son to the commissioners and presented him, saying, with pleasure and pride shining in his face, that he had resigned his chieftainship, having become very old, and had given it to him. The sense of fear among the older Indians showed itself by their refusal then to draw nearer the commissioners and share the shelter of the canopy. The latter, therefore, caused a portion of it to be removed so that they could be seen by their red brethren.

Silence once more fell over the conclave, and Red Cloud and Spotted Tail, amid murmurs of approbation in the Dakota tongue, advanced from opposite sides of the circle toward each other. Red Cloud, who preserved a stately dignity, stopped before reaching the centre and Spotted Tail was thus compelled to go the farther distance to meet him. He did not hesitate, however, but with a natural, lofty grace, showing him superior to petty scruples of pride and the living impersonation of Fenimore Cooper's North American savage, he made a merit of an intended humiliation, and raised himself in the estimation of whites and barbarians.[15] The scene was historical and pregnant with meaning to those who contemplated while gazing upon it the past, present, and future of the red race. The opinion that never again will a similar one be enacted, with the same significant surroundings, will surely not be disputed. The present is the last grand gathering of the greatest of the surviving Indian nations.

Spotted Tail and Red Cloud sat on the ground in opposite positions, and were immediately joined by Two Strike and Little Wound, both second in authority in their respective tribes. Other chiefs quickly followed their example, striding into the arena, and an inner circle being formed a council within a council was soon in progress. A ripple of uneasiness seemed to pass through the vast throng. Red Dog at this moment arose and spoke as follows, seemingly greatly excited:

"My friends, we are here to treat peacefully with the men sent to us by the Great Father. But it seems to me that it looks very bad for both the whites and the Indians to be here with their guns in council."

Before this speech a silent movement had been observed by Colonel Mills and Captain Egan, commanding the cavalry guard, and Sitting Bull had gone over to the spot where Young-Man-Afraid-of-His-Horses was seated and placed himself opposite him. While Red Dog was speaking a band of young men from the Oglala and Cheyenne camp had crossed the White River silently and placed themselves in the rear of the soldiers and council. Some had dismounted and thrown themselves among the grass and shrubbery, and others still remained on their horses, hidden by the tall bushes near the bank of the stream. When those visible were first observed, their guns were cocked. Little Big Man, astride of his powerful charger, was meanwhile keeping up a constant movement in the outskirts of the crowd, circling around and around with a few of his braves. Indians who had been sitting on the ground suddenly got up and mounted their horses. Instinctive perception of the imminent danger by this time had aroused the small group of white men seated in the centre of the perfect trap formed by the Indians. The first shot, the brief struggle and the finale of terrific butchery was confidently expected.

Your correspondent went to the rear of the canopy to observe the Indians who were lying in ambush, and found there General Terry and Colonel Comingo, both agitated. Colonel Mills mounted his best soldier, Corporal Ballard, on the finest horse in his company and sent him around the outer edge of the crowd, with an order to keep near Little Big Man, watch him closely, and on the smallest hostile signal to shoot him dead. Corporal Ballard is well known as a perfect marksman, and is rashly brave. He obeyed his orders. The cavalry were moved backwards a few paces, to enable them to manoeuvre easily. Captain Egan swore between his teeth to "give the red devils hell if a shot was fired." Orders were given, however, that Spotted Tail's and Red Cloud's people be not fired at.

Young-Man-Afraid-of-His-Horses had meanwhile seen the danger and knew its approach before the whites. Those who observed him say that he simply removed his pipe from his mouth and spoke a word to an attendant warrior, who quietly retired, and in a few minutes a band of Indians had driven the young bucks from their position in the rear, and had formed in line of battle to support the troops. Their leader, an old man on a white horse, meanwhile loudly exhorted them to courage and loyalty to the whites, reciting, as a refrain, his own brave deeds. The movement was as well and quickly executed as would have been possible for a company of United States soldiers.

For ten minutes longer there was the most intense suspense. An assurance then began to be felt that Little Big Man had seen his plans frustrated, and soon after he was observed on the inside of the conclave, sitting quietly on his horse, but wearing an angry and malicious expression on his face. He subsequently shouted loud disapprobation of parts of White Bull's speech.

Old-Man-Afraid-of-His-Horses was standing in the inner circle of chiefs, and joined in the council. Red Dog, after the moment of apprehension had passed, again came forward and addressed himself especially to Commissioner Beauvais. He said:

"You are in too much of a hurry to make this treaty. You can go around in the States in summer and winter and walk where you like. But you are afraid of staying out here too late in the season. We have fine weather here now and there is no reason why you should not remain here long enough to allow us to make up our minds about selling our country. It is not so plain to us yet. We have got an important business before us now and you must give us time to consider it."

He concluded by saying that the Two Kettles band were starving and that the commissioners had better give them some beef to eat or they would not remain longer at the council, but would go home.

White Bull, of the Sans Arc band, next delivered an effective harangue, in which he accused the Oglalas and Brules of petty jealousies and squabblings, and said that Red Cloud and Spotted Tail were fools. He said that he and his people had come there to do business and were ready now to make the treaty. They had long ago decided on what they should do. They should not remain here any longer than two more suns, when they would start for home. They had many hundred miles to travel, and the snow would soon cover the ground.

The principal chiefs said they would be ready to meet the commissioners again on Saturday, and the conclave then began to disperse. The Indians from the Standing Rock Agency came forward to the canopy and said that they would leave this country on Saturday for home. The resisted the persuasions of the commissioners and declared that they could not remain longer. They had business at home to attend to and wanted to return before winter. They were asked by President Allison about their position in regard to a treaty should one be framed with the other Indians. They replied that they would delegate their "father" or agent, Major Burke, to accept or reject it for them according to his judgment.

The commissioners got into the artillery ambulances and returned to the agency under escort. A band of Oglalas was stationed on an elevated point in the road to watch for their safety, as I was informed with signs when I rode up to them in advance of the general cavalcade.

Since the council of yesterday evidence has been accumulating of the reality of the danger of a general massacre. It was observed that at the critical time the half-breeds under the canopy, all of whom, an unusual fact, carried rifles, stole to the rear and disappeared in the brush along the river. Two of them, well known here as interpreters, ran down its banks four or five miles. All of them had received warnings from their Sioux relatives. They had been told that there would be trouble in the council and that a great many people would be killed. It has also been learned that the young braves who stationed themselves in the rear of the gathering, near the stream, were exactly equal in numbers to the troops on guard, and that each man had his special victim assigned him, who stood immediately in front of him, within easy range of his gun. Louis Richard, the interpreter for the commission, received warnings from several Indians to leave the council. He told them that he had been employed to interpret for the commission and that he should do it if it caused his death. During all the excitement Louis stood in the most dangerous place, directly in front of the commissioners, with a stolid countenance and no betrayal of the slightest knowledge of his peril. At the dispersion many of the elderly Indians were very earnest in their congratulations to the white men on the avoidance of a disturbance. One of them actually hugged your correspondent and shook him repeatedly by the hand, mistaking him for an amiable representative of the Great Father.

The loyalty shown by Young-Man-Afraid-of-His-Horse is in keeping with his record as a good Indian. The commission have discussed the propriety of recognizing him as the principal chief of the Oglalas, and certainly the great extent of his influence and his undoubted rank would justify such an act as wise and politic. Red Cloud's usefulness has gone, although he is too proud to believe it. He is only nominally a chief, having formerly been Old-Man-Afraid-of-His-Horses head soldier and was raised to power only by the will of the whites. He is not recognized by many of the best men of his tribe as their chief. Young-Man-Afraid-of-His-Horses not only deserves the reward promised him by the commission for his expedition to the north, but other and more valuable appreciation for his latest services.[16]

[Unsigned]

[*New York Herald*, Thursday, October 7, 1875]

[September 25, 1875 – Ed Welch report, about Red Cloud Agency, Nebraska]

The Great Council—Little Big Man after the Commissioners

Mr. Ed. Welch arrived in this city [North Platte] on Tuesday last [Sept. 28] direct from Spotted Tail and Red Cloud agencies. He made the trip in three days. When he left [ca. Sept. 25] the Indians were holding councils among themselves for the purpose of arriving at some conclusion as to what course they should pursue in the Black Hills matter. Owing to the hostile threats and demonstrations of Little Big Man, chief of the wild northern Sioux, the commissioners refused to hold any further intercourse with the Indians at the point selected for the council about nine miles from Red Cloud.

The last day of the council at this point (Crow Butte grounds) the movements of Little Big Man were so suspicious, that Red Cloud and Spotted Tail stationed their mounted warriors two deep so as to encircle the council grounds, for the purpose of defeating whatever evil designs the hostile Indians might have. It transpired on this day that Little Big Man was the identical brave who had threatened to kill a commissioner; and this fact in connection with the movements of his band of three hundred warriors, rendered the situation somewhat uncomfortable for the distinguished gentlemen composing the commission; insomuch, that they adjourned to the fort, and notified the Indians that they would have no further intercourse with them until the chief men of the tribes represented there had arrived at some definite conclusion as to what they would do. This was the state of affairs when Mr. Welch left.

[North Platte *Western Nebraskian*, Saturday, October 2, 1875]

[September 27, 1875 – Charles Collins, from Red Cloud Agency, Nebraska]

Red Cloud

(Special Correspondence of the *Bee*)

Red Cloud Agency [Monday] Sept. 27

Editor *Bee*

The excitement experienced by the commissioners and the other white spectators after the participation in last Friday's [Thursday's] proceedings at the council ground, and hearty congratulations at their escape is rapidly being supplanted by the hope that the Indians will to-day make some propositions by which some kind of treaty may be made. The head men of all the tribes interested in the Black Hills have been in council at Spotted Tail's camp since Friday.

About noon yesterday (Sunday) the principal chiefs, to the number of twenty, called on the commissioners and the latter, intent to discover what, if any, progress the chiefs had made looking towards the making of a treaty, gave them a first-class dinner at Dear's restaurant; with the understanding that they meet in the commissioners' room at two o'clock p.m. The Indians were present at the designated time, with the exception of Red Cloud. It being an inexcusable and traditional breech of Indian etiquette for any minor chiefs to speak on questions of general interest in the absence of ranking chiefs, a messenger was then dispatched to bring in the wayward chief. After a few minutes delay Red Cloud put in an appearance with a self-satisfied smile suffusing his strongly-marked and dusky features, apparently pleased at the idea that the council realized the fact that his presence was indispensable. Senator Allison instructed the interpreter to say they were glad to meet them; that they were anxious to return to their homes, and would like to know whether or not the Indians had come to any definite conclusion. To this the Indians answered in an equivocal manner. The commissioners then told them that they did not want to know what conclusion—if any—they had arrived at, but only whether or not they had come to any conclusion, supplementing the remark by an additional one, that unless the Indians had arrived at some definite idea as to what they wanted to do in the matter of treating for the Black Hills, it would be useless to go to the council ground to-day [Monday]. The Indians merely replied that they would meet the commissioners to-day, and then Red Cloud majestically wrapped his blanket around him and walked out of the room, followed by the other Indians.

The commissioners and other white men about the agency are just beginning to realize the dangerous position they occupied at the council-ground on Friday [sic]. Every new development since then shows that a preconcerted movement as thoroughly understood amongst the disaffected, that at a given signal they were to fire on the cavalry. Little Big Man, a chief from the wild northern camp, aided by a few bad followers, had, on Friday [sic] morning, threatened to shoot the first chief that spoke in the council in favor of making a treaty. This was thoroughly understood by Spotted Tail, Red Cloud and other chiefs, and this accounts for none of the chiefs addressing the commissioners. If Little Big Man should have fired the fatal shot, the cavalry, acting under instructions, on the first report of a gun, to fire into the Indians on the right of the council grounds without further orders, would have fired into friends and foes alike. The consequence would have been that not a single white man present would have survived to tell the tale of the council massacre. We are informed that large bodies of Indians were secretly amongst the hills in the vicinity of the agency. All of the ponies were driven up and other preparations made for moving camp on the first symptoms of a fight. After the return of the commissioners from the council ground, a guard has been stationed inside the agency stockade, which is still on duty. That the commissioners, without exception, were thoroughly scared, and had good reason to be so, is now clearly demonstrated. This morning, previous to the commissioners starting out, they all armed themselves, and took extra precautions against an attack from visible or invisible foes. The proceedings of to-day's council have been a signal failure, so far as the possibilities of making a treaty is concerned. The commissioners now admit that before any treaty can be made with the Indians that would be recognized or endorsed by the American people, the Indians will have to be toned down. They have been so humored and pampered by investigating committees, Indian agents and white men, who come on the reservations, that they have come to believe that the white man is their servant, and that it is their natural right to not only demand, but receive, anything they want. If an Indian agent or the government doesn't give an Indian what he asks for, he goes on the war-path, threatens to burn an agency, robs and scalps a few white men, comes to the agency, boasts of his prowess, and makes some more threats. The agent immediately empties his storehouse to him, and the government fills it up again. It is now well understood that to get plenty of rations and annuity goods, they have first to establish a reputation as being bad Indians, the government then gives them everything they want as a means of reconciliation. Good Indians at this and other agencies that we came in contact with during the treaty council, complain that they are neglected by the agent in the latter's zeal to reconcile the bad Indians who are continually committing depredations. But we ought not to complain of the Indians; human nature is the same everywhere. When any people, white or black, or copper-colored, have all their wants supplied without labor and without an equivalent, it is but natural that they would become aristocratic or haughty. The Indian draws his rations weekly of beef, flour, coffee, and all the other luxuries; he is annually supplied with blankets, tents, horses, etc., etc., for which he renders no visible equivalent, and as a consequence he comes to the very logical conclusion, that he must be some superior being. This was satisfactorily illustrated by a perusal of the speeches. Nebraskans will in a spirit of humility be perfectly satisfied to accede to the demand of Spotted Tail and other chiefs for an extension of the southern boundaries of their reservation into Nebraska as far as the middle of the North Platte River, establishing, as Spotted Tail and Red Dog requested, mounds along, and in the middle of that river, to show the gentle savage where he is secure from justice on his return raids from plundering and scalping frontier settlers. As an evidence of Indian oratory and the spirit of the Indians in council, I give you the following few samples by the head men of the Sioux nation assembled to talk with the commissioners at to-day's council. Red Dog, speaking for Red Cloud, said: "The Great Father picked you commissioners out to do business for him, but instead of coming here as peace commissioners, you are afraid and bring large numbers of troops to scare our people. We are six nations, and we have been fed by the whites for six generations; we are now in the seventh. Now I want you to guarantee us for ourselves, our children, and the white men and half-breeds among us, food, clothing, and everything we want for six generations more. We want to get back pay for all the unfulfilled promises made by former treaty commissioners; we want to get horses, wagons, cattle, clothing, etc., for each head of our Indian families. You have surveyed our lands; we want you to take the surveyors off our land; we want you to run the lines so that the southern line of our reservation will be extended into the State of Nebraska as far as the middle of the North Platte River; that to be boundary line; President asks for Black Hills, but head chief don't want to part with hills, except the centre, where the gold is. We won't sell the Powder River and Big Horn country; we don't want the whites to have any other road into Black Hills except the Custer's trail, where the thieves come through; don't want a road running through our reservation and all over our country."

Little Bear, chief at Cheyenne [River] Agency, said he "would try and tell the commissioners what didn't please him. When a man is on his own land he is not afraid to speak; if a man is on another man's land he ought not to want to quarrel; I am on my land and you are on my land. Our Great Father got a house full of money; if a man goes in and takes it out, will that suit everybody? These hills here of gold, all Indians watching it to get rich on it, last seven years; whites working hills. If a man owns anything he wants to get rich on it. You, gentlemen, come from the President looking for something, and so are we; so we will talk as gentlemen while you are here; what people has done in the hills we would like to get back pay. You came from President to hear what we say; I will tell you, so you can report to the Great Father; as long as Indians live we want them fed, we want our annuities distributed right; want to be helped and taken care of forever; council men are here, and we want to hear what the Great Father has to say; what the President does for us is very little; our agent been with us three years and a half, but now I'll give him back to our Great Father; land belongs to us, and we want to control; the interpreters we have there have filled their pockets, and now we can get along without them; want to get a Catholic priest for an agent; have had enough of the other; we want to derive a benefit for what we have; we want to have the privilege of selecting our own traders, half-breed or squaw men; when the President does anything at north of Cheyenne Agency he does it very small. From now henceforth we want more annuity goods than we have been getting; when we get annuity goods we would like to get the bills of them, so we could have one of our half-breeds look after them; when you have done all this, we will think of what you have to say to us."[17]

Spotted Tail – "You men sitting here were all drunk, and you threw a big blanket over my head; threw a big blanket over me and I was nearly smothered; have thrown the blanket off, and now I'll talk to you and tell you what I was afraid of; people want to buy land, if so, we want the Nebraska line changed."

Allison – "A new question. Our Great Father sent us out to treat for the Hills, and that is all we can now decide."

Spotted Tail – "Agencies here and other agencies elsewhere we want to occupy as long as our race exists. If Great Father should want to move us again we would want a great amount of pay as long as we live on this earth. We want to leave it with the President and get interest on it forever."

The amount paid must be such that the interest will support the Indians each year. Part of this each year will sell for something to eat and for buying annuity goods; he will trade some of it for stock and cattle and each year for mares. The next wagon he gets he wants them to be strong. The work cattle he got were old; wants some good work cattle each year; wants part of annuity in powder, lead and guns; "I want pay every year, and the people want clothing and sustenance for as long as they live; we will agree to this as long as the land does not fall to pieces. The agent has talked to my white friends and relations in a way I don't like; Great Father, give me tools to work and that is time; agent wants to drive away my white friends; these white men (squaw men) are my relatives, and with their help I can make fences, cut hay, etc. When I made treaty at Laramie I told you I wanted them to have the same rights as myself, whoever learns them right; I want the Catholic church and Catholic priest to take care of them, and learn them to write, as they will understand how to do business like white people." He don't want the troops to leave here from his agency and watch the Black Hills. His friends at lower Brule Agency, who live very poor, and I want President to send them agent.

Old Mandan (Two Kettles). "Here are two parties with arms, troops and white men on hand, but in the name of God want to hold a good council. Our Great Father has asked questions, but it seems we are not all of one mind; Great Father has a big safe; so have we in the Hills; that is the reasons why we can't come to conclusion. I want a great amount for Hills.[18]

"Great Father has promised us great things;

"Before we sell the hills, these people steal our hills as long as our tribe lives; want Great Father to furnish us with blankets, and what we want; your people are great and good people, and this day we want to do our business correct, and put at mouth of Cheyenne River all people who misuse us; we want you to remove them quietly. Everything that God has given me has been taken away from me; now I want a Roman Catholic to look after me; wants the Roman Catholic priest to make him wise and educate him. Now there is something we want, and we want our Great Father to grant it. We want 70 millions for the hills— you white people put your money out at interest, and half breeds in my tribe are all my relations, and like me, and guards got to treat them like me. Half breeds and white men are in my tribe; I want to select traders from them, so as to have several trading points on agency. Hereafter when our Great Father sends annuity goods, we want to pick out white men and see that bill is correct; we want telegraph operator at our line there; we come here to have a settlement, and there are some soldiers at our agency, and want to have power to remove them when we think we can do without them; want the President to give ammunition, guns, etc; in liberal quantities; every sensible man looks ahead, and he wants to have a home, a farm, and we want each Indian that runs a farm to have all these things. We want our agent."

Charles Collins

[*Omaha Daily Bee*, Tuesday, October 5, 1875]

[September 27, 1875 – "D," from Red Cloud Agency, Nebraska]

From our Special Correspondent

Red Cloud Agency

[Monday] Sept. 27th, 1875

Editor *Leader*

Another council to-day, the first since last Thursday. Red Dog, Little Bear, Spotted Tail, and White Bull were the speakers. They all wanted to sell the Black Hills, but wanted to be fed for seven generations to come, to be clothed, to have horses and wagons, etc. etc., and one wanted seventy million dollars for the Hills.[19] The council was a farce. The Indians talked all kinds of stuff, but made no real advance towards business or a treaty. They wanted their agents and interpreters changed, wanted the squaw men and half-breeds provided for, in short displayed their belief that the American government is run principally for the purpose of supporting in idleness a lot of breech-clout Indians, squaw men, and half-breeds. From appearances at present no treaty will be made, although it might have been done, in the opinion of those best informed, had the commission taken the proper method of dealing with the Indians; but as it is, the entire negotiations have been worse than a farce and failure.

D.

[*Cheyenne Daily Leader*, Tuesday, October 5, 1875]

[September 27, 1875 – Capt. Andrew S. Burt, from Red Cloud Agency, Nebraska]

An Offer to Sell the Black Hills

By Telegraph to *The Tribune*

Red Cloud Agency, [Monday] Sept. 27, via Fort Laramie, Sept. 28

The commission went to the council grounds this morning under a strong military escort, and also with an Indian guard. No apprehensions need be entertained now, as Little-Big-Man, the northern chief leading the discontented, has been suppressed by friendly Indians. The council was opened by Red Cloud, who presented Red Dog as his spokesman. Red Dog is the orator of the Oglalas. The next speaker was Little Bear of the Miniconjous. He indicated the conclusion of the Indians, that by the sale of the Hills they are to be cared for handsomely for all time. Spotted Tail followed Little Bear. He put a "poser" to the commission by asking to have Nebraska [the border] moved south. The chief wanted an answer at once, which, of course, the commission could not give. The commission are unanimous not to consider the demand made, which was for the payment of $3,500,000 a year for an indefinite period. They will attend another council to-morrow, and then withdraw, and see what the Great Father has to say. Two commissioners, Messrs. Ashby and Lawrence, with their clerk, will remain to deliver the horses promised to Young-Man-Afraid-of-his-Horses. On the same day the rest of the commission will be en route for home, with Lieut. Vroom's Third Cavalry escort.

[Unsigned]

[*New York Tribune*, Wednesday, September 29, 1875]

[1] William Quigley with his wife and two sons appears on a list of whites and mixed bloods living at the Spotted Tail Agency in 1875. E. A. Howard to CIA, June 3, 1875, Spotted Tail Agency Letters. John Whalen, in an interview with Eli S. Ricker, said Quigley was an Irishman who kept Spotted Tail well posted on government affairs. Jensen, ed. *Voices of the American West: The Soldier and Settler Interviews*, 327. John Bruguier, also known as "Big Leggins," whose father was French-Canadian and mother Lakota, was a noted interpreter, scout for the army, and intermediary between the army and Sitting Bull during the Great Sioux War. His biography appears in Josephine Waggoner, *Witness*, 120-26.

[2] See the *Omaha Herald*'s critical editorial commentary about Commissioner Ashby dated Sept. 2, 1875.

[3] The commissioner was undoubtedly G. P. Beauvais, who had once had an Indian wife or wives. "Mrs. Beauvais" and two daughters were listed in an 1875 census of Spotted Tail Agency. Hanson, "G. P. Beauvais," 42n36 and Spotted Tail Agency Letters.

[4] The alleged "Treaty Tree" stood well into the twentieth century. When it finally died, a portion of the trunk was displayed in the Crawford, Nebraska, park until it was swept away by a flash flood on the White River in 1991. Historical markers have been erected on "Old Highway 20," now a county road between Whitney and Crawford, Nebraska, designating the approximate site of the council and the tree.

[5] For the October 1874 "flagpole incident" at Red Cloud Agency, see Pt. 1, n.40.

[6] Red Cloud Agent Saville provided his own report on the visiting Indians to the commissioner of Indian affairs, which figures do not always match those in Senator Allison's letter. Saville's numbers from Cheyenne River, Standing Rock and Santee were the same, but he listed 300 Yanktonai from Fort Thompson (Crow Creek), 60 Lower Brulé (presumably also from Crow Creek), 50 Yankton, and 400 "Northern Indians not belonging to any agency." Saville to CIA, Sept. 23, 1875, Letters Received by the Commissioner of Indian Affairs, Red Cloud Agency, 1875-76, National Archives and Records Administration, Microcopy 234, roll 719. Perhaps Allison's totals had become garbled by the time they were published in the newspaper.

[7] These were the delegates from the non-agency bands who had been induced to attend by Young Man Afraid and his emissaries sent from Red Cloud Agency in August.

[8] Sioux Jim, whose Indian name was given variously as Poor Bear or Fishgut, was a son of Yellow Thunder and brother of Little Big Man. Powers, *The Killing of Crazy Horse*, 108, 488n. 4. According to William Garnett, Sioux Jim

belonged to the "Loafer band" of the Oglala and was killed at the Red Cloud Agency by American Horse in the fall of 1876. Jensen, ed., *Voices of the American West: The Indian Interviews*, 96-97, 284-85.

[9] Meaning the killing of Capt. William J. Fetterman and his command near Fort Phil Kearny on Dec. 21, 1866, by Indians allied under Red Cloud's leadership.

[10] Randall was a sometime trader and interpreter who had married a Brulé woman. He was sub-agent at the Whetstone Agency on the Missouri River for a time in the late 1860s. George E. Hyde, *Spotted Tail's Folk: A History of the Brulé Sioux* (Norman: University of Oklahoma Press, 1961), 179, 181.

[11] A few days earlier, Spotted Tail Agent E. A. Howard penned a letter to the commissioner of Indian affairs requesting permission to stop issuing rations to the "squaw men" at his agency "who embrace every opportunity to give council to the Indians in direct opposition to that which they ought to, and are a source of continual annoyance and trouble." Howard listed several exceptions by name, mostly former fur traders of French-Canadian ancestry who would be allowed to remain because they had spent most of their lives among the Indians and "are now old and incapacitated to earn a livelihood elsewhere." The exceptions list included James Bordeaux and Joseph Bissonette among its eighteen names. Howard to CIA, Sept. 20, 1875, Spotted Tail Agency Letters. For Howard's earlier effort to have various white men expelled from the agency, see Pt. 2, n.76.

[12] See Pt. 1, n.19 and Pt. 2, n.53.

[13] For more about this notable woman, see John S. Gray, "The Story of Mrs. Picotte-Galpin, a Sioux Heroine: Eagle Woman Learns about White Ways and Racial Conflict, 1820-1868," *Montana, the Magazine of Western History* 36 (Spring 1986): 2-21; and Gray, "The Story of Mrs. Picotte-Galpin, a Sioux Heroine: Eagle Woman Becomes a Trader and Counsels for Peace, 1868-1888," ibid., (Summer 1986): 2-21.

[14] A Miniconjou named White Robe signed the Manypenny agreement at Cheyenne River Agency on Oct. 16, 1876, "Report of the Sioux Commission," *ARCIA, 1876,* 355.

[15] It seems none of the correspondents could resist likening Spotted Tail to Cooper's idealized Indian.

[16] Young Man Afraid had previously received recognition for his role in defusing the volatile "flagpole incident" at Red Cloud Agency on Oct. 23, 1874. As a reward, Agent Saville presented Young Man Afraid with an ornate set of inscribed silver earrings bearing a horse motif. The earrings are displayed at the Knight Museum and Sandhills Center in Alliance, Nebraska, and their sto-

ry is told in "A Gift for a Great Hero," *Museum of the Fur Trade Quarterly* 48 (Winter 2012): 8-11.

[17] Little Bear, a Miniconjou headman and son of the hereditary chief White Hollow Horn. The band left the hunting grounds to settle at Cheyenne River Agency in 1874-75. His participation in the Black Hills Council marks Little Bear's transition to civil leadership. Personal communication from Kingsley M. Bray.

[18] A Two Kettle headman, correctly known as Long Mandan. He had participated in delegations to Washington, D.C. in 1867 and 1875. Personal communication from Kingsley M. Bray.

[19] According to Charles Turning Hawk, who was present at the council, the agency leaders had counseled among themselves and agreed on the "seven generations" plan. "Chief Red Dog got up and told them that if they did not sell the hills the whites would take them from them without paying for them." Once some of their children could learn to read and write, "the Inds. would figure with the Govt. & let it pay the Inds. to the seventh generation." Turning Hawk interview in Jensen, ed. *Voices of the American West: The Indian Interviews*, 325-26. Kingsley Bray believes the plan surfaced after the disrupted council session of Sept. 23 and gained the support of the Oglala Kit Fox warrior society that had maintained an attitude of "critical engagement" with U.S. government policies. Kit Fox Society endorsement led to the plan's adoption by the Oglala tribal council and the support of the Cheyenne and Arapaho who lived with the Oglala. Delegations from the other agencies, along with the "rejectionist/isolationist" delegation under Little Big Man, did not support the plan. Personal communication from Kingsley M. Bray. Spotted Tail's approach was similar though more open-ended than tying government support to a specific number of generations.

Part 4

Frustration and Failure,
September 29 – October 7, 1875

༄

S eptember 29, 1875 – Albert Swalm, from Red Cloud Agency, Nebraska]
Black-Hills Commission
Special Correspondence of *The Chicago Tribune*
Red Cloud Agency, [Wednesday] Sept. 29

Some portion of the American public will no doubt be surprised and chagrined at the failure of the Sioux Indian Commission to succeed in their efforts here; but the probabilities I mentioned in my first letter from Cheyenne, wherein the move of the Indian Ring was sketched, have become realities, and, being such of the most formidable shape, of course the commission fail to secure a cession of the Black Hills country. At the first I gave the facts that the Indians were being tampered with, and that an enormous amount would be demanded. My predictions, based upon information gained from the Indians themselves, have been more than verified; and, instead of $50,000,000 being asked, the demand is made in such manner that its fulfillment would amount to more than $100,000,000. All this is the result of a thoroughly-organized system of working the matter up among the redskins. From the commencement of the furor about the Black Hills to the present time, day and night have the agents of the Ring been busily at work getting the ideas of the Indians "toned up" to the notch that promised most stealing for those whose hands as well as hearts are most heartily engaged in the cause of the poor Indian. For this purpose, the half-breed element, and all the whites in the Indian country, have been enlisted, and sent in all ways to spread the most fabulous stories of the wealth of the country asked for. The hills and the valleys were literally dotted with nuggets, so that they could be picked up like stones; and the army wagons with Colonel Dodge's command were being loaded down with gold.

And the Indians believed, in a degree, many of the stories told them, and think that, in the Hills, they have a fortune for the whole Sioux nation that shall keep them from want, and make them rich eventually. They were assured by these industrious men of benevolence that the government would pay almost any price they might ask for the gold country, and also pay largely for the wagon-loads of gold already taken out. Every conceivable story that a pilferer could invent to sway an ignorant, uncivilized mind was told and retold a thousand times, and even to the extent of employing full-blooded Indians to make the circuit of tribes, telling a yarn that a humble but active disciple of the Ring had concocted. Indians will lie very easily and very often, both for pelf and for the nature that there is in lying. And they detract not a shade, for an Indian's imagination is not constructed on the diminutive scale.

To aid the good work of fastening a fearfully-rapacious treaty upon the people, there came from several sections, especially the Ring village of Cheyenne, all the loose political swashbucklers not too lazy to move to the field, who devoted their efforts to a great deal of blowing and to about an equal amount of bibulating. They were sure that the "great American sentiment of progress now permeating the land" would consign to everlasting damnation any commission that would let pecuniary views withhold from civilization the immense gold-fields of the Black Hills; and, in fact, that none but fools and misers ever offer to treat on the basis of a lease. To buy, and to buy at a generous price, not less than one aggregating many millions, was just the thing; and the blank-blank fools of the commission were not wise enough to see it. This was the sample of Cheyenne influence sent here; and alas! it failed in its efforts. There were some hearts sent home feeling very badly; but their intentions on the coffers of the public through this Indian business were very much worse.

The speakers of the Indians showed how wonderfully well the Ring-work had been done. Red Cloud wanted a light wagon, a heavy wagon, and six yoke of oxen, a pair each of hogs, chickens, sheep, and cattle, for each lodge, with houses built and civilized furniture put in them. His bill-of-fare demanded Texas beef, the best kind of pork, corn-meal, dried apples, rice, beans, salt, "red pepper for old folks," tobacco; and all this for seven generations to come.

Meanwhile, the government was to change the Nebraska state line from its present northern boundary to the Platte, and remove all the soldiers from Camp Robinson. Likewise, Red Cloud wanted all the claims for Indian depredations paid—not out of his money, but out of the Great Father's safe. Then he wanted to be paid for the non-fulfillment of certain portions of the treaties of 1868 and 1851. At that time he was doing a wholesale business by way of murdering whites and stealing things generally. He was at the Phil Kearny massacre and for distinguished action there was made a chief. Spotted Tail was in the same mood exactly; and so were Red Dog, Little Wound, who wanted to hunt buffalo on the Republican River; and Long Mandan, who wanted $70,000,000 cash besides the back-pay due him. Then the Cheyenne and Arapahoe cut-throats chimed in, indorsing all and added that, as the Great Father had detained some of their chiefs in the Pensacola prison, they must be released. There was hardly any limit whatever to their demands. There is where the tools of the big-bonanza treaty overdid their work. They caused too much of an elevation of ideas as to the value of the Hills. What the Ring card really called for was $45,000,000 in addition to the provisions of the treaty of 1868. They feel that they have been badly sold out by their own short-sightedness; but, as has been the custom, will at once lay new wires that lead to newer robberies. To kill the Ring business in our Indian affairs would cause too many funerals in high life, private and official. Still, the country would flourish just as well without their tricks that are exceedingly dark, as it does with them, and the tax-payer much better. In the usual November Thanksgiving, special mention should be made of their deliverance from wrong and premeditated robbery under the cloak of charity.

The 1868 treaty under which the Sioux nation is now controlled, is an exceedingly good one for the Indians. It gave them a reservation containing over 160,000 square miles. It is true that much of the land is worse than useless but there is plenty of good land for them. It provided for the establishment of only one agency, and that on the Missouri River. Now they have four on the river and two inland. Buildings were to be erected at one agency; they have gone up at six. They have the privilege of entering a quarter-section at any time on the reservation, and $100 worth of implements and seeds are given the farmer the first year; after that, $25 per annum. But the agricultural resources, as developed by the Indians, amount to nothing at all; not over 10 acres have been cultivated at Red Cloud and Spotted Tail. For thirty years, each male person was to receive a good, substantial suit of clothing, consisting of coat, pantaloons, flannel shirt, hat, and one pair of homemade socks. This has never been carried out on the part of the government. Blankets and breech-clout stuff are issued only; for shirts and hats poor Lo must look otherwise. This is a retarding feature, judged in a civilizing sense; and why civilized clothing was not issued, can only be answered by the incapables so long mismanaging these matters. The women were to receive a flannel skirt, or the goods necessary to make it, a pair of woolen hose, 12 yards of cotton cloth; and the children a suit of clothing, or the stuff to make it. In only a partial manner have these provisions of the treaty been carried out. Nothing is issued to the children in the clothing line to make them comfortable, and they are mostly all clothed from the purchase of goods with "hide money." For four years each Indian was to and did receive rations at the rate of 1 pound of meat and the same of flour per day. This has been carried on ever since the treaty; and for four years subsistence has been furnished without treaty-stipulation requiring it. Another provision required that, to each lodge removing to the reservation and commencing farming, one good American cow and one good, well-broken pair of American oxen, were to be given; but few have been demanded. In addition to the clothing allowance, "the sum of $10 for each person shall be annually appropriated for a period of thirty years, while such persons roam and hunt; and $20 for each person who engages in farming." Specifically, these appropriations were never made; they are now being made by furnishing subsistence after the treaty demand had ceased to exist. Schools were provided and, at some of the agencies, are in operation.

The propositions made to the Indians for the cession of the Black Hills and Big Horn country were as follows: For a lease of the Black Hills, the sum of $400,000 annually as long as the country was occupied by the government—$100,000 of which was to go for objects beneficial to their civilization, the balance for subsistence; for a purchase of the country, the sum of $6,000,000, payable in fifteen annual payments, under the same ruling as the lease as to its disposition. For the Big Horn country, the sum of $50,000 annually for ten years was offered. At the three propositions, the nose of the very high-priced Indian was very much turned up. To show how they were received, I will quote verbatim the remarks of Spotted Tail—Red Cloud was not present, and none of his representatives said anything:

Spotted Tail – "Now you have told us about the price for the Black Hills—our country. It seems that that amount of money would hardly last one year. It would not be enough to live on one year. The annuities and rations that our Great Father promised us before and agreed to give us, are more than the price that you have mentioned."

Senator Allison – "What we propose to give you here is in addition to what you have under the treaty of 1868."

Spotted Tail – "It is not the fault of my tribes or any of my people that no sale is made. It will be your fault. Now we want to let this thing rest a little while. The chiefs of my people have said that they would sell you the Black Hills, and they asked such prices, and they told you what they wanted besides the cash payments; and now you have said to the contrary. So we must let you carry these words to our Great Father. Let him decide. If he wants to borrow, we will think of it; and if he wants to buy, we will think of that. That is all I am going to say at present."

All of which was received with many "Hows" by the Indians.

Another Washington trip is wanted by the Indians. This evening Spotted Tail called on the commission and said that, as the Indians and the commission could not agree, he would ask them to lay all the papers in the case before the Great Father, and he would see them through it. When he does, if he wants to, he can send for the chiefs of this section, of the North, and of the Missouri River, and have all come to Washington. "Then," said Spotted Tail, "when we are away from our young men, who do not know anything, we can look these things all over in the right light, and make a good, strong treaty, and preserve peace forever." Red Dog, Sword, Young-Man-Afraid, Little Wound, and several other chiefs asserted to the words of the variegated caudal. The probabilities are that this will be done, and that perhaps President Grant may be able to overcome the influences that have been found so strong with the Indians here. If the value of the gold country, so-called, is carefully considered, the Washington authorities will not go above the figures of the commission. Popular furore, confined to a very few papers and a small number of people, may drive people into thinking that the only way out of the matter into peace will be the surrender of millions to a few cormorants that hover over and around Indian affairs. The gold product of the Black Hills, I predict, for the next ten years will not equal annually the price proposed to be paid for a lease; and, in less than half that time, the bubble will have collapsed entirely, and people will be wondering at the success that attends generally the greatest of humbugs.

The commission will meet at the Grand Pacific hotel, Chicago, Nov. 15, to make up its report.

[Unsigned]

[*Chicago Daily Tribune*, Saturday, October 9, 1875]

[The same letter appears in *The Fort Dodge Messenger*, Thursday, Oct. 28, 1875]

[September 29, 1875 – Charles Collins, from Red Cloud Agency, Nebraska]

West

(Special to the *Bee*)

Red Cloud Agency, [Wednesday] Sept. 29, via Sidney, Neb., Sept. 30

The following is the substance of the treaty: The commissioners submit a proposition to purchase the Black Hills, Big Horn, and Powder River country. The United States asks, first, to lease or purchase the right to the mines, raise stock, and cultivate the soil in the Black Hills. The boundaries are as follows: Beginning at the junction of the north and south forks of the Cheyenne River, and embracing all the territory between said river lying west of said junction to the 104th meridian of longitude west of Greenwich; the United States agreeing to pay therefore the sum of $400,000 per annum; U.S. reserving the right to terminate said license by giving two years notice by proclamation and the payment of the full amount stipulated for the time the license may continue, and at the expiration of the time, all private property reverts to the Sioux nation, and that of such amount, $400,000, as Congress shall determine, not less than $100,000 shall be annually expended in objects beneficial for civilization, remainder expended subsistence, or if the Sioux nation prefer it, to purchase only the Black Hills as above described, to pay them for it $6,000,000 in 15 annual installments, said sums to be annually appropriated for their subsistence and civilization; of which sum not less than $100,000 shall be expended for civilization; that the President of the United States shall under proper restrictions and regulations designate three routes to the Black Hills country as follows: One from the south between the 102d and 103d meridians; one from the east not farther north than latitude 43 ½°, until it reaches the 102d meridian, and one from the west not north of latitude 44°; also a branch road from some point on the Niobrara River to intersect either the eastern or southern route at some convenient point not west of the 103d meridian west of Greenwich. The commissioners furthermore propose to purchase all that portion which is known as the Bighorn country in Wyoming, which lies west of a line drawn up as follows: beginning at the northwest corner of the state of Nebraska, and running in a northeasterly direction until it reaches the Yellowstone River, where the 107th meridian west of Greenwich crosses said river, and to pay them for their interest therein $50,000 annually for 10 years, paid in American cows, live stock and agricultural implements, as the president may select, the treaty not being valid unless approved by congress. The commissioners propose, in case of the acceptance of said proposition, to distribute at once $50,000 in presents.
Charles Collins
[*Omaha Daily Bee*, Friday, October 1, 1875]

[September 29, 1875 – Charles Collins, from Red Cloud Agency, Nebraska]

(Special to the *Bee*)

Red Cloud Agency, [Wednesday] Sept. 29, via Sidney, Sept. 30

The commissioners submitted a proposition for treaty to the Indians on Wednesday, the text of which I already sent you. It will not be accepted by the Indians, and the commissioners are prepared to return home and submit report. The following is the summary of what the Indians demand, in payment for the Black Hills: 6 yoke of oxen and wagons; 1 span of horses and wagon; live stock; furniture, etc., and annuities of subsistence annually for 600 years. They also demand the appointment of agents and employees and removal of troops from all agencies on the reservations, and the removal of the Catholic clergy as religious instructors; only one road into the hills via Bismarck; the extension of the reservation to the middle of the Platte River in Nebraska, and an utter refusal to part with the Powder River and Big Horn country.

Their demands are considered preposterously unreasonable by the commissioners. The commissioners return Saturday.

Charles Collins

[*Omaha Daily Bee*, Friday, October 1, 1875]

[September 29, 1875 – Reuben Davenport, from Red Cloud Agency, Nebraska]

The Black Hills

Red Cloud Agency, [Wednesday] Sept. 29, via Fort Laramie, Sept. 30, 1875

The council closed this afternoon with an abandonment of the negotiations by the commissioners with the acquiescence of the Indians. All of the Missouri River Indians are now on their way home. Yesterday in a long talk the Indians repeated a list of their wants, as Red Dog, Spotted Tail and Spotted Bear [Two Bears?] had done on Monday.

They desired to have given them by the Great Father, in return for the Black Hills, the support of the nation for seven generations, or over 200 years. In addition they wanted yoke cattle, cows, sheep, horses, hogs, fowls, farming utensils, guns and ammunition, and, moreover, enumerated a hundred articles of food and clothing, which they wished sent them as annuity goods. They wanted houses, schools, sawmills and civilized furniture. Red Cloud emphatically asked for a subscription for the *New York Herald* for his agency. They declined to permit any other roads to the Black Hills but Custer's trail from Bismarck.

The portion which they would cede to the government was that where timber exists, retaining the foot of the hills. Certain agents, traders and interpreters, whom they named, they desired discharged, and wanted the citizens' claims for Indian depredations paid by the government. The request for Catholic missions was repeated and emphasized. Red Cloud wanted to live in peace, and asked that the bringing of whiskey on the reservation by Mexicans be stopped.

The Arapahoes spoke through Black Crow. The chief claimed the first right to the soil of this country, and asked exactly what the Sioux had asked. Little Wolf and Living Bear presented the case of the Cheyennes.

They asked that all Southern Cherokees [Cheyennes] who came here may be permitted to remain. Fast Bear, of the Wazhazha Brules wanted an agent from his own people. Crow Feather, Bad Heap, Flying Bird, and Standing Cloud made speeches of the same purport as all the rest. The wishes of the different bands seemed unanimous.

Wizac [Wizi] presented Commissioner Allison with a large council pipe for President Grant.[1] Fool Dog said that many of the chiefs would prefer to finish the council at Washington. The commissioners then referred to Big Horn Mountain, and promised to submit the proposition to lease or buy to-day.

This morning about one hundred chiefs met the commissioners. Little Wound made the first speech, repeating and indorsing what Red Cloud said yesterday. He hoped the Great Father would give them the privilege again of going down to the Republican. They wanted to hunt there this winter, as the young men reported buffalo there.

Senator Allison read the following formal proposition regarding the Black Hills: - [not transcribed, the proposal appears in Charles Collin's Sept. 29 letter above.]

Spotted Tail said he spoke for the tribe. The amounts offered were too small, and they could not agree. It was not the fault of the commissioners, nor of his tribe. They had better let the matter rest and postpone the treaty for the present. Spotted Tail apologized for saying on Monday that the commissioners were drunk. He meant only a jest.

Lone Horn rode into the council on horseback and claimed to own all the country.

The commission promised to take all the words of the Indians to the Great Father. It was evident there could be no agreement then and there, and they hoped to part as they had come, as friends.

The Indians feel insulted by Lone Horn's conduct, and after the council attempted to kill him. He is hid in the bush along the White River.

The closing hand shaking was most friendly. The Indians betrayed no disappointment. The commissioners will depart to-morrow.
[Unsigned]
[*New York Herald*, Friday, October 1, 1875]

[September 29, 1875 – Capt. Andrew S. Burt, from Red Cloud Agency, Nebraska]

The Crow Butte Council Over
By Telegraph to *The Tribune*
Red Cloud Agency, [Wednesday] Sept. 29, via Fort Laramie, W.T., Sept. 30

After the council yesterday, when enormous prices were put on the Black Hills by the Sioux, the commissioners became desirous not to submit any proposition for the purchase of the Hills. At to-day's council a protocol, drawn by Messrs. Ashby and Lawrence, was presented to the chiefs therefore, which, after reciting a desire for peace, offered to buy the right to mine in the Black Hills for $400,000 per annum, this right to terminate at any time on a year's notice by the United States. It was next proposed to purchase the Big Horn country for $50,000, paid annually for ten years, the money to be expended in food and stock. Furthermore, it was proposed that if the protocol be accepted, $50,000 be expended in presents, to be distributed among the bands. This protocol was left with the Indians to discuss this winter. They think, however, that a sale is made for $70,000,000.

Lone Horn of the Miniconjous disturbed the council by riding up and delivering from his saddle a violent speech against the Brules and Oglalas for trying to sell his country, the Black Hills. Little Wound and Spotted Tail spoke, dwelling principally on their wants about agents. The council closed with "Hows" and handshakes.

The commissioners, except Messrs. Ashby, Lawrence, and Swalm, leave on Thursday afternoon for Fort Laramie.[2] The Crow Butte Council for the sale of the Black Hills is ended, and nothing accomplished.
[Unsigned]
[*New York Tribune*, Friday, Oct. 1, 1875]

[October 1, 1875 – Reuben Davenport, from Red Cloud Agency, Nebraska]

The Grand Council
Red Cloud Indian Agency, Nebr. [Friday] Oct. 1, 1875

The Grand Council has ended in nothing. There seems to be little surprise or disappointment among the Indians, and still less among the "squaw men," who have been the mysterious scene-shifters in the farce.

The honorable commission, however, departed yesterday filled with chagrin and nervously apprehensive of public criticism. Two of their number they delegated to remain behind them a few days, to supervise the presentation of the one hundred horses promised to Young-Man-Afraid-of-His-Horses and his band. They are Messrs. Beauvais and Ashby. The horses are now on the way here.

The last days of the council were marked by the small attendance of the chiefs and head men. Red Cloud was not present when the commissioners delivered their valedictory to the Indians, but was a spectator at the sun-dance of the Arapahoes then in progress a dozen miles away. Red Dog and other important personages were also absent. Whether this fact showed a lack of respect for the commissioners or was intended to impress them with the idea that the chiefs were, after all, not anxious to sell their country, even for the enormous price which they had named, I do not know. But those few who gathered near the bank of the White River seemed better to understand the value of time than ever Indian did before, and probably knew then that the result of the negotiation could only be failure. On Tuesday Red Cloud repeated the speech which Red Dog had, on Monday, in delivering for him, managed so badly that the interpreters could not construe it. He said:

"All you white people who are gathered here have for days drawn the sky down upon me, so that it has pressed heavy upon my head. To-day the sky seems to have risen back to its proper station. It was my intention that the Black Hills should be sustenance for my children as long as they should live. That is what I thought in 1868, and I sit here holding that treaty in my hand. But since the Great Father wants to buy that country I want from him support for our people for seven generations. We have already lived six generations, and I am of the seventh. We will yet live so much longer. I want the money which you shall pay us for the Black Hills put at interest among the white people; and with the interest I want to buy wagons and cattle. We have a great deal of small wild game here which we can depend on for food. I want the Great Father to provide us with guns and ammunition, with our interest. We want Texan steers for the seven generations to come. We want the white people and the Great Father to grant it because I grant their wishes to-day. I want you to grant us the best kind of coffee, crackers, corn, meat, sugar, provisions, beans, rice, dried apples, saleratus, and soap. I want some pepper for the old people. I want for each head of a family a light wagon and span of horses; six yoke of working cattle, breeding stock of cows, sheep, hogs, and fowls. I am an Indian. You try to make a white man out of me. At this agency this winter I want white men to build houses for all my Indians. I have been in white people's houses and have seen their chairs, sofas, tables and beds. I want the same kind of furniture for my people. The sawmill near the agency I thought to be mine, but found I was mistaken. I want the Great Father to give me a sawmill, to be my own. I want a mower and a scythe. Then I do not want you to forget that I want a subscription for the *New York Herald* for my agency.

"It may be that the white people will think I ask too much; but these Black Hills reach to the skies and are full of wild and tame beasts. I think that the Black Hills are worth more than all of the white people's country. I know well and declare plainly that God placed those hills there for my wealth. You are going to take them away and make me poor. Therefore do I ask so much for them. I will now tell you the portion of that land which I will sell you. It is the portion of the country inside the ridge circling the outer edge of the Hills. I will keep the foot hills because there is game in them, but no gold. Now you have seen the mixed blood in my tribe. My father and I raised these orphan half breeds and I love them. I will not part with them. I want them served by the Great Father the same as I shall be served. They were born and reared on this soil and we are all of one family."

Lone Horn, the garrulous and pretentious chief of the Miniconjous, at this point began a speech in the centre of the ring in loud and ranting tones. Red Cloud, however, did not allow himself to be interrupted, but proceeded with his address.

"I want," he said, "no other road to the Black Hills but the thieves road from the Missouri River—the road made by Long Hair (General Custer) and his men last year. I tell this to General Terry especially, because I believe him to be the most trusty man among you." Reverting again to the subject of the half-breeds, he said he wanted all the hired work about the agency to be done by them. He wanted them to plough, sow and reap for him; to issue the rations and make the hay. He mentioned certain men whose claims against the government for damage done to them by Indians in 1868 he desired paid. He also wanted Catholic missions established. "I mean to say plain things. What I don't like I will not speak of behind your back, but will mention boldly. There is a trader at my agency named Dear. I don't want him any more. From this day forth I discharge him. My reservation is my home, and I should be able to regulate it as suits me. Nevertheless a saloon is kept there by this man Dear. So I say so. I want to live at peace and be good friends with the whites, but whiskey is brought in here and is drank at Dear's. It would make a false people of us and I want it stopped. The troops which are placed at the post have done no good for me. They are still destroying my timber and cutting my hay. I want the Great Father to remove them further away. I want the Great Father to take the northern line of Nebraska and move it back to the middle of the Platte River. I want the surveyors to build mounds in the middle of the river to mark the boundary. In the bends of the river, on this side, are my great hay fields."

Red Cloud concluded by asking that all his words be repeated to the Great Father, and hoping that the Great Father would not think his demands too great to be granted. The other chiefs who spoke their minds between this time and the close of the council, with the exception of references to their own agencies, repeated only what Red Cloud had said. There had evidently been a formal agreement beforehand as to what should be asked of the whites. The Indians from the Cheyenne River Agency were very earnest in desiring the discharge of their present agent and interpreter, and asked for half-breeds in their places. They also desired that the traderships should be given to half-breed Indians.

I have already given by telegraph the proposition made by the commissioners to the Indians and their response. On the evening of September 29, the day of the dissolution of the council, the commission were followed to the agency by several chiefs. Spotted Tail was at their head. He was rather grieved that no clear understanding had been reached between his people and the whites, and his manner was rather dejected. He, with several companions, came into the room occupied by the commissioners in the stockade and sat down. In the course of conversation Spotted Tail proposed that he and the other principal chiefs of the Sioux should go to Washington to finally settle the question of the Black Hills. He said:

"In this council what you said to us we did not understand, and what we said to you, you did not understand. But all we said you have on paper and you can take it to the Great Father. He may be able to understand it, and when he has looked at it, if he wants to do so, he can send for us, the chiefs of this country, and of the North and the Missouri, and we can all meet at his house in Washington. I wish this to be done."

Red Dog, Sword, Little Wound and Young-Man-Afraid-of-His-Horses, who were present, said that they agreed with the words of Spotted Tail. Red Dog said:

"I was one of the last to come to the whites, but now I listen to them. I never dispute my Great Father's word. Myself and my friend, Blue Horse, always obey it. Whatever Spotted Tail says I agree with. If we can get the chiefs to go to the Great Father's house, we can agree to perform some business and will sell you any land that you want."

Spotted Tail – "We could not agree with you here and now, nor you with us."

There is no doubt that the failure of this negotiation is to be attributed mainly to the ignorance of the majority of the commission of the proper method of treating with the Indian and the miserable interpretation of both the Sioux and English languages in council. Neither party in the negotiation thoroughly understood the other. The commission were aware of this, and could have remedied it by employing more efficient interpreters. They could also have modified their proposition so that it could have been more fully comprehended. Its "borrowing" phase was to the majority of the Indians a dark mystery, and it remained one to the end. I am assured by the best authority that the Sioux do not know the method of counting 1,000,000, but mistakenly suppose it to be 100,000. Their price of $70,000,000 for the Black Hills therefore, is in reality but $7,000,000, only $1,000,000 more than the offer of the commission. A competent interpreter should have rendered their demand according to its real significance in English, and a treaty might have been consummated. On so small an error sometimes hangs an important result. It is possible that my authority upon this point is mistaken but I am confident that he is not.

Constant raids by the youth of the Sioux nation upon the frontiers of settlement may be anticipated during the autumn and early winter. Parties of adventurers are beginning once more to move toward the Black Hills. Twenty of them recently left this agency and went directly north. The Dakota braves want only a provocation. They have imbibed a great idea of the strength of their nation from the displays made during the great council, and the presence of troops there undoubtedly annoyed and angered them. The treacherous disposition of a large number was sufficiently shown by the bloody trap set on the very council ground, but destroyed by the prompt loyalty of Young-Man-Afraid-of-His-Horses. Crazy Horse is expected here daily with his principal warriors. He comes to attend the council but what course he may pursue when he learns of its fruitless termination it is difficult to predict. He may proceed to fulfill the threats which he made in August; and indeed it is uncertain whether that may not be the object of his southern movement.
[Unsigned]
[*New York Herald*, Saturday, October 16, 1875]

[October 5, 1875 – Albert Swalm, from Red Cloud Agency, Nebraska]
Indians at Red Cloud
Red Cloud Agency, [Tuesday] Oct. 5, 1875

At no time has there been more than three thousand Indians present at the council. In the camps round about there were perhaps twenty-five thousand men, women, and an everlasting lot of children. Like some of the old bucks we read about in the Bible, many of these Indians go into the family business at a wholesale rate, and as they have nothing in the world to do but to eat beef, sleep, and steal horses, you see at once that the increase is rapid.

At one time, when 200 chiefs and head men were in the council circle, the sight was one of great picturesqueness—something after the story that Fennimore Cooper tells in one of his books, but on that day the whole outfit came within a point of being massacred by the young bucks, and that has spoiled all the romantic that was in it for me. But while I was looking at the stalwart bucks lazing around, I could not help thinking that the Lord was allowing a great many good bodies to go to waste out here, when they could be raising corn and hogs. In an economic sense, the Sioux Indian does not average high.

The Indians are generally well mounted, and not less than fifty thousand horses were grazing here when the council commenced. They were mostly ponies, but an occasional horse and mule could be seen which some poor misguided Indian had stolen from the whites. Several white men saw their property in the herds, but the law did not permit them to take it. The Indian must be protected in his rights!

The most brutal sight one can witness in the Indian country is only afforded when the "Sun Dance" occurs, and its brutality is such that one only cares to see it once, and would then gladly forget its hellish orgies. For several days the Sioux, Cheyennes, and Arapahoes have been making grand arrangements for this dance, and yesterday came the finale. For twenty-four hours previous a general dance and singing had been going on at the camp five miles above here; at times as many as two hundred warriors were in the happy circle, while three big drums gave out noise enough to start three or four pandemoniums, with the not very musical voices of a large number of squaws thrown in to add an additional feature of the horrible. The object of the "sun dance" is to test the courage of the young warriors to endure physical pain, under the most trying circumstances, the one enduring most coming out with the barbaric honors. At ten o'clock seventeen young warriors, stripped entirely naked, save a limited breech-clout, came into the circle and were operated upon. This operation was performed by a medicine man, horribly rigged out. The first one to come up was a magnificent looking fellow from the Cheyennes, all bone and muscle, and in glorious health. The medicine man cut first four gashes about three inches long, on the shoulders, near the point. With a smooth stick of hard wood he made a hole underneath the slits he had cut, each taking in an inch or more in width, and through which hole he passed a buffalo thong, and tied it tightly. Then the breast was served in the same manner, after which one thong was fastened to a fourteen feet pole. To the other thong was tied a large beef head—a long horned Texan, with about ten feet of thong between the back and the head. The young warrior then jumped into a lively dance, getting a song of some sort in keeping with the performance, jerking that bull head around so fast that at times it was four or five feet above the ground—all the time pulling as best he could at the thong fastened to the pole by jumping back and swinging upon it. At times the flesh on back and breast seemed to stretch out about eight or ten inches, and when let up, would close down with a pop. The ropes in the breast fastenings were the first to break, one breaking at the top of the cut, the other at the lower end. The top one hung down full four inches, and this the medicine man cut off dexterously. It was put through an incantation, when the bloody, sweaty warrior was put through a race of about forty yards with that bull head hanging to his back. At one bound the horns stuck well in the ground, and with a vigorous pull the thongs broke, and a warrior was made. He was a terrible looking object, and so nearly exhausted that he had to be helped away. During the last half of his torture he uttered not a word, nor did he open his mouth, nor even wince. His wounds were washed and bound up, presents made to him of horses and robes, and he [was] recognized as a brave man. There were sixteen more performances of like nature, save that no other ones took the double ties on back and breast. Thirteen were tied by the back, the others by the breast. The fat fellows got away with the business very quickly, but the lean, lank and more muscular fellows had long and tough jobs with it. One fellow, breaking in a frantic effort, and falling under the heels of my horse, resulted in a peeled head for the Indian as well as a sore back. I confess that I only remained to see two of the victims go through the ordeal, gaining from my companion, a half-breed interpreter, the statistics concerning the fat and lean fellows, who had enough Indian in him to stomach the whole of the bloody brutality. The warriors who went through the ordeal were all from the north—those who have but little to do with the whites, and that little mostly in the way of scalps and horse stealing. The more civilized fellows have learned better than to make such confounded fools of themselves.

On Saturday a friendly Indian who had conferred the pleasure upon me of smoking cigars quite generously invited me to come to his tepee, up the canyon, that night, as he was going to have a feast and he desired that Col. Beauvais and Capt. Ashby, of the treaty commission, should also come. Sword is the name of the entertaining party, and the "invite," while not presented on a salver, or even printed on or written on tinted paper, was accepted, entirely for the novelty and not for the boiled dog.[3] We were bid to come early, and at sundown were at Sword's canvas mansion. A multitude of children, with a double number of dogs, welcomed us in truly aboriginal fashion. Sword immediately designated to his squaw the particular dog that was his choice for the pot. The same was caught and tied by a short rope to a stake and the female "went for" the dog with a club. Striking at the head, she missed and hit him on the nose. He filed his objections to that sort of treatment, and raised a fearful howl. This brought out three other squaws with clubs and a dozen dogs, and from that on it was "nip and tuck" with the dogs and squaws in getting punishment in on that tied dog. Finally the clubs beat life out of it, and it was ready for the next step. It was thrown on a quick brush fire, which singed off all the hair. The squaws scraped it well, took out the entrails, cut the carcass to pieces, put it in a large camp kettle, and set it "a bilin." So far there had been lots of fun for the visitors. In about two hours the dog was pronounced done, and the feast ready. Some twenty prominent Indians had been invited in—and they never go back on a feast. Each one of the visitors was seated on a robe between two Indians, and each man was furnished with a pan. Two Indian soldiers were detailed to "dish out" the dog, and I am confident that they did so. To Col. Beauvais, who is of St. Louis, was given the whole head, which set in his dish, grinning at him like—well, there is nothing so much on the grin as a dog's head boiled. Possibly your readers cannot obtain an adequate idea of such a sight save only in one way—boil a dog's head, set it in a pan and gaze at it by the light of a pine knot. I positively decline to state what your correspondent received in his dish, but Capt. Ashby, who is from Nebraska, had his pan garnished with an elegant hind leg, and a few joints of tail. Bade to come to a feast, it must have been a grave breach of Indian hospitality not to partake, but Col. Beauvais, who is an old Indian trader, informed the whites that if they did not wish to eat that dog, a release could be purchased. None of the visitors were hungry, and it took twenty dollars to convince the Indians that they were not so. The dog was entirely eaten up, the bones being picked as clean as though flesh had never covered them.

S.

[*Fort Dodge Messenger*, Thursday, October 21, 1875]

[October 7, 1875 – Albert Swalm, from Red Cloud Agency, Nebraska]

The Indian Council
Special Correspondence of *The Chicago Tribune*
Red Cloud Agency, [Thursday] Oct. 7

The manner in which horse and other contracts are filled in the Indian country was fully exemplified at this agency on Wednesday and to-day, and its description will not be without interest to that portion of the public that foots the tax bills. In making the preliminary arrangements for the treaty for the Black Hills, a party of about eighty-five Indians, made up from the Oglalas, Brules, Cheyennes, and Arapahoes, under the command of an Oglala chief, Young-Man-Afraid-of-his Horses, was sent north to the Powder and Tongue Rivers country, to endeavor to bring in the wild Sioux. For this service each man was promised a horse by the sub-commission. The contract was ordered by Commissioner Smith to be let through J. W. Daniels, a special agent in charge of matters of that kind for the treaty commission. As an item showing the complete connections the Ring has, I have only to say that one Ward, a contractor of the firm of Ward & Mason, arrived at Red Cloud the same day the courier brought the telegram order from the commissioner to Chairman Allison. The dispatch came to Fort Laramie by telegraph, and the query is, How did the firm that had been doing all the horse contracting for this section learn of the order at least four days before its delivery here? They must have got it a few hours after its issue in order to bring Ward here in the time he arrived. There is nothing like having a good circuit when matters of this kind come around for the fattening of the Ring. All this may be said in a parenthetical way, and now to the manner of fulfillment.

Daniels let the contract to Ward & Mason, of Cheyenne, and J. W. Dear, a trader at this agency. The price was set at $124, delivered here, the contract calling for young American horses bought east of the Missouri River, to be not under 3 or over 6 years old, and sound in every respect. The horses were to be delivered to some members of the commission, and Capt. W. H. Ashby, of Nebraska, and Col. G. P. Beauvais, of St. Louis, were detailed for that purpose. The animals arrived Wednesday, and after a few days' feed on agency hay, were announced as ready to be inspected. The commissioners did so, and found that about thirty first-class horses were in the lot, sixty were from fair to medium, and ten were the sickest looking ten I ever had the misfortune to see. The ninety horses were considered as filling the contract, but the other ten were promptly and positively rejected. This was an unusual thing, and never occurred here before. Anything that wore hair and did not have split hoofs had been passed heretofore as being all right, and was paid for at high rates. The contractors refused to allow the ninety to be branded and issued, and there was a general consultation, in which the whole Ring resident here participated. Col. Beauvais, who was for nearly forty years a trader among the Sioux, explained to the Indians why the horses were not issued, and they all said "how" to his determination to have ten good horses, or the bad ones thrown out. The Indians said that such a thing had never been done for them before; that they always had to take "rats" for good horses, and that their hearts were very glad that a better time was in store for them. Three hours afterward the commission rooms were crowded with chiefs and head soldiers, demanding that the whole lot of horses be accepted and issued. It was suspected at once that the contractors had been "sweetening" the Indians, and Col Beauvais accused some of the chiefs of the same. This they acknowledged, and it was afterwards fully proven by one of the half-breeds who had assisted in the matter.

An answer was given to the effect that the horses would not be accepted under any consideration, save in full compliance with the contract; and that if they meant to force things to an issue the commission would pack up and move to Camp Robinson. The Indians were told to go home and the commission would settle the matter in their own way, and that when the horses had been received in proper manner, they would be issued, but in no other way. Col. Beauvais, being greatly respected by the Indians, met with obedience to his request, and the Indians departed. Meanwhile the contractors set up a very mournful howl about hard times, the scarcity of the "irredeemable," the time they would have to wait for their pay, and so on to an almost unlimited extent. To all of which the commission said: "Nay—fill the contract with good horses, take out the wrecks, or we shall reject the whole outfit and go home." All the half-breeds and the dead-beats were set to beating their tom-toms concerning the excellencies of the rejected horses and the utter hellishness of the commission in interfering with the smooth running of affairs of the Ring. From being "exceedingly pleasant" gentlemen, the commissioners became suddenly, "___ ___ galoots, who did not know a good horse from a jackass." Still, the commissioners took matters serenely, amused themselves at the exhilarating game of "Don Pedro," and awaited the developments. All this is the history of Wednesday. To-day the contractors came around very much in the same mood as yesterday, but were willing, if the commission would wait ten or fifteen days, to replace all rejected stock, the commission to accept the ninety and give a receipt for one hundred, the number called for by the contract. This was in accordance to usage in this country, but the commissioners failed to see the matter in that light. Matters then came to a climax, in which it was proposed to reject the entire lot, which was a point the contractors could not meet. So the ninety were delivered, and an outside swap made to bring in one more good horse, making ninety-one. The Indians were then made recipients of the horses, each man being compelled to make his mark on a receipt for the horse. One-half of them refused to put the pen to paper; but would touch it when held away from it by the clerks—so far does superstition carry them. For perfect foolishness the Indians here will carry away the world's first premiums. One noble red, carrying the name of Chips refused to sign a receipt in any form, but wanted to have the horse. The commission refused, and Chips now proposes to go to the wild bands north and fight the whites next spring. His refusal was made in grand style, and he moved away as though he had everlastingly smashed the white man. Moon Eagle, a son of the rather lively Black Twin, said that he would not sign a paper for the best horse in the outfit. The commission might tie one to the fence and he would take it, but not a scratch of a pen would he give. Two of the Indians signed their own names, and did it very well. They belonged to the Oglalas.

Another phase of Indian cussedness was manifested after the distribution. To the Oglalas twenty-nine horses had been given—some good and some only average—and then each Indian was mad because he was not specially favored. Even Young-Man-Afraid was enraged because he did not get two good horses instead of one, and also a fine mare for his wife. I left him about making a trade of his fine bay presented him for two of the condemned hacks and the contractors seemed anxious to make the dicker. The contract called for good American horses, of uniform size and condition—and yet they were willing to trade two for one. Such is the charity shown by the whites to the poor Indian (?).

A party of eighteen warriors from the bands of the Black Twin and Crazy Horse, who make their home near the Powder River, and are hostile, came in the other day, and are still here. Moon Eagle, the son of the Black Twin, was interviewed by your correspondent, and in substance he said: "Our people have heard many bad rumors concerning the doings of the Indians here, and that they had sold the Black Hills. My father's band and that of Crazy Horse, in all about 400 lodges, are determined not to sell the country, and are now moving into that section, being camped on a creek this side of the Little Powder. There is a great deal of game there, and the buffalo come in great plenty. We don't want anything from the Great Father, and we will keep his people from taking our land. Some of our men will go through the Black Hills soon, and see what has been done. If we find any men there we shall take them out,"—he meant to kill them—"and we want all the horses we can get. None of our people will come to the agency. Our hearts are happy when we are away from the whites, and we are glad that our brothers have not sold the Hills, for they do not own them." This is the straightened out substance of his talk, and it is referred to Gens. Sheridan and Crook for future action. There is no doubt in the least but that there will be an outbreak next spring by these northern bands. Already several hundred of the young men of the Oglalas have left the agency and gone north, and more are preparing to go. These are the same turbulent fellows who came so near causing an outbreak at the council-ground, and only yesterday I heard some of them boast of it, and upbraid the old men for their timidity on that occasion. These hostiles are well armed, but generally poor shots. They have an abundance of ammunition, plenty of horses, and are just the fellows that need to make the acquaintance of Gen. Crook. And I hear whisperings that ample preparations are being made for the business. The commission will close its work here on the 10th and then leave for home, awaiting only the arrival of saddles to end their business with the Indians.[4]

[Unsigned]

[*Chicago Daily Tribune*, Saturday, October 16, 1875]

---

[1] Wizi was a cousin of White Ghost, Lower Yanktonai head chief at Crow Creek Agency. Personal communication from Kingsley M. Bray. Wizi is pictured in an 1884 painting of the Crow Creek Agency by William Fuller that appears in Raymond De Mallie, ed., *Handbook of North American Indians*, "Plains," V. 13:2 (Washington, DC: Smithsonian Institution: 2001), 783. The original is at the Amon Carter Museum in Fort Worth, Texas.

[2] As subsequent letters reveal, Ashby and Beauvais were the two commissioners who remained behind.

[3] This man was an Oglala shirt-wearer and the older brother of Hunts-The-Enemy. He died in 1876. Subsequently, Hunts-the-Enemy took his brother's name, Sword, and later became known as "George Sword." Bray, *Crazy Horse*, 449n.25.

[4] On Oct. 16-17, as Colonel Richard Dodge was en route from Fort Laramie to Cheyenne after closing up his Black Hills expedition, he fell in with Beauvais and Ashby also returning home from their work at Red Cloud Agency. Kime, *Black Hills Journals*, 246.

Appendix One

Editorials on the Black Hills Council

❧

Omaha Daily Herald, [Wednesday] September 29, 1875
Red Cloud and the Commission

It is fashionable to abuse Red Cloud, the famous chief of the Oglalas. The Black Hills Commission ignored the ablest living Indian on their advent to his country to negotiate the purchase of the Black Hills because it was said he had lost his old power with his people and, because he resented their manifestations of contempt, they deposed him from his old rank, putting Young-Man-Afraid-of-his-Horses in his place. They would not heed his counsels when he advised the commission to hold the Great Council inside the stockade as a precautionary measure of safety, and it was held outside. The result is known. The refusal to act on the advice of Red Cloud caused him to stay away from the council and came near costing the lives of every white man connected with it. Nothing but the loyalty to their honor of friendly Indians whom Red Cloud and Spotted Tail had trained to peace with the whites saved the commission and all associated with them from destruction at the hands of the wild braves of the northern tribes.

Red Cloud may be abused and derided by men who can neither understand nor do justice to the man who, more than any and all others, Spotted Tail alone excepted, brought peace and security to the frontier. But the wise fools who thus deal with him long since ceased to deny to him a noble fidelity to his engagements. Red Cloud has more brains than the whole commission put together, always excepting Ashby, and if they had heeded his counsels, the flat failure of the negotiations for the purchase of the Black Hills might have been avoided. He suspected there was danger of an outbreak at the council but probably did not know the fact. The supreme wisdom and bad whisky that direct the

293

proceedings of the more loyal and pious part of the commission came near costing their own lives and a bloody tragedy. Fortunate it is for them and the country that they escaped the consequences of their own folly.

Omaha Daily Herald, [Thursday] September 30, 1875
An Ignominious Failure

The Indian commission, controlled, if not composed by men who know nothing about the management of Indians, are solely responsible for the failure of the negotiations to purchase the Black Hills. These men blundered from the outset. The self-constituted managers of the commission have been on a general spree for the last month, and have botched everything connected with this most important transaction. They swaggered over Red Cloud who saved their lives in a critical emergency, and assumed the airs of men who neither understood the gravity of their mission nor the means whereby its objects could be accomplished. Instead of removing causes of jealousy among the various savage tribes interested in the sale of their country it will probably turn out that everything was done to increase that jealously. It is a fact that will not be disputed that a very large majority of the Sioux were willing to negotiate for the sale of the Black Hills region. Some of the northern Indians were opposed to it, most likely from the circumstance that they had no notice of the movement to buy their country until they were called by messages to attend the Grand Council. No step was taken to conciliate the disposition of these savages before the council assembled to sell their country, and they came to it wholly unprepared to treat for its sale.

The preposterous trifling that disgusted the red men with a serious proposition to lease the Black Hills was another source of irritation. It was entirely worthy of the average stupidity of the heavy men of the commission, and produced universal disgust among both white men and Indians. The political Cheap Johns sent out to meet men or more character and sense than they possess, supposed that these Indians were a set of fools, and that they could be induced to part with a vast and valuable country for a song. Their want of ordinary judgment could be pardoned if it did not inflict great injury upon the people of the West. Still indulging a faint hope that these commissioners may succeed in their blundering endeavors to purchase the Black Hills, we are only too fearful that the whole thing will terminate in an ignominious collapse and a disgraceful failure.

Sioux City Daily Journal, [Thursday] September 30, 1875
Indian Treaties

We dare say the commissioners on the part of the United States now at Red Cloud with a view of making a new treaty with the Sioux Indians are pretty thoroughly disgusted with "the noble red" upon general principles. It is certainly a humiliation to them personally, and something of a humiliation upon the dignity of the United States, that they should be compelled, in their efforts to protect the interests of the Indian and provide for his present and future necessities, to hedge themselves in with bayonets, and be constantly on the alert against the treachery of the people they are commissioned to serve. The demands made upon them by the untutored, preposterous in the extreme, can hardly fail of filling their minds with contempt for the rascals it is proposed to Christianize and civilize. It can hardly appear otherwise than sheerest nonsense to them that they should be called upon to treat with these dusky children as reasonable and responsible human beings. The Indians have no comprehension whatever of the relations they sustain to the government, nor of self-dependence, nor of manly honor, nor of decency in any form. They possess no pride of any worth, and beg and steal with every indication of self-justification and self-appreciation of importance. It is folly to reason with them for reason is beyond them; and it is idle to appeal to them in the name of right, because they have no comprehension of what right is. An irrepressible conflict exists between them and the whites, and in the very nature of things it cannot be otherwise. This conflict cannot be quieted by wrong assumptions. There is nothing of value to either race to be gained by the superior getting down to the level of the inferior. The Indians as it is appreciate no influence aside from an influence of force. If they can get food and clothing, horses and guns, through threatenings, the majority of them will be satisfied; but they fall under no obligation to the hand that answers their demands, and as the demands are met they only make them the more exacting. A poor white who receives assistance from the public treasury accepts the same in humility and with a sense of degradation; but these lazy vagabonds of Indians are only flattered thereby and rendered more insolent, exacting, and worthless. What the Indians in their ignorance and depravity consider best for themselves is totally at variance with the judgment of the whites. It is time that the business became practical—that the sentimental part of it were wiped out. This country has no occasion for any royalty in pauperism. If the Indians are willing to work, give them the opportunity; if they are capable of better lives, strive in justice to lead them therein. But if they insist upon being what the majority of them now are, justice demands nothing more than that they be kept from starvation, if that. The government should provide for them as cities and towns provide for their poor and worthless, in the most economical manner and on a basis of charity. Men who grow rich in feeding and clothing and guarding the Indians will not agree to this; but the policy is just to the Indians and just to the whites who have to meet the enormous bills that are annually piled up on account of the Indian service. The Indians, for the present, if not forever, are to be controlled by the power of coercion and not by the power of reason, and the sooner the theory is accepted, the better. Such farces as that now playing at Red Cloud should be dropped on.

New York Tribune, [Friday] October 1, 1875

Little surprise will be caused by the abrupt termination of the council for the sale of the Black Hills. It has been manifest from the first that while the wilder tribes did not wish to sell at all, the more peaceable ones were willing to part with their rights only at an exorbitant price. There was another subject in which they were far more profoundly interested. They wanted honest dealing at the agencies. For the sake of that, their chiefs had made a long journey to Washington, and obtained little satisfaction even in promises. During this council that subject was occasionally brought up, despite the efforts of the commissioners to stifle it. It was the last topic urged by the Indians amid the "hows" and handshakings with which the council broke up. It is the real cause of the failure of the council. Indians have as much common sense as white men, and they perceive clearly that until the whole agency system is remodeled or swept away, they will never get more than a fraction of what belongs to them. With fair and square dealing and direct payment in prospect, the negotiations for the sale of the Black Hills would have reached a very different conclusion.

Sioux City Daily Journal, [Sunday] October 3, 1875
Black Hills
Return of Charley Collins from the Red Cloud Fizzle

Charley Collins, of this city, returned last evening from Red Cloud Agency, where he has been in attendance upon the Grand Council, which has proved such a grand failure.

He left the agency Thursday evening [Sept. 30], after the treaty proposed by the commissioners had been submitted, and was the bearer of dispatches which impelled him to make time. He rode to Sidney, a distance of 140 miles, in seventeen hours and a half. From thence he proceeded to Omaha, reaching there Friday night [Oct. 1], and finished his journey leisurely, arriving here as stated.

After the treaty was submitted the Indians asked three days to consider it, as they would do in any event, but it was a foregone conclusion, as announced by telegraph at the time, that the labor of the commission had been lost. Our dispatches give the story of the last hours of the commission at Red Cloud, their departure, etc., and it is not necessary to speak further of them here.

Mr. Collins says the commission blundered from the start. He attributes their mistakes to their utter lack of knowledge of Indian character and Indian methods, and says the membership are now fully aware of their errors. Their first mistake, he says, was in not going to Chadron Creek, and thus keeping faith with the Indians. The trouble over the selection of a council ground came of jealousies among the Indians, which were promoted rather than allayed by the indecision of the commissioners.

The chief cause of failure, however, is to be found in the manner in which the commissioners approached the Indians upon the subject of the purchase. The Indians were told of how much the Great Father desired to do for them, of what immense value the Black Hills are to the whites, and all that, and the Indians were forthwith prepared to make extravagant demands. Moreover the commissioners did not approach the Indians through such avenues, chief of which is to be named the "squaw men," in which the "noble reds" are found most tractable.

Mr. Collins' idea is simply this, and it seems to be well supported by the experience of the past, that the commissioners should have presented their treaty forthwith and asked the Indians to sign; stating what they would give, and not stopping to indulge in the foolishness of asking what the Indians would take.

The commissioners, undertaking to deal in high honor with the Indians directly and solely, occupied weeks in listening to the extravagant demands of the Indians, and then proposed to give $6,000,000 instead of the $70,000,000 etc., the Indians had demanded. The way could not have been more surely paved for failure.

Mr. Collins feels confident that men knowing how to have gone at the matter rightly could have made a treaty easily, and much below the figure the present commissioners were willing to agree to. In point of fact, the purchase of the Black Hills is not, according to Mr. Collins' idea, to cost the government anything, for he reckons that the expense of feeding and clothing them is to be incurred whether they surrender the Black Hills or not.

Cheyenne Daily Leader, [Saturday] October 9, 1875

Quite a general hullabaloo was raised all over the country, when the news was telegraphed that the Commissioners who went to talk to Red Cloud and a lot of other copper-colored, breech-clouted gentlemen, came very near losing the tops of their heads, in consequence of the thirst of Little Big Man for blood. The first news gave everybody the shivers who read the dispatches. Gone up sure, some said! Another Modoc affair, ejaculated others! But since the danger has passed and the sky in the direction of Red Cloud has brightened, it is now certain that the Commissioners were not the object of the savage vengeance that looked so threatening for a while there. We gather the following facts in relation to the matter from reliable sources:

The Indians had been in council for some days previous and were unable to agree among themselves. The Uncpapas and Minneconjous chiefs understood that the Commissioners wanted to buy their country. They were opposed to selling it. On the day before they were to meet the Commissioners, a long wrangle took place in the Indian council. Spotted Tail and Red Cloud were dictatorial to their brother Indians, and finally boasted that they would meet the Commissioners the next day and make a treaty or bargain for the sale of the Black Hills. Then White Bull, an Uncpapa chief, rose up and shook his long bony finger at Spotted Tail and said: "We came here from our homes far away in the North to meet you here in council, and to talk about the sale of the Black Hills to the whites. Until this council tells you what to say to the Commissioners, if you speak to them about the sale of any part of this country we will kill you. This council has not determined upon what shall be done yet, and no one can speak for it and live, unless it asks him to do so." There were how! hows! without number when White Bull concluded, and Spotted Tail was silent.

Little Big Man singled out Red Cloud and said to him that if he spoke to the Commissioners until the council told him to, that he would kill him as soon as he opened his mouth. Red Cloud intimated that Little Big Man could not muzzle him, and that he would indulge in free speech on the morrow; but he did not, as the story will show. The council broke up that day in bad blood; the Northern Indians vowing death to the chief or chiefs who attempted to swap away their country without their consent. This was the real cause of the trouble.

When the Commissioners met on the following day the Standing Rock Agency Indians rode up singing within one hundred yards of the Council tent under which the Commissioners sat. They were all armed, and refused to dismount, giving as the reasons therefor, that there was likely to be some trouble among the Indians and that they desired to protect the Commissioners and the whites present, from injury and harm. Red Cloud kept away until he had been sent for three times. He came unattended, and after shaking hands with the members of the Commission, quietly sat down among the whites. Later Spotted Tail came dressed up in his best clothes and Red Cloud met him. They spoke together for a few minutes and then were seated. It was then that Little Big Man came riding up naked, on a splendid horse, with his rifle in his hand. The young braves of his band began arranging themselves behind the cavalry, so as to cover the group of Commissioners and whites where Red Cloud and Spotted Tail were sitting. What followed has been correctly reported. These Indians say it was the fixed determination of the followers of White Bull and Little Big Man to kill Red Cloud and Spotted Tail that day, if they spoke in favor of the sale of the Black Hills. A single shot would have brought on an indiscriminate slaughter, for which none of the whites would have escaped. But the trouble was among the Indians alone. Neither Spotted Tail or Red Cloud said a word about selling the Black Hills; the Commissioners and the whites present had a good scare of it and adjourned as soon as it was seemly to do so, and talked with bated breath of the dangers through which they had passed.

It is agreed upon all hands that had a shot been fired even by accident, there would have been a fearful massacre. Three of the best shots among the Standing Rock Indians had been detailed to kill Little Big Man at the first disturbance. Some of Red Cloud and Spotted Tail's Indian soldiers had also been detailed for the same purpose and were to do the same good office for Lone Horn and White Bull, if occasion required. The firm and temperate threat of Sitting Bull, one of Red Cloud's soldiers, that he would kill with his own hands the Indian who fired the first shot had an excellent effect in inducing the young bucks of the northern bands to delay firing it.

Cheyenne Daily Leader, [Saturday] October 9, 1875

A good deal of small merriment is being displayed by certain newspapers of the ha! ha! order, because a Sioux chief who had some idea of what he was talking about, asked seventy million dollars for the Black Hills. There is not quite as much sense and propriety in these ill-proportioned guffaws and jeers as there was in the Indian's demand. There is some excuse for the inflated price asked for the Hills because they are really worth the money, but they can be obtained for less than a tenth of it; but there is no excuse whatever for the class of newspapers we refer to, displaying the densest ignorance concerning the Black Hills, without interruption.[1]

People are getting tired and disgusted with these ignorant displays of geography, topography, and the mineral wealth of the Black Hills.

Cheyenne Daily Leader, [Tuesday] October 12, 1875
The Ring Village of Cheyenne

Some obscure scribbler writing to the *Chicago Tribune* from Red Cloud Agency, under date of September 29th, [Albert Swalm] inflicts a column and a half of stuff upon the readers of that paper, worth reading. That is, it is worth reading if the reader desires to learn something of the asinine qualifications of the average *Tribune*'s Red Cloud correspondent, in describing persons and things out in this region of country. He pictures a gigantic job, which it seems, with singular foresight, this astute correspondent had previously foretold, which was to be worked up for the proposed treaty with the Sioux for the benefit of the mythical ring fellows of "the ring village of Cheyenne." And the "ring village" was duly represented, somehow, at the late council, if this correspondent tells the truth; for he says "there came from several sections, especially the ring village of Cheyenne, all the loose political swash-bucklers, not too lazy to move to the field, who devoted their efforts to a great deal of blowing, and to about an equal amount of bibulation." We have made diligent inquiry and ascertained that not one of our political swash-bucklers was absent from the ring village during the time of the council. All were present and answered to their names at roll call. This may be relied upon. Wonder if the bibulous martinet, who scrawled the correspondence, would not like to be a political swash-buckler himself, Eh?

Appendix Two

George Armstrong Custer's Opinion
about the Black Hills Council

ॐ

The Black Hills Negotiations

Gen. Custer's Opinion

Major-General George A. Custer arrived in this city [New York] on Thursday last, [Sept. 30] fresh from Bismarck, Dakota, and is stopping at the Hotel Brunswick. Very naturally he has "his opinion" on the recent negotiations with the northern Indians and very politely expressed it yesterday to a [New York] *Herald* correspondent with whom he entered into conversation:

Correspondent – "What do you think, general, of this morning's news about the Black Hills negotiations?"

General Custer – "It has terminated somehow in the same manner as I anticipated. I believe the commissioners meant well, but they were not sufficiently well acquainted with the Indian character, to bring their negotiations to a successful issue."

Cor. – "Where do you think they were in error?"

Gen. – "First, in letting the Indians have so much of their own way. Indians are like children that get spoiled if they are petted, and had the commissioners been firm and backed up by strength, they would have executed their mission with considerable honor to themselves."

Cor. – "Do you apprehend any troublesome times to follow this disagreement on terms?"

Gen. – "Not at present, because they have not time, but next spring I fancy there will be plenty of work."

Cor. – "How will this decision affect the mining in the Black Hills?"

Gen. – "Properly carried out, it will prevent all gold digging or squatting in the Black Hills, but ousting white men—pioneer frontiersmen who are risking their lives in search of fortune—is a job that United States troops do not like. Besides if things go as I expect, they will have plenty to attend to, to keep off the Sioux."

Cor. – "How do you account for the monstrous demands that have been made by the Indians?"

Gen. – "It is the result of holding the council right in the heart of the Indian country, where the chiefs had the squaw men (the whites married to squaws) to advise them. Each of those men were anxious to make the payment as large as possible in order that he might reap the benefit through his squaws. They should have held the council at some spot remote from the Indian agencies and ordered the different tribes to consult among themselves and when they had arrived at a decision, send delegates to represent them at the council. The chiefs would then have been away from the squaw men and in a position to listen to reason."

Cor. – "What do you think of the country?"

Gen. – "I think it a fine country, and I am anxious to see it opened to the whites, as I am satisfied it will afford a livelihood for thousands. Again, I know a number of men who have been waiting for the signing of the treaty to go into the Hills, and now that they find the negotiations have fallen through, they will go all the same and probably get into trouble."

Cor. – "I see, General, that the Indians are anxious for permission to hunt this fall on the Republican."

Gen. – "Yes, they are always harping on game when they are in their own country and object to selling land because it is their hunting country, but when they come to Washington they beg for food, as they acknowledge that there is not sufficient game to feed them. The fact of the matter is, they are too much pampered and require a little different treatment. An equitable and just arrangement should be made, and after a certain show of strength, in order to convince them that business is meant, there will be no difficulty in bringing them to fair and reasonable terms."

Cor. – "Do you think the opening of the Black Hills will be of assistance towards the solution of the Indian question?"

Gen. – "Yes, I do, as it will gradually force the wild Indians to the reservations and accustom them to government rations. As long as the Black Hills, Powder River, and Big Horn section is closed to the whites, the Indians will have a country where they can get up their raiding parties and make mischief. After they have been on a reservation a short time, they will get accustomed to agricultural pursuits and settle down."

Cor. – "Do you think that Indians take naturally to tilling the soil?"

Gen. – "Certainly not; but they can be quietly educated to it. It would be well to accustom them first to raising stock, which they would not think derogatory to their manhood. They would become quite interested in that pursuit as soon as they discovered that they could trade a couple of oxen or five or six sheep for a pony. The latter is their market base and they would take pride in rearing any animals of nearly a similar value."

Cor. – "Do you anticipate any trouble this fall from the Sioux?"

Gen. – "Hardly this fall, as I think they will wait until the grass is plenty next spring. They will probably raise a trouble then, and make traveling a little dangerous around the Black Hills country."

Gen. Custer then arose, as he had an appointment to keep, and the *Herald* reporter, after listening to a short disquisition from the gallant cavalry chieftain on the merits of the runners at Jerome Park, tendered his thanks and retired—*New York Herald*, 2nd inst. [Saturday, October 2, 1875]

[*Cheyenne Daily Leader*, Saturday, October 9, 1875]

Appendix Three

"Spotted Tail's Description of the Other World," 1875

❦

Happy Hunting Grounds
Spotted Tail's Description of the Other World
Correspondence of *The Chicago Tribune*

"I want you to tell me somewhat of your religious belief," said a correspondent, talking with Spotted Tail.

Spotted Tail, after quite a pause proceeded, in answer to the question put by the correspondent and Maj. Howard, to talk very gravely, the following being substantially what he said:

"Most Indians believe in the Great Spirit, in a heaven, and in a hell; but some are unbelievers and think that when they die they are no more, just like the deer and the horse. There are but two worlds, the one on which we live and that one where the Great Spirit dwells. The spirit world is more than ten thousand times larger than this, its hunting fields have no end and the game there is inexhaustible. Its flowers are more beautiful than any we have ever known, and its maidens are as lovely as the color of the clouds before a setting sun, and never grow old. The land does not have to be cultivated there; but every kind of good fruit, and in the greatest abundance, hangs upon the trees and vines, continuously waiting to be plucked. Nothing ever dies there, and the wants of all who go there are constantly and forever supplied without the necessity of any work. All good men, whether they are white or red, go to heaven, but a great difference will exist between the conditions of the races of men and individuals there and what they are here. Everything nearly will be reversed. The wealthy here will be poor there; the powerful and great here will be humble there. The Indians, who have been overpowered by the intelligence and skill of the white man here, will

305

have a better chance there. Everything which has been taken from them here will be given back to them there, even to his gun, his dog, and his pony. Here, the Great Spirit has been on the white man's side; there, he will lean to the cause of the Indian and then, said the chief, his eyes flashing in the meantime a fearful realization of the present condition of his people, "we'll fight it out, and we'll not be driven from our hunting grounds like the sneaking, savage wolf. The bad men of all nations will go down into the center of the earth, and be excluded from the spirit land."

Correspondent – "But tell me. You know that when you die—when your people die—they rot like the horse and dog, and their bodies go into the air and water. How is it that you are to go into the spirit land and do everything there as individuals very much after the same manner that you do here?"

Spotted Tail – "We go there as spirits, and there get new bodies, which the white man cannot kill."

Correspondent – "Have you not heard through your commissioners about Jesus Christ, the son of the Great Spirit?"

Spotted Tail – "Yes, I have heard all about Him; how good He was; what great things He did; how He would help the bad man to be good, and how He would lead all who would listen to Him to the Great Spirit, His Father; and I have heard also how the white man killed Him. The Indian never would have done that; he never would have murdered the son of the Great Spirit. He would rather have loved Him better than his own life; would have given Him anything and all he had, and for Him would have gone upon the war path and conquered the world. It was for a long time after I first heard about Jesus Christ that I did not understand how the white man could have killed Him; but when I got better acquainted with the whites, when I realized the fact that they had no respect for the rights of the Indian, would take away his home where he was born, murder him and his children, despoil his women and rob him of his winter's food, I then very readily understood how they could even kill the Son of the Great Spirit as they did."

Correspondent – "Do the Indians often pray to the Great Spirit?"

Spotted Tail – "Yes; on most occasions, whether great or small."

Correspondent – "Does the Great Spirit answer their prayers?"

Spotted Tail – "Yes; He always answers the good man. He has given us all we have, and is always present to give us more if we only do no wrong."

[Presumed Albert Swalm]

[*Fort Dodge Messenger*, Thursday, December 9, 1875]

[1] Given the economic benefits that Cheyenne realized as an outfitting point for the gold rush, it is not surprising that the newspaper upheld the view that the mineral wealth of the Black Hills was of immense value.

Bibliography

ॐ

Allen, Anne Beiser. "Scandal in Niobrara: The Controversial Career of Rev. Samuel D. Hinman." *Nebraska History* 90 (Fall 2009): 114-29.

Agonito, Joseph. "Young Man Afraid of His Horses: The Reservation Years." *Nebraska History* 79 (Fall 1998): 116-32.

Anderson, Grant K. "Samuel D. Hinman and the Opening of the Black Hills." *Nebraska History* 60 (Winter 1979): 520-42.

Annual Report of the Commissioner of Indian Affairs, 1875. Washington, DC: GPO, 1875.

Annual Report of the Commissioner of Indian Affairs, 1876. Washington, DC: GPO, 1876.

Barry, Louise, comp. *The Beginning of the West: Annals of the Kansas Gateway to the American West, 1540-1854.* Topeka: Kansas State Historical Society, 1972.

Benkelman (Nebraska) News-Chronicle

Berkhofer, Robert F. Jr. *The White Man's Indian: Images of the American Indian from Columbus to the Present.* New York: Alfred A. Knopf, 1978.

Bray, Kingsley M. "Teton Sioux Population History, 1655-1881." *Nebraska History* 75 (Summer 1994): 165-88.

_____. "Spotted Tail and the Treaty of 1868." *Nebraska History* 83 (Spring 2002): 19-35.

_____. *Crazy Horse: A Lakota Life*. Norman: University of Oklahoma Press, 2006.

Bourke, John G. "The Medicine Men of the Apache." *Ninth Annual Report of the Bureau of American Ethology, 1887-1888*. Washington DC: Smithsonian Institution, 1892.

Brown, Mable, comp. "The Wyoming Portion of the Custer Expedition of 1874 to Explore the Black Hills." *Annals of Wyoming* 46 (Fall 1974): 263-80.

Buecker, Thomas R. "Red Cloud Agency Traders." *Museum of the Fur Trade Quarterly* 30 (1994): 4-13.

_____. "'The Men Behaved Splendidly': Guy V. Henry's Famous Cavalry Rides." *Nebraska History* 78 (Summer 1997): 54-63.

_____. *Fort Robinson and the American West, 1874-1899*. Lincoln: Nebraska State Historical Society, 1999.

_____. *Fort Robinson and the American Century, 1900-1948*. Lincoln: Nebraska State Historical Society, 2002.

_____, and R. Eli Paul, eds. *The Crazy Horse Surrender Ledger*. Lincoln: Nebraska State Historical Society, 1994.

Chadron (Nebraska) Democrat

Cheyenne Daily Leader

Chicago Tribune

Clow, Richmond L. "The Sioux Nation and Indian Territory: The Attempted Removal of 1876." *South Dakota History* 6 (Fall 1976): 456-73.

Conard, Jane. "Charles Collins: The Sioux City Promotion of the Black Hills." *South Dakota History* 2 (Spring 1972): 131-71.

DeMallie, Raymond J. "Touching the Pen: Plains Indian Treaty Councils in Ethnohistorical Perspective." In *Ethnicity on the Great Plains*, ed. Frederick C. Luebke. Lincoln: University of Nebraska Press, 1980.

_____, vol. ed. Plains. V.13, pt.2 of *Handbook of North American Indians*, series ed. William C. Strudevant. Washington, DC: Smithsonian Institution, 2001.

Department of the Platte. Letters Received, 1866-1878. Fort Laramie National Historic Site.

Dobbs, Hugh, comp. *History of Gage County, Nebraska*. Lincoln, NE: Western Publishing and Engraving Co., 1918.

Fort Dodge (Iowa) Messenger

Fort McPherson, Nebraska. Post Returns, 1875. Records of the Office of the Adjutant General. RG94. National Archives and Records Administration.

Gray, John S. "Frank Grouard: Kanaka Scout or Mulatto Renegade?" *Chicago Westerners Brand Book* 16 (October 1959): 57-64.

_____. "The Story of Mrs. Picotte-Galpin, A Sioux Heroine: Eagle Woman Learns about White Ways and Racial Conflict, 1820-1868." *Montana, the Magazine of Western History* 36 (Spring 1986): 2-21.

_____. "The Story of Mrs. Picotte-Galpin, A Sioux Heroine: Eagle Woman Becomes a Trader and Counsels for Peace, 1868-1888." *Montana, the Magazine of Western History* 36 (Summer 1986): 2-21.

Greene, Jerome A. *Fort Randall on the Missouri, 1856-1892*. Pierre: South Dakota State Historical Society Press, 2005.

Hanson, Charles E., Jr. "Geminien P. Beavais." In Vol. 7, *The Mountain Men and the Fur Trade of the Far West*, ed. LeRoy R. Hafen. Glendale, CA: Arthur H. Clark Co., 1969.

_____. "Joseph Bissonette's Last Trading Post." *Museum of the Fur Trade Quarterly* 16 (Fall 1980): 2-3.

Hanson, Charles E., Jr. and Veronica Sue Walters. "The Early Fur Trade in Northwestern Nebraska." *Nebraska History* 57 (Fall 1976).

Hanson, James A. "A Gift for a Great Hero." *Museum of the Fur Trade Quarterly* 48 (Winter 2012): 8-11.

Hanson, James A. and LaRee Wyatt. "The Battle of Crow Butte." *Museum of the Fur Trade Quarterly* 45 (Fall/Winter 2009): 4-68.

Hedren, Paul L. "Camp Sheridan, Nebraska: The Uncommonly Quiet Post on Beaver Creek." *Nebraska History* 91 (Summer 2010): 80-101.

Heitman, Francis B. *Historical Register and Dictionary of the U.S. Army*. 2 Vol. Washington, DC: GPO, 1903.

Hudson, David, Marvin Bergman, and Loren Horton. *The Biographical Dictionary of Iowa*. Iowa City: University of Iowa Press, 2008.

Hughes, J. Donald. *American Indians in Colorado*, 2d Ed. Boulder, CO: Pruett Publishing Co., 1987.

Hutton, Paul Andrew. *Phil Sheridan and his Army*. Lincoln: University of Nebraska Press, 1985.

Hyde, George E. *Spotted Tail's Folk: A History of the Brule Sioux*. Norman: University of Oklahoma Press, 1961.

Jensen, Richard E., ed. *Voices of the American West, Vol. 1: The Indian Interviews of Eli S. Ricker; Vol. 2: The Soldier and Settler Interviews of Eli S. Ricker*. Lincoln: University of Nebraska Press, 2005.

Kappler, Charles J. *Indian Affairs: Laws and Treaties*, 2 Vol. Washington, DC: GPO, 1904.

Keller, Robert H., Jr. "Episcopal Reformers and Affairs at Red Cloud Agency, 1870-1876." *Nebraska History* 68 (Fall 1987): 116-26.

Kime, Wayne R., ed. *The Black Hills Journals of Colonel Richard Irving Dodge*. Norman: University of Oklahoma Press, 1996.

Kingsbury, David L. "Sully's Expedition against the Sioux in 1864." *Collections of the Minnesota Historical Society* 8 (1898): 449-62.

Larson, T. A. *History of Wyoming*, 2d ed. Lincoln: University of Nebraska Press, 1978.

Lazarus, Edward F. *Black Hills, White Justice: The Sioux Nation versus the United States, 1775 to the Present*. New York: Harper Collins Publishers, 1991.

LeCompte, Janet. "Antoine Janis." In Vol. 8, *The Mountain Men and the Fur Trade of the Far West*, ed. LeRoy R. Hafen. Glendale, CA: Arthur H. Clark Co., 1971.

(Lincoln) Nebraska State Journal

McChristian, Douglas C. Fort Laramie: *Military Bastion of the High Plains*. Norman, OK: Arthur H. Clark Co., 2009.

McDermott, John Dishon. "John Baptiste Richard." In Vol. 2, *The Mountain Men and the Fur Trade of the Far West*, ed. LeRoy R. Hafen. Glendale, CA: Arthur H. Clark Co., 1965.

Mallery, Garrick. "On the Pictographs of the North American Indians." *Fourth Annual Report of the Bureau of American Ethnology, 1882-83*. Washington, DC: Smithsonian Institution, 1886.

Mattes, Merrill J. *Indians, Infants, and Infantry: Andrew and Elizabeth Burt on the Frontier*. Denver, CO: Old West Publishing Co., 1960.

_____. *The Great Platte River Road*. Lincoln: Nebraska State Historical Society, 1969.

Morton, J. Sterling, succeeded by Albert Watkins. *Illustrated History of Nebraska*. 3 Vol. Lincoln: 1905-13.

New York Herald

New York Tribune

(North Platte) Western Nebraskian

Olson, Gary D. "Relief for Nebraska Grasshopper Victims: The Official Journal of Lieutenant Theodore E. True." *Nebraska History* 48 (Summer 1967): 119-40.

Olson, James C., *Red Cloud and the Sioux Problem*. Lincoln: University of Nebraska Press, 1965.

Omaha Daily Bee

Omaha Weekly Bee

Omaha Daily Herald

Parker, Watson. *Gold in the Black Hills*. Pierre: South Dakota State Historical Society Press, 2003.

Poore, Ben: Perley, comp. *Congressional Directory*, 3d ed. 47th Cong., 1st Sess. Washington, DC: GPO, 1882.

Powers, Thomas. *The Killing of Crazy Horse*. New York: Alfred A. Knopf, 2010.

Red Cloud Agency. Letters Received by the Commissioner of Indian Affairs, 1875-76. Microcopy 234, roll 719. National Archives and Records Administration.

Reilly, Hugh J. *Bound to Have Blood: Frontier Newspapers and the Plains Indian Wars*. Lincoln: University of Nebraska Press, 2011.

"Report of the Sioux Commission." *Annual Report of the Commissioner of Indian Affairs, 1876*. Washington, DC: GPO, 1876.

Report of the Special Commission Appointed to Investigate the Affairs of the Red Cloud Indian Agency, July 1875. 3 Vol. Washington, DC: GPO, 1875.

St. Germain, Jill. *Broken Treaties: United States and Canadian Relations with the Lakotas and the Plains Cree, 1868-1885*. Lincoln: University of Nebraska Press, 2009.

Sioux City Daily Journal

Spotted Tail Agency. Letters Received by the Commissioner of Indian Affairs, 1875-76. Microcopy 234, roll 840. National Archives and Records Administration.

Spring, Agnes Wright. *The Cheyenne and Black Hills Stage and Express Routes*. Glendale, CA: Arthur H. Clark Co., 1949.

"Swalm, Albert." *Annals of Iowa* 14 (July 1924): 398-99.

Tallent, Annie D. *The Black Hills, or The Last Hunting Grounds of the Dakotahs*, 2d ed. Sioux Falls, SD: Brevet Press, 1974.

Thrapp, Dan, comp. *Encyclopedia of Frontier Biography*. 3 Vol. Lincoln: University of Nebraska Press, 1991.

Triggs, J. H. *History of Cheyenne and Northern Wyoming*. Omaha, NE: Herald Publishing House, 1876.

Waggoner, Josephine. *Witness: A Lakota Historian's Strong Heart Song of the Lakotas*. Ed. Emily Levine. Lincoln: University of Nebraska Press, 2013.

Wilson, George, comp. *Portrait Gallery of the Chamber of Commerce of the State of New York*. New York: Press of the Chamber of Commerce, 1890.

Woods, Lawrence M. *Wyoming Biographies*. Worland, WY: High Plains Publishing Co., 1991.

Index

❧

Page number followed by "i" designates illustration
Page number followed by "n" designates endnote

"Great Father," (*continued*) 276, 277, 279, 280, 282, 283, 284, 291, 297

Great Sioux Reservation, 9, 10, 12, 16, 70, 94n37, 214n44

"Great Spirit," 45, 49, 305. *See also* religion

Greeley, Horace, presidential candidate, 216n62

Green River County (UT), 89n4

Grouard, Franklin, Sandwich Islander and Sitting Bull band member, 148, 166, 167, 216n68

hair, human, as Lakota robe decoration, 198

"Happy Hunting Grounds," 305

Hare, Bishop William H., 62, 97n63, 216n65

Harlan, James, Secretary of the Interior, 199, 218n89, 219n91

Harmon, William, soldier and husband of Mrs. Galpin's daughter, 218n84

Harney City (DAK), 32, 91n12, 97n60

Harney Peak (DAK), 54, 66

Harney, Gen. William S., 1868 Fort Laramie Treaty commissioner, 81, 101n92

Harney's Gulch (DAK), 59

Harris, Benjamin, Red Cloud Agency investigation commissioner, 89n2

Harrison, W., recorder of mining district, 61, 82, 97n61

Hawk Springs (WY), 209n2

Hawk Spring Ranche (WY), 113

He Dog, Oglala, 224i

Henderson, Sen. J. B., 1868 Fort Laramie Treaty commissioner, 101n92

Henry, Capt. Guy V., Third U.S. Cavalry, Company H, 42, 94n35, 98n70, 119

Hewitt, Capt. Christian C., Lt. Col. Bradley's aide-de-camp, 179

High Backbone, Fetterman Massacre planner, 216n63

High Lance, Great Council delegate, 94n36

Hinman, Rev. Samuel D., commission member, 6, 13-14, 20, 30, 50, 54, 71, 72, 84-86, 93n30, 96n55, 110, 117, 127-28, 135-36, 149, 150, 161-62, 165-66, 170, 175, 185-86, 202, 219n97, 221i, 235, 253; description of, 201

Hofman, Lt. William, in charge of garden at Camp Sheridan, 38, 40

Homestake Mine (DAK), 214n44

Horse Creek Treaty. *See* Fort Laramie Treaty of 1851

Horse Creek (NE), 9, 113, 183, 197, 211n11

horses: appropriations 27, 125, 194, 268, 282; bribes, 157, 190, 197; culture, 14, 42, 72-73, 77, 119, 154, 207; grieving, as part of process, 43, 189; raided, 35, 41, 44-45, 82, 91n13, 92n20, 189, 198, 215n36, 286; reward 19, 44, 135-38, 282, 287, 289, 290-91; transportation, 9, 30, 63, 114-15, 150, 189, 191, 193, 232, 234, 242, 245, 251, 255-57; wealth, 46-47, 100, 116, 121, 152, 170, 190, 194, 206, 233, 240, 264, 286

Hotel Brunswick (NYC), 301

housing, government provided for Lakota, 120

Howard, E.A., Spotted Tail Agency agent, 80-82, 101n90, 122, 126, 148, 152, 166, 177, 190, 207, 305

Howe, Evan T., relative of Senator Howe, 110n, 210n3

CPSIA information can be obtained
at www.ICGtesting.com
Printed in the USA
FSOW02n0230220216
17157FS

9 780933 307377